# SOLICITING
# INTERPRETATION

# SOLICITING INTERPRETATION

*Literary Theory and*
*Seventeenth-Century English Poetry*

*Edited by*

## Elizabeth D. Harvey

*and*

## Katharine Eisaman Maus

The University of Chicago Press
*Chicago and London*

*Elizabeth D. Harvey* is assistant professor of English at the University of Western Ontario. *Katharine Eisaman Maus,* associate professor of English at the University of Virginia, is the author of *Ben Jonson and the Roman Frame of Mind.*

The University of Chicago Press, Chicago 60637
The University of Chicago Press, Ltd., London
© 1990 by the University of Chicago
All rights reserved. Published 1990
Printed in the United States of America
99 98 97 96 95 94 93 92 91 90 5 4 3 2 1

Library of Congress Cataloging-in-Publication Data

Soliciting interpretation : literary theory and seventeenth-century
  English poetry / edited by Elizabeth D. Harvey and Katharine Eisaman
  Maus.
      p.   cm.
   Includes bibliographical references.
   Contents: The monarchy of wit and the republic of letters / David
Norbrook—All Donne / Annabel Patterson—From the superfluous to
the supernumerary / John Guillory—Joyning my labour to my pain /
Rosemary Kegl—Jonson and the amazons / Stephen Orgel—
Shakespeare's sonnets as literary property / Arthur Marotti—
Jacobean poetry and lyric disappointment / Jane Tylus—Dating
Milton / Jonathan Goldberg—Masculine persuasive force / Stanley
Fish—Unspeakable love / Gordon Braden—That ancient heat /
Michael Schoenfeldt—The constant subject / Maureen Quilligan.
   ISBN 0-226-31875-3 (alk. paper).—ISBN 0-226-31876-1 (pbk. :
alk. paper)
   1. English poetry—Early modern, 1500-1700—History and criticism—
Theory, etc.   I. Harvey, Elizabeth D.   II. Maus, Katharine
Eisaman, 1955-
PR543.S6   1990
821'.309—dc20                                                89-20680
                                                                  CIP

# Contents

v

# Acknowledgments

We are grateful for support and travel funds provided by the Social Sciences and Humanities Research Council of Canada, a Faculty of Arts Research Professorship from the University of Western Ontario, and a Princeton University Class of 1932 Bicentennial Preceptorship. The members of a graduate seminar on Donne, Herbert, and Marvell at the University of Western Ontario in 1988–89 offered stimulating and insightful responses to the volume as a whole and to a number of essays, and Heather Dubrow, Leah Marcus, Mary Nyquist, and Nancy Vickers gave invaluable advice at crucial junctures. Finally, we have been fortunate in our contributors, whose promptness, fine essays, and patience have eased the necessarily drawn-out process of preparing a volume of this nature.

EDH
KEM

# Introduction

"New philosophy calls all in doubt," wrote John Donne in 1611, and many of his critics in the 1980s could say the same about the effect of recent literary theory upon their own interpretive practices. A decade ago, it seemed that our conception of seventeenth-century poetry had been definitively shaped by T. S. Eliot's rehabilitation of the metaphysical poets and by the powerful strategies of reading developed by the New Critics. In the past few years, however, explorations of gender, ideology, power, and language in the Renaissance have not only provided radically new understandings of familiar texts but have also forced us to reexamine the critical, historical, and cultural presuppositions on which our readings are based.

It is sometimes said that the distinguishing feature of much recent literary criticism, in contrast to the criticism of a previous generation, is its fascination with history.[1] In itself, this might seem a curious formulation, since many of the most significant critics of the early and mid-twentieth century make explicit or implicit literary-historical claims. When T. S. Eliot describes a "dissociation of sensibility" that divides the culture of the modern world from the culture of Donne, and when Cleanth Brooks attributes that rupture to the rise of scientific method,[2] they are making a historical argument, albeit perhaps a rudimentary one, about the difference between a Renaissance poet and his twentieth-century readers. Reflecting upon the role of history in literary theory and criticism in *The Theory of Literature,* a comprehensive "guide to critical practice" published in 1949, René Wellek holds that "they implicate each other so thoroughly as to make inconceivable literary theory without criticism or history, or criticism without theory or history, or history without theory or criticism" (p. 30). Countless books and articles published in the forties, fifties, and sixties examined how the poetic techniques of Donne or Jonson influence their poetic successors, or how Milton revises epic forms inherited from Virgil, Dante, and Spenser, or

ix

how Renaissance poetry reflects the Christian beliefs of the society in which it was created.

What is "new" about the "new historicism" is not so much the fact that it is historicist, as the fact that it conceives the relationship between literature and history in a new way. Many recent critics have been redefining the kinds of history that might be important for a reader to know. Even in the era of high formalism, criticism of seventeenth-century poetry often admitted the relevance of certain forms of history—religious history, for instance, or the history of genres. What it eschewed were kinds of history that threatened the ideality of what Eliot calls the "ideal order" of canonical texts: kinds of history that made those texts seem too topical, too politically polemical, too imbued with prejudice, too much the consequence of a writer's particular professional or economic situation. It was considered appropriate, for instance, to read Donne's "The Canonization" in terms of a tradition of religious paradox but improper to speculate about Donne's relationship to the woman the poem purportedly addresses, because a great poem ought to remain uncontaminated by, or at least properly distanced from, the vicissitudes of biography. It was respectable to explore Shakespeare's modification of the inherited conventions of the sonnet form but less respectable to investigate ways in which the taste of the patrons who financed him might have affected the quality and character of his art. For the first project represents literature as a category apart, developing either according to its own specifically aesthetic logic, or according to more general laws that apply to all intellectual or spiritual endeavors. The second suggests that literary production is contingent upon extra-literary factors of the most baldly material kind.

The past decade or so has witnessed a variety of challenges to the older notion of the intellectually respectable use of history and biography—those uses, that is, that could coincide even with a formalism that sometimes purported to do without them. These challenges derive from a conviction that Cleanth Brooks's precept that the critic discuss "poems as poems" has implausibly divided literature from politics and social life. T. S. Eliot's attempt to distinguish between the man as poet and the man as suffering human being, and the related New Critical attempt to elevate and protect literature from material contingency have in fact, many recent critics claim, drained it of some of its most powerful kinds of significance. Moreover, discussing literature in terms of the material history of cultures and individuals—precisely the kind of history an older literary criticism eschewed—becomes for some recent critics a tool for counteracting an ideological system that uses aestheticism or spirituality to conceal politically oppressive tactics. Stephen

Greenblatt, Louis Montrose, Leah Marcus, and Jonathan Goldberg, among others, have explored the way Renaissance literary texts represent and are determined by structures of political authority: by upheavals attendant upon the Reformation and its aftermath, by the consolidation of sovereign power in the sixteenth century and its subsequent dispersal in the seventeenth, by changes in family structure and relations between the sexes, by the challenges posed to a traditional worldview by the English experience in the New World. Richard Helgerson, Annabel Patterson, Stephen Orgel, and Arthur Marotti have clarified the more local and perhaps more urgent demands placed upon a seventeenth-century writer by the facts of his professional situation—the way his relationship to patrons, printers, and fellow writers defines his sense of a literary career and of appropriate literary undertakings. Recent work on the issue of gender in the Renaissance, evidenced by such anthologies as *Rewriting the Renaissance: The Discourses of Sexual Difference in Early Modern Europe,* have demonstrated how deeply the patriarchal bias of scholarship, in early modern Europe and in the present, has affected the categories of value and strategies of reading that determine the texts we choose as representative of the period and the kinds of history we see as illuminating them.

Many of the influential recent critics of Renaissance literature were the students of the very New Critics whose theoretical assumptions they reject. They acquired from their teachers a sensitivity to paradox, ambiguity, and incongruity that allows them to escape what the New Critics often feared was the inevitably simplifying tendency of historical explanation, its willingness to take complex literary expression for blunt statement of fact. Considered purely as readers, they are just as ingenious as their mentors were. But whereas the New Critics tended to take paradox as the expression of a necessarily contradictory but eternal human truth—the simultaneity of death and life, disorder and harmony, sensuality and spirituality, weakness and strength, and so forth—their successors are likely to see paradox or contradiction as the site of some unresolved conflict, a strategy of management and containment as well as of revelatory expression. Thus, while quite eclectic in their use of theoretical models, many recent critics find most consistently helpful those writers who can help articulate those strategies: Marx, Althusser, Foucault, Freud, Derrida, Lacan, Irigaray. Critics now working on Renaissance literature are far more likely than their predecessors to interpret their task as demystification rather than celebration, maintaining a skeptical distance from the belief structures of the writers they discuss.

As a proliferating variety of histories have come to replace a monolithic "tradition," literary critics have had to confront the reasons they are likely to see certain kinds of history as especially relevant to their endeavor. They have become, in other words, intensely aware of the ways in which preoccupations in the present affect their construction of the past. This, too, is hardly unprecedented. In *The Verbal Icon* W. K. Wimsatt, for instance, stresses the inescapability of the critic's modernity:

> Understanding is derived not only from historical documents but also from our own living and thinking of the present. . . . We are bound to have a point of view in literary criticism, and that point of view, though it may have been shaped by a tradition, is bound to be our own. Points of view cannot be slipped in and out of our minds like lantern slides. Our judgments of the past cannot be discontinuous with our own experience or insulated from it. (pp. 255, 258)

But while Wimsatt uses this perception to set limits on the usefulness of history for the literary critic, more recent critics see themselves *and* the objects of their study as immersed in a historical situation that can neither be eluded nor denied. Thus Stephen Greenblatt, in *Renaissance Self-Fashioning,* writes that "It seemed to me the very hallmark of the Renaissance that middle-class and aristocratic males began to feel that they possessed . . . shaping power over their lives, and I saw the power and the freedom it implied as an important element in my sense of myself" (p. 256). Jonathan Dollimore's critique of the essentialist foundations of humanist subjectivity in *Radical Tragedy,* and Francis Barker's similar attempt in *The Tremulous Private Body* to reveal the instability and historical contingency of the bourgeois idea of the subject, are quite frankly inspired by the possibility of change in the present. Jean Howard has persuasively argued that the recent readings of the Renaissance "resonate with some of the dominant elements of postmodern culture" (pp. 6–7): they are characterized by a "clash of paradigms and ideologies, a playfulness with signifying systems, a self-reflexivity, and a self-consciousness about the tenuous solidity of human identity" (p. 6). This attitude toward both literary and nonliterary texts emphasizes irresolvable gaps and contradictions rather than the closure or *concordia discors* privileged by an earlier criticism. It is a version of historicism often heavily influenced by poststructuralist literary theory, which has altered our sense of language as a stable medium, of a text as self-contained, and of discourse as the property of an individual author. But this general description ought not to conceal the very different intellectual pedigrees and theoretical allegiances among the most influential critics of Renaissance literature today. The "new historicism" of critics such as Jonathan Goldberg or Patricia Parker, who focus on the intertextuality of Renaissance writing and on the absence of closure, differs in premises as well as in style from the more narrative and biographical methods of Greenblatt, Helgerson, or Patterson.

Often more implicitly than explicitly, the new methods of reading have altered the sense of the canon by attending to a different group of texts. The poetic practices of such writers as Sidney and Nashe, long over-shadowed by their seventeenth-century successors, have come to seem freshly engaging. An emphasis on the social context in which works of art are created and consumed has lent a new excitement to the criticism of Renaissance drama. The disintegration of boundaries between liter-ary and nonliterary discourse has rehabilitated the journal, the history, the travelogue, and the rhetorical treatise as worthy of close critical scru-tiny. The inclusion of gender as a category of analysis has meant not only that familiar, male-authored texts are approachable now from dif-ferent perspectives but also that a stable sense of a canonical group of Renaissance texts is beginning to be disrupted. This challenge derives from an unprecedented interest in women writers and from a corollary awareness that to privilege a patriarchally constructed canon is also to value male experience over female experience, the public over the pri-vate, and established genres like epic over less conventionally esteemed forms like autobiography and letters. As scholars such as Joan Kelly have demonstrated, the term "Renaissance" celebrates the rebirth not of culture in general but of male culture in particular. Analyses that take into account the material condition of women and that consider the dis-courses of sexual difference in the early modern period are reshaping our sense of periodization, the texts we choose to consider, and the ways in which we read them.

We believe, however, that recent changes in the methodology of read-ing Renaissance texts have important consequences not only for previously neglected or undervalued literature but for the texts that used to be absolutely central to the New Critical project: the lyric and epic poetry of the earlier seventeenth century. With the eclipse of formalism, some of these texts have suffered a certain relative neglect or margin-alization—a displacement that has been particularly striking in the case of Donne. Until very recently, criticism of metaphysical poetry has tended not to engage in the new ways of reading that poststructuralist theory has made possible,[3] but rather to enlarge upon the insights pro-duced by New Critical strategies, and thus to leave unquestioned the suppositions that attribute value to this particular group of poets in the first place.

By design, therefore, *Soliciting Interpretation* focuses not upon the texts that many new historicists and poststructuralists have found most immediately intriguing, but upon the very works and genres privileged by New Criticism. It does so, however, not by unselfconsciously endorsing the canonical status of Donne, Herbert, Milton, Jonson, and Shakespeare, but by calling into question the mechanisms of their canonization. In a recent essay on Eliot, Brooks, and canon formation, John Guillory has argued that the formation of the New Critical canon required various kinds of silence: silence about the differences among literary works (so that canonical authors were made to agree with one another); silence about meaning (so that the text was imagined as the repository of an unparaphrasable truth); silence about the complicity of interests that valorized particular texts by claiming to discover their intrinsic excellences. The essays in *Soliciting Interpretation* break this silence. To read seventeenth-century poems with explicit attention to the construction of the author figure in relation to certain ideological formations (as Jonathan Goldberg or Rosemary Kegl does) or to consider them intertextually, paying articulate attention to issues of subjectivity and voice (as Gordon Braden or Maureen Quilligan does), or to analyze their rhetoric in terms of its mimetically sexual power or impotence (as Stanley Fish does), or to situate them with respect to the historical operations of power within the court (as David Norbrook, Annabel Patterson, or Stephen Orgel does) is to violate the premises upon which an older criticism operated.

Nor is the focus upon traditionally canonical authors meant to be exclusive. Some of the essays in the volume address writers who used to be nearly or entirely ignored, showing how they might be integrated into a fuller understanding of the seventeenth-century literary context. For the inclusion of these authors is not a simple accretive process; our focus upon them obliges us to reconsider the process of canonical consensus, reassessing what is valuable, what has "interest." Similar concerns affect the way the collection has been assembled and organized, since to disregard the self-contained category of "Metaphysical" poetry and situate discussions of Donne and Herbert in a critical context alongside essays on Milton, Jonson, and the Jacobean Spenserians disrupts the grouping of texts by Eliot and the New Critics, which often privileged a monarchical and Anglo-Catholic inheritance at the expense of possible alternatives. While the collection might be neater in shape if all the essays focused upon a single author, Donne for instance, it would in that case risk re-inscribing the very categories from which many of these interpretations seek to free themselves.

*Soliciting Interpretation* gathers essays by critics and scholars who are currently reshaping our sense of the function and nature of seventeenth-century poetry. They are not a monolithic group. Their common interest in a "historicist" criticism, for instance, should not obscure significant differences in their theoretical orientations. The first group of essays disagrees over the adequacy of Foucault's conception of power for historicist critics; in the second group of essays, Goldberg's skepticism about the motives of scholarly narrative has very different consequences from Marotti's more empiricist premises. The contributors to this volume take issue vigorously with their predecessors, with one another, and even with themselves: Norbrook's essay argues against his own influential recent book, and Fish revises the assumptions about authorial control that have informed his powerful readings of Milton, Herbert, Bacon, Bunyan, and others. As a collection, the essays depict a literary landscape that might seem unfamiliar, devoid of the familiar stylistic frontiers that used to define the boundaries between, for example, the "metaphysicals" and the "cavaliers," and which tended to isolate Milton from all the other writers of his century. Old landmarks are not obliterated, but their relation to their surroundings has been reconceived.

The title of the volume evokes the etymological sense of the word "solicit"—to disturb, to dislocate—as well as the sense still current, to tempt or entice. Jacques Derrida writes:

> Structure is perceived through the incidence of menace, at the moment when imminent danger concentrates our vision on the keystone of the institution, the stone which encapsulates both the possibility and the fragility of its existence. Structure then can be *methodically* threatened in order to be comprehended more clearly and to reveal not only its supports but also that secret place in which it is neither construction nor ruin but lability. This operation is called (from the Latin) *soliciting*. In other words, *shaking* in a way related to the *whole* (from *sollus*, in archaic Latin, "the whole," and from *citare*, "to put in motion"). (p. 6)

Our title draws simultaneously on this Derridean "historico-metaphysical threatening of foundations" and on John Guillory's activation, in chapter 3 below, of the etymological associations of the word in his analysis of Raphael's admonition to Adam in *Paradise Lost*, "Solicit not thy thoughts with matters hid." The kinds of interpretive activity represented in this volume seek to disturb a totalizing account of the early seventeenth century, not in order to substitute one hegemonic system with another but rather to solicit further discussion by making hidden consensus about value and meaning manifest.

The interesting points of intersection among the contributors to this volume occur less in their shared enthusiasm for particular authors or in a shared interpretive method than in a common interest in particular critical issues. We have tried to reflect this fact in the organization of the essays, juxtaposing those which might fruitfully be considered together. But our three categories are hardly mutually exclusive; moreover, none of the essays fit comfortably under a single rubric. Many of the authors explicitly devote themselves to storming barriers separating the history of sexuality, the history of genre, and the history of economics, or the barriers dividing the editorial concerns of textual scholarship from the politics of writing and reading.

The essays in the first section represent divergent conceptions about the ways in which a literary text can be "political." For David Norbrook and Annabel Patterson, political stances are conscious authorial choices, clear to a reader who possesses a vivid and detailed sense of the political options available to writers at particular historical moments. John Guillory, Rosemary Kegl, and to a lesser extent Stephen Orgel, work by contrast from a model of cultural history in which ideology is conceived as both more pervasive and less consciously articulated.

Patterson and Norbrook reread Donne in biographical terms, showing how a fallaciously apolitical and aestheticizing bias has skewed much earlier criticism, even when it has tried to place Donne in a historical context. In "The Monarchy of Wit and the Republic of Letters," David Norbrook closely examines Donne's complicated views on monarchy. He argues that the received view of Donne as politically and religiously conservative is seriously incomplete, a claim that represents a major revision of Norbrook's own previous account of Donne. Norbrook takes issue not only with himself but with many recent "new historicist" critics, whom he sees as working from an "unpolitical" Foucauldian model of power as irrational self-aggrandizement, rather than as collective pursuit of rational goals. In "All Donne," Annabel Patterson shows how our conception of Donne's poetics is altered by an awareness of his role in two significant Jacobean political episodes: the chaotic 1610 Parliament and the trial of his patron, Somerset, for the murder of Thomas Overbury. Patterson asserts that the traditional approaches to Donne, both biographical studies and those which make a point of eschewing biography, ignore the significance of Donne's political commitments and avoid confronting the implications of a depoliticized construction of the author.

In "From the Superfluous to the Supernumerary: Reading Gender into *Paradise Lost*," John Guillory, more receptive than Norbrook and Patterson to the influence of Foucault, argues that recent feminist and antifeminist readings of Milton are both grounded in a modern "master discourse of sexuality" which is only anachronistically applied to Milton's text. Seeking to resolve the vexed question of how a reading of *Paradise Lost* can be simultaneously feminist and historicist, he analyzes the way superfluity in the prelapsarian Eden is represented as feminine in Books VII and VIII. He shows how the signs of gender difference in *Paradise Lost* are not attributable to the psychology of the characters, but rather are inextricable from economic concerns, and best understood in the context of the scientific and economic discourses nascent in the mid-seventeenth century.

In "Joyning my Labour to my Pain": The Politics of Labor in Marvell's Mower Poems," Rosemary Kegl shares with Guillory an interest in the relation between economic issues and issues of gender, both of which she sees addressed in Marvell's pastoral poetry. She points out how the figure of the mower is simultaneously privileged and overpowered in the poetry, just as in mid-seventeenth-century England actual mowers seemed the beneficiaries of an enclosure agriculture (because their strenuous labor demanded a high daily wage) even while suffering an actual displacement (because they had been deprived of their traditional rights to the land and compelled to perform seasonal wage labor.) Kegl sees the representation of women in the poems in similarly complex and problematic terms: Juliana is evoked only to be silenced, erased, and contained. Kegl connects this kind of double representation to the politics of seventeenth-century "gardens of rarities" which detached biological and ethnographical specimens from originally politicized contexts and meanings.

"Jonson and the Amazons" owes more to Freud than to Foucault or Marx, but by refusing to segregate the analysis of gender from the analysis of other issues Stephen Orgel, like Guillory and Kegl, suggests ways of fruitfully combining methods of inquiry that have usually been pursued separately and imagined as requiring different kinds of critical attention. Orgel examines the way Ben Jonson's *Masque of Queens* rewrites the ideology of the Elizabethan court, taking over the classical, chivalric, and Petrarchan *topoi* with which female sovereignty had been represented, and altering them to reflect the changed circumstances of James's rule. Orgel argues that Jonson uses the Perseus myth in this masque to fashion a hero whose valor takes the form of overcoming the Medusa, incorporating the "feminine" rhetorical power which the Gorgon's head confers. The deeply ambivalent representations of female power in *The Masque of Queens* provide both poet and king with a fantasy of masculine self-sufficiency which underlies Jacobean conceptions of literary and political authority. But Jonson has to do more than reassure a single nervous sovereign about the transfer of power from a queen to a king; for in fact various members of the Stuart royal family were his patrons, and their interests did not always coincide. Both *The Masque of Queens* and *Oberon,* the masque that follows it, address the implications of a chivalric ideology that can be made to represent both the king's pacifism and the increasing militarism of the heir apparent.

In different ways, the essays by Arthur Marotti, Jane Tylus, and Jonathan Goldberg explore the circumstances of textual production and reception in the seventeenth century. Their analyses take into account the material conditions of writing in the Renaissance, the philosophy and history of editing (both seventeenth-century and modern), and an often thematized sense of relationship with literary predecessors. Read together, these essays suggest how critics working from quite different methodological premises might challenge the view of the text as a literary artifact abstracted from the ideological context in which it was originally written and read. Marotti and Tylus, moreover, in their concern about the details of seventeenth-century editorial practice, help illuminate from an unexpected angle Renaissance conceptions of intertextuality and literary tradition with which Gordon Braden, Maureen Quilligan, and Stephen Orgel are likewise concerned.

In "Shakespeare's Sonnets as Literary Property," Arthur Marotti analyzes the manuscript and print history of Shakespeare's sonnets from the time of their presentation to a patron and their circulation among his "private friends," through their various incarnations in seventeenth-century printed editions. He sees the sonnets as texts caught between two notions of literary property—that of a system of manuscript transmission and that of a print culture. The fate of the sonnets reflects not only the processes of institutionalizing literature at work in the English Renaissance but also the way certain poems continue to be treated as texts of the very manuscript culture they help bring to an end. Marotti examines not only the material transmission of the sonnet texts in the seventeenth century but also the way the sonnets obsessively refer to themselves as commodities, texts in which the poet has a "proprietary" interest. Although the poems are supposedly written for an individual patron, the poet or publisher could circulate them among a large readership, claiming that they are enduring poetic monuments that will outlast both author and patron. This gesture disrupts or complicates the patronage relationship and points towards the public possession realized by subsequent editing and criticism.

In "Jacobean Poetry and Lyric Disappointment," Jane Tylus examines the political and poetic aims of the English Spenserians. She shows how anthologies of pastoral poetry like *England's Helicon,* which seem to divorce pastoral from its political and cultural subtexts, nonetheless reflect a sophisticated sense of the political implications of inherited generic categories. Through her analysis of Jacobean editorial theories, she, like Marotti, investigates changing conceptions of literary property and the emergence of the notion of an enclosed and stable text. Her discussion of the revision of pastoral genres in the seventeenth century has some affinities with Rosemary Kegl's, although she is more concerned with the way pastoral becomes a way of establishing a refuge from the structures of authority at court than with the way pastoral reflects political strategies for controlling the laboring classes.

In "Dating Milton," Jonathan Goldberg likewise destabilizes some traditional editorial notions, but by questioning not so much the unity and self-identity of the text as the unity and self-identity of the author. Working from the indeterminate date of Milton's "When I consider how my light is spent," a sonnet that directly addresses issues of poetic identity and poetic career, Goldberg investigates the scholarly fictions involved in attempts to reconstruct the Miltonic "I" and fix a time and place in which it speaks. Goldberg maintains that seductive but implausible narratives about the development of individuals and cultures are central not only to traditional literary-historical scholarship but also to some recent new-historicist accounts (so that, for instance, Eliot's modernist account of the dissociation of sensibility is recapitulated in Francis Barker's Foucauldian history of the subject in *The Tremulous Private Body.*) Goldberg enlarges his discussion to treat problems posed by the editorial positioning of the authorial voice in three other Miltonic texts: the autobiographical passages in *The Reason of Church Government, An Apology for Smectymnus,* and the *Second Defense of the People of England.*

Stanley Fish, Gordon Braden, Michael Schoenfeldt, and Maureen Quilligan discuss, from different perspectives, the particular forms of anxiety that result when seventeenth-century poets modify the traditional rhetoric of sexual desire to serve what seem to be new erotic or religious purposes. In "Masculine Persuasive Force: Donne and Verbal Power," Stanley Fish reads Donne's poetry as an exploration of creative linguistic force, a power that is figured in terms of a sexualized domination or submission. Fish shows how the *Elegies, Satires, Songs and Sonnets,* and religious lyrics are informed and motivated by Donne's self-reflexive hunger for and revulsion against verbal power: what Fish calls "linguistic bulimia." Donne's antimimetic theory of language asserts that verbal representation is not constrained by the world but in fact produces reality. His rhetorical virtuosity thus allows him to exert control over a world that had disappointed him, and, at the same time, to realize that the infinite plasticity of language renders such victories meaningless.

Braden, Schoenfeldt, and Quilligan share with Fish a conviction that the Renaissance literary imagination is deeply involved in disturbances of gender identity, but instead of relating these disturbances to a tradition of sophistic rhetoric, they see the seventeenth-century revolution in erotic discourse constituting itself as an ambiguous struggle with, and adaptation of, Petrarchan tropes and forms. In "Unspeakable Love: Petrarch to Herbert," Gordon Braden examines the legacy of Petrarch in the context of Renaissance individualism. In a culture increasingly conscious of articulate speech as a source of power, the paralysis of speech in the face of overwhelming longing (the paradigm of the Petrarchan lover) enacts an important discipline on the acquisitive self. Braden shows how Petrarch's poetry inaugurates a thematics of speech and the subject which is both perpetuated and transformed first in Sidney, for whom speechlessness results not only from the unattainability of the lady but from the anxiety of influence, and then once more in the Protestant poetics of George Herbert.

Michael Schoenfeldt makes a different kind of argument for the relation of Herbert's poetry to secular love poetry, pointing out the sexual implications of the ways in which Herbert attempts to imagine and address God in his lyric poetry. In "'That Ancient Heat': Sexuality and Spirituality in *The Temple*," Schoenfeldt argues that Herbert's poetry represents and is motivated by a simultaneously energizing and guilty inability to transcend the flesh in the worship of the divine. The intersection of spiritual and physical desire becomes the subject of a poem like "Paradise," in which linguistic pruning or "paring" analogically expresses the excision of desire that would constitute the poet's Eden. The eroticism in *The Temple* is not merely phallic, however. Although he recognizes the conventional expressions of misogyny in Herbert's poetry, Schoenfeldt sees in poems like "The Bag" a representation of a Christ whose vulnerability becomes a sexualized femininity which constitutes the essence of humanity and compassion. Schoenfeldt argues that the "anxious eroticism" of Herbert's poetry derives from an early seventeenth-century context which witnessed the early stages of a progressive privatization of sexuality; to dismiss the erotic implications of the lyrics is to retreat from history.

In "The Constant Subject: Instability and Female Authority in Wroth's *Urania* Poems," Maureen Quilligan shows how some Petrarchan paradigms change in the hands of a female author describing female characters and experience, in a tradition in which the articulation of desire has been an exclusively male prerogative, and in which the lady is imagined as silent or absent. Her essay has especially interesting affinities with Braden's, since she too is concerned with the way a poet in the Petrarchan tradition can articulate a place from which to speak by exploiting the very conventions that would seem to silence her. The title and form of Wroth's prosometric pastoral romance were designed to recall her connection with her uncle, Sir Philip Sidney. Not only does Wroth draw on family relationships in an extratextual sense, but family relationships are also inscribed within the romance, both as a theme and as a system of echoes. Whereas in Sidney's *Arcadia* Urania is the absent, lamented beloved, she is at the center of Wroth's poem, but because she does not know her family, she mourns her lack of identity. This self-less condition paradoxically allows her to insert herself into the well-defined position of the Petrarchan speaker. Urania comments upon the historical belatedness of this position by speaking her extempore sonnet in the voice of Echo, a figure who can, of course, only say what has already been said. Her lament is itself a comment, Quilligan argues, on the appropriation of Petrarchan discourse by a woman, a discourse the very incompleteness and repetitiveness of which become the mark of gender.

The essays in this volume are deeply skeptical of many of the received ideas about a literature that is itself sensitive to the disruption of epistemological, social, and economic certainties. What emerges in the collection is not a new consensus but a skeptical interrogation of numerous received ideas along a variety of fronts. The value of the collection, we believe, lies not in its pretensions to definitive readings but in the way it unsettles established modes of interpretation.

Katharine Eisaman Maus
Elizabeth D. Harvey

## Notes

1. Two of many essays discussing the phenomena are Miller's and Howard's.

2. T. S. Eliot, "The Metaphysical Poets"; Cleanth Brooks, *Modern Poetry and the Tradition,* p. 203.

3. Some exceptions to this general rule are Rajan, Marotti, and Docherty. Tillotama Rajan, "'Nothing Sooner Broke': Donne's *Songs and Sonets* as Self-

Consuming Artifact," *ELH* 49 (1982): 805–28; Arthur F. Marotti, *John Donne: Coterie Poet* (Madison: University of Wisconsin Press, 1986); Thomas Docherty, *John Donne Undone* (New York: Methuen, 1986).

## Works Cited

Francis Barker. *The Tremulous Private Body: Essays on Subjection.* New York: Methuen, 1985.

Cleanth Brooks. *Modern Poetry and the Tradition.* Chapel Hill: University of North Carolina Press, 1939.

———. *The Well Wrought Urn: Studies in the Structure of Poetry.* New York: Harcourt, Brace, 1947.

Jacques Derrida. *Writing and Difference.* Trans. Alan Bass. Chicago: University of Chicago Press, 1978.

Jonathan Dollimore. *Radical Tragedy: Religion, Ideology, and Power in the Drama of Shakespeare and His Contemporaries.* Chicago: University of Chicago Press, 1984.

T. S. Eliot. *Selected Essays.* New York: Harcourt, Brace, and World, 1964.

Margaret Ferguson, Maureen Quilligan, and Nancy J. Vickers, eds. *Rewriting the Renaissance: The Discourses of Sexual Difference in Early Modern Europe.* Chicago: University of Chicago Press, 1986.

Jonathan Goldberg. *James I and the Politics of Literature.* Baltimore: Johns Hopkins University Press, 1983.

———. *Voice Terminal Echo: Postmodernism and English Renaissance Texts.* New York: Methuen, 1986.

Stephen Greenblatt. *Renaissance Self-Fashioning.* Chicago: University of Chicago Press, 1981.

———. *Shakespearean Negotiations: The Circulation of Social Energy in Renaissance England.* Berkeley: University of California Press, 1988.

John Guillory. "The Ideology of Canon Formation: T. S. Eliot and Cleanth Brooks." *Critical Inquiry* 10 (1983): 173–98.

Richard Helgerson. *Self-Crowned Laureates: Spenser, Jonson, Milton, and the Literary System.* Berkeley: University of California Press, 1983.

Jean E. Howard. "The New Historicism in Renaissance Studies." In *Renaissance Historicism: Selections from English Literary Renaissance,* ed. Arthur F. Kinney and Dan F. Collins. Amherst: University of Massachusetts Press, 1987, pp. 3–33.

Leah S. Marcus. *Politics of Mirth: Jonson, Herrick, Marvell, and the Defense of the Old Holiday Pastimes.* Chicago: University of Chicago Press, 1986.

Arthur F. Marotti. *John Donne, Coterie Poet.* Madison: University of Wisconsin Press, 1986.

J. Hillis Miller. "The Triumph of Theory, the Resistance to Reading, and the Question of the Material Base." *PMLA* 102 (1987): 281–91.

Louis Adrian Montrose. "'Eliza, Queene of Shepheardes,' and the Pastoral of Power," *English Literary Renaissance* 10 (1980): 153–82.

―――. "Of Gentlemen and Shepherds: The Politics of Elizabethan Pastoral Form." *ELH* 50 (1983): 415–89.

David Norbrook. *Poetry and Politics in the English Renaissance*. London: Routledge and Kegan Paul, 1984.

Stephen Orgel. *The Illusion of Power*. Berkeley: University of California Press, 1975.

Stephen Orgel, ed. *Patronage in the Renaissance*. Princeton: Princeton University Press, 1982.

Patricia Parker. *Literary Fat Ladies: Rhetoric, Gender, Property*. New York: Methuen, 1987.

Annabel Patterson. *Censorship and Interpretation*. Madison: University of Wisconsin Press, 1984.

René Wellek and Austin Warren. *Theory of Literature*. New York: Harcourt, Brace, 1949.

W. K. Wimsatt. *The Verbal Icon: Studies in the Meaning of Poetry*. Lexington: University of Kentucky Press, 1954.

I

# THE POLITICS OF
# POETIC REPRESENTATION

# I

# The Monarchy of Wit and the Republic of Letters: Donne's Politics

## David Norbrook

*Here lies a King, that rul'd as hee thought* fit
*The universall Monarchy of* wit
*Here lies two Flamens, and both those, the best,*
*Apollo's first, at last, the true Gods* Priest.[1]

In 1633 the phrasing of Thomas Carew's elegy for Donne had powerful political connotations. Europe was polarized between rival power blocs and rival cultural models. On the one hand there were the Habsburg powers, the spearhead of Counter-Reformation reaction throughout Europe, who were accused of aspiring to a universal monarchy. Where their influence was felt, representative political institutions were eclipsed; and an independent intellectual life gave way to a theatrical public world of secular and religious ritual.[2] The Habsburgs' archenemy was the Dutch Republic, a problematic political entity but one which permitted religious toleration, relative freedom of the press, and a thriving bourgeois economy. In the long term, absolutism was to be defeated; but that victory seemed by no means inevitable in the mid-seventeenth century, and in the short term the extinction of independent intellectual life became a reality in many parts of Europe.[3] In the 1630s it seemed to many Britons that the king was moving towards the Habsburg model, refusing to aid Protestants abroad and sponsoring a more ritualized state church; he was contrasted unfavorably with Gustavus Adolphus of Sweden, who actively aided the Protestant cause. Later in 1633 the Swedish king was killed at Lützen, and his death was passionately mourned in England. The following year Carew's friend Aurelian

3

Townshend wrote to him calling on him to canonize Gustavus Ado-
lphus with the same zeal as he had shed tears "on the herse Of divine
Donne."[4] Carew's reply politely refused. His argument begins as a mod-
est *recusatio,* declaring that neither Virgil, nor Lucan, nor Tasso, nor
even Donne, "worth all that went before," could do justice to the Swed-
ish king, and urging Townshend to return to the peaceful arts of
masquing. Carew lacks the enthusiasm of some of his compatriots for
the Protestant militancy of the ruler he elsewhere called, with barely
concealed disparagement, "the royall Goth."[5] For Carew, it seems, Do-
nne's poetry is bound up with a monarchist, High Anglican culture
which is antagonistic to the values of Protestant militancy.

In the 1633 elegies Donne became canonized as a pillar of the mon-
archy and High Anglicanism. This image of him as quintessentially a
monarchist poet has predominated from Walton's *Life* prefaced to the
1640 *LXXX Sermons* down to the New Criticism and beyond. In *The
Well Wrought Urn,* Cleanth Brooks took Donne's lyrics as central in-
stances of an "incarnational" poetry whose vivid, concrete images
corresponded to the ritual of the old monarchical order later disrupted
by Puritanism; the urn analogy implies a view of poems as timeless,
transcendent objects to be contemplated, rather than as agents in a his-
torical process.[6]

In recent years, of course, this notion of poetry as transcending its
society has been sharply challenged; but the effect of this challenge has if
anything been to reinforce the notion of Donne the monarchist. In an
impressive, ground-breaking series of sociological studies, David Aers
and Gunter Kress have drawn on Mark Curtis's notion of the "alienated
intellectual" produced by an educational system whose supply of gradu-
ates exceeded the demand for official positions. Such figures could
become politically oppositional; but, Aers and Kress argue, as a Catholic
in origin Donne lacked the Puritan conviction that was an essential com-
ponent of a radical ideology. Lacking any coherent ideology, and
rejecting the social isolation that resulted from holding to his Catholic
origins, he could therefore easily become incorporated in the monar-
chical establishment—in Gramscian terms a "traditional" intellectual
rather than an "organic" intellectual of emergent social groups. Though
Aers and Kress are more open than other recent critics to utopian mo-
ments in some of Donne's earlier poems, they emphasize how quickly
such moments collapse.[7] Though they acknowledge the possibility of
opposition, they tend to see any form of office-holding as a complete
capitulation, and the direction of their analysis is therefore pessimistic:
purity is bought at the cost of practical efficacy.

Such pessimism has deepened in many recent "new historicist" critics who have emphasized the impossibility of any sustained opposition to dominant power structures. Thus Jonathan Goldberg has declared not only that Donne's self-constitution was essentially "absolutist" but also that for Donne "there seems to be no alternative"; Goldberg finds absolutism as much in the early lyrics as in the later sermons.[8] In the fullest sociological analysis to date, Arthur Marotti is able to give a more nuanced picture but nonetheless sees Donne as essentially a conservative coterie poet, the monarch of an exclusive inner circle of wits who disdained the wider republic of letters. Marotti emphasizes the role of Donne's poetry in reinforcing social status or bidding for wealth and court position.[9]

These recent critics have made a decisive contribution in helping to banish simplistic notions of poetry as serenely transcending its society and political structures. But in resisting traditional depoliticization, the new political criticism may depoliticize poetry in new ways. Indeed in criticism strongly influenced by Foucault and poststructuralism there is a conscious resistance to analysis in political terms, insofar as the concept of "politics" seems to be bound up with outmoded humanist notions of self-determination and rationality. The problem with this rejection of politics is that it risks replicating a structure of the very absolutist thought that is being critically analyzed. The classical republicanism which became the basis of the Renaissance and Enlightenment critique of absolutism made a central distinction between states confined to the naked exercise of power, the will of one monarch, and states in which power gave way to politics, the exercise of rational decision-making by autonomous agents. Renaissance republicanism tended to distinguish absolutist from republican orders precisely because only the latter permitted a fully political life to emerge.[10] The Elizabethans were assimilating the civic humanist notion that participation in politics is a right, a responsibility, and an essential means of self-fulfillment. It would of course be naive to take such claims entirely at face value; Foucauldian critics can point to all kinds of ways in which this opposition between absolutist politics and more democratic power was itself a mystification. Nonetheless, we do not necessarily gain in sophistication by ignoring such distinctions and analyzing Renaissance England as if it were Louis XIV's France. Such elisions are made possible by the ubiquitous linkage in modern criticism of the terms "subject" and "subjection": if the distinction between subject and citizen is the central mark of transition from absolutism to republicanism, current theoretical terminology tends to blur this distinction until it appears insignificant.[11] Critics who have focused on Donne's half-shameful presentation of his pursuit of power seem almost to share the old Augustinian view that he was being presumptuous in seeking power at all. The assumption that Donne and his contemporaries were fundamentally irrationalists, their minds dazzled by spectacular images of authority, has influenced the reading of Donne's poetry and prose. The metaphor of the "monarch of wit" is taken fairly literally, with the emphasis placed on the irrational, coercive power of figures and tropes. Donne is obviously a forceful and persuasive writer; but an analysis which paid closer attention to the contexts of his writings would, I think, qualify the view of his unequivocal absolutism.

I do not want to argue, against the current consensus, that Donne was a full-fledged oppositional figure. His discourse was very different from the combination of humanism and strong Protestantism that motivated an increasingly radical poetic tradition from Spenser to Milton. Where Spenserians like Drayton urged the need for the poet to address a wide public through the new medium of print, Donne confined most of his poetry to a private coterie. In criticizing the vogue for "Metaphysicall Ideas, and Scholasticall Quiddityes," William Drummond was in tune with a humanist tradition that opposed linguistic elegance to the barbarism of scholastic philosophy; Donne's celebratedly "metaphysical" poetry reflects his refusal to exalt the classical so firmly at the expense of more idiosyncratic interests in byways of medieval and Spanish literature and theology.[12] These differences of course reflect his Catholic background at a time when the norms of public poetic discourse had been set by a strongly Protestant humanism.

It was because of such differences that in a recent study of Renaissance public poetry I was ready to accept the high-church monarchist reading—to the extent of describing Donne quite mistakenly as a bishop.[13] In trying to remedy this error, I would like also to reexamine the common factors that may have counterpoised the differences. The social forces that were helping intellectuals to gain increasing confidence in their public role were operating on Donne as well, albeit mediated through his distinct personal background. When viewed more closely, Donne's final apotheosis as Caroline monarchist looks much less clear-cut and inevitable: he never achieved a finally secure standpoint in the Caroline regime. The quest for a standpoint is a unifying motif of Donne's writings. He constantly seeks to put his feet down on the ground, to become part of a society from which he feels alienated. And yet he desires also to maintain a critical distance, a standpoint outside the existing social order from which he can criticize it. I shall try to show that his writings never abandoned this latter, critical perspective;

and that if nonetheless he did seek a standing within society, this aim reflected a sense of the limitations of the quest for a purely transcendent critique at least as much as a capitulation to absolutism. Donne's position as an intellectual was less traditional than hindsight may make it seem.

I

Conventional discussions of Donne's lack of any coherent ideology begin with his apostasy from his childhood religious faith—and also from the legacy of his most eminent predecessor as a writer in his family, Sir Thomas More. One side of this legacy was formed of traditional pieties: we are told that one of More's miraculously divided teeth was passed down in the Heywood family.[14] John Carey of course makes Donne's apostasy from his Catholic background the central fact of his career.[15] But some of More's writings, most notably *Utopia,* transmitted a critical, politically rationalistic humanism, strongly influenced by classical republicanism (Utopia has a figurehead prince, but he is elected).

The more secular aspect of More's and Erasmus's legacy was problematic for the Counter-Reformation church. As the Tridentine church elevated More with increasing vehemence as an anti-Protestant hero, so his texts had to be more strictly purged of anticlerical comments: many cuts were made from the *Utopia* and other works in the 1565 Louvain edition, which was issued as a counter to the Erasmian Basel edition—the one that Donne owned.[16] The *Utopia* was taken up by intellectuals whose own relation to authority was problematic. The first Italian translation was issued by Ortensio Lando and Francesco Doni, two outspoken social critics who were fiercely opposed to the effects of Habsburg influence in Italy and saw the continuing republicanism of Venice as a glimmer of utopian hope.[17] Donne knew and borrowed from Lando's *Paradossi,* and we know from *Ignatius his Conclave* that he followed the process by which the values of Machiavelli's prince drove out republicanism from Italy; Donne translates the "civilitate" which has been lost as "all civility & re-publique," contrasting both cultural and political forms under a monarchy with those of a republic (even though the narrator at this point is hardly reliable, the usage is interesting).[18] Lando signed several of his works as "A Citizen of Utopia" or "Utopian lover of truth," and many later Renaissance Utopias carried "Utopia" as place of publication on their title pages: More's Utopia may have been an imaginary state but his work's circulation helped to outline a space for an international republic of letters, an ideal community to which entry was freely offered to those with ability and whose values were critical of tradition, struggling to replace the arbitrary exercise of power by rational political debate. Though Habermas does not date the full emergence of the bourgeois public sphere until the late seventeenth century, its emergence was already rapidly accelerated as soon as printing was invented. The term "republic of letters" was a metaphor, but the implications of its values ran counter to absolutism.[19] The *Utopia* sets up a characteristic contrast between the systematically distorted communication (to borrow Habermas's term) of absolutist courts, where policy is governed by private, personal impulses and mystified by dazzling images, and the equal participation in public discourse in More's ideal republic. But there is a further tension between the strong impulse to retreat from public corruption and an awareness that such a Stoic withdrawal, standing self-sufficiently in one's own circle, may be selfish and irresponsible. The dazzling paradoxes of *Utopia* leave the reader, and indeed the author, with no secure place to stand.

The legacy of More, then, would for Donne have been highly problematic: to be loyal to a papacy which had grown far more rigid in the mid-sixteenth century was to support the suppression of the utopian republic of letters; to be loyal to a Protestant monarchy which took harsh punitive measures against his kindred was not an attractive alternative. Nor did these contradictory positions seem to offer an intellectually coherent middle way. In *The Courtier's Library* he mercilessly satirizes Erasmus's attempt to find "Equilibrium in two volumes, or the art of reaching stability in controversy." (To decide about transubstantiation Donne's Erasmus writes "yes" and "no" on equally-sized slips of paper and weighs them to see which is the heavier.)[20] In the 1590s Lipsius was giving a new authority to a neo-Stoic role for the intellectual, that of standing above public religious and political controversies, accepting a permanent dissociation between the public world and the inner republic of letters. As opposed to Luther's "Here I stand," Lipsius's neo-Stoicism affirmed that the intellectual could stand in his own autonomous circle: a state of perfection symbolized by his friend Plantin's emblem of the compasses.[21] Another aspect of More's legacy, however, was the belief that Stoic self-sufficiency could be an evasion of social responsibility, and Donne's close friend Ben Jonson, who was converted to Catholicism for several years, took the broken compass as his emblem. Donne found it equally hard to be an apostate, to stand outside, and to stand in the middle.

Given these conflicting pressures, it is not surprising that in the 1590s Donne, far from being firmly monarchist, wrote even more mordantly antimonarchical poetry than any of his contemporaries. But it is possible to exaggerate the monarchism of the period generally: absolutist elements in the polity were being countered by growing political elements. A number of theorists saw England as a mixed polity, a *dominium regale et politicum* in Fortescue's phrase, and medieval theories of limited monarchy had been given a new humanist cast by writers like Thomas Starkey. Republicanism pure and simple was hardly a practicable option in England before the Civil War, and even seventeenth-century republicans often allowed an element of monarchical power; the crucial point was that the claims of political participation from below were strongly asserted against absolutists who would deny them.[22] Parliamentarians were growing in self-confidence in Donne's lifetime. In 1610 his former patron Lord Ellesmere could complain that Britain was becoming a democracy.[23] Sir Henry Wotton, a man with much Italian experience, commented in 1614 that M.P.s were behaving like Venetian senators and forgetting that when they left the House they would "return . . . to their natural capacity of subjects."[24] In Renaissance London a traditionally strong civic consciousness, one of the presences behind More's Utopia, was growing rapidly, and the city was a center for the dissemination of news as well as commodities.[25] It is right to see Donne as a coterie poet, but we should also remember that he was the son of an ironmonger and would thus have always been slightly distanced from the sons of county gentry. Barbara Everett sees him as quintessentially a London poet, addressing a "metropolis of letters," manifesting an intellectual rather than a social elitism, and this is an important distinction. In common with most Elizabethan writers, Donne certainly lacks the broader concern for the less wealthy social groups that is found in More and earlier sixteenth-century writers—or in his contemporary, Joseph Hall, a poet, utopian writer, and later bishop. But there is less routine sneering against citizens than in many of his contemporaries.[26] The elegies and satires go beyond their Roman models by depending for much of their wit on an informed knowledge of current affairs, including an ability to criticize the inaccuracy of the available news-sheets. The boldness of the 1590s satire of course provoked a reaction; the intellectuals had moved a long way beyond the borders of acceptable discourse. Nashe found to his cost that London was not Venice and he could not be an English Aretino, and Donne did not risk publishing his satires. In this wider context it is not surprising to find Donne oscillating so insecurely between self-assertion and self-depreciation. I. A. Shapiro has suggested that Donne's extraordinary misjudgment in marrying the daughter of a social superior in 1601, an odd act from someone whose only concern was to ingratiate himself with his patrons, may have been fuelled by the access of confidence, the sense of being a rightful participant in public processes, that derived from his election to Parliament that year.[27]

But participation meant compromise, the inescapable dilemma of the *Utopia,* and the author of the Third Satire did not find compromise easy. The voice is that of a critical intellectual who has set aside all traditional religious prejudices and institutional loyalties, distancing himself equally from the opposed political poles of the Spanish Inquisition and the "mutinous Dutch" and yet not finding the correct position in the *via media* either. To find truth it is necessary to "stand inquiring" for a time, to withdraw from public activity, and yet this is not a Stoic self-sufficiency but a process, not just willing but doing; it is really truth that stands still while the inquirer must be constantly on the move, not in a simple linear way but spiralling slowly upward. And the truth has public implications: though the poem ends with a bleakly disillusioned view of all power, it also insists that one religious position is the correct one, so that ideological choices can be made between different powers. The poem's brusque imperatives reveal Donne's uneasy awareness that the critical audience to which it is addressed as yet scarcely exists.

## II

Donne eventually did take up a public stand; and one of his reasons for doing so was to gain wealth and power. John Carey exaggerates, however, in presenting Donne as "spending . . . twenty years straining every nerve to get a secure foothold" at court.[28] The dialectical movement of the Third Satire, or of the debate in *Utopia,* better describe his career than a linear movement towards power; and he never really did gain a secure foothold. It is significant that his first known allusions to *Utopia* come from the period when he entered public office under Sir Thomas Egerton. In his verse letter to Sir Henry Wotton, "Sir, more then kisses, letters mingle Soules," he says that writing to Wotton helps him to "ideate"—a word he generally uses elsewhere in reference to the ideal republics of Plato and More.[29] What Donne is trying to "ideate" in this letter is some standpoint from which he can criticize his society without becoming implicated in its power structures. As in More's *Utopia,* the debate is made especially problematic by the fact that his contempt for the public world is set against an equally vehement contempt for evasive retirement. Rejecting a simple opposition between court and country or court and city, Donne concludes that no part of society is untouched by corruption:

I thinke if men, which in these places live
Durst looke for themselves, and themselves retrive,
They would like strangers greet themselves, seeing than
Utopian youth, growne old Italian.

(I, 182)

That last line makes its moral point by a political analogy with the
process by which the old republican culture of the Italian city-states had
become extinguished by an absolutist court culture. Donne sees each
individual as undergoing a similar process in his own life, a process of
absolute alienation from a pristine republican self. He goes on to imag-
ine Wotton as achieving a kind of self-sufficiency, but this is less simple
than the Stoic retreat Wotton had counseled in the poem that he had
addressed to Donne; not a traditional balance of opposing humors but a
radical self-purgation that leaves the individual in and yet not of the
world, "as / Fishes glide, leaving no print where they passe, / Nor mak-
ing sound." This analogy, like that of the high hill, combines the sense of
movement with that of a kind of self-sufficiency, but not simply a Stoic
standing on firm ground.[30] Such an analogy retains the sense of self-
alienation, however, and the only valid community the poem envisages
is the republic of letters, specifically in the letters with which humanist
intellectuals can mingle their souls. Wotton's world at this stage was that
of the energetic but confined intellectuals around Essex, and Donne
perhaps echoes "The World" by Francis Bacon, whose writing always
tended to move, not unlike Donne's, between radical utopian visions
and overinsistent public deference.[31]

It would be easy to exaggerate the anticourtly element of the verse
letters: Marotti describes "Sir, more then kisses" as "patently disin-
genuous" because both Wotton and Donne were energetically pursuing
preferment. If Stoicism could be a pose, however, so could ambition;
and Marotti goes on to point out that Wotton was "following an Earl
whose political fortunes were clearly declining," a course of action
which seems totally inexplicable if the analysis is purely in terms of the
will to power.[32] But to see the 1590s court purely in terms of the strug-
gle for personal power is to suppress significant political factors. One
reason the earl's fortunes were declining was precisely that he was fol-
lowing a political line that the queen considered dangerously "popular"
and was flirting too much with men of radical political views. Essex had
inherited the political alignments built up by Leicester, who had been
accused of constructing his own "commonwealth," a state within a state
made up of followers who were anxious for England to play a decisive

part in shifting the balance of European politics away from Habsburg ascendancy, and who built up their own republic of letters, establishing close contact with republicans and religious radicals on the Continent. As part of his campaign to unify anti-Habsburg forces, Essex had recently commissioned Wotton to write a lengthy defense of the Aragonese rebellion against Philip II; Wotton wrote that since the people were the creators of the king they had every right to depose him, and cited the examples of the depositions of Edward II and Richard II. Essex wanted to have this treatise published, but not surprisingly only a Spanish-language edition for foreign consumption was allowed to appear.[33] One could call Wotton's text coterie literature in the sense that it was not published; but it was not written to give a smug sense of aristocratic solidarity, it was precisely because its implications tended towards a widening of the sphere of public political activity that it had to remain private. Undoubtedly much of Donne's disdain for print was a product of the kind of elitism Marotti chronicles; but it is worth remembering that works might also be withheld from print for political reasons.[34]

Donne kept a certain distance from the Essex circle, in which militant Protestant views were dominant, and he had connections with Essex's rivals Ralegh and Northumberland.[35] But his continuing correspondence with Wotton reveals his concern at the gradual decline of the earl's, and consequently of Wotton's, fortunes, and alludes to the constraints placed on correspondence by censorship. The years before Essex's rebellion saw increasing political tension and a tightening of censorship culminating in the ban on satire in June 1599. In a letter probably to Wotton about 1600 Donne declares that "to my satyrs there belongs some feare"[36]; and the censors in 1633 were to hesitate before allowing their publication, and trimmed them of antimonarchical comments. The fact that Donne did not publish these poems in the 1590s makes them count as coterie poems, but no other form of circulation would have been possible for the more polemical passages. This political context helps to explain the violence of Donne's reaction when reading Dante at this time: he was so angry at Dante's condemnation of Celestine's "gran rifiuto" in rejecting public office that he threw away his copy of the book.[37] Retiredness to Donne seems much more honorable than ambition. His later comments in *The Courtier's Library* reveal his muted sympathy with Essex even after his rebellion in 1601 and his bitterness at Bacon's betrayal of Essex. Ten years after Essex's fall Donne dated his "death" to that period.[38]

III

It was in the period of the most acute political tension, between Essex's confinement and his rebellion, that Donne fell in love with Ann More. It would be possible to read his secret marriage as part of his ruthless search to ingratiate himself with power, but it was certainly an inept attempt; and for the next few years his quest for public employment was intermittent. He did not write a poem greeting James's accession, and in 1604 a friend had to write to him asking why he made himself such a stranger to the Court.[39] This period is normally accepted as that of the greatest, most original *Songs and Sonets;* and the recurrent exploration of new private worlds in these poems represents a displaced, or redefined, utopianism in a period of extreme alienation from the public world. If More, Sidney, and Spenser created massive literary "golden worlds" dealing with public themes, Donne, inhibited from sharing all their political values, compresses comparable literary ambitions into his little rooms: the best *Songs and Sonets* represent in effect the implosion of epic aspirations.[40] William Empson, Donne's most eloquent champion in the present century, repeatedly argued for this utopian impulse in Donne's lyrics, an impulse that led to a radical rethinking of conventional hierarchies and a search, however flawed, for a more equal kind of relationship with the women of the poems. On Empson's reading, Donne's portrayal of the lovers' creating their new world has a science-fiction aspect, breaking out of the religious and geographical confinements of *terra firma* altogether; he draws parallels also with the radical antinomian experiments of some of the Protestant sects.[41] Support for utopian readings can be derived from the recurrent puns on the word "more," which may allude both to Donne's wife and to his utopian ancestor.[42] Aers and Kress speak of the *Songs and Sonets* as creating poetic "antiworlds."[43]

Whatever his eccentricities of argument, Empson does seem to me to have located a genuine radical impulse in these poems, and to have been justified in objecting to the mean-mindedness of neo-Christian critics of the Cold War epoch who tried to bring the lyrics back in line with a conservative cultural pessimism. Eliot and Brooks did this by reading back the alleged religious conservatism of the later writings into the lyrics, and seeing the blasphemous use of conventional religious language as testifying to an underlying orthodoxy. More recently, the terms of the argument have been transformed: both deconstructionist criticism and the "new historicism" have repudiated transcendental readings. The new theorists, however, have sometimes ended up sounding remarkably like the neo-Christians.

Deconstruction has radically inverted the conventional description of Donne as a "metaphysical" by seeing him as an antimetaphysical poet, undermining the nascent Cartesian "metaphysic of presence" by denying any attempt to fix on a coherent meaning, identity, or ideology.[44] Poststructuralism can take on many different political inflections, and one recent deconstructionist study, Thomas Docherty's *John Donne, Undone,* agrees with Empson in finding utopian potential in the lyrics. But the tone was set for much recent criticism by a Paul de Man essay which used Empson as a warning against "certain Marxist illusions"—the "illusions" de Man believed inherent in any attempt to construct a large-scale historical interpretation.[45] Tillotama Rajan's de Manian reading of the *Songs and Sonets* finds that Donne "defeats" the "romantic humanism" Empson had admired in the major lyrics "by self-irony." The poems are a "dramatization of the dialogue between human aspiration and the acknowledgement of post-lapsarian wit"; but the "dialogue" proves to come down in favor of a mature resignation in the face of the Fall. Rajan's essay ends with a qu ion from that old favourite of the *contemptus mundi* school, *The Second Anniversary.*[46]

In response to what have often seemed the ahistorical categories of deconstruction, "new historicists" have called for stricter contextualization; but they have tended to share with deconstruction an insistence on the illusory character of any attempt at conscious control of one's social context. That celebrated lyric "The Sunne Rising," once regarded as a triumphantly optimistic poem, has come to epitomize social defeat and confinement. Empson valued Donne's insolent decentering of the traditional cosmic imagery that linked monarch with sun; the sun finds its standpoint in the poet's final stanza, the room where Donne's exultant "I" is modulating into the solidarity of "us." On Empson's view, "instead of dignifying the individual by comparison to the public institution, he treats the institution as only a pallid imitation of the individual. All the imaginative structures which men have built to control themselves are only derived from these simple intimate basic relations, and the apparently fantastic compliment is no more than brutal fact."[47] Recent criticism has claimed rather that Donne's subjectivity was inexorably determined by the dominant discourse, so that we must expect to find his poems replicating precisely the authoritarian values they try to escape. Carey insists that "if kings can be supreme only by being kings, then kings are still supreme. The private world is valued only as it apes the public." In describing the woman, here as elsewhere, as a "girl," Carey emphasizes the almost pedophiliac desire to dominate an inferior which has become accepted as the prevailing note in Donne's poetry. If such an authoritarian figure does voice contempt for kings, then it can only be the product of "jealousy."[48] Marotti sees Donne's "furtive erotic activity" as a manifestation of "displaced anger," Donne's facade of enjoyment of carnality with his wife being merely a displacement of his "frustrated needs" for worldly advancement.[49] While Empson saw Donne's reluctance to publish these lyrics as part of his safeguarding of a radically innovative private utopia from the conventionally minded, Marotti sees it as an aristocratic expression of disdain for the lower orders. And for Goldberg the poem provides a neat illustration of the new historicist double bind: in comparing himself to princes the speaker reveals that he is himself "absolutist."[50]

That there are tensions and insecurities in the poem can be readily conceded; and the voice of Donne's speaker, offering an emergent nuclear family as a new paradise, is obviously open to a feminist critique. The emergence of the "bourgeois public sphere" was related to the increasing confinement of women to a private, domestic sphere. Empson did not mince words in speaking of Donne as "gradually killing his wife by giving her a child every year."[51] The double bind constructed by some new historicists is too neatly symmetrical, however: subversion is always and inevitably contained, any attempt to distance oneself from the public world ends up by reproducing its structure. But if Donne failed to model his erotic utopia in "The Sunne Rising" on the austere discourse of republican virtue, it was not necessarily because of repressed absolutism. Donne was seeking a metaphor for a certain male postcoital mood of expansive exhilaration.[52] For such an unregenerate mood, the popular image of the king as a figure of unrestrained bounty and excess may seem a more appropriate analogue; but it would be literal-minded to infer that the user of such an analogy necessarily wishes the realm to be permanently ruled by one individual in such a frame of mind. Indeed, by parodically appropriating a Christ-like or monarchical status to himself, Donne undermines the claims of such discourses to transcendent status. The monarchical symbolism in the *Songs and Sonets* derives in part from the Stoic notion of the man who withdraws from the public world to become king of himself. But Donne's king cannot stand by himself: as the recurrent sexual puns on that word indicate, he is incomplete without some kind of mutual relationship.[53] Donne's most famous emblem for standing together is the compass simile from "A Valediction: Forbidding Mourning." As has been seen, the compass could be a figure of Stoic self-sufficiency, while the broken compass implied the inevitable failure of such aspirations. Donne's figure rejects both a purely individualistic humanism and a pessimistic antihumanism. He revises a probable source-poem by Guarini in which the lover is the active compass, the woman the still center; in Donne the two lovers are mutually supportive legs of the compass, and while the woman remains the less active partner, the sense of mutuality is reinforced by the meter's syllabic stiffness.[54]

The figure of the precariously standing compasses testifies also to the extreme precariousness of this private utopia. The recurrent geographical and cosmological images combine a joy in turning the outside world inward with a fear of intimacy and desire for distance. Whether Donne's universe is Ptolemaic or Copernican, the end of "The Sunne Rising" brings the sun terrifyingly close; in "The Canonization" the lovers can stand securely not in the poet's stanzas but only in a funeral urn. In "The Extasie" ultimate fulfillment appears in a miraculous suspension, a standing outside the body. In "A Lecture upon the Shadow" the noon lovers vainly try to stand in eternal sunlight. Donne's utopianism at this time seems to have had a manic-depressive element, and in *Biathanatos* he writes wistfully of the fact that suicide is tolerated by More's Utopians.[55] Aers and Kress have pointed out that Donne's lack of ease with inwardness, his sense of the imminent collapse of a private self into nothingness, is found in the *Holy Sonnets* as well as the *Songs and Sonets*—in order to "rise, and stand" he must have God ravish him. They contrast the greater sense of inwardness found in Fulke Greville; alienated Protestant intellectuals could at least look to some kind of collective power-base and could situate themselves in relation to an intellectual tradition, but Donne was at this stage still critically detached from the Foxean Protestant tradition.[56] In terms of radical rethinking of sexual relationships, Spenser perhaps makes a more appropriate comparison: Spenser has a broader public frame of reference to draw on than Donne. While from a deconstructionist perspective Donne's lack of any sense of a coherent self may seem laudable, it may also reflect political precariousness.

IV

That Donne did move back to the public world after his period of enforced retreat may, then, testify not only to insatiable ambition but also to some desire for a more broadly based political context for his writing. Much attention has recently been paid to Donne's flattery and ingratiation in his attempts to gain royal favor. It is certainly true that in *Pseudo-Martyr,* where he firmly denied subjects' right to resistance, he vigorously repudiated his earlier critical stance towards monarchy.[57] His quest for advancement culminated in his courting of the royal favorite Somerset, and his poetic celebration of the latter's marriage to Frances Howard, whose expediently manipulated divorce from the earl of Essex had outraged large sections of public opinion. The royal favor to the house of Howard was widely seen as a growing alignment with "hispaniolized" courtiers who allegedly favored Spanish absolutism against Protestant constitutionalism. Donne's poetry certainly never reveals the anti-Spanish fervor of his contemporaries the "Spenserian" poets; he had had his portrait as a young man painted with a Spanish motto and a defiantly Catholic cross, and his conceited style, though not necessarily the more exploratory aspect of his sexual politics, may owe something to Spanish mannerism.[58] He could compare the countess of Bedford to the Escorial, and accept patronage from Sir Robert Drury, who was anxious to sell his military services to the king of Spain and who was alleged to have abused that Puritan hero Frederick V of the Palatinate.[59] Suspicions about his Catholic past may explain why he could not find a home in the court of Prince Henry, which became a center for those disaffected with royal policy.

If Donne's Jacobean poetry is not clearly "oppositional," it is nonetheless by no means unambiguously absolutist. Theories of inevitable containment can certainly find support in Donne's recurrent statements of self-annihilation, of the dependence of his personal identity on courtly power structures. Such language does reflect the precariousness we have noted in the lyrics. At the same time, we should be wary of taking it at face value. In his verse letters Donne constantly displaces courtly hyperbole from the monarch on to other people, whether patronesses or little girls. As Marotti has shown, Donne maintained a sharply satirical stance towards the Jacobean court in some of his prose writings; and even his public poetry maintained a degree of independence.[60] Even his flattery of Somerset does need to be seen in the context of the turbulent period after the deaths of Cecil and Essex when the whole structure of the court was in turmoil and significant changes of direction seemed possible. It is certainly true that there was a shift to the right at this time, and that someone with Donne's background would have been unlikely to gain much advancement had a more militantly Protestant faction been in the ascendant. But Donne's rise at such a time does not necessarily prove that he was firmly aligning himself with the "Spanish faction," any more than was the case with another figure whose rise at the same time earned him some unpopularity, Fulke Greville. The earl of Somerset's reputation has inevitably been retrospectively clouded by the lurid story of his wife's complicity in murder; but a close scrutiny of his political career suggests that he was not quite the monster of Italianate vice created by the subsequent legend.[61] Donne was introduced to him by a patron to whom he was much closer, James Lord Hay, who like many Scots lords preferred a French to a Spanish

alliance; in the period when Donne was courting the favorite he was
moving closer and closer to the Howards and an alignment with Spain,
but this could not necessarily have been foreseen from the beginning.
The more Rochester moved towards the Howards the more Donne be-
came cut off from other patrons such as the countess of Bedford, who
was coming under Puritan influence. Donne's writings at this time re-
veal a politically and personally inept attempt to forestall growing
polarizations at court. While writing a complimentary poem to Frances
Howard's sister, he also joined in the cult of Prince Henry's great friend
Lord Harrington, in an attempt to maintain the favor of his sister the
countess of Bedford. He sat in the ill-fated Parliament of 1614; as An-
nabel Patterson has pointed out, many of his friends there took up an
oppositional stance, and we should not be too ready to assume that his
part in it was merely that of servile acquiescence to the royal will.[62]

Donne's poetic praise of James himself at this time was relatively
muted. In the epithalamium for the wedding of Frederick and Eliz-
abeth, he does not mention the king at all—a striking silence. The
epithalamium for Somerset's wedding is in any case a decidely am-
bivalent piece, a court poem framed by a country poem, an occasional
poem written after the occasion, an epithalamium that is an epitaph for
its own poet. James's is a court, says Allophanes,

> where all affections do assent
> Unto the Kings, and that, that Kings are just . . .
> Where the Kings favours are so plac'd, that all
> Finde that the King therein is liberall
> To them, in him, because his favours bend
> To vertue, to the which they all pretend.
>
> (I, 134)

The convoluted syntax in this passage, and the "bend" and "pretend,"
seem almost to undermine the overt praise of the court's plain-dealing
and openness. As Annabel Patterson has pointed out, the name "Al-
lophanes," which can mean "one in another guise" or "one who seems
like another," is on one level an index of Donne's self-alienation, that of
the aging Utopian reduced to currying favor from the Italian youth.[63]

Donne was certainly uncomfortable about his role at this time; but
his writing needs to be seen in context. Late in 1614 he began assem-
bling a collection of poems to be dedicated to Somerset. About the same
time Samuel Daniel seems to have been planning a similar collection, a
group of poems on leading court figures whom Donne had also
praised—Prince Henry, the countess of Bedford, Lord Harrington,
and Somerset himself. Like Donne, Daniel eventually decided that

Somerset's reputation made the project impossible; but it is clear from the letter he wrote in support of the disgraced favorite that he thought his character worth defending, and this at a time when Daniel had nothing to gain by doing so.[64] The comparison with Daniel brings out the complexity of the questions of agency and courtly discourse. On the one hand, the picture of Donne as isolated egotist and careerist has partly been created by critics who have themselves isolated his career and neglected to set him in a wider political context. On the other hand, the comparison also heightens the extreme effusiveness of Donne's language of compliment as against Daniel's more measured tones. To speak of the discourse of power as something one had either to accept or to subvert *en bloc* is to overlook the degree to which that discourse could be refashioned by individual choices. Donne did choose to flatter, and he did gain preferment.

V

That preferment was ultimately in the church rather than the state; and this phase of Donne's career has been viewed as an ultimate capitulation to an authoritarian hierarchy. Simpson and Potter, in the standard edition of the sermons, effectively restate Walton's picture of Donne as a leading member of the High Church party headed by Archbishop Laud.[65] It is unfortunate that the dominant picture of Donne's career has been retrospectively simplified by Walton's 1640 hagiography, and that Sir Henry Wotton, a far more intelligent and politically astute figure than Walton, did not live to write his projected life of his friend.[66] Unfortunately, too, historians of the Jacobean church have paid little attention to Donne. An adequate analysis of his career will need to be done by those versed in theology as well as in stylistics, attentive to the content and context of the sermons as well as their royalist purple passages; and a full analysis seems likely to qualify the absolutist model.

First of all, it is important to remember that the church Donne entered in 1615 was very different from the church at the time of his death, that it was not so much the last bastion of the "traditional intellectual."[67] It was, of course, a state church committed to suppressing autonomous religious life. And the crushing of the presbyterian movement had put an end to the project of making the church a more "political" institution, one in which officials were elected instead of power's being passed down from above. But a genuine attempt was being made to win over dissenters by persuasion, by political means rather than by naked power. After all, the official theology of the church was widely considered to be a Calvinist one; and this allowed moderate Puritans to assume high office without too many qualms, while feeling a bond of sympathy with dissenting brethren. This Calvinist position also meant that the church could be seen as one member of an international Protestant community, rather than as a unique national institution. On the other hand, figures like Overall and Andrewes who dissented from the Calvinist position could gain advancement provided that they did not make their dissent too explicit. Donne was friendly with both these men; but it is interesting that the person who most actively encouraged him to enter the church was associated with the Calvinist wing. Bishop Thomas Morton is taken by Patrick Collinson as a prime example of that group of moderate churchmen—which included another of Donne's friends, Joseph Hall—who tried to keep the church relatively open to different views, and have been labeled without too much of a sense of oxymoron as "Puritan bishops." Clarendon found Morton suspiciously "popular," soft on puritan dissenters, and Laud so much suspected him that he set a spy to follow him.[68] Men like Morton and Hall cut across the conventional historical categories. They were firm monarchists, inheriting Foxe's cult of secular sovereignty against the papists and associating rebellion with popery. We need to remember that the cult of monarchy had two sides: in the Foxean tradition it was an essential bulwark against Catholicism, and many Puritans accused the Laudians of trying to undermine the king's authority. Thus exalted panegyrics of monarchy might function as a coded criticism of interference by high-flying clerics in secular affairs: this point needs to be borne in mind in considering Donne's rhetoric of praise. Though clearly distinct from the Laudian high-flyers, Hall and Morton were not hostile to ritual and could speak of episcopacy in elevated terms. They can be regarded as Calvinists in theology—Morton defended the Calvinist position at the Hampton Court conference—but their position on predestination was a modified one.[69] It was another member of this group, John Williams, who later claimed credit for Donne's advancement to the deanship of St. Paul's; though he supported alignment with Spain in the 1620s, Williams was to become a leading opponent of Laud.[70] At a higher political level, the traditional story that has James himself putting pressure on Donne to enter the church is plausible in the light of recent research that suggests the king played a more active and intelligent part in ecclesiastical policy than has often been assumed.[71]

This relative openness of the earlier Jacobean church does not quite sanction Empson's genial comment that the good thing about Anglicanism was that it kept Christianity at bay.[72] It must, however, qualify the new orthodoxy, which sees Donne's lust for power and domination as giving him an underlying emotional sympathy for the Counter-Reformation church, but argues that he betrayed this true loyalty for the thrill of wielding repressive power in an authoritarian institution at home. The church was, undeniably, a state apparatus; James's policy can plausibly be seen as one of containing dissent over the long term by short-term compromises.[73] That process might, however, have been a relatively gentle and gradual one had not external events forced a radical shift in direction not long after Donne entered the church. In 1619 James's son-in-law, Frederick V of the Palatinate, was elected king of Bohemia, an event that was to plunge Europe into the Thirty Years War. James's attempt to mediate between the opposing factions was regarded by many Protestants as effectively a capitulation to the Habsburg powers with their aspirations to universal monarchy; and faced with the storm of popular protest against his policies, James gradually became persuaded that royal authority could only be salvaged by siding more decisively with the conservative faction in the church.

Whatever his earlier history, one would expect the careerist, absolutist Donne of the current critical orthodoxy to have aligned himself unequivocally with the High Church party at this stage. But the record, which still requires full investigation, does suggest a more complex picture. As the crisis in Europe deepened, Donne, having apparently overcome some of his earlier prejudices against "German schismes," took a keen interest in the fate of Continental Protestantism. His name is found along with Archbishop Abbot's and a few others in a cipher concerned with international Protestantism.[74] Donne made a great public occasion of his departure to Germany on Doncaster's futile mission to settle the Bohemian crisis. Donne's sense of the gravity of the international crisis is indicated in his "Hymne to Christ, at the Authors Last Going into Germany," where he declares his willingness to sever national roots in the name of a suprapersonal godliness.[75] The German poet Weckherlin greeted Doncaster on his arrival on the Continent as offering renewed hope for the international Protestant cause.[76] The earl of Pembroke, a leading court supporter of the Protestant cause, spoke highly of Donne in a letter to Doncaster.[77] At The Hague Donne preached two sermons which, Paul Sellin has recently argued, indicated his support for the official Calvinist position recently approved at the Synod of Dort against Arminian factionalism; earlier he had supported the Huguenot leaders against a similar revisionist movement in their ranks.[78] Donne's preaching and poetry were both warmly admired by his Dutch translator, Constantin Huygens, who was an orthodox Calvinist.[79]

In 1619, however, James was still supporting the Calvinist line, so that Donne was doing no more than expressing the official view.[80] As the

crisis intensified, however, and James began to back away from the Jaco-
bean compromise, Donne does not seem to have followed him with
alacrity. An important basic qualification is that it became harder and
harder to take a public stand contrary to the royal view: censorship re-
strictions became ever stricter, and his superiors at London, first Mon-
taigne and then Laud, were keen to enforce conformity in sermons.
Some preachers nonetheless braved the law by attacking royal policy;
whereas it has become notorious that Donne himself preached in de-
fense of the restrictions. But it seems that it was precisely because he was
not regarded as a partisan of the conservatives that James regarded him
as a suitable person to justify his policies in public. And yet contempo-
raries noted signs of unease. When he was called on to preach in defense
of the censorship in 1622, a contemporary reported that he did not seem
satisfied with the position he was defending; he was prepared to give
Elizabeth her due as well as James.[81] As David Nicholls has recently
pointed out, the parallels Donne draws between God and the king are
not always absolutist in their implications: he stresses God's pluralistic
delegation of power through the Trinity.[82] In Donne's less public writ-
ings at this time, political metaphors are used in a way that is far from
unproblematically absolutist. There is a remarkable passage in the
*Devotions* where he uses the traditional body politic imagery in a dis-
tinctly edged way: at a time when it was feared that James was losing his
grip on public affairs, Donne compares the king to the heart, the council
to the brain, and says that even though the heart may not be the strongest
part of the body we should still care for it because its failure would lead
to the collapse of the whole system.[83]

   Under King Charles, Donne maintained a critical distance, even at
the cost of speedy advancement. In a sermon preached in 1626 he
praised the wise decisions of the Synod of Dort.[84] A glance at the index
to the sermons will reveal the striking fact that Donne's references to
Calvin steadily increased under Charles's reign as the Arminians
gathered strength. It is true that often this was a strategy by which he
could defend some of the ritual innovations of the Caroline church by
showing that even Calvin did not approve of them; and indeed on many
points Calvin was more traditionalist than his followers.[85] But Donne
went out of his way to praise Calvin at a time when he was growing out
of fashion. In 1626–27 Donne was insisting that his difference with the
Puritans was simply one of discipline, of church order, not of theology.
While insisting that episcopacy was the best form of church govern-
ment, he refused to disparage other Reformed churches which did not
have bishops.[86] Donne's preaching practice does bear out his far from
bland concept of the *via media*: his concessions to Laudian ritualism are

countered by moves to include broader sections of Protestant opinion. He recalls figures such as the Waldenses and Jan Hus, pioneers of reformation who were esteemed by the Calvinist churchmen more than the Laudians.[87] He preferred evangelical "zeal" to the "decency" that was so much a feature of High Church rhetoric.[88]

Annabel Patterson has recently drawn attention to a sermon of April 1627 over which Donne took particular care as a statement of his religious position, and which was felt by the king to go against his policies.[89] His brief here was to defend church and king against mounting criticisms, which were concentrated by the forced loan. Sermons published that spring and summer were so high-flying in their defenses of hierarchical order that Archbishop Abbot himself refused to license one of them.[90] In this context Donne's central text, "Take heed what you hear," could take on an ambivalent tone, and as Patterson has pointed out, Donne included some oblique criticisms of Charles and found himself in trouble with the authorities. And it was in this charged context that Donne gave his fullest characterization of the Anglican *via media*:

> From extream to extream, from east to west, the *Angels* themselves cannot come, but by passing the middle way between; from that extream impurity, in which Antichrist had damped the Church of God, to that intemerate purity, in which Christ had constituted his Church, the most Angelicall Reformers cannot come, but by touching, yea, and stepping upon some things, in the way. He that is come to any end, remembers when he was not at the middle way; he was not there as soon as he set out. It is the posture reserved for heaven, to sit down, at the right hand of God; Here our consolation is, that God reaches out his hand to the receiving of those who come towards him; And nearer to him, and to the institutions of his Christ, can no Church, no not of the *Reformation,* be said to have come, then ours does.[91]

A soon as Donne has set up the figure of the *via media* he starts to deconstruct it: precisely because it is a way, a process, the middle is constantly changing its position; and the church is, and ought to be, moving towards a state of greater purity. Although earlier in the sermon he has declared that truth is now firmly embodied in the Visible Church, *as a City upon a hill* (VII, 396), Donne now sees the church as mobile, an angel which scarcely puts its feet on the ground, engaged in a search not unlike that of the Third Satire—or the imagery of the Invisible Church that was regarded with suspicion by the Laudians. Herbert's "The Church Militant" got into trouble with the censors in 1633 for suggesting that "Religion stands on tip-toe in our land," implying that idolatry at home might force it further westward.[92] The word "purity" was a charged one in this time when the Laudians were redefining "Puritan" to condemn not just separatists but mainstream Calvinists. In his sermons, however, Donne tried to avoid polemical oversimplification of the term "Puritan," going so far as to declare that he himself wanted to be a puritan.[93] In the 1627 sermon he attacks the "brackish taste" of easy syntheses of the Catholic and Protestant positions, and launches a panegyric of the "holy animosity" of Martin Luther. In a sermon commissioned to defend censorship he celebrates the Reformation as above all a matter of publication, of making texts more widely available. Shortly before his death, Donne seems to have been revising for publication some sermons which defended the theological line taken at Dort.[94]

A crucial element in Laudianism was a downgrading of preaching in favor of ritual. Donne certainly did defend some of these changes; but again hindsight tends to distort the picture. The St. Paul's of the triumphant Caroline church was a reconstructed building which epitomized monarchical authority. The scheme for reconstruction had begun under James as part of the preparations for a new, more absolutist architecture for the Spanish match; when negotiations fell through the reconstruction lapsed, but Laud resumed it with characteristic energy on becoming bishop of London. So that the old structure could be encased in classical blinkers, the houses around the cathedral were demolished, despite complaints that Inigo Jones was an absolute architectural "*monarch*" and did not consult residents properly.[95] And, as a significant part of the changes, the old sermons at Paul's Cross were shifted inside the cathedral: Laud had already cut down the length of the sermons and insisted that he be given copies in advance, for the outdoor setting seems in itself to have contributed to the atmosphere of civic political consciousness and controversy that sometimes spilled over into the sermons' content, and a remarkable number of preachers risked making anti-Spanish comments.[96] Conversely, the activities of gossiping and exchanging news that had traditionally taken place inside the cathedral, making it a political center in its own right, were banished to the somewhat inhibiting environment of Inigo Jones's stately portico. The new ethos is exemplified by Waller's poem on the new building:

> Which Spouse-like may with comly grace command
> More then by force of argument or hand.
> For doubtfull reason few can apprehend,
> And war bring ruine, where it should amend.
> But beauty with a bloodlesse conquest findes
> A welcome sovereignty in rudest minds.[97]

Rational political and theological debate are rejected in favor of the power of courtly beauty. Denham was to allude to these lines in *Cooper's Hill*, the poem that established norms of political "balance" amongst generations of subsequent conservative poets.

One might expect Donne to have been in the forefront of those calling for these changes. But there is no evidence that he took any initiative over the rebuilding of St. Paul's, and Laud felt that he had been deplorably lax about keeping a reverent atmosphere in the church; work did not begin in earnest until after Donne's death.[98] The religious polarization after 1640, when Puritans not only abandoned the Laudian alterations but let the cathedral itself become generally dilapidated, inevitably blurred the distinctions between Donne and the Laudians. Donne's St. Paul's was above all a place of preaching; in a central Protestant tradition, he had a special affection for St. Paul as a master of the word.[99] Donne's relations with Laud were strained. Though by 1630 there was a plan to make him a bishop, his advancement under Charles was not meteoric.[100]

In this context Carew's elegy looks more complex. He singles out as a common factor in Donne's career as preacher and as poet a particular boldness and independence of mind: it is Donne in the pulpit, not at the altar, who is commemorated, and when he moves on to the secular verse it is to find the same verbal force which serves as a reproach to his own generation—Carew tries to roughen his couplets against the grain of the bland flow that Waller was starting to popularize. And yet he denounces himself as one of the "Libertines in Poetrie." Donne is heard as a voice from a vanished era; and this was true ecclesiastically as well as politically, for the relatively open, easygoing church Donne had entered in 1615 was very different from the more authoritarian apparatus the Laudians were trying to perfect. There is evidence that Carew himself was not particularly happy with the current state of policy. Interestingly, another elegist declares that the true judges of his preaching are not the clergy, who are partial, but those who are without faction, the marquis of Hamilton, the earls of Southampton, Pembroke, and Dorset, and the countesses of Bedford and Huntingdon.[101] One person's impartiality is of course another's faction, and all of the names here mentioned are of those who were regarded as patriots sympathetic to the Protestant cause and resistant to "hispaniolization." Another elegist, Sir Lucius Cary, called on Laud to preach Donne's funeral sermon; but this Laud chose not to do.[102] One attentive reader of the poems and elegies, the Puritan republican Robert Overton, was to find in them a sanction for his criticisms of court life and a pattern for his own marriage, which was consciously based on spiritual equality.[103]

"Let others carve the rest," declares Carew before offering an inscription for Donne's monument. Donne had composed his own inscription; and monument and inscription offer another index of his uneasy relationship to the Caroline establishment. I have tried to show that his relation to that establishment had not been as single-mindedly careerist and sycophantic as is often assumed. And yet the fact is that his margin for maneuver was very limited. Donne's role as court spokesman prompted him late in life to return to the *Utopia* and to find a renewed relevance in Hythlodaeus's comments about the inevitable corruption of discourse at courts; in the margins he wrote comments like "ship monie" and "cryers up of y$^e$ Kings prerogative."[104] Donne may have worried that he himself was one of those "cryers up," that he had indeed left himself no alternative. And his sense of his difficulty in achieving an independent place to stand in the world of courtly power—a difficulty which, as has been seen, marks all his poetry from the Third Satire onward—seems to be represented in his own monument.

The construction of an elaborate funeral monument could be seen as a gesture in support of Laud's ceremonialism: in the year of Donne's death John Weever lamented the neglect of monuments and praised Laud.[105] But the monument is hard to interpret, and there is some doubt about how far it reflected Donne's own wishes. Helen Gardner has argued that the traditional story about Donne's posing in his shroud is a melodramatic flourish, part of Walton's somewhat uncritical canonization of Donne. She points to the oddity of the statue's composition: the way the folds fall is more appropriate to a recumbent figure, and his eyes are closed as if lying awaiting the resurrection; yet he is standing up as if the folds are falling off him and he has been awakened by the Last Trumpet. Gardner suggests that Stone may originally have been commissioned to make a recumbent figure, and that half-way through it was discovered that there was no room, so he was put upright instead. The ruffed shroud that now covers his feet seems not to have been there in the original monument and may have been added to soften the incongruity of his standing on what Gardner describes as an "absurdly small" urn.[106] There is perhaps a suggestive symbolic truth in the idea that Donne's presence was such an embarrassment that they could not decide where to put him; and that posterity has naturalized his image in order to make him fit in more easily. But the monument as it survives does seem appropriate to the inscription Donne composed, which ends, after its tribute to James I: "here, though in falling [western] ashes, he looks towards Him whose name is rising [the east]."[107] Even now that at last he has achieved a secure niche, he is always already embarked on a journey in which there is no middle way, only an end and a beginning, and he has but a precarious foothold on his well-wrought urn.

## Notes

This is a revised version of a paper delivered at the English Institute, Harvard University, on 29 August 1986. I am grateful to the English Institute and to Annabel Patterson, who organized the session on "The Canonization of Donne," and to Frank Romany and an anonymous reader for comments on earlier drafts.

1. *The Poems of John Donne,* ed. Herbert J. C. Grierson, 2 vols. (Oxford: Oxford University Press, 1921), 1:380. Citations from Donne's poetry come from this edition unless otherwise stated.

2. See S. L. Adams, "Spain or the Netherlands? The Dilemma of Early Stuart Foreign Policy," in Howard Tomlinson, ed., *Before the English Civil War* (London: Macmillan, 1983), pp. 79–101. The Spanish-Dutch polarity is much developed in the pamphlets of Thomas Scott: contrast his *The Spaniards Perpetuall Designes to an Vniuersall Monarchie* (n.p., 1624) with *The Belgicke Pismire* (London, 1622), with its praise of the godly, industrious Netherlands as a realization of More's Utopia (p. 90).

3. On the emergence of the "public sphere" in the late seventeenth century see Jürgen Habermas, *Strukturwandel der Öffentlichkeit: Untersuchungen einer Kategorie der bürgerlichen Gesellschaft* (Neuwied: Hermann Luchterhand Verlag, 1962), pp. 26ff.

4. *The Poems and Masques of Aurelian Townshend,* ed. Cedric C. Brown (Reading: Whiteknights Press, 1983), p. 48.

5. Carew, "To the New-yeare, for the Countesse of *Carlile,*" cited by Michael P. Parker, "Carew's Politic Pastoral: Virgilian Precepts in the 'Answer to Aurelian Townshend,' *John Donne Journal* 1 (1982):101–16, n. 22. Parker links the poem with Virgil's eclogues, but the poet's self-conscious refusal to deal with public themes is surely modeled rather on the Roman elegiac poets. Kevin Sharpe has argued that there is "a tension within the poem that may reflect Carew's ambivalent attitude to royal foreign policy": *Criticism and Compliment: The Politics of Literature in the England of Charles I* (Cambridge: Cambridge University Press, 1987), p. 147. Sharpe argues that Carew is not rejecting the Protestant cause but turning from politics to the higher realm of poetry; but such a choice itself had its political dimension.

6. Cleanth Brooks, *The Well Wrought Urn* (New York: Harcourt, Brace, 1947), chap. 1.

7. David Aers and Gunther Kress, "Vexatious Contraries: A Reading of Donne's Poetry," in *Literature, Language and Society in England, 1580–1680* (Dublin: Gill and Macmillan, 1981), pp. 23–48, 49–74.

8. Jonathan Goldberg, *James I and the Politics of Literature: Jonson, Shake-*

*speare, Donne, and Their Contemporaries* (Baltimore and London: Johns Hopkins University Press, 1983), p. 219.

9. Arthur F. Marotti, *John Donne, Coterie Poet* (Madison: University of Wisconsin Press, 1986).

10. For a brief historical account, see Bernard Crick, *In Defence of Politics,* 2d ed. (Harmondsworth: Pelican Books, 1982).

11. For fuller discussion, see my "The Life and Death of Renaissance Man," *Raritan,* 8, no. 4 (Spring 1989): 89–110.

12. William Drummond, "A Letter on the True Nature of Poetry," in *Poems and Prose,* ed. Robert H. MacDonald (Edinburgh and London: Scottish Academic Press, 1976), p. 191.

13. David Norbrook, *Poetry and Politics in the English Renaissance* (London: Routledge and Kegan Paul, 1984), p. 257.

14. R. C. Bald, *John Donne: A Life* (Oxford: Clarendon Press, 1970; corrected paperback edition, 1986), p. 25.

15. John Carey, *John Donne: Life, Mind and Art* (London and Boston: Faber and Faber, 1981), pp. 113ff.

16. Sir Geoffrey Keynes, *A Bibliography of Dr John Donne,* 3d ed. (Cambridge: Cambridge University Press, 1958), p. 218. Donne comments on hard-line Catholics' distaste for More's Lucianic, satirical side in *Pseudo-Martyr* (London, 1610), p. 108; for other comments on Catholic censorship, see pp. 47ff., 102, 114. Cf. Donne's attack on the suppression of Aristotelian writings in *Biathanatos,* ed. Ernest W. Sullivan II (Newark: University of Delaware Press, 1984), pp. 31ff.

17. Paul F. Grendler, *Critics of the Italian World, 1530–1560: Anton Francesco Doni, Niccolò Franco and Ortensio Lando* (Madison: University of Wisconsin Press, 1969), pp. 29–33.

18. John Donne, *Ignatius his Conclave: An Edition of the Latin and English Texts,* ed. T. S. Healy, S. J. (Oxford: Clarendon Press, 1969), p. 57. For evidence of Donne's close reading of Machiavelli, see Paul F. Grendler, "Francesco Sansovino and Italian Popular History, 1560–1600," *Studies in the Renaissance* 16 (1969):164. But see Sydney Anglo, "More Machiavellian than Machiavel: A Study of the Context of Donne's *Conclave,"* in A. J. Smith, ed., *John Donne: Essays in Celebration* (London: Methuen, 1972), pp. 349–84.

19. Elizabeth L. Eisenstein, *The Printing Press as an Agent of Change: Communications and Cultural Transformations in Early-Modern Europe,* one-vol. ed. (Cambridge: Cambridge University Press, 1980), pp. 136ff.; Paul Dibon, "L'Université de Leyde et la République des Lettres au 17e siècle," *Quaerendo* 5 (1975):5–38 (26–32); Fritz Schalk, "Von Erasmus' Res publica litteraria zur Gelehrtenrepublik der Aufklärung," in *Studien zur Französichen Aufklärung* (Frankfurt: Vittorio Klostermann, 1977), pp. 143–63. Sir Henry Wotton was using the phrase in the 1590s: *Life and Letters of Sir Henry Wotton,* ed. Logan Pearsall Smith, 2 vols. (Oxford: Clarendon Press, 1907), 1:312; an Italian friend praised him as holding high place "nella Republica dè Letterati": Orazio Lombardelli, *I Fonti Toscani* (Florence, 1598), p. 4.

20. John Donne, *The Courtier's Library, or catalogus librorum aulicorum incomparabilium et non vendibilium,* ed. Evelyn Mary Simpson (London: Nonesuch Press, 1930), pp. 49–50.

21. On Donne and Plantin's emblem, see Josef Lederer, "John Donne and the Emblematic Practice," *Review of English Studies* 22 (1946):182–200 (197ff.), and Doris C. Powers, "Donne's Compass," *Review of English Studies* 9 (1958):173–75.

22. After a period when the existence of ideological conflict in pre–Civil War England was effectively denied, the pendulum has been swinging back to a considerable degree: see, e.g., J. P. Sommerville, *Politics and Ideology in England, 1603–1640* (London and New York: Longman, 1986).

23. *Proceedings in Parliament, 1610,* ed. Elizabeth Read Foster, 2 vols. (New Haven and London: Yale University Press, 1966), 1:276: "the popular state ever since the beginning of his Majesty's gracious and sweet government hath grown big and audacious, and in every session of parliament swelled more and more."

24. *Life and Letters of Sir Henry Wotton,* 2:137.

25. Richard Cust, "News and Politics in Early Seventeenth-Century England," *Past and Present* 112 (1986):60–90.

26. Barbara Everett, "Donne: A London Poet," *Proceedings of the British Academy* 58 (1972):245–73 (273, 261). Everett does, however, stretch definitions to make London "courtly" (p. 266).

27. I. A. Shapiro, "John Donne and Parliament," *T.L.S.,* 10 March 1932, p. 172.

28. Carey, *John Donne,* p. 63.

29. Cf. Donne, *Biathanatos,* p. 91: "that Author purposed onely like *Zenophon,* or *Plato,* or *S.ʳ Tho: More,* to *ideate* and forme, then to write a credible History"; and *Pseudo-Martyr,* p. 4: "that forme of a State which *Plato* Ideated."

30. David Aers and Gunter Kress, "'Darke Texts Needs Notes': Versions of the Self in Donne's Verse Epistles," in *Literature, Language and Society in England, 1580–1660* (Dublin: Gill and Macmillan, 1981), pp. 23–48, find the poem's Stoic stance "simple-minded" (p. 41) but note that there are signs of unease with pure Stoicism.

31. *Life and Letters of Sir Henry Wotton,* 1:312.

32. Marotti, *Donne,* pp. 119–23.

33. Gustav Ungerer, *A Spaniard in Elizabethan England: The Correspondence of Antonio Pérez's Exile,* 2 vols. (London: Tamesis Books, 1974–76), 1:210, 252–53; 2:298, 303–4. Marotti makes Wotton's move to the Venetian ambassadorship a cynical abandonment of old allegiances (*Donne,* p. 323 n.11), but this overlooks his intellectual interests and his readiness to defend Essex after his fall (Ungerer, *A Spaniard,* 2:322).

34. Cf. Christopher Hill, "Censorship and English Literature," in *Collected Essays of Christopher Hill, vol. 1: Writing and Revolution in the Seventeenth Century* (Brighton: Harvester, 1985), pp. 32–72.

35. R. E. Bennett, "John Donne and the Earl of Essex," *MLQ* 3

(1942):603–4; cf. M. van Wyk Smith, "John Donne's *Metempsychosis,*" *Review of English Studies,* n.s., 24 (1973):17–25, 141–52. Donne's Catholicism was a factor in distancing him from Essex; but it should be remembered that Essex was courted by a number of Catholic writers, such as the poets William Alabaster and Henry Constable, who favored Henry IV's moderate Gallicanism over Jesuit and Habsburg militancy and thus sided with a "Puritan" foreign policy: see, e.g., John Bossy, "A Propos of Henry Constable," *Recusant History* 6 (1961–62):228–37. On the strong Catholic participation in Essex's rebellion, see also M. E. James, "At a Crossroad of the Political Culture: The Essex Revolt, 1601," in *Society, Politics and Culture: Studies in Early Modern England* (Cambridge: Cambridge University Press, 1986), pp. 416–65 (436).

36. *John Donne: Selected Prose,* chosen by Evelyn Simpson, ed. Helen Gardner and Timothy Healy (Oxford: Clarendon Press, 1967), p. 111.

37. Ibid., p. 110.

38. Donne, *The Courtier's Library,* pp. 51–52; *Letters to Severall Persons of Honour* (London, 1651), p. 122, cited by Everett, "Donne: A London Poet," p. 263.

39. Bald, *Donne,* p. 144. Dennis Flynn, "Donne's Catholicism: II," *Recusant History* 13 (1975–76):178–95 (180), points to the difficulty of reconciling this and other evidences of a lack of full-hearted careerism in Donne at this time with the thesis about his power-hunger, and suggests that religious scruples were a continuing factor. Marotti, p. 160, suggests that Donne may have held back from seeking office because of "poverty and family obligations," the reasons he advances elsewhere for Donne's desperately seeking office.

40. In 1601 Donne was working on a mini-epic, *Metempsychosis,* which attacked Cecil and possibly even Elizabeth, and seems to view Essex with a certain degree of sympathy: see Janel M. Mueller, "Donne's Epic Venture in the *Metempsychosis,*" *Modern Philology* 70 (1972):109–37, and van Wyk Smith, "Donne's *Metempsychosis.*"

41. William Empson, "Donne and the Rhetorical Tradition," *Kenyon Review* 11 (1949):571–87; "Donne the Space Man," *Kenyon Review* 19 (1957):337–99; "Donne in the New Edition," *Critical Quarterly* 8 (1966):255–80; 'Rescuing Donne', in *Just So Much Honor: Essays Commemorating the Four-Hundredth Anniversary of the Birth of John Donne,* ed. Peter Amadeus Fiore (University Park and London: Pennsylvania State University Press, 1972), pp. 95–148. That Donne's poems were read in just this way by at least one Puritan saint can be demonstrated by the case of Robert Overton: see n. 103 below.

42. Cf. Marotti, *Donne,* p. 139, and Thomas Docherty, *John Donne, Undone* (London and New York: Methuen, 1986), pp. 198ff.

43. Aers and Kress, "Vexatious Contraries," p. 57; cf. Gunther Kress, "Poetry as Anti-Language: A Reconsideration of Donne's 'Nocturnall upon S. Lucies Day,'" *PTL* 3 (1978):327–44.

44. See the pioneering article by Jean-Marie Benoist, "La géométrie des poètes métaphysiques," *Critique* 27 (1971):730–69.

45. Paul de Man, "The Dead-End of Formalist Criticism," in *Blindness*

*and Insight: Essays in the Rhetoric of Contemporary Criticism,* 2d ed., Wlad God-
zich, ed. (London: Methuen, 1983), p. 240. Relative evaluation of Empson's and
de Man's contributions will ultimately rest on the validity of de Man's assump-
tion that all forms of biographical, sociological, and historical inquiry are
necessarily secondary to, and less "rigorous" than, pure linguistic analysis. For
the argument that that assumption is disabling for many forms of political cri-
tique, see Terry Eagleton's comments on Empson and de Man in *Against the
Grain: Essays 1975–1985* (London: Verso, 1986), pp. 156ff., and cf. 53–56, 136–
38. Eagleton was writing before the recent revelations about de Man's wartime
support for the Nazi "revolution." The implications of that episode are very
complex and still under debate; it has at least served as a reminder that the
assault on Enlightenment "humanism" as the central evil of modernity has
come in the present century as vigorously from Heidegger on the right as from
the left, and that some important historical and political distinctions have
sometimes been blurred in the generalized critique of humanism.

46. Tillotama Rajan, "'Nothing Sooner Broke': Donne's *Songs and Sonets*
as Self-Consuming Artifact," *ELH* 49 (1982):805–28.

47. Empson, "Donne the Space Man," pp. 347–48.

48. Carey, *John Donne,* p. 109.

49. Marotti, *Donne,* pp. 156–57.

50. Goldberg, *James I and the Politics of Literature,* pp. 111–12.

51. On the nuclear family as recuperation of the poem's revolutionary
moment, cf. Docherty, *John Donne, Undone,* p. 37; Empson, "Donne the Space
Man," p. 345.

52. But see Christopher Rick's analysis of the majority of the lyrics as ex-
emplifying "post-coital sadness and revulsion": "Donne After Love," in Elaine
Scarry, ed., *Literature and the Body: Essays in Populations and Persons (Selected
Papers from the English Institute),* n.s. 12 (Baltimore and London: Johns
Hopkins University Press, 1986), pp. 33–69.

53. Cf. Ilona Bell, "The Role of the Lady in Donne's *Songs and Sonets,"
Studies in English Literature 1500–1900* 23 (1983):113–29; though Bell's "lady"
is as unsatisfactory as Carey's "girl."

54. The potential ramifications of the compass analogy are endless: see John
Freccero, "Donne's 'Valediction: Forbidding Mourning' ", *ELH* 30 (1963):335–
76, and for a virtuouso series of deconstructive readings, Docherty, *John Donne,
Undone,* pp. 73ff.

55. *Biathanatos,* pp. 62–63.

56. Aers and Kress, "Vexatious Contraries," pp. 66ff. Barbara K. Lewalski,
*Protestant Poetics and the Seventeenth-Century Religious Lyric* (Princeton: Prince-
ton University Press, 1979), chap. 8, corrects earlier overemphasis on the Catholic
element in Donne's devotion but arguably makes his Protestantism in the early
Jacobean period too unproblematic—see the mordant comment about Foxe in
*The Courtier's Library,* p. 58. John Stachniewski, "John Donne: The Despair of
the '*Holy Sonnets,*' " *ELH* 48 (1981):677–705 (697–98), argues that Donne's Cal-
vinism springs from social anxiety rather than intellectual conviction. See also

Dominic Baker-Smith, "John Donne's 'Critique of True Religion,'" in Smith, ed., *John Donne: Essays in Celebration*, pp. 403–32.

57. Donne, *Pseudo-Martyr*, pp. 172–73; *The Sermons of John Donne*, ed. George R. Potter and Evelyn M. Simpson, 10 vols. (Berkeley and Los Angeles: University of California Press, 1953–62), 7:427.

58. Dennis Flynn, "Donne's First Portrait: Some Biographical Clues?" *Bulletin of Research in the Humanities*, 82 (1979):7–17; Empson, "Donne the Space Man," p. 346. In a letter of 1623 Donne told Buckingham that he had more Spanish authors than any other nationality in his library. Of course, not all Spanish writers were absolutists; and as Bald, *Donne*, p. 446, points out, in its charged political context the letter can be held to constitute an oblique warning to the favorite, who was under pressure to convert: "they do not show us the best way to heaven, yet they thinke they doe."

59. R. C. Bald, *Donne and the Drurys* (Cambridge: Cambridge University Press, 1959), pp. 53–54; Drury had opposed the earl of Leicester's faction (pp. 73–75) and at the time of Overbury's disgrace was courting the house of Howard as well as Somerset (Wotton, *Life and Letters*, 2:28).

60. Marotti, *Donne*, pp. 183–95.

61. See P. R. Seddon, "Robert Carr, Earl of Somerset," *Renaissance and Modern Studies* 14 (1970):48–68.

62. For a revaluation of the events of 1613–14 in Donne's career, see Annabel Patterson, 'All Donne,' chapter 2 below.

63. Patterson, "All Donne," p. 000; see also the illuminating reading by Heather Dubrow, "'The Sun in Water': Donne's Somerset Epithalamium and the Poetics of Patronage," in Heather Dubrow and Richard Strier, eds., *The Historical Renaissance: New Essays on Tudor and Stuart Literature and Culture* (Chicago: University of Chicago Press, 1988), pp. 197–219.

64. For the parallels between Donne and Daniel, see John Pitcher, *Samuel Daniel: The Brotherton Manuscript. A Study in Authorship* Leeds Texts and Monographs New Series No. 7 (Leeds: The University of Leeds School of English, 1981), pp. 73–74.

65. Recent criticism of the sermons, by concentrating on style rather than context, has tended to confirm the High Anglican analysis: thus Stanley Fish contrasts Donne's humble Anglican preaching with that of the Puritans, who were without exception "self-glorying" in their foolish belief that "understanding, in the sense of a rational clarification, is possible": *Self-Consuming Artifacts: The Experience of Seventeenth Century Literature* (Berkeley: University of California Press, 1972), pp. 70–71.

66. On the ways Walton's lives reflected his strong high-church royalism, see David Novarr, *The Making of Walton's "Lives"* (Ithaca, N.Y.: Cornell University Press, 1968), pp. 213–14, 222, 243.

67. See Patrick Collinson's fine overview, *The Religion of Protestants: The Church in English Society, 1559–1625: The Ford Lectures 1979* (Oxford: Clarendon Press, 1982).

68. Nicholas R. Tyacke, "Puritanism, Arminianism, and Counter-Revo-

lution," in Conrad Russell, ed., *The Origins of The English Civil War* (London: Macmillan, 1973), p. 139; Collinson, *The Religion of Protestants,* pp. 83ff.; Bald, *Donne,* pp. 202ff.

69. See Hall's *Via Media: The Way of Peace in the Five Busy Articles, Normally Known by the Name of Arminius* (1627), in *Works,* ed. Philip Wynter, 10 vols. (Oxford: Oxford University Press, 1863), 9:488–519; cf. Peter White, "The Rise of Arminianism Reconsidered," *Past and Present* 101 (1983):34–54 (50).

70. Bald, *Donne,* pp. 375–76.

71. Kenneth Fincham and Peter Lake, "The Ecclesiastical Policy of King James I," *Journal of British Studies* 24 (1985):169–207.

72. Empson, "Donne the Space Man," p. 378, cf. pp. 344–45.

73. Tyacke's thesis of a stable, broadly Calvinist church disrupted by Laudian innovation, a thesis broadly supported by Collinson, has been challenged by White, "The Rise of Arminianism Reconsidered," who argues that there was never a fully Calvinist orthodoxy. More recently, Peter Lake has challenged both views, arguing both that there was a Calvinist consensus and that it nevertheless covered deep inner contradictions which emerged under the pressure of the international crisis: "Calvinism and the English Church, 1570–1635," *Past and Present* 114 (1987):32–76.

74. Bald, *Donne,* p. 314 n.2.

75. On the diplomatic significance of this mission, see Paul R. Sellin, *So Doth, So Is Religion: John Donne and Diplomatic Contexts in the Reformed Netherlands, 1619–1620* (Columbia: University of Missouri Press, 1988).

76. Weckherlin translated some of Donne's epigrams: see Bald, *Donne,* pp. 353–54, and for a fuller account my *Poetry and Politics in the English Renaissance,* pp. 216, 228, and "'The Masque of Truth': Court Entertainments and International Protestant Politics in the Early Stuart Period," *The Seventeenth Century* 1 (1986):97–100.

77. Bald, *Donne,* p. 351.

78. Ibid.; Paul R. Sellin, "John Donne: The Poet as Diplomat and Divine," *Huntingdon Library Quarterly* 39 (1975–6):267–75, and *John Donne and "Calvinist" Views of Grace* (Amsterdam: VU Boekhandel, 1983); cf. E. Randolph Daniel, "Reconciliation, Covenant and Election: A Study in the Theology of John Donne," *Anglican Theological Review* 48 (1966):14–30; Gosse, *Life and Letters of John Donne,* 1:297.

79. Paul R. Sellin, "John Donne and the Huygens Family, 1619–1621: Some Implications for Dutch Literature," *Dutch Quarterly Review* 12 (1982–83):193–204; cf. Rosalie L. Colie, *"Some Thankfulness to Constantine": A Study of English Influence upon the Early Works of Constantijn Huygens* (The Hague: Martinus Nijhoff, 1956), chap. 4. As an index of the complexities of ideological cross-currents, it seems that Hugyens, who figures for Sellin as an orthodox Calvinist, may have been introduced to Donne's poetry by his friend Sir Robert Killigrew, who was an Arminian: Nicholas Tyacke, "Arminianism and English Culture," in A. C. Duke and C. A. Tamse, eds., *Britain and the Netherlands, 7: Church and State Since the Reformation* (The Hague: Martinus Nijhoff, 1981),

pp. 94–117 (110). Donne's name does not however figure prominently in Tyacke's survey, though Samuel Brooke, brother of his friend Christopher, was an Arminian.

80. See Lake, "Calvinism and the English Church, 1570–1635," pp. 53ff. As a qualification to Sellin's argument one must point to the differences detailed by Lake between the Dutch Reformed orthodoxy and the considerably diluted version of this predestinarian position introduced by the English delegation (pp. 56ff.). Donne's own position on predestination seems to have been still further diluted (cf. David Nicholls, "The Political Theology of John Donne," *Theological Studies* 49 [1988]:45–66), but this is a topic on which I feel unable to speak with confidence; my concern is with the political context of the theological positions.

81. *Sermons,* IV, 182ff.; for discussion, see Annabel Patterson, *Censorship and Interpretation: The Conditions of Writing and Reading in Early Modern England* (Madison: University of Wisconsin Press, 1984), pp. 97ff. Those who went further, of course, ran severe risks: Thomas Winniffe, who was to succeed Donne at St. Paul's, was sent to the Tower in 1622 for a sermon in which he attacked Gondomar, the Spanish ambassador: *The Court and Times of Charles the First,* ed. R. F. Williams, 2 vols. (London: Henry Colburn, 1848), 2:104.

82. David Nicholls, "Divine Analogy: The Theological Politics of John Donne," *Political Studies* 32 (1984):570–80.

83. Goldberg, *James I and the Politics of Literature,* pp. 81–82, notes "republican" elements in the *Devotions.* See also Robert M. Cooper, "The Political Implications of Donne's *Devotions,*" in Gary A. Stringer, ed., *New Essays on Donne* (Salzburg: Institut für Englische Sprache und Literatur, 1977), pp. 192–210.

84. *Sermons,* VII, 127; cf. Sellin, *John Donne and "Calvinist" Views of Grace,* pp. 31ff.

85. E.g. *Sermons,* IV, 373; VII, 430; X, 91, 103, 128, 175.

86. *Sermons,* VII, 328; X, 130.

87. *Sermons,* VIII, 264, 321; X, 155.

88. Cf. Madelon E. Heatherington, "'Decency' and 'Zeal' in the Sermons of John Donne," *Texas Studies in Literature and Language* 9 (1967):307–16.

89. Patterson, *Censorship and Interpretation,* pp. 100–105.

90. Samuel R. Gardiner, *History of England from the Accession of James I to the Outbreak of the Civil War, 1603–1642,* 10 vols. (1884), 6:203–10; a particularly unctuous sermon by Isaac Bargraves, delivered on March 27, held up as exemplary a man who offered to go to sea in a ship without mast or tackle if ordered to do so by those in authority: *A Sermon Preached Before King Charles* (London, 1627), pp. 19–20. The fact that the king encouraged such mindless obedience was widely noted and censured: *The Court and Times of Charles the First,* 1:214–15. For protests about the impossibility of voicing Calvinist views in sermons, see Lake, "Calvinism and the English Church, 1570–1635," pp. 63–65. There is at least some significance in the negative evidence that while audiences were tremendously vigilant for signs of Arminianism in sermons by figures like Mainwaring and Wren, Donne seems to have attracted very little public notice at all.

91. *Sermons,* VII, 409.

92. Cf. my *Poetry and Politics in the English Renaissance,* p. 276. Herbert's own political stance is currently undergoing revaluation; Bishop Williams also played a large part in his ecclesiastical career.

93. For Donne on the term "Puritan," cf. *Sermons,* II, 58; IX, 157ff., 166.

94. Sellin, *John Donne and "Calvinist" Views of Grace,* pp. 9, 52–53.

95. Per Palme, *Triumph of Peace: A Study of the Whitehall Banqueting House* (London: Thames and Hudson, 1957), pp. 22–25, 314. See also W. R. Matthews and W. M. Atkins, eds., *A History of St. Paul's Cathedral and the Men Associated With It* (London: Phoenix House, 1957).

96. Miller Maclure, *The Paul's Cross Sermons, 1534–1642* (Toronto: University of Toronto Press, 1958), p. 13. For conservative alarm in 1629 at "statising discourses" calling for the election of new governors, cf. p. 250.

97. Waller's poem is printed, with a discussion of its relation to *Cooper's Hill,* by Brendan O Hehir, *Expans'd Hieroglyphicks: A Critical Edition of Sir John Denham's "Cooper's Hill"* (Berkeley and Los Angeles: University of California Press, 1969), pp. 276–83.

98. Bald, *Donne,* p. 402, notes that "there is no hint that he made any effort" to raise funds for Paul's as he had done for the Lincoln's Inn chapel (whose completion he offered as testimony that the Protestant doctrine of faith did not undermine good works [*Sermons,* II, 234]). Shortly after his death, a commission "placed the blame" for profanation of St. Paul's "squarely upon the Dean and Chapter"; Bald responds by citing records of one case when Donne did exercise discipline (*Donne,* pp. 403ff.; cf *Sermons,* IX, 15). See also Bald, *Donne,* pp. 505–6, 515, 375.

99. Richard E. Hughes, *The Progress of the Soul: The Interior Career of John Donne* (New York: William Morrow, 1968), pp. 253ff. It is significant that the new church built in the 1630s in Covent Garden for the Puritan-leaning earl of Bedford took Paul as its patron.

100. Janel L. Mueller argues that Donne paid the price in lack of advancement for his "salutary and rare restraint" in controversy: *Donne's Prebend Sermons* (Cambridge, Mass.: Harvard University Press, 1971), p. x.

101. Donne, *Poetical Works,* 1:387. On the political allegiances of those named by the elegist, cf. S. L. Adams, "Foreign Policy and the Parliaments of 1621 and 1624," in Kevin Sharpe, ed., *Faction and Parliament: Essays in Early Stuart History* (Oxford: Clarendon Press, 1610), pp. 144–45; on Edward Sackville, earl of Dorset, see my *Poetry and Politics in the English Renaissance,* p. 220. There seems to have been a rising amount of tension between poets and clerics just after Donne's death. When in 1632 a veteran critic of the Stuarts, Thomas Dekker, tried to publish a poem on the restoration of St. Paul's, he was obstructed by ecclesiastical censorship. Complaining that "upon a Poett, especially the looke with a Frontispicuous superciliosity," he defiantly declared that "I licence my selfe." F. D. Hoeniger, "Thomas Dekker, the Restoration of St. Paul's, and J. P. Collier, The Forger," *Renaissance News* 16 (1963):181–200 (194).

102. Donne, *Poetical Works,* 1:380.

103. Overton's adaptations of Donne and his elegists, which are to be found

in his commonplace book "Gospell obseruations" at Princeton University Library, came to my attention as the present article went to press; I am working on a fuller study of the manuscript.

104. J. B. Gleason, "Dr. Donne in the Courts of Kings: A Glimpse from Marginalia," *Journal of English and Germanic Philology* 69 (1970):599–612.

105. John Weever, *Ancient Funerall Monuments* (London, 1631), sig. A1v; for attacks on the growth of sects and stern reminders of the times when they had been punished by burning at the stake, see pp. 54ff. Weever praised Mercers' Company for their recent refurbishing of the monument to More's friend Colet (p. 369). Sir William Dugdale, *The History of St. Paul's Cathedral in London from its Foundation* (London, 1658), sig. A3r, cites an attack by Ralegh on Puritan iconoclasm; for the Donne memorial, see pp. 62–63.

106. Helen Gardner, "Dean Donne's Monument in St. Pauls," in *Evidence in Literary Scholarship: Essays in Memory of James Marshall Osborn,* ed. René Wellek and Alvaro Ribeiro (Oxford: Clarendon Press, 1979), pp. 29–44; see also Nigel Foxell, *A Sermon in Stone: John Donne and His Monument in St. Paul's Cathedral* (London: Menard Press, 1978). At this stage in his career Stone was moving towards a naturalism in which the precise fall of folds was very carefully reproduced: Margaret Whinney, *Sculpture in Britain, 1530–1830* (Harmondsworth: Penguin, 1964), pp. 26–27.

107. On the inscription, see Foxell, *Sermon in Stone,* p. 10, who notes that the translation given by Bald misses the double meanings. Claiming that Donne was an absolutist down to his "last words," Goldberg, *James I and the Politics of Literature,* p. 219, omits the inscription's actual last words after the reference to James. It is interesting that Donne alludes to his service of James but not of Charles.

## 2

# All Donne

*Annabel Patterson*

Yet I would not have all yet,
Hee that hath all can have no more.
"Lovers' Infinitenesse"

In the first decade of the reign of James I, at the end of Michaelmas
term, perhaps in 1610, a meeting took place at the Mitre Tavern, in Fleet
Street, London. We know of its existence from a Latin poem that de-
scribes it; and thanks to that poem, we know that its tone was both
festive and intellectual, a "convivium philosophicum." The poem sur-
vives in several forms, one of them in the hand of John Chamberlain,[1]
who, by retailing in his letters to Dudley Carleton across the Channel
the most significant political gossip, was a kind of touchstone of Jaco-
bean culture. We care about this meeting of like minds, or we should
care, not only because John Donne was one of the participants, but be-
cause the event offers precious evidence of how a writer subsequently
canonized may be resituated in his original environment, and of how
"literary" assumptions may be profitably modified by cultural history.
Finding Donne at this meeting and pursuing its heuristic implications,
we can test the evaluative accounts and images of him that have been
produced so far, from his early hagiographer Isaac Walton to his subse-
quent biographers Edmund Gosse,[2] R. C. Bald[3] and John Carey,[4] not to
mention English New Criticism, for which Donne came to serve as one
of the primary exemplars, and all that has followed from it.

We know from the poem who were Donne's companions on this oc-
casion, which may have been one of a series of meetings of a "Mermaid
Club." They included Lionel Cranfield, whose financial efficiency
would eventually make him earl of Middlesex and treasurer of En-

gland;[5] Arthur Ingram, financier and soon-to-be secretary of the north;[6] Inigo Jones, already James I's architect in more than one sense, but in December 1610 appointed surveyor of the works in Prince Henry's household; one of the two Sir Henry Nevilles; Sir Robert Phelips, son of the master of the rolls; Sir Henry Goodyer and Christopher Brooke, with both of whom Donne would maintain an intimate correspondence; John Hoskyns, author of *Directions for Speech and Style,* a rhetorical manual, but also a lawyer who in 1623 would become one of the king's sergeants-at-law;[7] Richard Martin, known wit, who on behalf of the sheriffs of London had presented James on his accession with a remarkably challenging speech attacking monopolies and warning James against the use of "an unlymmitted power";[8] Hugh Holland, best known now as the author of a mediocre sonnet in the first Shakespeare Folio; Richard Connock; John West; and Thomas Coryat, in whose honor this particular dinner was given and whose known activities help to date it.[9] As Shapiro points out, although several of these men (Brooke, Goodyer, Martin, Hoskyns, Holland, and of course Donne himself) wrote poetry, this was not a *literary* gathering. Rather, the occasion represents the convergence of unusual men, most of them in early middle age, most of them ambitious and some already clearly on the way up, in a forum in which the distinctions (or choices) between business, politics, cultural image-making (or breaking) were not yet hard, not yet incised by the interaction of personal temperament, circumstance, and conviction.

Like Phelips, Connock, and Jones, Coryat was attached (loosely) to Prince Henry's household, but would proffer his *Crudities* in specially bound copies to each of the members of the royal family. Donne, if the banquet took place in November 1610, was at this stage less notable as a poet than as the author of *Pseudo-Martyr,* published in January 1610 in support of the Jacobean oath of allegiance. Eight of the group (Donne, Brooke, Martin, Hoskyns, Phelips, Connock, Goodyer, and West) were members of an Inn of Court. Nine, including Donne, already had participated in active political life by serving as a member of Parliament, Donne and Martin in Elizabeth's last Parliament, as was also true of both the Nevilles.[10] Brooke, Ingram, Goodyer, Holland, Phelips, and Hoskyns were elected to James's first Parliament which had been meeting between 1604 and the summer of 1607, and which in February 1610 was recalled after a noticeably long prorogation. This was a Parliament which, however unsystematically, contested James I's theoretical insistence on unlimited monarchical power, resisted Salisbury's attempt, through the Great Contract, to resolve the king's financial difficulties, declared impositions (Salisbury's short-term solution to the deficit) unconstitutional, called for the reform of "grievances" generally, and heard from some of its members remarkably strong statements on the limits of the royal prerogative. Brooke, Martin, and Hoskyns had already distinguished themselves as active and outspoken champions of issues that could loosely be termed liberal—fair elections, free speech, the liberties of the subject.[11] Phelips, who was younger, would become an opposition leader in 1621. All of these men, except West, Ingram, and Connock, contributed mocking but affectionate verses to Coryat's eccentric travelogue; but there was not a professional writer, such as Ben Jonson, among them on this occasion, and the composition of the group puts the literary amateurs in the minority.

The poem opens jokily, introducing the participants with Latin pseudonyms. The rules of the game are established in the opening stanza, which links "Gruicampus" (Cranfield) with "Christopherus vocatus Torrens" (Christopher Brooke) and "Johannes Factus"; and they are followed by "Ne vile aestimet Henricus," an allusion to the already punning family motto of the Nevilles, "Ne vile velis." In the contemporary translation produced by John Reynolds, then a fellow of New College, some of these jokes get broader, as in Martin "Pewter-Waster," or Goodye[a]r "Twelve-month-good," or, sometimes, the original point gets lost. "Johannes Factus" reappears as "John ycleped Made." We can recognize him nonetheless; or perhaps better. This symbolic naming reminds us that the wit of "John Donne, Ann Donne, undone" is only one witness to the continuous social construction of a self, in which group identity and personal identity are interdependent constructs, and for which, in Donne as in other writers alert to the difficulty of self-construction, onomastics performs as a strong linguistic symptom of that difficulty. Despite the skepticism that has subsequently accrued to this personal pun,[12] with its micronarrative of marital disaster, its relationship to the collegial identity game suggests that it may be Donne's own pun after all.

As a social text, the poem challenges Donne's readers today to survey what has so far been made of "John ycleped Made" and what has been done, or left undone, with a vast collection of similar facts about "Johannes Factus." The fact is, like Donne's presence at that academic dinner, much of what is known of his sociohistorical environment has been disregarded in critical practice as having no explanatory value, no bearing at all on our understanding of "Donne," the literary entity. How did this happen? Some of the answers are obvious. As perhaps *the* author in whom the critical enterprise was invested at the stage when its antihistorical procedures became both a doctrine and a discipline, Donne has not attracted the attention of those who, having shunted the

New Criticism onto a siding, have been driving the express trains of a renovated historicism through Renaissance and seventeenth-century texts, documents, and records of every kind. Some of this has been, possibly, poetic justice; attention has been lavished on Ben Jonson, in proportion as Eliot and his colleagues rendered him virtually invisible. Some has been, surely, the effect of the way Donne entered the canon, and for years our pedagogy, as solely a lyric poet, since lyric has been the least inviting of the genres to the New Historicism.[13]

But in this bypassing, Donne's own advocates have been complicit, most frequently by not opening all his work to discussion. The inaugural volume of the *John Donne Journal* contained an eloquent plea for a more equitable, less synecdochic study of the poems,[14] as compared to the obsession with the *Songs and Sonets* that has defined the field since Grierson's famous anthology; but the appeal was not extended to Donne's prose. Since then, Thomas Hester brought the satires into view,[15] and Arthur Marotti scrupulously reviewed all the poetry of compliment;[16] but it was still possible for Thomas Docherty to produce a book that, while chastising others for ignoring "the historical culture which informed [Donne's] writings, and the ideology which conditioned the act of writing or 'authority' itself,"[17] contained one sentence on *Biathanatos,* and remained entirely silent on the works, from *Pseudo-Martyr* and *Ignatius his Conclave* to the more political sermons, in which Donne engaged directly with contemporary problems of authority in both church and state.

The critical decree that Donne was "essentially a poet," articulated with unintentional irony by the editors of his sermons,[18] and the exclusions that stem from this now outdated belief, can and will be canceled by new editions designed for the classroom which set the poems alongside generous selections of the prose.[19] But merely enlarging the canon will not in itself produce the conditions for understanding the complex process of social conditioning and self-construction Donne so remarkably illustrates, and which, perhaps more than for any other Renaissance poet, his own writing and other forms of self-representation consciously evoke.[20] For, by another irony of the literary institution, it is precisely those critics who preceded, ignored, or challenged the modernist effacement of "context" that have, through their own findings, created a disincentive. For we now face as the ruling paradigm, in the aftermath of R. C. Bald's definitive modern biography and John Carey's extension of it into psychobiography, the spectacle of John Donne the careerist, marked by a devouring ego and a prevailing sense of expediency; while the intellectual and psychological complexity that were assumed by the New Critical style of reading have been narrowed to the linked imperatives of "apostasy" and "ambition," each with its matching arts. Told by Carey that we might not have had the *Songs and Sonets* at all had it not been for the "thwarted, grasping parasitic life that Donne was forced to lead," and that "the egotism manifest throughout his career is what impels the poetry" (p. 91), one might well wonder whether the postmodern critique of subjectivism, for all its excesses, did not have some prophylactic value. Carey's book is not only a perfect example of the anthropological "synthesizing operations" that Foucault wished to eliminate from cultural analysis;[21] it also exemplifies a danger that Foucault did not articulate, namely, that the psychological profile of an author so produced will either attract or repel.

I infer, however, that Carey's study of Donne was in its own way a work of iconoclasm. Its critique of Donne for selling out to the Jacobean church and state is in striking contrast to the values of Sir Edmund Gosse, as expressed in the following account of Donne's fame as a preacher:

> [He] belonged to an age in which the aristocratic element exercised a domination which was apparently unquestioned. Although of middle-class birth, the temperament, manners, and society of Donne were of the most distinguished order. The religious power of democracy had not been discovered. . . . The Rebellion, and still more the success of the Re-bellion, driving men and women of incongruous classes close to one another in the instinct of self-protection against the results of a common catastrophe, began the democratization of the pulpit. But of Donne we must think as untouched by a least warning of such a political upheaval. He belonged, through and through, to the old order; was, indeed, in some ways, its most magnificent and minatory clerical embodiment. . . . This unity of purpose, this exaltation of a sovereign individuality, made to command in any sphere, gave to the sermons of Donne their extraordi-nary vital power; and if this particular charm has evaporated . . . it is that the elements in ourselves are lacking, that we no longer breathe the aristocratic Jacobean atmosphere.[22]

And Carey boldly converted to a post-Freudian analysis materials that for Bald were simply the occasion for moral evaluation. For looking at the middle period of Donne's life, the period immediately before his decision to take orders, Bald was forced to admit that it did not present "a particularly edifying spectacle": from his letters, especially, Donne appeared to Bald "as one who had mastered at last the arts of the courtier, and it is clear, even when he finally turned to the Church, that he did not intend to abandon those arts, but to rise by them" (p. 301). Here, surely, lies the origin of Carey's thesis, complete with the term— arts—that he would make structural. Bald struggled with the evidence, and wished to give Donne the benefit of the doubt—"the truth seems to be," he wrote, "that these qualities in him were not essential and permanent traits of his character; rather, they were symptoms of his despair" (p. 301); but he (and Gosse behind him) nevertheless created the premises on which Carey's more sinister portrait was erected.

But perhaps we are now capable of retelling Donne's story with a different emphasis. If we could purge from the idea of an *oeuvre* the ideal of coherence, we might be able to look at the whole Donne and see him not as a monster of ambition but as a mass of contradictions, many of which were known to himself and warily or wittily expressed as self-division; and if we can reframe the historical goal as cultural analysis, rather than biographical criticism (with its almost irresistible tendency to judge), we might be able to focus on what Foucault called discursive relations:

> Relations between statements (even if the author is unaware of them; even if the statements do not have the same author; even if the authors were unaware of each other's existence); relations between groups of statements . . . (even if these groups do not concern the same, or even adjacent fields; even if they do not possess the same formal level. . . . ); relations between statements and groups of statements and events of a quite different kind (technical, economic, social, political).[23]

To speak more simply, before we evaluate Donne's conduct and his writing, we need to ask what his friends and contemporaries were doing and saying at about the same time, and what were their shared conditions of material and intellectual practice. We may in the process be able to draw some inferences about the relationship not only between principle and self-interest, which is a vexed issue in early seventeenth-century historiography,[24] but also about that between personal friendship and concerted political action. And, finally, this essay will have something to contribute to the topic of wit, as a literary phenomenon resistant to definition but perhaps more intelligible now as a cultural practice *of* resistance, a symptom of energies and ideals that the system repressed or marginalized—in short, of linguistic grace under pressure.

What Donne's friends were doing that evening in the Mitre Tavern, where we began, was talking politics:

> The king of religion doth out-beare,
> The people doe allegiance sweare,
>           Citizens usurize it.
> .   .   .   .   .   .   .   .
> Prince Henry cannot idly liven,
> Desiring matter to be given
>           To prove his valour good.

And Charles, the image of his father,
Doth imitate his eldest brother,
    And leades the noble blood.
The Chancellour relieveth many,
As well the wyse as fooles, or any
    In humble-wise complayninge,
The Treasurer doth help the rich,
And cannot satisfy the stitch
    Of mendicants disdayninge.
Northampton, seeking many wayes,
Learning and learned men to rayse,
    Is still negotiated.
And Suffolk, seeking in good sorte,
The king his household to supporte,
    Is still defatigated.[25]

The culture outlined here, however crudely, is both familiar in its broad outlines and not familiar enough. As the guests at the *convivium philosophicum* have been identified by a comic onomastics, the major figures on the Jacobean scene of state are identified each by one salient characteristic: James's obsession with the oath of allegiance, and its scholarly defense against the pope and Cardinal Bellarmine, a defense in which Donne himself was at the moment engaged; Prince Henry's restlessness ("Princeps nescit otiari") with his minority, and perhaps also with his father's policies of nonintervention in Europe, a role that he took over from the Protestant activists of the preceding reign;[26] Charles, already revealed as not his own man, and soon to succeed as the heir who would, unlike his stronger older brother, act as his father's "image" in his pacific foreign policy and deep resistance to parliamentary government; the chancellor, Donne's old employer Sir Thomas Egerton, seemingly contrasted in point of charity with Treasurer Cecil (Salisbury) who only "doth help the rich," or, as the Latin text puts it more accurately, "summos," those at the top of the hierarchy, for the very good reason that the budgetary deficit prevented a wider distribution ("Sed quoniam non habet nummos, / Invident mendicantes"; "But because he has no money, those who beg for it are jealous"). The list is completed by the two most powerful members of the Howard family, Henry, earl of Northampton, lord privy seal, whose role as patron of scholars is singled out for special and favorable mention,[27] and his nephew Thomas, whose attempts as lord chamberlain of the royal household to manage without funds might well have left him "defatigated." But what explains the selection of these figures is also what links the participants at the dinner—economics. The poem is an emblem of the power to give and the need to receive, and its honorary guest, Coryat, is a focus both of mockery and a certain real admiration. The poem moves to the larger scene of conflict by class and occupation: the nobility are erecting buildings, the bishops are consecrating them, the gentry are selling their lands, and, while the peasants struggle ("dum rustici contendunt"), the legal profession grows rich ("juridicus lucratur"); and it concludes:

> Thus every man is busy still,
> Each one practising his skill,
>   None hath enough of gayne.
> But Coryate liveth by his witts,
> He looseth nothinge that he gets,
>   Nor playes the fool in vayne.

If we build the whole poem, along with its cultural message, back into Donne's cultural context, it will help us to see what has been excluded, and where the distortions might have been avoided. Bald, for example, cites only the first stanza of the Mitre Tavern ballad, where Donne himself is named. Carey, bent on his representation of Donne as a man peculiarly obsessed, avoids this episode altogether. Both underemphasized the category of the political; but we especially need this category to explore the most problematic section of Donne's career, the one that he himself elided in formulating the polar opposites of Jack and the Doctor, those five or six transitional years which served as his threshold between lives, which mark his passage from outsider to one of the most notable spokesmen for the establishment. Bald, significantly, called these the "Steps to the Temple." We might rather call this the time when Donne was leading a double life. We might begin to understand this doubleness by considering another underrated or excluded text that belongs in the environment of the Mitre Tavern ballad. *Elegy 14,* "A Tale of a Citizen and His Wife," contains at its center a neat example of what Foucault would call "discourse," actually introduced by that very term. As the speaker attempts to make contact with the citizen whose wife is making eyes at him behind her husband's back, he tries to find a set of contemporary issues likely to engage a London merchant:

> To get acquaintance with him I began
> To sort *discourse* fit for so fine a man:
> I ask'd the number of the Plaguy Bill,
> Ask'd if the Custome Farmers held out still,
> Of the Virginian Plot, and whether Ward
> The traffique of the Inland seas had marr'd,
> Whether the Brittaine Burse did fill apace,
> And likely were to give th'Exchange disgrace;
> Of new-built Algate, and the More-field crosses,
> Of store of Bankerouts, and poore Merchants losses.

And the citizen, his tongue finally loosened by the theme of "Tradesmens gaines," launches into a heated critique of the Jacobean economy in its relation to the power structure:

> He rail'd, as fray'd me; for he gave no praise,
> To any but my Lord of Essex dayes;
> Call'd those the age of action; true (quoth Hee)
> There's now as great an itch of bravery,
> And heat of taking up, but cold lay downe,
> For, put to push of pay, away they runne;
> Our onely City trades of hope now are
> Bawd, Tavern-keeper, Whore and Scrivener;
> The much of Privileg'd kingsmen, and the store
> Of fresh protections make the rest all poore;[28]

As Grierson worked through the series of topical references,[29] the poem appeared to situate itself in late 1609 or early 1610. Aldgate was rebuilt by 1609, and on April 11, 1609 the "Britain Bourse," constructed by Salisbury to draw financial business away from the City, was formally opened and so named by the king. The reference to "Custome Farmers" refers to a transaction initiated by Salisbury in 1604, with Arthur Ingram as his agent, by which the so-called Great Farm of the Customs was leased out to merchant syndicates, who from their profits, so the justification went, would lend money to the Crown; but by 1609/10 they were becoming increasingly reluctant to do so. There were two expeditions sent to Virginia in 1609, one in May and one at the end of the year. The reference to Ward, a notorious pirate, though less chronologically specific, also relates to this period. There were numerous complaints from the Venetian ambassador, and the issue of pirate control was raised in the 1610 Parliament. As for the "Plaguy Bill," 1609 was a particularly bad year for plague. There were no theatrical performances at court during the winter of 1609–10, and, more to the point, on September 29, 1609, James issued a proclamation further proroguing Parliament until February 9, citing plague as the primary reason.[30] Another proclamation on September 22, this time affecting the legal profession, adjourned part of Michaelmas term, also on account of plague.[31] Perhaps most interesting of all, Grierson discerned in the citizen's complaint echoes of yet another royal proclamation, this time on March 25, 1610. If he was right, *Elegy 14* belongs to the late spring of 1610, when many of the group at the Mitre Tavern were convened at Whitehall, and there protesting, among other things, the publication of Dr. John Cowell's *The Interpreter,* a book dedicated to Archbishop Bancroft and devoted to the praise and mystification of the royal prerogative—that is to say, to the divine right of kingship.

But what makes this allusion provocative is the fact that phrases from the proclamation seem to have been lifted, not only out of context, but into an opposing "discourse," one might even say a discourse of opposition. James's strategy in publishing the proclamation had been to preempt the parliamentary attack on Cowell, which had probably been led by Richard Martin,[32] by claiming that he himself was outraged by this unwarranted intervention by an amateur into constitutional theory. Yet the method he chose to discredit Cowell in public was to deliver a broad attack on *all* public discussion of these issues, and to combine this prohibition with a lament for the good old days:

> The later age and times of the world wherein we are fallen, is so much given to verball profession, as well of Religion, as of all commendable Morall vertues, but wanting the action and deedes agreeable to so specious a profession, as it hath bred such an unsatiable curiosity in many mens spirits, and such an itching of the tongues and pennes of most men, as nothing is left unsearched to the bottome, both in talking and writing. . . . And therefore it is no wonder, that men in these our dayes do not spare to wade in all the deepest mysteries that belong to the persons or State of Kings or Princes, that are gods upon Earth: since we see . . . that they spare not God himselfe. And this license that every talker or writer now assumeth to himselfe, is come to this abuse, that . . . many men that never went out of the compasse of Cloister or Colledges, will freely wade by their writings in the deepest mysteries of Monarchie and politique government.[33]

To counter this "license" of talk and writing, James ended by proclaiming a new campaign for "better oversight of Books of all sorts before they come to the Presse"; in other words, an increase in censorship.

The phrases that Grierson discerned as carried over into the citizen's protest were the lament for "action and deedes," and a complaint against the "itching" of tongues and pens. Yet during the transfer, if such it were, the nostalgia for an "age of action" has become the clearly seditious claim that the only age of action was "my lord of Essex dayes." These lines connect with the political analysis, such as it was, of the Mitre Tavern ballad. There it was Prince Henry who yearned for action in a society, as the *Elegy* phrases it, "put to push of pay," repeating Essex's role as the incarnation of the nation-as-hero in a precapitalist, still partly chivalric culture; while three of the participants had had connections with Robert Devereux, second earl of Essex: Donne, who had volunteered for the two expeditions against Spain in 1596 and 1597; Sir Henry Goodyer, who was knighted by Essex in Ireland in 1599; and Sir Henry Neville, who was implicated in Essex's rebellion in 1601, and despite protesting his innocence spent three years in the Tower, to be released only on James's accession.[34]

Although *Elegy 14* appeared in the 1635 and 1669 editions of Do-
nne's poems, and was accepted by Grierson with mild hesitation, Shaw-
cross defined it as "having generally been rejected," and omitted it from
his own edition, "in conviction of [its] spuriousness and in hope of help-
ing rid Donne of [its] inferiority."[35] Helen Gardner had earlier
discarded it from hers, with a revealing justification:

> Although some students of Donne would not regard it as impossible that
> he should write an improper poem in 1609, at the time that he was writ-
> ing *Pseudo-Martyr* and the "Holy Sonnets," it is surely in the highest
> degree unlikely that he would produce a weak *pastiche* of his earlier style,
> echoing phrases and lines from his own fourth Satire and Elegies at a
> time when he had developed a new style.[36]

Finding myself among those improper persons, I suggest that Gard-
ner's exclusion of *Elegy 14* begs precisely those questions the poem
demands we answer, and that she was motivated by a moral and evolu-
tionary theory of Donne's development not so very different, finally,
from Walton's hagiography. Conversely, I would argue that the *Elegy*
was produced when Donne could not himself decide between Jack and
Dr. Donne. The fact that "the Plaguy Bill" also echoes *The Canonization*
("When did the heats which my veines fill / Adde one more to the pla-
guie Bill?") is only one of the signs that the sharp break between "early"
and "mature" work was a wishful critical construction. In *The Courtier's
Library*, an unpublishable collection of satirical gibes (in Latin) at local
issues and figures, Donne included two items that implied, however
obliquely, continued support of Essex after his trial and execution: "The
Brazen Head of Francis Bacon: concerning Robert the First, King of
England," an attack on Bacon for his role in the earl's indictment; and
"An Encomion on Doctor Shaw, Chaplain to Richard III, by Doctor
Barlow," which equated Barlow's sermon at Paul's Cross in 1601, as an
attempt to manipulate public sympathy away from Essex, with Shaw's
"sycophantic defence" of the murder of the Princes in the Tower.[37]

Neither Bald nor Carey mentions *Elegy 14*, the latter being therefore
able to conclude that although "James's court was far more obviously
corrupt and degenerate than Elizabeth's, Donne never ventured any
criticism of it at all."[38] On the contrary, the poem reiterates, as Gardner
knew, the strategy of Donne's fourth satire, where Donne imagines
himself trapped on his way to court by a seditious malcontent, who
forces him to listen to his "Libells . . . 'gainst each great man," "names
a price for every office paid," and thus renders him complicit against his
will in the language of treason. "I . . . felt my selfe then," wrote Donne
in the late 1590s, "Becomming Traytor, and mee thought I saw / One of

our Giant Statutes ope his jaw / To sucke me in."[39] I have argued else-
where that this sedition-by-proxy, this creation of a socially dangerous
persona to do his libeling for him, was one of Donne's personal solutions
to the restraints imposed on his culture by political censorship.[40] In
*Elegy 14,* he returned to this strategy of self-division, and extended it to
the Jacobean state. By placing his satire in the mouth of a discontented
Londoner, pretending all the while to be shocked at what is said, and
flirting, while it is said, with the citizen's wife behind his back, Donne
in effect divides himself into two voices, the one asserting its loyalty but
demonstrating its frivolity, the other supposedly being rejected as trea-
sonous yet carrying a certain obvious conviction. "I am no Libeller, nor
will be any," says the narrator, in introducing his citizen decoy, and dis-
misses his "harsh talke" as "void of reason." But as he listens, the
narrator once again begins to "sweat for feare of treason." From this
perspective, *Elegy 14* becomes a significant exhibit in the cultural after-
life of the Essex rebellion, a tribute to the role played in that episode by
difficult intellectuals like Donne and his friends.

Carey berated Donne for apparently abandoning Essex as soon as his
fall from favor was apparent, citing a letter of Christmas 1599: "My
lorde of Essex and his trayne are no more mist here then the Aungells
which were cast downe from heaven nor (for anything I see) likelyer to
retourne."[41] I, however, find it impossible to tell from this statement
whether or not Donne was of the Devil's party, with or without know-
ing it. John Hoskyns must have been writing his rhetorical manual in
1599, while Essex was still in Ireland, but evidently much in mind; for
with characteristic imprudence Hoskyns chose to illustrate synecdoche,
taking the part for the whole, by an example of political deputy-ship:
"one may say that the Earl is gone into Ireland for E:R.[the queen]";[42]
Sir Henry Wotton, who had been Essex's secretary and may well have
introduced to him his good friend Donne, hastily detached himself
when the breach with the queen seemed irreparable, and awaited in
Venice James's accession. We know what happened to Neville, whose
integrity was celebrated by Jonson in one of his epigrams (no. 109),
though in terms so general as to be entirely innocuous. But Sir Thomas
Roe, another of Donne's correspondents, wrote a flaming satire about
the Jacobean court that partly corroborates the citizen's complaint in
*Elegy 14.* Roe's speaker, like Donne's in the fourth satire, went to court
(but after 1603), and found there "Kings were but men":

> What Treason is, and what did Essex kill,
> Not true Treason, but Treason handled ill;
> And which of them stood for their Countries good,

Or what might be the cause of so much Blood.
He said she stunck, and men might not have said
That she was old before that she was dead.
His Case was hard, to do or suffer; loth
To do, he made it harder, and did both.
Too much preparing lost them all their Lives,
Like some in Plagues kill'd with preservatives.
Friends, like land-souldiers in a storm at Sea,
Not knowing what to do, for him did pray.[43]

Whoever attributed this poem to Donne, adding it to his satires in the 1669 edition, obviously believed that its tone and opinions were compatible with the five that preceded it; but Roe's Jacobean satire also tells us much about the confusion and guilt, what one might call the survivor-complex, that affected those who had looked to Essex as a focus for their own alienation and who, when the mortal danger of their allegiance dawned on them, "not knowing what to do," chose to be ineffectual.

We will need to return to *Elegy 14* and its theme of financial corruption in order to understand the demise of the 1610 Parliament and the so-called "Addled" Parliament of 1614, of which Donne himself was a member. In between, we can continue to follow the Mitre Tavern ballad as a rough guide to Jacobean "issues" (keeping good faith with Donne's prose), by considering *Pseudo-Martyr* (1610) and *Ignatius his Conclave* (1611), the pamphlets by which Donne entered the local controversy concerning the oath of allegiance. We know that Donne had done so at the urging of Bishop Thomas Morton, and apparently not without internal resistance. His dedication of *Pseudo-Martyr* to James begins, "As Temporall armies consist of Press'd men, and voluntaries, so doe they also in this warfare,"[44] leaving it open to interpretation which category he himself belonged to. The following year he published, both in English and Latin, and anonymously, *Ignatius his Conclave,* an anti-Jesuit satire so violent in its contempt for what had once been his own church that it might seem to establish his voluntary acceptance of this new polemical role. In it, the persona of the fourth satire, he "who dreamt he saw hell" in the Elizabethan court, becomes a Jacobean author who fell into an "Extasie" and "saw all the roomes in Hell open to [his] sight," with Ignatius Loyola as *diabolus in cathedra.*[45] Yet here too occurs a curious self-division, not now between speaker and libeler, but between the real and the fictional author, or between fictional author and fictional editor. "Dost thou seeke after the Author?" wrote Donne in the preface, "It is in vaine."[46] For the only thing known of him was conveyed to the fictional editor by a friend of the author's, in a letter, as follows:

> The Author was unwilling to have this book published, thinking it unfit
> both for the matter, which in it selfe is weighty and serious, and for that
> gravity which himselfe had proposed and observed in an *other* booke
> formerly published, to descend to this kind of writing. . . . At the last he
> yeelded, and made mee owner of his booke, which I send to you to be
> delivered over to forraine nations, (a) *farre from the father:* and (as his
> desire is) (b) his last in this kinde. Hee chooses and desires, that his *other*
> booke should testifie his ingenuity, and candor, and his disposition to
> labour for the reconciling of all parts. This Booke must teach what hu-
> mane infirmity is. . . . (pp. 3–5; emphasis added)

This extraordinary passage speaks to the pressures on the self of the do-
mains of law and authority, those territories entry into which Lacanian
theory has identified with social and linguistic maturity, and subsumed
under the Name-of-the-Father. But if Donne intuits the point at which
psychoanalysis will merge with sociology, he offers himself and his
readers a strategy for self-management that Lacanian theory, with its
stress on irreparable bondage, overlooks. Dividing himself between au-
thor and editor, reluctant utterer and eager promoter, dividing his
utterance between *this* book, written in the alienated voice of satire, and
the *other,* written from the "reconciling" perspective of the official pro-
pagandist, Donne found a way to speak ambivalence. Even in the
physical presence of his two books, the official polemic a handsome
quarto, the anonymous satire a tiny, unreadable octavo, he showed his
resistance to the move expected of him (by himself among others), the
move from sardonic outsider to institutional spokesman. And though
by this strategy he may not have been able to reconcile both sides of him-
self, his appeal to "humane infirmity" is both disingenuous and ingen-
uous at the same time, demanding for himself the toleration that his
project denied to others.

The text of the *Conclave* is no less peculiar than its preface. As the
preface concludes by observing "how hard a matter is it for a man . . . so
thoroughly to cast off the Jesuits, as that he contract nothing of their
naturall drosses, which are Petulancy, and Lightnesse" (p. 5), the ironies
of the text are so rebarbative that it looks suspiciously as if the author had
reserved to himself the Jesuit strategy of "Mentall Reservation, and Mixt
propositions" (p. 55). The *Conclave* consists in a demonic competition,
presided over by Lucifer, between all the greatest innovators in contem-
porary thought, in theology, science, or the "Arts," "or in any thing
which . . . may so provoke to quarrelsome and brawling controversies:
For so the truth be lost, it is no matter how" (p. 13). Among the contes-
tants, then, are Copernicus, Paracelsus, Machiavelli, Aretino, Columbus,
and Ignatius Loyola, who will win; and in the course of putting his own

case forward Machiavelli complains that the followers of Ignatius "have brought into the world a new art of Equivocation . . . have raised to life againe the language of the Tower of Babel, so long concealed, and brought us againe from understanding one an other" (p. 27). Conversely, Ignatius, who has argued against Copernicus's claims as insufficiently perverse ("those opinions of yours may very well be true" [p. 17])[47] attacks Machiavelli (his most formidable rival) on the grounds that his teachings have worked against the kingdom of Rome:

> for what else doth hee endeavour or go about, but to change the forme
> of common-wealth, and so to deprive the people (who are a soft, a liquid
> and ductile mettall, and apter for our impressions) of all their liberty: &
> having so destroyed all civility and re-publique, to reduce all states to
> Monarchies; a name which in secular states, wee doe so much abhor. (pp.
> 55–57)

This astonishingly backhanded compliment to those absolute monarchs who had removed their states from papal jurisdiction is at the heart of the *Conclave's* main argument, which is that the Jesuits, like the devil himself, are vowed to the destruction of monarchies. Yet the result is a statement that monarchies come into existence by depriving the people "of all their liberty" and "having . . . destroyed all civility," a curious defense of James I and Elizabeth. The irony, though, cannot be intended to function by a simple discrediting or inversion of all that Loyola says, for that would nullify his malice and deprive the pamphlet of its point.

Self-division and equivocation are also the dominant symptoms of another roughly datable and (one might well feel) disreputable text produced in the winter of 1613/14. We know that Donne had by this time already profited from the greatest scandal of James's reign, in which Frances Howard's divorce from the third earl of Essex and remarriage to Robert Carr, earl of Somerset and still the reigning favorite, was accomplished at the cost of Sir Thomas Overbury's life. On September 14, 1613, Overbury, who had tried to prevent the divorce, died in the Tower, poisoned, it was subsequently charged, by the countess through her accomplices. Donne, in the meantime, had not only sought out Somerset as a new patron but had accepted the position as his secretary that Overbury's imprisonment had vacated. By mid-December rumors were circulating that there had been foul play; so that Donne already knew how he had fulfilled one of the most horrible of the charges laid by the seditious speaker in his own fourth satire, where the first-person persona learns unwillingly "who by poyson / Hasts to an Offices reversion."[48] Yet early in 1614 Donne contributed semi-anonymously, as did

Sir Thomas Roe, to the second edition of Overbury's *Characters,* a col-
laborative volume that became *the* best-seller of 1614, capitalizing on
what was known and what was suspected of his all-too-convenient
death, and adding to his own "Characters" a series of satirical portraits
that rendered, at very least, a skeptical account of Jacobean culture.

We also know that Donne was late in contributing his own verse trib-
ute to the Somerset-Howard marriage. He may have been very late
indeed. Although the "Ecclogue" that prefaces the epithalamion is
dated December 26, 1613, the date of the marriage, we know from his
private correspondence that Donne did not begin it until several weeks
later. The function of the "Ecclogue" is, in fact, to explain the delay in
the poem's completion and delivery; and it provides the most sharply
delineated version in Donne's work of that formally divided self to
which he apparently had recourse when attempting to deal with am-
bivalence, here personified as Idios ("one's own,"[11] "pertaining to one's
self") and Allophanes ("appearing otherwise," or, perhaps, "the face of
the Other"). In their dialogue, Allophanes reproaches Idios for his ab-
sence from court on this great occasion of the marriage, only to be told
that even in the country Idios so reveres the king and his style of govern-
ment that he is not, in spirit, "from Court."[49] Yet the language in which
Allophanes records the virtues of James and Carr treads that slippery
line whereby the claim for good is rendered as a denial of the converse
imputation. It is a court "where it is no levity to trust, / Where there is
no ambition, but to'obey, / Where men need whisper nothing, and yet
may;" and the question of Carr's own role in that structure is addressed
in the most oblique manner possible:

> . . . the King's favours are so plac'd, that all
> Finde that the King therein is liberall
> To them, *in him,* because his favours bend
> To vertue, to *the which they all pretend.*
> (11. 81–84; emphasis added)

While the discreetly unnamed recipient of the king's favors supposedly
is merely the conduit of those favors to "all" who desire them, and the
king's liberality is supposedly proven by the favorite's selfless virtue, the
mobility of "all" as a qualifier may expand to include suitors, Carr, king,
all. And all are then governed by the ambiguous concluding verb "pre-
tend," which in Donne's day already carried, along with the neutral
meaning "profess," the alternative, deceitful connotation that is now the
only meaning.

It is then not entirely surprising that the language Idios himself uses
to explain his delayed eulogy is scarcely that of celebration:

>                                    . . . I knew
> All this, and onely therefore I withdrew.
> To know and feele all this, and not to have
> Words to expresse it, makes a man a grave
> Of his owne thoughts; I would not therefore stay
> At a great feast, having no grace to say.

(11. 91–96)

If one reads these lines without a prior assumption that Donne when he wrote them was utterly cynical, they express rather clearly and painfully the particular version of the inexpressibility topos that actual and self-inflicted censorships had arranged. The crucial "whisper," in Donne a sign of political opposition or "sedition,"[50] is here introduced (through denial) in order to explain the deadly gap between knowing all and telling only part of it; while the powerful and indecorous image of the marriage celebrant becoming a "grave of his own thoughts" reintroduces the necrophilic imagination of Donne's first satire,[51] and reveals, after all, what generic affiliates this pretended pastoral confesses to.

Writing to his close friend Sir Robert Carr, Somerset's cousin, about the Other, Donne considered, without stating, his options as a client. "I had rather like the first best," he began:

> not onley because it is cleanliest, but because it reflects least upon the other party, which, in all jeast and earnest, in this affair, I wish avoided. If my Muse were onely out of fashion, and but wounded and maimed like free will in the Roman Church, I should adventure to put her to an Epithalamion. But since she is dead, like Free-will in our Church, I have not so much Muse left as to lament her losse. Perchance this business may produce occasions, wherein I may express my opinion of it, in a more serious manner.[52]

This extreme awkwardness can scarcely excuse the fact that Donne actually contributed a reasoned argument in support of the "nullity," the divorce imposed on Essex; but it helps to explain the tone of Donne's epithalamion, so much more truthful, even its evasions, than Ben Jonson's purely conventional one.[53] The connection between poetic spontaneity and theological free-will, killed by the Calvinist doctrine of the state religion that Donne now professed, serves as another symptom of the internal strain his apostasy was still causing, and inextricable here from the social determinism of clientage.

This brings us back to the citizen's complaint against "privileg'd kingsmen," in *Elegy 14*, which Grierson understood as an attack on monopolies, but which could obviously carry a larger reference to the Scottish favorites and the entire patronage system. And the citizen's

charge that the age of action has been replaced by one of financial cor-
ruption ("put to push of pay, away they run") may also imply a charge
against even those parliamentary activists who had committed them-
selves to fight monopolies. As the 1610 Parliament ground its way
towards stalemate, it was rumored that efforts were being made by the
king's councillors to dismantle the opposition. On December 10, the Ve-
netian ambassador, Marc Antonio Correr, wrote to his employers:

> The business in Parliament has gone from bad to worse. Meantime they
> will try to win over some of those who have shown most opposition, and
> if they do not succeed Parliament will be dissolved altogether, so that the
> constituencies will elect new members. There are those who say that the
> King will never summon Parliament again, but his need of money is
> against that, and maybe this rumour is put about to frighten many of
> them.[54]

In fact, as the dissolution approached, four of the most determined op-
positionists, Lewknor, Fuller, Wentworth, and our John Hoskyns were
sent for by Salisbury for a private conference.[55] On December 31, Cor-
rer continued his report:

> Certain persons have been approached with a view to inducing them to
> bow to his Majesty's wishes and desires (I have information on this point
> from a good quarter, but it would only weary your Serenity).

He added (again recalling for us the Mitre Tavern ballad) that nothing
had been done "about the Prince's demand to be freed from his minor-
ity as regards the exercise of his prerogative . . . perhaps because, in the
present disagreements, they are doubtful of the issue."[56] And on Janu-
ary 21 Correr reported the dissolution of Parliament, which, after a
series of adjournments, was dissolved by royal proclamation (in the
middle of a prorogation) on December 31:

> This step, which is unusual, as Parliament is usually prorogued, and the
> rumour that the King intends to issue privy seals for the amount of one
> million six hundred thousand crowns, give rise to some talk. This loan
> once obtained his Majesty will summon a new Parliament; care being
> taken that those hostile to him shall not be re-elected. He will all the
> more readily obtain subsidies to pay back the loan, in that everyone will
> have an interest in voting it, and all the money will pass into the hands of
> the nobility. Some cry out that it is not well to exclude those who have
> forgotten their personal interest in the service of their country; others
> are unwilling that his Majesty should achieve by indirect ways what was
> refused him in Parliament. All the same . . . if he gains the Parliamen-
> tary leaders he will secure a return of a majority of members that suit his
> taste.[57]

Diplomatic reports are often, especially by revisionist historians, treated with a certain skepticism, dependent as they were, in Kevin Sharpe's words, "upon information, even rumour, from courtiers, M. P.'s, and newsmongers." Yet Sharpe also admits that "at times their reports may reflect the views of a courtier who spoke his mind but would not commit his opinion to the dangerous permanence of paper";[58] and Correr's report has precisely that quality of *talk* that Foucault called discourse, and that therefore connects with both *Elegy 14* and the Mitre Tavern ballad.[59]

It also connects, probably, with a joking letter written by Donne to Sir Henry Goodyer, and published, without a date, in the *Letters to Severall Persons of Honour*.[60] In it Donne speaks of "two millions confiscated to the Crown of England" and asks his friend to tell their other friends how they might each get their share of the pickings:

> acquainte M. Martin from me, how easie it will be to get a good part of this for Virginia. Upon the least petition that M. Brooke can present he may make himself whole again, of all which the Kings servants M. Lepton and master Waterouse, have endammaged him. Give him leave to offer to Mr. Hakevill enough to please himself, for his *Aurum Reginae*. And if Mr. Gherard have no present hopefull designe upon a worthy Widow, let him have so much of this as will provide him that house and coach which he promised to lend me at my return. If M. Inago Jones be not satisfied for his last Maske (because I hear say it cannot come to much) here is enough to be had: This is but a copy, but if Sir Ro. Cotton have the originall he will not deny it you.

Edmund Gosse believed, I think correctly, that the grouping of names in this letter, and the predominance of those who were M. P.s in 1610—Goodyer, Martin, Brooke, Cotton, and William Hakewill, who delivered the great speech against impositions at the end of the fourth session[61]—not only helps to date it but explains the mysterious and exaggerated "millions" that the Crown was supposed to have confiscated.[62] And one might add that, with the mention of Inigo Jones, five of the persons named were also present at the Mitre Tavern dinner.

This letter helps to explain the *tone* of the Addled Parliament, that *parlamentum inchoatum* (as John Chamberlain called it),[63] for which writs were finally called in the spring of 1614 (even, perhaps, while Donne was finishing his leaden tribute to Somerset). The grease that rendered the political territory unstable was, not surprisingly, self-interest. One of the questions that exercised the Commons in the few weeks between April 14 and June 7, when James dissolved them, was whether their proceedings had been destabilized by bribery. As Sir John Holles complained in a letter:

a schism is cast into the House by reason of some interlopers between the
K. and the Parliament, whom they term undertakers, so named, because
they have promised that the Parliament shall supply the King's want to
his contentment . . . nor for that they envy these undertakers' reward
but that they foresee a perilous consequence by this precedent to the
State, when kings heartened by this success shall hereafter practise the
like; and sprinkling some hires upon a few shall . . . so by little and little
steal away the liberty and at the next opportunity overthrow Parliament
itself.[64]

And even before the Privy Council had advised James to issue the writs
for the election, Donne himself had written to a friend that "It is taken
ill, though it be but mistaken that certain men (whom they call under-
takers) should presume either to understand the house before it sit, or to
incline it then, and this rumour beforehand, which must impeach, if it
do not defeat their purposes at last."[65] Despite the cautious neutrality of
this statement, its very occurrence would seem to align Donne more
with Sir John Holles than with Sir Henry Neville of Berkshire, whose
own contriving to bring the Parliament into being was not only con-
strued as "undertaking" but probably introduced this new, political
meaning of the word. Neville had committed himself to negotiate with
the "patriots" in the Commons on the basis of his friendship with them;
and, claiming to speak "as one that lived and conversed inwardly with
the chief of them that were noted to be the most backward and know
their inwardest thoughts in that business," offered to "undertake for
most of them" that the king would find them "willing to do him
service."[66]

Apart from Neville and Donne himself, the Mitre Tavern group was
powerfully represented in the 1614 Parliament: Lionel Cranfield,
Arthur Ingram, Sir Robert Phelips (whose father had provided Donne
with his seat), Richard Connock, John Hoskyns, and Christopher
Brooke were all elected, along with Donne's friends Sir Thomas Roe,
Walter Chute, and Sir Henry Wotton. Sir Thomas Egerton, Donne's
old employer, now Lord Ellesmere, was lord chancellor in the upper
House; and continuing his role as a firm supporter of the Crown and an
advocate for granting its royal supply was Donne's father-in-law, Sir
George More. This short and troubled session, therefore, economically
represents Donne's environment, in both personal and political terms,
in the months immediately preceding his decision to take orders; and
we should pause to see what routes his colleagues took before passing
judgment on Donne's own performance.

There is no doubt that some of Donne's friends vehemently adopted
an oppositionist stance, among them Roe, Brooke, Hoskyns, and Phe-

lips. Hoskyns made himself particularly vulnerable, and by the end of the session had managed to compare the condition of England in the hands of the Scottish favorites with that of Sicily under Angevin domination in the thirteenth century, which had resulted in the notorious uprising known as the Sicilian Vespers. It is not without irony that Hoskyns had begun his *Directions for Speech and Style* with a warning against "Carelesse speech" and "the indilligence of an idle tongue."[67] When James lost his patience and dissolved the Parliament on June 3, Hoskyns was one of four members sent to the Tower, where he remained for a full year. One of the more poignant records of this event is a poem reportedly sent to James by Hoskyns's wife as an appeal for his release. In it, the prisoner looks "out of the caves mouth cutt in stone" while his wife tries to explain to their little son why his father is incarcerated. "My father nere was so unkinde," says the child, "Who lett him then to speake his mynde?" and his mother replies: " 'tis Caesar's will, / Caesar can hate, Caesar can kill":

> The worst is tolld, the best is hidd:
> Kings know not all, oh would they did.

The substance of the appeal is that Hoskyns was loyal to James "in person & in purse" when others "aymed at broken hope of doubtfull state," that is to say, at disrupting parliamentary process for their own ends; and it concludes with the wife's realistic observation, "he that offends not doth not live."[68]

On the other hand, Cranfield, who had been made surveyor-general of customs the previous summer, was identified as a possible profiteer, and humbly submitted his records to the inspection of the house. Sir Arthur Ingram, recently knighted as a result of having loaned money to the king, had been managing the income which Suffolk derived from pensions on the English and Irish customs, and owed his seat in the house to Northampton.[69] Sir Henry Wotton defended the king's right to impose, and demanded an explanation from Hoskyns of the Sicilian Vespers allusion, thus making it impossible to ignore. And Richard Martin, who in 1610 had directly sparred with Salisbury, chaired the committee of the whole, and extravagantly introduced a private bill which, in lieu of hanging, or enforced villeinage, proposed to deprive the divine-right advocates in the clergy of all their dignities,[70] now declined to run for reelection. Bacon, who provided James with a list of those who, he thought, had been bought off before the 1614 Parliament was called, stated that "Martin has money in his purse."[71] He was, Chamberlain wrote to Carleton, "loth to venter his fortune upon his slipperie tongue," and now appeared before the Commons in a very dif-

ferent, commercial role, as a special counselor to plead for the support
of the Virginia project. There "he fell to ripping up what had passed
since theyre sitting, taxing them for theyre slow proceding, for theyre
disorderly cariage, and schooling them what they shold do . . . wher-
with he so discontented them . . . yt was agreed he shold be called to
the barre and aunser his misdemeanure." "Thus you see," concluded
Chamberlain, that though "he abstained from being of the parlement
for feare of beeing transported and doing himself harme, Yet yt was *in
fatis* that he shold shame himself in that house."[72]

What then should we make of Donne's own contributions to this epi-
sode, when his friends and colleages went their several ways as con-
science, prudence, bravado, and financial incentives directed? There is
no record of his having spoken in the Commons, though he was named
to important committees. One, in May, was to prepare a conference with
the Lords so that both Houses could present a joint petition to the king
against monopolies. (It included all the members of the Privy Council,
as well as Hoskyns, Brooke, and Neville, and Sir George More). The
others were a series of select committees appointed to deal with a con-
stitutional crisis, in which Richard Neile, bishop of London, declared
that the Commons had no business meddling with impositions, that
they were a *noli me tangere.* "Proud Prelate," said Sir William Strowde
in the Commons; and Sir Edward Hoby, "Woe to that Time, wher an
humble Petition of the grieved Gentry of England shall be called an
entering upon the King's Prerogative."[73] But both Ellesmere and Sir
George More defended Neile. Ellesmere himself had earlier been ac-
cused in the house of lining up undertakers, and had only been saved
from more serious consequences than formal reprimand by virtue of his
age and distinguished record of service. The pressures on everyone were
evident, and Donne more than others must have experienced those pres-
sures as the pull of divided allegiances.

For Bald, the absence of evidence that Donne participated in the de-
bates meant that he did not, although the official records are, to say the
least, elliptical. *"No doubt,"* wrote Bald, arguing from silence, "he
judged it the part of discretion not to run the risk of expressing himself
too openly or of giving offence. He seems to have been a good commit-
tee-man [and what a derogatory phrase that is] but he *probably* kept out
of the debates *quite deliberately,* less he should spoil his chances with the
King or the leading members of the Government," (p. 289; emphasis
added). By the time Carey retells the story, that "no doubt" and "proba-
bly" have hardened into statement: "Christopher Brooke and other
*former* friends of Donne vehemently opposed these abuses of royal
power. . . Donne discreetly held his tongue" (emphasis added). When

added to the misleading statement that Donne acquired his seat through "court influence" (p. 87), when in fact he owed it to the father of one of the leading oppositionists, Carey's language suggests betrayal of friendship, another form of apostasy. Yet the record of how those friends themselves behaved demands, at worst, a more equitable distribution of our scorn, and, at best, a more realistic assessment of political behavior, then as now. Not only were the lines of force and the patterns of loyalty far less clearly drawn than Carey assumes, but the dangers of misspeaking, as exemplified in the diametrically opposite cases of Hoskyns and Martin, were far more evident. If these were the conditions of political activism, and Donne had little reason to imagine their alteration, it is perhaps no coincidence that one of Donne's love poems goes under the title of "The Undertaking" and begins (and ends) as follows:

> I have done one braver thing
> Then all the Worthies did,
> And yet a braver then doth spring,
> Which is, to keepe that hid.[74]

Perhaps we now know when this otherwise unnoticeable poem was written.

Among other signs of strain[75] in the epithalamion that Donne was, almost concurrently, writing for Somerset, the most incongruous is the metaphor that opens the penultimate stanza, entitled "The Bridegroomes Comming":

> As he that sees a starre fall, runs apace,
> And findes a gellie in the place,
> So doth the Bridegroome hast as much,
> Being told this starre is falne, and findes her such.
>
> (ll. 204–7)

It turns out that this was also an aspect of the Addled Parliament's semantics, an image of disintegration and the collapse of political integrity. The Commons Journal for May 14 noted that "divers [are] taxed. as Stars of the last Parliament, now Jelly," and that there was thereby an "implicit concluding, that there are still Undertakers."[76] Can this be merely a coincidence? I doubt it. It looks as though Donne were still struggling with this poem as the *parliamentum inchoatum* struggled with its own conscience. On June 1, when the Speaker delivered the king's message that unless the Parliament proceeded to vote him a supply he would forthwith dissolve it, we can hear Donne's world in shambles. "[This is] The Ship, wherein we all fail," said Sir George More, and "If we neglect this, which must now be done, the Commonwealth will receive the prejudice." Sir Thomas Roe warned, "That this is a Dissolution, not of this, but of all parliaments." John Hoskyns protested, "This is a Parliament of Love. All the Arguments now used, Arguments of Fear," a premonitory warning of what was about to happen to himself; and Mr. Ashley's remarks are incoherence rendered with a dramatic force that one does not expect of public documents: "Basileus. Basis populi. Bring, bring; Give, give; Spend, spend. The Question only, who to begin. King, or People."[77] Division and confusion mark the public arena and the writerly psyche; and both belong to the peculiar discursive formation of 1614, to that aspect of Jacobean culture that we have so far been unable to recuperate with adequate sensitivity, when the rules of public and private behavior were under major strain, and everyone had to make, as it were, a separate treaty with circumstances.

Perhaps the most telling statement was made after the session was over, when Sir John Holles was deciding whether his constituency should contribute to the forced loan. His advice was yes: "for, if only Nottingham look upon the commonwealth, Lincoln, Derby, Leicester, York, in a word all their other neighbours upon the King," their "obstinacy and stoutness" would redound to the discredit of the commissioners; and, turning to the ethical issue, he added:

> These foreseeings and cogitations decline me something from that *quod oportet* and draws me with the throng into the broad high way of *quod convenit*, which, though not so honest as the other, yet (as our nowadays wise will have it) more courtly and civil; so as I hold it expedient rather to *errare cum Aristotele*, to give as our fellows do, than to offer with one finger to stay a falling house.[78]

Such troubled testimony in others (which has important implications for parliamentary history)[79] permits in the "literary" arena a more generous view of Johannes Factus and John-ycleped-Made than the one that is currently in place. And if this kind of evidence will not (as it should not) release the "essential" Donne into our custody, or give us the whole picture, at least these transitional years in his career form a bridge between Jack and the Doctor, and remind us as, as did *Ignatius his Conclave,* "what humane infirmity is." This essay has emphasized, too, the continuity between the Elizabethan satirist and the Jacobean aspirant for something significant to do. And when Donne eventually succumbed to James's insistence that he take orders, it may have been less out of naked ambition than out of despair for any secular change. As Roe's poem declared that the friends of Essex, "not knowing what to do," turned to prayer, and as the Addled Parliament showed what happened to those who spoke their minds,[80] so Donne's *Second Anniversary,* published in 1612, linked his preacherly future with his satirical past (and both with a prophetic metaphor of poisoning) in a statement of absolute vocational nihilism:

> With whom wilt thou converse? what station
> Canst thou choose out, free from infection,
> That will not give thee theirs, nor drinke in thine?
> Shall thou not find a spungie slacke Divine
> Drinke and sucke in th'instructions of Great men,
> And for the word of God, vent them agen?
> Are there not some Courts (and then, no things bee
> So like as Courts) which, in this let us see,
> That wits and tongues of Libellers are weake,
> Because they do more ill, then these can speake?
> The poyson's gone through all.[81]

## Notes

1. See I. A. Shapiro, "The 'Mermaid Club'," *Modern Language Review* 45 (1950): 6–17. Shapiro used the text in John Chamberlain's papers in the Public Record Office (*State Papers Domestic,* 14/66/2). Another version was printed in A. Clark, ed., *Aubrey's 'Brief Lives'* (Oxford, 1898), 2:50–53.

2. Edmund Gosse, *The Life and Letters of John Donne,* 2 vols. (London, 1899).

3. R. C. Bald, *John Donne: A Life* (New York and Oxford, 1972). This is, to date, the definitive biography of Donne, and while I shall have cause to differ with it in evaluation, I wish here to record my debts.

4. John Carey, *John Donne: Life, Mind and Art* (New York, 1981).

5. For Cranfield, see Menna Prestwick, *Cranfield: Politics and Profits under the early Stuarts* (Oxford, 1966).

6. See Anthony Upton, *Sir Arthur Ingram* (Oxford, 1961).

7. For Hoskyns' life and writings, see L. B. Osborn, *The Life, Letters and Writings of John Hoskyns, 1566–1638,* (New Haven, 1937). The *Directions,* unpublished, were prepared as a gift for a young gentleman of the Middle Temple.

8. Richard Martin, *A Speach delivered to the kings Most Excellent Majestie in the Name of the Sheriffes of London and Middlesex* (London, 1603). This was, not surprisingly, republished in 1643.

9. The question of dating has been overcomplicated by Clark's assertion that the phrase, "in clauso Termini Sti. Michaelis" meant September 2, on the basis of the fact that the feast of St. Giles was September 1. R. C. Bald, *A Life,* p. 191, clearly puzzled by this, since the Latin clearly translates as "at the end of Michaelmas Term," that is, on or about November 28, observed that "'the feast of St. Giles in the Fields' is a jest, the point of which is now lost," and that "the

month and day of the gathering are uncertain." The poem refers to Coryat's return in October 1608 from his European tour, which resulted, in March 1611, in *Coryats Crudities,* his extraordinary travelogue. Since Coryat left England again on September 12, 1612, the dinner must have taken place during November of either 1608, 1609, or 1610. It could not have been in 1611, as Bald suggests, since Donne, as Bald also states, was by then in France with Sir Robert Drury (pp. 191, 245). Shapiro argues against 1609 and 1610 on the grounds, unpersuasive to me, that Chamberlain could only have copied out the poem with the intention of sending it to Carleton, who was in England in the fall of both years. There is much to be said for positing late 1610 for this occasion, since Coryat would then have been engaged in preparing the *Crudities* for the press, and collecting the parodically commendatory verses by his friends.

10. The problem of identity here is insoluble. The choice is between (1) Sir Henry Neville of Abergavenny (1573–1641), author of one of the commendatory poems in *Coryats Crudities,* who was raised a Catholic, knighted by Essex at Cadiz, married the daughter of Elizabeth's treasurer, Thomas Sackville, earl of Dorset, and sat in the Parliaments of 1601 and 1604. (2) Sir Henry Neville of Billingbear, Berkshire (1564–1615), Abergavenny's cousin, a member of Parliament from 1584 onwards, ambassador to France for Elizabeth and knighted in 1599, but implicated in Essex's conspiracy, stripped of his offices and imprisoned in the Tower from July 1601 until James's accession, when he and Southampton were released together. R. C. Bald may be forgiven for blending both figures together. Shapiro, in identifying the Mitre Tavern guests, "assumed" that the Neville present was Abergavenny, on the grounds of the poem assigned to him. However, the majority of the contributors to Coryat's volume, with its fifty-six commendatory poems, were not at the dinner; and there are aspects of Abergavenny's profile which seem to render him the less likely candidate. He was of higher rank, as the heir to a barony, than any other of the participants; he had probably been educated abroad in a Catholic university (though entered as M. A. Oxford in 1594); his connections, through his marriage, were with the court rather than the Inns of Court; and four days after Essex's rising Abergavenny had revealed to the government a proposal made to him by Captain Thomas Lee to put the queen under duress until she signed a warrant for the earl's release. Sir Henry Neville of Berkshire, on the other hand, had like Martin and Hoskyns been educated (though a decade earlier) at Oxford; was, like several of the Mitre Tavern participants, a friend of Prince Henry; and had become one of the hero-victims of the Essex rebellion and its aftermath. While Abergavenny's crypto-Catholicism, not professed until 1614, might have connected him to Donne, the other Sir Henry's friendship with Brooke, Hoskyns, and other parliamentarians became, as we shall see, a matter of record in 1614. For biographies of both men, see P. W. Hasler, *The History of Parliament: The House of Commons, 1558–1603* (London, 1981), 3:123–25.

11. See Wallace Notestein, *The House of Commons, 1604–1610* (New Haven, 1971). The extent to which this group, which also included Sir Edwyn

Sandys, Nicholas Fuller, Thomas Hedley, Thomas Wentworth, and William Hakewill, constituted an organized opposition in the Commons has been much disputed by revisionist historians; but Notestein's decision, to refer to them as the "opposition" as yet uncapitalized, seems the right compromise. "It is hardly to be doubted," he concluded, "that they held quiet conferences, decided on lines of argument, arranged who would present them, and weighed with one another possible motions and resolutions" (p. 434).

12. Compare Bald, *A Life,* p. 139.

13. Witness the efforts of Chaviva Hosek and Patricia Parker, as editors of *Lyric Poetry: Beyond New Criticism* (Ithaca, 1985), to amend this.

14. John R. Roberts, "John Donne's Poetry: An Assessment of Modern Criticism," *John Donne Journal* 1 (1982):55–67, especially 62–63.

15. See Thomas Hester, *Kinde Pity and Brave Scorn: John Donne's Satyres* (Durham, 1982).

16. See Arthur F. Marotti, *John Donne, Coterie Poet* (Madison, 1986).

17. See Thomas Docherty, *John Donne, Undone* (London and New York, 1986), p. 1. Docherty updates his topic primarily by his allegiance to deconstructive criticism. He avoids all but the most passing reference to Donne's biography, and understands history as the history of philosophy, or at best the history of science.

18. See George R. Potter and Evelyn M. Simpson, eds., *The Sermons of John Donne,* 10 vols. (Berkeley and Los Angeles, 1953–62), 1:83.

19. The Modern Library edition by Charles Coffin (New York, 1952), which offered precisely that format, has been out of print for about three decades; but an excellent replacement, in the Oxford Standard Authors series, is forthcoming, edited by John Carey.

20. Compare the argument of Ernest Gilman, in "'To adore, or scorn an image': Donne and the Iconoclastic Controversy," *John Donne Journal* 5 (1986), that "the surviving portraits offer a series of shifting, carefully contrived poses that vividly reflect the several different selves Donne would fashion for himself—the resolute 'gentleman volunteer' at eighteen, the fastidious melancholiac at twenty-three, the sober courtier at thirty-four, the august divine at forty-nine" (p. 68).

21. Michel Foucault, *The Archaeology of Knowledge,* trans. A. M. Sheridan Smith (New York, 1976), especially pp. 27–29.

22. Gosse, *Life and Letters,* 2:236–37.

23. Foucault, *Archaeology of Knowledge,* p. 29.

24. See especially T. K. Rabb and D. M. Hirst, "Revisionism Revised," *Past and Present* 92 (1981):55–99.

25. See Clark, ed., *Brief Lives,* 2:52–53.

26. Compare also the comments of the Venetian ambassador, Marc Antonio Correr, on December 31, 1610: "The King came back to London yesterday; he is quite free from the worry which usually disturbs him excessively; for his Majesty is wont to say that while Parliament is sitting it is interregnum for him. Certain persons have been approached with a view to

inducing them to bow to his Majesty's wishes and desires; . . . this vile system is being continued, but as yet with small results. About the Prince's demand to be freed from his minority as regards the exercise of his prerogative, nothing more has been said owing to the want of time, as is stated, but perhaps because, in the present disagreements, they are doubtful of the issue" (*Calendar of State Papers Venetian,* 12, art. 153, p. 102).

27. See Linda Levy Peck, *Northampton: Patronage and Policy at the Court of James I* (London, 1982), especially pp. 58–62, which deal with Northampton's commissions to Sir Robert Cotton, Edmund Bolton, Francis Thynne, and others, who between 1603 and 1614 supplied him with the legal precedents for his speeches and, in the trial of Father Henry Garnet, the materials for *A True and Perfect Relation of the whole proceedings against . . . Garnet,* (London, 1606), of which Northampton was known to be the author.

28. Donne, *Poetical Works,* ed. H. J. C. Grierson (Oxford, 1928), pp. 95–96. I refer to this paperback version of the first volume of Grierson's edition on the grounds of its accessibility. The pagination differs from the original two-volume edition (Oxford, 1912), which contains annotation.

29. Grierson, *Poetical Works* (1929), 2:84.

30. See James Larkin and Paul Hughes, eds., *Stuart Royal Proclamations,* 2 vols. (Oxford, 1973), 1:232–33.

31. *Stuart Proclamations,* pp. 230–31.

32. See Elizabeth Read Foster, ed. *Proceedings in Parliament,* 2 vols. (New Haven, 1966), 1:25.

33. *Stuart Proclamations,* 1:243.

34. If the Neville in question were Abergavenny, he too had been knighted by Essex at Cadiz in 1596; although, as noted above, he had acted as a government informer in February 1601.

35. John Shawcross, ed., *Complete Poetry of John Donne* (Garden City, N.Y., 1967), xxiii.

36. Helen Gardner, ed., *The Elegies and The Songs and Sonnets* (Oxford, 1965), xxxix.

37. See E. M. Simpson, ed., *The Courtier's Library, or Catalogus Librorum Aulicorum* (London, 1930), pp. 51–52. Simpson dates the *Library* circa 1609. It may have been revised in 1610 or 1611. In a letter to Sir Henry Goodyer printed in the 1633 edition of Donne's *Poems* (p. 352), Donne asked for the return of several of his manuscripts, including a *Catalogus librorum satyricus,* so that he could revise them.

38. Carey, *John Donne,* p. 64. Carey did, however, note that "the thought of government spies and butchers like Topcliffe . . . never failed to turn his stomach. They are still among the targets in *The Courtier's Library,* which probably received its final form as late as 1611" (p. 36).

39. Donne, *Poetical Works,* p. 145.

40. See my *Censorship and Interpretation* (Madison, 1984), pp. 92–94.

41. Carey, *John Donne,* p. 71. For the letter, see Bald, *A Life,* 117–18.

42. See Osborn, *John Hoskyns,* p. 103.

43. Printed by Grierson in an appendix, *Poetical Works,* p. 375.

44. John Donne, *Pseudo-Martyr,* ed. F. J. Sypher (Delmar, N.Y., Scholars' Facsimiles, 1974), A2.

45. *Ignatius his Conclave,* ed. T. S. Healy (Oxford, 1969), pp. 5–7.

46. The Latin is still more potent: "Autorem quaeris? Frustra."

47. Healey, ed. *Ignatius his Conclave,* xxx, suggests that Donne did not wish to satirize Galileo and was uneasy with the attack on Copernicus.

48. Donne, *Poetical Works,* p. 144.

49. Ibid., p. 118.

50. See *Censorship and Interpretation,* pp. 100–101.

51. See *Satire 1*'s opening lines: "Leave mee, and in this standing woodden chest,/Consorted with these few bookes, let me lye/In prison, and here be coffin'd, when I dye" (*Poetical Works,* p. 129).

52. *Letters to Several Persons of Honour* (1651), ed. M. Thomas Hester (New York, 1977), p. 270.

53. An signed autograph copy of Jonson's epithalamion, presumably the one delivered to Somerset, is pasted into a copy of the 1640 folio edition of his *Workes* in the British Library.

54. *Calendar of State Papers Venetian,* vol. 12, art. 151, p. 100.

55. See Foster, *Proceedings,* 2:344.

56. *Calendar of State Papers Venetian,* vol. 12, art. 153, p. 102.

57. Ibid., art. 164, p. 110.

58. Kevin Sharpe, "Parliamentary History, 1603–1629: In or Out of Perspective?" in *Faction and Parliament,* ed. Kevin Sharpe (Oxford, 1978), p. 13. It is worth noting that Sharpe (p. 12) cites the Venetian ambassador's report in 1607, that James had "reached such a pitch of formidable power that he can do what he likes," but not the subsequent reports which indicate oppositional behavior in the Commons.

59. Correr's information was, however, wrong as regards the loan. This did not occur until after the abortive session of 1614. In 1611 James and Salisbury instead fell back on a large-scale sale of baronetcies.

60. *Letters to Severall Persons of Honour,* pp. 55–56.

61. See Foster, *Proceedings,* 2:170. The speech was printed in 1641 by Hakewill himself, as an accurate copy with the legal precedents given in full. See William Hakewill, *The Libertie of the Subject: Against the Pretended Power of Impositions* (London, 1641).

62. Gosse, *Life and Letters,* 2:555-56. That Donne refers to "my book" and his disappointed hopes of a reward for it also helps to date the letter, since 1610 was the only year in Donne's life when he had only a single book in print. The mysterious references to Lepton and Waterhouse cannot be fully explicated; but in September 1608 John Lepton joined Jonas Waterhouse as king's agent attached to the Council of the North, and on July 4, 1609 Lepton, identified as "the king's servant," was given a royal protection against his creditors. See *Calendar of State Papers Domestic,* 1603–1610, art. 36, p. 459, art. 47, p. 525; and 1611–1618, art. 65, p. 66.

63. John Chamberlain, *Letters,* ed. Norman McClure, 2 vols. (Philadelphia, 1939), 1:539.

64. Sir John Holles to Lord Norris, 28 April 1614; H. M. C. Portland MSS. 9:27.

65. Gosse, *Life and Letters*, 2:34.

66. For Neville's *Advice* to the king, which was subsequently circulated in the Commons in order to embarrass him, see S. R. Gardiner, *History of England from the accession of James to the outbreak of civil war*, 10 vols. (London, 1883–84), 2:389–94. That there was anything disreputable in this has been denied by Clayton Roberts and Owen Duncan, "The Parliamentary Undertaking of 1614," *English Historical Review* 93 (1978):481–98. But it is worth noting that Roberts subsequently published a second version of his argument in *Schemes and Undertakings: A Study of English Politics in the Seventeenth Century* (Columbus, Ohio, 1985), which makes Henry Neville the heroic pioneer of undertaking, and Margaret Thatcher as the inheritor who brings it to perfection: "She, and only she, can undertake to manage the Queen's affairs in Parliament successfully" (p. 251).

67. See Osborn, *John Hoskyns,* p. 116.

68. See ibid., pp. 206–8.

69. See Upton, *Sir Arthur Ingram,* pp. 65, 69. Upton recorded that Ingram had kept discreetly silent about impositions in 1610, and would be silent again in the great debates in 1628–29; yet, though closely associated with the court, he managed, partly because of his strong Protestantism, "to keep a foot firmly planted in both camps until the time came to make a choice" (p. 252). When that time came, in the 1640s, he emerged as a strong supporter of the revolutionary government.

70. See Foster, *Proceedings,* 1:118, 143: 2:327–28. Parliamentary historians seem to have missed the outrageous humor of this speech, which Martin delivered on November 14, in the knowledge that the "contract is like to break." Obviously referring to Cowell, among others, he arraigned those "which preach in pulpits and write in corners the prerogative of a king, and dare put into the King (who hath as much natural goodness as a man can have) that which hath made him do things here which he never did in Scotland, nor his predecessors in England." Therefore, Martin continued, "to preserve our liberties . . . I thought it necessary to draw a bill. I had at first made it somewhat sharp; but 'twas short, I would but have hanged them . . . but I was advised by some of my friends to spare that. I then thought of a course that it would be fit to make such slaves (who by such base means as the selling of the liberty of the people and the laws would seek to prefer themselves) villeins so that they and their posterity might feel that bondage which they would lay upon others; but this I was dissuaded from too." Already secure in his reputation as a wit, Martin must have known that the tone of his speech would be well understood as a mixture of jest and earnest; but the reference to advice of his friends contributes to our sense of a group action.

71. See Clayton Roberts, "The Parliamentary Undertaking," p. 481: "Yelverton is won, Sandys is fallen off; Crew and Hyde stand to be Serjeants; Brooke is dead; Neville has hopes; Berkeley I think will be respective; Martin has money in his purse; Dudley Digges and Holles are yours." In what sense

Brooke was dead is not clear; certainly not literally; and Bacon was wrong at least about the inclinations of Sir John Holles.

72. Chamberlain, *Letters*, 1:525, 531.

73. *Journal of the House of Commons*, 1:494; 496.

74. Donne, *Poetical Works*, p. 9.

75. For more of these signs, see Heather Dubrow, "'The Sun in Water': Donne's Somerset Epithalamium and the Poetics of Patronage," in *The Historical Renaissance*, ed. Heather Dubrow and Richard Strier (Chicago, 1988), pp. 197–219.

76. *Journal of the House of Commons*, 1:485.

77. Ibid., 1:506. There are fuller and less incoherent versions of these remarks in Maija Jansson, ed., *Proceedings in Parliament, 1614 (House of Commons)* (Philadelphia, 1988), pp. 417–37; but the point remains that what the official parliamentary journalist heard was chaos.

78. Sir John Holles, *Historical Manuscripts Commission, Rutland*, 9:139.

79. For one thing, it questions Kevin Sharpe's certainty ("Parliamentary History," p. 19) that in the summer of 1614 "the country gentlemen gave generously to a voluntary contribution which brought in at least as much as a subsidy," a statement intended to support Conrad Russell's position, "that the Commons never successfully used, and seldom tried to use, the weapon of withholding supply in order to gain advantages." What one man stated, others may also have felt, imagining themselves also in the minority.

80. In a memorandum (*Historical Manuscripts Commission Rutland*, 9:138) describing the end of the Addled Parliament, Sir John Holles related how very closely the statements of members were scrutinized for seditious implications. Wentworth was imprisoned "for interpreting the prophet Ezekiel and the ii. of Daniel to imposing kings," and for citing as examples Philip II of Spain and the recently assassinated Henry IV of France; Sir Walter Chute, for having spoken "against building stately houses and the fruit of impositions going to them and not to the king who (till they were laid down) should not with his consent be supplied"; Christopher Neville, a younger member of the Abergavenny family, for showing "the miseries of the times," and for comparing the "Bills of Grace, as they came pared to us, to 'potticaries' boxes," i.e., tiny containers. Two members who were not imprisoned also had their words "questioned," Sir Edwin Sandys (whom Bacon had believed "fallen off") "for his speech on elective and successive kings, and his rehearsing two verses in Juvenal *Ad generum Cereris sine caede*"; and Sir John Savile "for alleging he had warning from some of his neighbours not to give anything that should confirm the impositions." And, added Holles, "All those lawyers and gentlemen, who were assigned to parts in the conference propounded and refused by the Lords, concerning impositions, were commanded to bring their papers thereabouts, which upon Thursday they brought to the Council chamber door at Whitehall and there burnt them."

81. Donne, *Poetical Works*, p. 236.

# 3

# From the Superfluous to the Supernumerary: Reading Gender into *Paradise Lost*

*John Guillory*

I

The argument I propose to make in this paper is suggested by a pedagogical problem arising from students' responses to the representation of women in Milton. I refer to the circumstance of a surprising willingness on the part of our students to embrace immediately the severest judgment upon Milton's representation of women, when the question of gender is opened in feminist terms. In order to forestall the decline of analysis into the mere accusation of misogyny, which loses sight altogether of the question of representation, one is forced to emphasize strongly the historical determinants of Milton's position, and thus in a peculiar sense to defend Milton. In considering the context of this classroom dialogue, I have had occasion to meditate upon the fact that the peculiar script of the dialogue—a short-circuiting of analysis— is produced by the same liberal consensus that makes possible, to begin with, a feminist reading of Milton. Within this consensus it is difficult to dispel the notion that the sexual subjection of women was everywhere and always the same thing, until it was definitively challenged several years ago. I also note somewhat ruefully that the appeal to the historicity of sexual subjection is precisely the defense adopted by antifeminist critics in response to the feminist critiques of Milton published over the last decade. Hence Joan Webber, to name only one of several, dismisses Sandra Gilbert's reading of Milton as *anachronistic,* as an example of reading gender into Milton's epic, where the question of gender ought

not to be distinguished from the whole theological/ethical system con-
stituting the horizon of thought in Milton's time.[1] Whether Milton
expresses the intrinsic sexism of this system, or the transhistorical sex-
ism of the male gender, in either case the choice of his text for feminist
analysis in the classroom appears to be without any more complex justi-
fication than the particular gusto he appears to lend to the expression of
sexual hierarchy.

If it is not easy to convey in the classroom the historicity of sexual
subjection—not impossible but not easy—this problem is preemi-
nently an effect of dissemination, of the deformation of a feminist
discourse as it spreads out to fill institutional spaces. But the unintended
effects of dissemination are not only a problem for feminist historical
scholarship; they are also the problem of any historical discourse—
even, let us say, the problem of theology itself in the seventeenth century.
The very difficulty of establishing the relation of gender issues to the
theological system—a difficulty which is registered by our students as a
disinclination to be sufficiently impressed by the importance of theology
to this issue, or by the traditional Milton scholar's inclination to be only
too impressed by theology as the supreme court of reference for
Milton's text—has the salutary consequence of bringing to the fore the
social relations of discourse per se. In this context, the unreflective re-
sistance of students to the discourse of theology, while it does represent a
resistance to the difference of other historical cultures, might also be
understood as a belated replication of a resistance that surely charac-
terized men and women of the seventeenth century when they strug-
gled with one another, whenever the most important immediate con-
cern in their lives was simply their relations as sexed human beings. One
might reasonably hypothesize that the "no" of a seventeenth-century
wife to some particular demand of her husband required no theorized
position of resistance to the hegemonic "patriarchal" discourse, but only
the exigencies of an irreducibly concrete circumstance of struggle to
which the principle of "he for God only, she for God in him" was simply
irrelevant. It is a fallacy of historicism, an *idealist* fallacy, to assume that
discourse determined nondiscursive practice. I am reminding myself,
then, by reflecting briefly upon the micropolitics of the classroom, that
no discourse of any age wears its crown easily, that it always exists in a
relation of conflict not only with other discourses but with the multiple
and contradictory practices of everyday life. It seems to me far from un-
historical to deny the master discourse of theology the last word in
interpretation of Milton, even if it must have the first word: rather, this
refusal ought to permit one to observe the real social relations of com-

plicity and conflict between discourses and practices, as these relations constitute the only truly historical condition of human life, which is the condition of continuous change.

If the latter point is valid, it follows conversely that the feminist reading of Milton can be seen to emerge from a prior discourse of sexuality itself, which for our own time is the master discourse of everyday life. We have articulated, for example, a far more intense and complex sexual discourse than a political, a fact which can be confirmed easily enough by contrasting the subtlety and dimension of the sexual lexicon with the poverty of the political, which makes do with trivial and manifestly inadequate clichés of liberalism and conservatism. This is not to say that there exists no theoretically sophisticated political discourse, but that it remains, in comparison to the sexual, relatively undisseminated. One might go farther and say that even the most advanced theoretical recognition of a "sexual politics" really means that we have admitted politics into the master discourse wearing the guise of the sexual. We like to see power itself in sexual terms, as a dynamic of desire. Milton, of course, liked to see sexuality in theological terms, as a sign of universal hierarchy within the little world of the household. Here I would like to situate myself at a slight tangent to the feminist reading of Milton in order to acknowledge that it does indeed read gender into *Paradise Lost,* first because it reads gender as already in Milton a sexual *discourse,* which it may not yet be, and second because this discourse is for us but not for Milton a psychological discourse, a psychology of the sexes. A concept of gender difference need not refer to psychology at all in order to function socially as the discursive authorization of the practice of sexual subjection. Moreover, in order for there to be a psychology of sexual difference, there must appear first, historically, a *biology* of difference, or of what Thomas Laqueur, in a recent article in *Representations,* calls a biology of incommensurability. According to Laqueur, this biology displaced a classical and Renaissance concept of gender constructed on an internal *homology* of the sexes rather than an internal difference, a system in which men and women were different more in degree than in kind: "Thus the old model, in which men and women were arrayed according to their degree of metaphysical perfection, their vital heat, along an axis whose telos was male, gave way by the late eighteenth century to a new model of difference, of biological divergence. An anatomy and physiology of incommensurability replaced a metaphysics of hierarchy in the representation of women in relation to men."[2] It is this biology which psychology, and in particular, psychoanalysis, both subsumes and overthrows in order to construct itself as a *discourse.*[3] Before the advent of a scientific biology, then, the hierarchy of gender had no more ultimate material basis than the strength differential of male and female bodies, that is, the immediate physical power of men over women, which simply replicates the relation of gods to men.

Let us grant that in Milton, as in his contemporaries, there is no language of sexuality which is not capable of subordination to theology, to a metaphysics of hierarchy. Whatever might determine locally the specific practices of sexual subjection, these practices can always be defended—raised to the level of discourse—by an appeal to the metaphysics of hierarchy. In Milton, then, as in his contemporaries, there is no psychology of the sexes, in the strict sense of a psychological discourse. From the vantage of this skepticism, it becomes immediately apparent why both feminist and antifeminist readings of Milton have for the most part proceeded as readings of the psychology of characters in his poem, and in fact, why these readings have been so much concerned with the character of Eve, as though she had a psyche, with its feminine secrets. The feminist and antifeminist positions in the current debate cohabit the *same* discourse of sexuality. Consider, for example, Barbara Lewalski's response, in *Milton Studies* 6, to Marcia Landy's feminist critique, in *Milton Studies* 4: "[Landy's] analysis of familial roles and relationships in *Paradise Lost,* culminating in a description of Milton's Eve as a wife relegated to domestic tasks and valued chiefly for her procreative role, seems to me to miss what is most important in Milton's presentation of the 'two great sexes which animate the world.'"[4] Lewalski goes on to argue that what is most important is "our common humanity," and thus she falls back on an ethical-theological system that subordinates questions of gender as simply less important than other questions. But this nostalgia for a universal ethics (which turns out to be a Renaissance humanist ethics) is belied by a willingness to argue about Eve as though she were a person. Perhaps as interesting as her defense of Eve, however, is her quotation of *Paradise Lost,* Book VII, line 151, at the end of her sentence. In context Milton is not referring to male and female persons at all:

> and other Suns perhaps
> With their attendant moons thou wilt descry
> Communicating Male and Female Light
> Which two great sexes animate the world.[5]

When we look at a phrase like "Male and Female Light," it would appear that we are simply looking at the metaphoric extension of sexual difference to objects that are clearly ungendered in nature. But I believe that supposition is a mistake, though it is a mistake that permits both Lewalski and her antagonists to translate the question of gender into a psychology of the sexes, a psychology of their innate qualities or capabilities, and thus to reduce the object of interpretation to male and female characters in the poem. Against this method I would argue, first, that Adam and Eve are relatively uninteresting as characters, as representations of people. This is not to say that in a full taxonomy of character types Adam and Eve are not simply another type of character, but rather that the easy attribution of motivation to their behaviors fails to consider precisely the taxonomical variety of character types. Hence mistakes that critics no longer make about characters in even the most "realist" fictions appear commonly in discussions of Adam and Eve, and particularly in the reading of Eve. It seems only obvious (if, within the discourse, hard to see) that Milton constructs his characters in *Paradise Lost* in a very ad-hoc fashion; their behavior is determined by the pressures upon the text at any given moment and much less upon any overarching conception of their psychological individuality.[6] In this they are rather like characters in classical epic—they are *ethos* rather than *psyche*—but Milton's critics have kept the debate about gender going by supplying them with a depth and complexity of motivation they do not possess, or need to possess for the narrative purposes of the poem. I shall return to this point later.

Second, and more important, I would propose that there is no real discursive difference for Milton between the expressions "Male and Female Light," and "male and female persons." The gender assignments in both expressions function in exactly the same way. I do not mean to argue, of course, that actual male and female bodies do not occur in nature, but that the sex-gender system, obviously enough, is everything that is superimposed in a given social context upon morphologically different bodies. The superimposition of masculine and feminine upon two heavenly bodies—the sun and the moon—is not conceptually different from the gendering of two different kinds of human bodies. Biology is just less important to Milton than hierarchy, than "greater" and "lesser." The anti-essentialist argument I am making here is very well established within feminist theory, but it oddly resists application in the controversy over Eve.[7] Reading gender into *Paradise Lost* by means of reading character permits and even provokes a regression into an essentialist psychology of the sexes, either feminist or antifeminist, and thus an erasure of Adam and Eve as discursive entities, as signs of gender.[8] As such entities they have a complexly mediated relation to the way people—seventeenth-century men and women—might actually have lead their lives.

What I propose to do now is to dislodge these gender signs forcefully away from male and female characters and to look at how they track across other aspects of the poem, or other bodies we would say are *ungendered* (because our discourse is centered on psyches), but which Milton calls gendered because his language of sexuality is conceptually subordinate to the hegemonic theological discourse, whose first principle is the principle of hierarchy. In fact, I would argue that the crisis with respect to gender in *Paradise Lost* occurs in Book VIII, which takes place in the absence of Eve; and what I hope to discover is not just another example of sexism, or sexual difference as sexual subjection, but the specific way in which gender terms interact with other discourses than the theological, discourses which abrade against the master discourse, or mesh poorly with it. I do not think the question of gender, as it arises in *Paradise Lost,* destabilizes the hierarchy of discourses by in any way resisting that hierarchy: Milton's intentions are very clear on this point. He does everything he can to affirm the immemorial and necessary subjection of women. Rather I want to show that the problem of gender catalyzes the operation of two other nascent discourses—the economic and the scientific—which do indeed produce a destabilization of the hierarchy of seventeenth-century discourses as the final result of interaction with them. In Milton's text this destabilization is marked by the attempted reinscription of gender within the domain of the alternative discourses, a displacement which will eventually (though not for Milton) permit an even more forceful assertion of sexual subjection.

II

My first exemplary text, by means of which I hope to set up a reading of Book VIII, is drawn from the hexameral narrative of Book VII, which Milton may actually have composed somewhat earlier than the remainder of *Paradise Lost:*[9]

> And God said, let the Waters generate
> Reptile with Spawn abundant, living Soul:
> And let Fowl fly above the Earth, with wings
> Display'd on the op'n Firmament of Heav'n.
> And God created the great Whales, and each
> Soul living, each that crept, which plenteously
> The waters generated by thir kinds.
> And every Bird of wing after his kind;
> And saw that it was good, and bless'd them, saying,
> Be fruitful and multiply, and in the Seas
> And Lakes and running Streams the waters fill;
> And let the Fowl be multipli'd on the Earth.
> Forthwith the Sounds and Seas, each Creek and Bay          398
> With Fry innumerable swarm, and Shoals                     399

> Of Fish that with thir Fins and shining Scales
> Glide under the green Wave, in Sculls that oft
> Bank the mid Sea: part single or with mate
> Graze the Seaweed thir pasture, and through Groves
> Of Coral stray, or sporting with quick glance
> Show to the Sun thir wav'd coats dropt with Gold,
> Or in thir Pearly shells at ease, attend
> Moist nutriment, or under Rocks thir food
> In joined Armor watch: on smooth the Seal,
> And bended Dolphins play: part huge of bulk
> Wallowing unwieldy, enormous in thir Gait
> Tempest the Ocean: there Leviathan
> Hugest of living Creatures, on the Deep
> Stretcht like a Promontory sleeps or swims,
> And seems a moving Land, and at his Gills
> Draws in, and at his Trunk spouts out a Sea.
>                         (VII, 387–416)

Lines 387–98 are a fairly straightforward redaction of Genesis, and they rely heavily on repetition, even to some extent on the parataxis of the biblical text. Readers may differ as to the actual quality of these lines, but I suspect that they are so demonstrably atypical of Milton's verse style as to sound flat by comparison with his more usually periodic mode. I am preceded in noticing the difficulty with the lines by the greatest literalist among Milton's critics, Dr. Bentley, who suggested in his 1723 edition of *Paradise Lost* that the lines are so bad they should simply be deleted. Bentley raises a typically logical objection: "Why should Raphael be so tied up to the Letter in Genesis, who makes this narrative thousands of years before Genesis was writ."[10] Now this is not a bad point at all if one feels that Milton is rhetorically inhibited in lines 387–98, tied down to the letter in Genesis. But in the passage beginning "Forthwith" the shackles apparently fall from the bound imagination. The rhetorical difference in the second passage is relatively easy to describe as an exuberant indulgence in Miltonic hypotaxis—and let the grammar take care of itself. The difference is also unmistakably marked syntactically by the partial displacement of "and" by "or" as a grammatical connective (*or* with mate, *or* sporting, *or* in thir pearly shells, *or* under Rocks, *or* swims). And this connective suits what amounts to a semantic distinction between the two processes represented in the two sets of lines: the distinction between the "omnific" creating word, figurally described as an act of insemination, and the process that results from this act, the process of birth, generation, or "multiplication." Now what does it mean to describe the *rhetorical* difference between the two passages as a gender difference? Obviously

Milton has "appropriated" the female function of generation to facilitate the rhetorical project of recreating creation itself. The opening of the womb is an opening for a display of rhetorical extravagance: "God said, Let the earth bring forth soul living in her kind. . . . The earth obeyed, and straight / Opening her fertile Womb teemed at a birth / Innumerous living creatures." But I want to return to Dr. Bentley's remark, which gives the right context for this act of appropriation. It is only possible when Milton goes beyond the text of Genesis, which he is able to do by going *behind* it. That is to say, he discovers, behind the text of Genesis, the agent who was written out of the text, the mother deity of Mediterranean creation myths. Nothing, of course, is more conventional in the hexameral tradition than this supplementing of the lack in the text of Genesis. What is different is only that the rhetorical power of Milton's narrative is bound, umbilically as it were, to the figure of the mother, who momentarily exists as an agent embodied in matter itself (*mater*). What in Renaissance rhetoric would be called *copia,* however, need not be gendered at all. What matters is that the gender sign can be moved about in this way.

Nor is the anxiety determining the appearance of the gender sign difficult to identify, since it impacts upon the poem as the priority in every sense of the father's text, his word. To recover the agency of the mother is to recover by a kind of imaginary recollection the temporal experience of the human infant, for whom the mother's care is primary. I would like to characterize the rhetorical exuberance of Milton's creation narrative—so fructifying, after all, to an entire genre, the loco-descriptive poem of the eighteenth century—as "pre-Oedipal." I do not mean by this term to invoke a fully psychoanalytic context of interpretation, but rather a wholly imaginary "pre-psychoanalytic," a time before one must think within psychoanalysis in order to think the psyche at all, a time before we need a theory of the father's intervention, or the father's prohibition. Nor does it matter that for us no such time has ever existed, that the infant does not know the mother as such, or that theories of the pre-Oedipal tend to backdate the agon constitutive of sexuality (for example, in Melanie Klein's drama of object relations). So far as Milton's Eden is concerned, as an imaginary textual envelope of the pre-Oedipal, there is only the mother, even if her agency must be named by the deluded recollection of the male. And this Eden is a world in which nothing is forbidden to desire, in which there is only abundance, a superfluity of everything, sheer multiplication.

The pre-Oedipal moment of the hexameral narrative is framed, or historically localized, by the topically suggestive invocation to Book VII, which unequivocally sexes the muse as female, and rewrites Milton's relation to the muse as the story of Orpheus, a story that expresses precisely a fear of abandonment by the mother: "Nor could the Muse / Defend her son." Perhaps we should say that this is a more honest account of pre-Oedipal sexuality. But the ephemeral invocation of this mother in what was evidently a period during which Milton's very physical safety was uncertain wishfully opposes her care to the "real" abandonment of revolutionary England, if not of Milton himself, by the Father God. His abandonment provokes a regression into a pre-Oedipal narrative which seeks to escape the very losses which accumulate as history itself. I would like to take note of this moment of regression at a later point in the poem, likewise consequent upon the sense of impending abandonment by the father. This moment occurs near the end of Book IX, when Adam and Eve must acquire clothing to conceal from each other their newly perceived nakedness:

> So counsell'd he, and both together went
> Into the thickest wood, there soon they chose
> The Figtree, not that kind for Fruit renown'd,
> But such as at this day to *Indians* known
> In *Malabar* or *Decan* spreads her Arms
> Branching so broad and long, that in the ground
> The bended Twigs take root, and Daughters grow
> About the Mother Tree, a pillar'd shade
> High overarch't, and echoing Walks between;
> There oft the *Indian* Herdsman shunning heat
> Shelters in cool, and tends his pasturing Herds
> At Loopholes cut through thickest shade: Those Leaves
> They gather'd, broad as *Amazonian* targe,
> And with what skill they had, together sew'd,
> To gird thir waist, vain Covering if to hide
> Thir guilt and dreaded shame; O how unlike
> To that first naked Glory. Such of late
> *Columbus* found the *American* so girt
> With feather'd Cincture, naked else and wild
> Among the Trees on Isles and woody Shores.
> (IX, 1099–1118)

What Milton makes of the institution (in both senses) of clothing has never received much attention, but that is doubtless because Milton's critics have not been disposed to consider clothing an institution. It is possible to cast upon the near naked savages the same troubled sidelong glance of the European colonizers who marveled at their surprising fashion of Edenic *couture*. The institution of clothing, while it conceals anatomical difference, may be said to institute sexual difference, as a properly semiological distinction, as socially constructed. The genesis of clothing is one story of the origin of gender difference, if not the only one. When Milton elaborates his image of the fig tree out of the scattered leaves of colonialist writing, his choice of a text in which this tree is described as a mother (Gerard's *Herball*) is overdetermined by a scenario of regression. All that is left of Eden is this tree, a mother tree to set against the father's tree of prohibition. The matrilineal proliferation of this tree makes a little world, or an other world in which labor itself is leisure, a suspending of the consequences of the fall hinted by the passage's slight evocation of Renaissance pastoral. If the life of the savages "at this day" seemed to the colonizers at first like an unfallen existence, this is to say that some human beings (if they were human beings) seemed to have found a loophole in the father's decree of judgment. And the consequence of this judgment might be said to be sexual difference itself; to escape it means to return to a world all mother. Milton's desire to think the worker in this colonial context without thinking sexual difference is betrayed subtly but irrevocably by the easy figural transformation of the fig leaves into the shields of the Amazons: again, a male fantasy of female enclosure. The Amazonian shields fend off the consequences of sexual difference, but necessarily after the fact, after the experience of such difference, and in retreat from it.

If it was no longer possible in the seventeenth century to produce a redaction of the Genesis narrative which was not thoroughly contaminated by the pseudo-Edenic images of colonialist writing, the ambivalence with which the Edenic life of the savage is contemplated carries over into *Paradise Lost* first as the fear of encroaching wilderness expressed by Adam and Eve throughout the middle books, but even more as the difference between the mother and the savage woman, the Amazon. The split-gender image of mother/Amazon rehearses the same ambivalence one finds in the invocation to Book VII, which almost goes so far as to hold the mother responsible for failing to shield the body of Orpheus from the savagery of the maenads, "the race of that wild rout that tore the Thracian bard / in Rhodope." The mother's care is implicitly repudiated as an illusion, a fantasy, like the Eden which reverts to wilderness before the eyes of Adam in Book IX: "these wild woods forlorn." To put this in the bluntest words, there never was a mother.

In the "true" Judeo-Christian Eden, of course, the mother as *agent* has always already disappeared into the earth itself, the dust, and only her *gender* remains: the female earth. I would like to raise at this point a question about the possibility of regarding the imaginary relation of the infant to the mother as a model of an economy, an Edenic economy, but this would not mean merely a further figural expansion of the garden's abundance but a formulation analogous to the pre-Oedipal, an imagi-

nary economy, an economy that never was. This imaginary system of
infinite consumption coexists with what must be acknowledged as the
*real* economy of Milton's paradise. Here is Raphael explaining the func-
tioning of this economy:

> But knowledge is as food, and needs no less
> Her Temperance over Appetite, to know
> In measure what the mind may well contain,
> Oppresses else with Surfeit. . . .
>                    (VII, 126–29)

This oppressive surfeit is converted into waste in Milton's digestive
analogy, which presumably elaborates the conventional system of vir-
tues and vices, represented in this instance by "temperance." The
digestive analogy is embodied mythologically by the forbidden tree;
and *its* economy, which is the real economy of Milton's paradise, is not
based on unlimited abundance or superfluity, but on the principle de-
scending etymologically from the word fruit: *frugality.* This concept,
though it has an ethical precursor in temperance, cannot be reduced to
an ethical concept, since it already describes in Milton's time an in-
creasingly prevalent mode of specifically economic behavior, the
rational dispensation of goods, time, and labor definitively analyzed by
Max Weber in *The Protestant Ethic and the Spirit of Capitalism.*[11] The
"spirit" of capitalism is, to be sure, the displacement of ethics itself into
the domain of economy, of rational self-interest, a displacement too
complex to untangle here because it stands for an ongoing debate about
the transition from feudalism to capitalism. In the simplified landscape
of Eden, the "transition" is registered by a practice of expenditure de-
signed to minimize waste; so while the branches of the trees in Book
VII are said to hang with "copious fruits," in the "real-world" economy
of paradise this surplus has to be daily collected and disposed of:

> . . . branches overgrown,
> That mock our scant manuring, and require
> More hands than ours to lop their wanton growth
> These blossoms also, and those dropping gums,
> That lie bestrewn unsightly and unsmooth,
> Ask riddance if we mean to tread with ease.
>                    (IV, 628–32)

Their daily labor holds off, just barely, the reversion of the garden into
wilderness. The question of what Adam and Eve do with the excess or
surfeit they prune from the superfluity of the garden—is it converted to
compost, or perhaps transported to some out-of-sight garbage dump
where angelic sanitation workers cart it away?—is thus not as naive as it

may sound, because it is just this pruning process, the continuous re-
moval of waste, which becomes the occasion of the quarrel in Book IX,
and of the fall.

At this point one might wish to determine more exactly the relation
between gender and the concept of *superfluity,* as a term which inhabits
two incompatible economies, meaning abundance in one, waste in the
other. Here one would have to consider Adam's famous question to
Raphael at the beginning of Book VIII, since this question is about
nothing other than the total economic organization of the cosmos itself,
although it takes the local form of a question about the distinction be-
tween the Ptolemaic and Copernican constructions of the universe:

> When I behold this goodly Frame, this World
> Of Heav'n and Earth consisting, and compute
> Thir magnitudes, this Earth a spot, a grain,
> An Atom, with the Firmament compar'd
> And all her number'd Stars, that seem to roll
> Spaces incomprehensible (for such
> Thir distance argues and thir swift return
> Diurnal merely to officiate light
> Round this opacous Earth, this punctual spot,
> One day and night; in all thir vast survey
> Useless besides; reasoning I oft admire,
> How Nature wise and frugal could commit
> Such disproportions, with superfluous hand
> So many nobler Bodies to create,
> Greater so manifold to this one use,
> For aught appears, and on thir Orbs impose
> Such restless revolution day by day
> Repeated while the sedentary Earth,
> That better might with far less compass move,
> Serv'd by more noble than herself, attains
> Her end without least motion, and receives,
> As Tribute such a sumless journey brought
> Of incorporeal speed, her warmth and light;
> Speed, to describe whose swiftness Number fails.
>                    (VIII, 15–38)

When Adam opposes the term "superfluous" with the arithmetic
frugality of Nature, he sets the economic problem of Book VIII against
the superfluity of Book VII, and in a deep sense inaugurates a repudia-
tion of that retrospectively imaginary economy. In Adam's account of
his creation, God says to his newly awakened creature, "Fear here no
dearth," but Adam experiences almost immediately a sense of lack, spe-
cifically a sexual lack. God's words are immediately followed by the

prohibition of the tree, and indeed Book VIII is all about prohibition. Every topic of conversation in Book VIII concludes with a prohibition, but the effect of this insistence is to conflate the act of disobedience with an intemperateness of consumption, with the principle of waste or excess. To lose this sense of difference from the hexameral narrative is not only to reduce Adam's question to the terms of the theological discourse, where it simply has an ethical valence, but also to miss how pervaded the question happens to be by the language of sexual difference (the sun and the earth are again he and she). I offer as a distinguished example of the reduction of economy to theology Sanford Budick's interpretation of the passage quoted above, in an interesting recent book on Milton, *The Dividing Muse*. Budick paraphrases Adam's question as follows: "Why should there be a part of the cosmic field of vision that is excluded from our sight; who else but man could be at the center of all earthly perception, all symbolic consciousness; why should any part of universal knowledge be excluded in any way."[12] In this reading a desire for more knowledge comes into conflict with the disciplining of desire that is for Milton an ethical principle derived from the theological discourse. So Adam's question is supposed to indicate an incipient pride, an avidity for knowledge that needs to be tempered; but there is no indication of a prideful motive in the lines of the text. And in fact I would argue that there is no question of Adam's motivation at all in this passage, that Milton is just interested in this subject. This is one of the passages in *Paradise Lost* that must be read wrongly—by means of imputing a motivation—in order to credit the hegemony of the theological discourse with a stability it does not possess. Adam is in fact asking a question about the energic economy of the cosmos; he does not understand why the stars and planets travel at such tremendous speed merely to vary day and night, when so much energy might be saved by having the earth spin round on its axis. It is Adam who asserts the principle of frugality, which Raphael in turn *affirms* by asserting the frugality of knowledge itself. Of course if God is God, all things are possible, even the unimaginable speed of the stars and planets as they revolve around the earth. If there is no reason why Adam should be troubled about the waste of energy (and what difference would it make to him?) the question of waste must derive from elsewhere. It could not have been generated from *within* the discourse of theology. It has no status as a question within that discourse.

It will not do, then, to sully Adam's motives by associating his question with Eve's in Book IV about why the stars shine at night. Milton's critics have conventionally used this association in order to set Eve up, even though her question is likewise about the energic economy of the cosmos, about who left the lights on. Budick uses Eve's question literally as a pre-text to impute to her a motive which at this moment does not appear in the text. Budick says about her departure from the scene of Adam's and Raphael's conversation: "The moment is a proud one for Eve . . . she departs with the intoxicating realization that her thoughts are to crown—or unsettle—the entire colloquy."[13] Of course Milton nowhere says anything about Eve's departing in a state of pride, much less intoxication. Budick is just making this up, inventing a complexity of motivation. But to say this is to remark how we read gender in *Paradise Lost* in the wrong way, by reading characters wrongly. Nevertheless there must be an impressive determination behind such reading, and this determination indexes the force of the present discourse of sexuality. For Budick the bad motive that Adam goes on to purge in his conversation with Raphael sticks to Eve; she apparently departs only to tend her flowers, and yet she is condemned for prideful curiosity. Budick is thus able to associate this original bad motive with a female agent without pretending to do more than to read her character. Eve is firmly indicted for her "unwillingness to accept incomplete perceptual dominion of her world," as though she *had* asked Adam's question, but for some reason did not stay for an answer. The fact that Milton will go on to attribute to Eve all possible bad motives in eating the forbidden fruit is quite irrelevant to the present case. The point is that one must pretend to divine a psychic state of Milton's Eve in order to detect in the very unconcern with which she departs the scene of Book VIII the pride that goes before the fall.

III

The question of gender is in fact much larger than Eve, and fills the book from which she is absent. What intrinsic connection is there, after all, between the book's two subjects of conversation, astronomy and sex? The relation between them is not at all self-evident, but ascertaining this relation is perhaps the only way in which we might describe how we get from the world of Book VII to the world of Book IX.

The moment of transition from the subject of astronomy to the subject of sex is, as it happens, the clearest testimony to the fact that the two subjects are for Milton the *same* subject. Here is Raphael's last word on the question of astronomy:

> Whether the Sun predominant in Heav'n
> Rise on the Earth, or Earth rise on the Sun,
> Hee from the East his flaming road begin,

> Or Shee from West her silent course advance
> With inoffensive pace that spinning sleeps
> On her soft Axle, while she paces Ev'n,
> And bears thee soft with the smooth Air along,
> Solicit not thy thoughts with matters hid.
>                        (VIII, 160–67)

As with Adam's question at the beginning of the book, it would seem easier to dismiss as irrelevant the gendering of the sun and the earth as "he" and "she." Yet Alastair Fowler, in his perceptive note to this passage, hints at a covert allegory of sexual hierarchy.[14] Briefly paraphrased the lines might go as follows: The sun "predominant" in heaven rises on the earth in the Ptolemaic system, and this system would then seem to accord more closely with the sexual hierarchy as it is immemorially authorized. Yet this predominance of the sun also means that the female earth is at the center of the universe, a position Raphael was at pains to reassure Adam held no significance in hierarchical terms ("Yet not to Earth are those bright Luminaries/Officious"). The geocentric system also requires that motion be attributed to the sun in measure necessary to get it around the earth in twenty-four hours (as Raphael says, "speed almost spiritual"). Milton is able to accept this superfluous expenditure as granted to the male-gendered sun, but only in order not to have the earth rise on the sun. When he comes to envision the motion of the earth in a hypothetical heliocentric system, however, he is careful to efface the moment of the woman on top; to do this, he must project onto an astral screen an image of economy, of frugality now associated not with the man but with the woman. We can go even further than this, and say who this woman is. She is the housewife, who is *silent, inoffensive,* and who, as the center of the domestic economy, spins upon her axle, which is nothing but the distaff. Astronomical relations in this allegory are intended to give us back not a reflection but a repetition of our domestic relations. This earth who "paces Ev'n" also conceals within the qualifier "Ev'n" the name of the housewife who is to embody domestic economy, and who is praised by Adam in Book IX for "studying household good." Equated with the earth itself, she *bears* Adam—maternally—as he was born out of the earth, even though we know that Eve was herself born out of Adam's side. At this point there is no way definitively to *position* her.

If we were to step back from this picture now, and try to look at it whole, we might see an image of domestic bliss, a hearth scene, but what we *cannot* see is whether the sun or the earth is at the center of the universe. If that question were decidable, the sexual hierarchy would be confirmed by *either* or *neither* the Ptolemaic or the Copernican system. In the Ptolemaic system do we see a sun that circles the earth in eternal homage to a female center, or a sun that rises on the earth in an aggressive gesture of sexual dominance? In the Copernican system do we see an earth that rises on the sun in a surprising inversion of sexual hierarchy, or an earth that quietly bears the burden of domestic economy? Clearly Milton *desires* the second alternative in each case, but the former possibilities cannot be wholly effaced; the discourse of astronomy, as a nascent scientific discourse, cannot confirm from its exterior and semiautonomous authority the hierarchy of the sexes. Yet Milton looks to the stars for this confirmation, to the scientific discourse. The fact that this discourse is called upon to confirm the sexual hierarchy measures not a weakening in the practice of sexual subjection but in the *discourse authorizing this practice,* the hegemonic discourse of theology. The very indeterminacy of the astronomical theory, its capacity to trouble with alternative hypotheses, is a measure in turn of its strength, as it draws other discourses and practices into its orbit of gravitational attraction.

The moment at which the discourses confront each other upon the privileged battleground of gender is nevertheless a moment in which the practice of sexual subjection is itself groundless, because it is the moment at which this practice begins to shift its discursive allegiance. The long-term effect of this transformation is that it will no longer be possible to assign gender to heavenly bodies; they will pass into a neutrality that only recalls gender as a charming poeticism of a prescientific discourse. And this recollection necessarily misrecognizes the true status of that poetic discourse, which did not exist merely to yield graciously to its scientific successor. The gender of the heavenly bodies was of the essence of that discourse, an inextricable feature of prescientific astronomy. The neutering of the stars and planets marks precisely the passage of sexuality into the domain of science, but into its "proper" domain: the medical practices, hygenic programs, and psychological therapies that define for us the realm of the sexual by *restricting* that realm to the bodies and minds of human beings.

It is no wonder, then, that Raphael retreats from the field of astronomy with the dogmatic gesture of a discourse which can no longer defend itself: "Solicit not thy thoughts with matters hid." The word "solicit" in the line bears the force of its Latin etymon, *sollus ciere,* to shake whole, to shake up the whole system. The more Milton's narrative accumulates discourses, or is invaded by their exteriority, the more he risks this solicitation. This is not to attribute to Milton subversive intentions, nor is it to credit the random discharges of semiosis with a capacity to

disable the logic of the argument. We are looking in the middle books of
*Paradise Lost* at an effect neither of subversion nor of linguistic indeter-
minancy but of the continuous, conflictual transformation of discourses
and practices, an effect of *pure change.* That effect is conditioned by the
fact that no discourse is not, as in *Paradise Lost,* a mixed discourse, just as
no genre is not a mixed genre. Such mixtures are inherently volatile, the
miscegenations which produce the monstrous forms of change. For this
very reason, and however contradictory it may seem, the subjection of
women as a practice does not fade away with the eventual recession of
the master discourse of theology. Sexual difference still means sexual
subjection, but not because theology makes it so. The subjection of
women, as a form of domination, would in any case, regardless of dis-
cursive practice, seek to perpetuate itself, merely because it is to the
material advantage of men; and women would in any case resist this
domination, wherever they perceive it to be in their interest or power to
do so. Nevertheless the subjection of woman under the discursive re-
gimes of biology and psychology, and within the institutional practices
of medicine and therapy, is not the same subjection as the subjection of
women under a hegemonic theology. To understand the discursive in-
stability of sexual subjection in Milton is at least to begin to understand
how sexuality itself can be constituted as a discourse, not simply a prac-
tice but an autonomous theoretical discourse authorizing a new
configuration of practices. Such discursive autonomy does not become
possible until the deposition of theology and the rise of hegemonic eigh-
teenth-century discourses—political economy, natural philosophy,
polite letters—out of which sexuality pieces together the discursive
existence whose history has been recounted in Foucault's now familiar
narrative. In the meanwhile, let us say that the momentary groundless-
ness of subjection in Book VIII—Adam's failure to devise a theory of
sexual subjection: "All higher knowledge in her presence falls de-
graded"—determines the simple and otherwise puzzling fact that the
narrative occasion of the fall is the failure of the male to control the
movement of the woman—what Adam describes as Eve's "strange de-
sire of wandering." She is herself a planet, a wanderer. Yet this narrative
looks forward to another regime of subjection, visible on the horizon as
a discourse within which Adam's question to Raphael might be defini-
tively answered, or within which every *body* knows its place.

When Eve returns in Book IX, she returns as the embodiment of a
new set of historical anxieties, all of which were formulated in her ab-
sence in Book VIII. The excursus on astronomy rejoins the question of
economy, and Eve now re-asks Adam's question, translated, brought

home from the stars to the little world of the *domus*. Let us not waste time, she says, let us not waste energy; we can dispose of the garden's surplus more efficiently apart. But the position of these earthly bodies with respect to one another can no more be determined than the position of the heavenly bodies. The rhetoric of frugality is so mobile that Eve now can advocate this principle in a context relevant not to "post-lapsarian" society in general but rather to Milton's own. The context is the division of labor, and specifically the labor of the woman, what Adam calls "household good." This problem is not yet represented within a discourse of political economy, for which indeed the gender of the laborer is irrelevant. Nevertheless it is economy itself which erupts onto the surface of the poem at this point, as something more than the theological discourse can handle. Because no discourse can answer the question Eve asks, she herself spins out of the control of any representational program. What, then, does she stand for (or fall for) in the end? Does she stand, as she certainly does in Book IV, for the garden and its infinite abundance; or does she stand, as she appears in Book IX, for a very unparadisal, suspiciously contemporary world in which the superfluous, the wasteful, is stigmatized by a new, economic ethos? She stands both within the surplus and against it, not because of who she is, but because the female gender is the *place* where these principles overlap. Thus Adam holds precisely contradictory views of this place which is Eve: she is "so absolute and in herself complete," that she seems "as one intended first, not after made / Occasionally." This Eve might well *be* Adam's mother, since he puts her first, and the bower to which they retire in the evening, as a paradise within paradise, might well be a truly pre-Oedipal place and time, where no tree of prohibition stands, no father's voice intrudes. This Eve is the very superfluity of paradise itself: "What seemed Fair in all the World, seemed now Mean / Or in her summed up, in her contained." She is *another* paradise; but this paradise is also, says the Adam of Book IX, *redundant,* in his word, supernumerary, like the rib from which Eve is formed: "Well if thrown out, as supernumerary to my just number found." The question of gender in the poem cannot be isolated from the sequence of narrative economies defining a trajectory from the superfluous to the supernumerary. To trace this trajectory is in a sense to have gotten nowhere, to have traced a retrograde motion; but it is also to recognize the impossibility of describing coherently the character or motivation of Eve. It is to discover behind the struggle of Milton's fictional agents the giant forms of discourses in conflict, the permanent revolution Milton might have known under another name, as trepidation of the spheres.

## Notes

1. The articles and books considered directly or indirectly are as follows: Sandra Gilbert, "Patriarchal Poetry and Women Readers: Reflections on Milton's Bogey," *PMLA* 93 (1978):368–82; Marcia Landy, "A Free and Open Encounter: Milton and the Modern Reader," *Milton Studies* 9 (1976):3–36; Christine Froula, "When Eve Reads Milton: Undoing the Canonical Economy," *Critical Inquiry* 10 (1983):321–48; Barbara Lewalski, "Milton on Women—Yet Once More," *Milton Studies* 6 (1974):3–20; Joan Mallory Webber, "The Politics of Poetry: Feminism and *Paradise Lost,*" *Milton Studies* 14 (1980):3–24; Diane Kelsey McColley, *Milton's Eve* (Urbana; University of Illinois Press, 1983). I have not considered in the following pages the two most recent and without doubt the subtlest defenses of Milton against the charge of misogyny, James Turner's *One Flesh: Paradisal Marriage and Sexual Relations in the Age of Milton* (Oxford: The Clarendon Press, 1987), and Joseph Wittreich's *Feminist Milton* (Ithaca: Cornell University Press, 1987). For reasons that will become clear at a later point, I do not wish to enter at all into this debate. My subject is the relation of sexual subjection as a historical practice to statements about gender within the discourses of theology, natural philosophy, and economics. Milton's alleged misogyny is in my view beside the point, since what Milton expresses in his writing is always more than what he personally "feels" about women. This something more is what participates in seventeenth-century discourses.

2. Thomas Laqueur, "Orgasm, Generation, and the Politics of Reproductive Biology," *Representations* 14 (1986):1–41.

3. As will be apparent, the concept of discourse here employed draws generally upon the work of Foucault, specifically upon *The Archaeology of Knowledge,* trans. by A. M. Sheridan Smith (New York: Harper and Row, 1972). The relation between discursive and nondiscursive practices is an unresolved question in *The Archaeology,* but its very difficulty opens up for Foucault his inquiries into the institutional practices of medicine, incarceration, and sexuality. The discourse approach to Renaissance literature is exemplified by the recent collection, *The Politics of Discourse: The Literature and History of Seventeenth Century England,* ed. Kevin Sharpe and Stephen Zwicker (Berkeley: University of California Press, 1987). Of the essays in that volume I would point especially to Michael McKeon's "Politics of Discourses and the Rise of the Aesthetic in Seventeenth Century England," which looks at the fate of theology from a perspective analogous to my own.

4. Barbara Lewalski, "Milton on Women," p. 4.

5. All quotations from *Paradise Lost* are taken from *John Milton: Complete Poems and Major Prose,* ed. by Merritt Y. Hughes (New York: The Odyssey Press, 1957).

6. I would emphasize that I am not arguing against the utility of psychoanalysis in reading Milton, but for shifting the object of interpretation to other structures than characters, or characters conceived in other terms than those implied by current feminist readings. Hence the conviction of Milton on the

charge of misogyny (or his exoneration from this charge) seems again and again to depend upon whether Eve is seen as thoroughly abject, or pluckily independent and dignified.

7. For a useful statement of what is at stake in this distinction, see Toril Moi, *Sexual/Textual Politics: Feminist Literary Theory* (London: Methuen, 1985). I would cite also the work of Alice Jardine on the "putting into discourse" of the woman, *Gynesis: Configurations of Woman and Modernity* (Ithaca: Cornell University Press, 1985). The productive debates within feminism, to which I make no contribution here beyond a simple extrapolation, have unfortunately had little effect upon the consideration of gender in Milton's work. I would point, however, to the exceptional methodological advance of Mary Nyquist in "Fallen Differences: Phallogocentric Discourses: Losing *Paradise Lost* to History," in *Post-Structuralism and the Question of History,*" ed. Derek Attridge et al. (Cambridge: Cambridge University Press, 1987), 212–43. Nyquist proposes, as I do here, a discursive rather than a character analysis.

8. It is worth emphasizing that Adam and Eve are introduced as iconic signs first of the human in general, and then of gender (IV, 287–320)—the latter not by reference to the biological distinction of male and female but by the cultural construction of gender (contemplation and valor vs. softness and grace). This distinction is in turn signified not by genital difference but by the respective length of Adam's and Eve's hair. The elaborated description of hair in this passage foreshadows the crucial function of clothing as the virtually universal semiotic of gender difference which operates precisely by concealing anatomical distinction of the genitals.

9. See the argument of Allan H. Gilbert, *On the Composition of Paradise Lost* (Chapel Hill: University of North Carolina Press, 1947).

10. Richard Bentley, *Milton's Paradise Lost* (London, 1732), annotation to lines 387–98.

11. Max Weber, *The Protestant Ethic and the Spirit of Capitalism,* trans. Talcott Parsons (New York: Charles Scribner's Sons, 1958).

12. Sanford Budick, *The Dividing Muse: Images of Sacred Disjunction in Milton's Poetry* (New Haven: Yale University Press, 1985), p. 101. While Kester Svendsen, in *Milton and Science* (Cambridge: Cambridge University Press, 1956), is certainly right to derive Milton's "science" from the medieval, encyclopedic tradition, it is too easy to say that "One must recognize that for Milton, as for the encyclopedists, problems in natural philosophy reached their last solution only in divine philosophy" (p. 44). Milton may very well attempt this conceptual subjugation through Raphael's discourse (repeated by Milton's critics), but we are also entitled to ask why the irrelevant astronomical problem is belabored if it is not a problem *for* divine philosophy.

13. Budick, *The Dividing Muse,* p. 102.

14. *The Poems of John Milton,* ed. John Carey and Alastair Fowler (London: W. W. Norton, 1968), p. 824. The explication of this passage by reference to the theological code still prevails in criticism of the poem, for example, in the recent work by Kathleen M. Swaim, *Before and After the Fall: Contrasting Modes in Paradise Lost* (Amherst: University of Massachusetts Press, 1986), p. 80: "The

discourse generally explicates the relationship and interrelationship between Sun and earth and therefore between God and man." Swaim notes in passing "an analogy for masculine and feminine to guide Adam in his own relationship to Eve." But such habitual derogations of the gender question prevent one from seeing that the passage enacts the failure of what was, to begin with, not an analogy, but a culturally functional homology. Gender difference has the same *function* in both the earthly and the heavenly regions of the universe: to mark once again, however apparently redundantly, the principle of hierarchy.

# 4

# "Joyning my Labour to my Pain": The Politics of Labor in Marvell's Mower Poems

*Rosemary Kegl*

This chapter analyzes the ways in which Andrew Marvell's mower poems[1] emphasize labor and, in so doing, participate in seventeenth-century struggles both over class and over gender. I argue, first, that Marvell's depiction of seasonal wage labor and of rural festivities promotes an economic structure which exploits wage laborers and, second, that his lovelorn mowers undercut women's demands for social change. The category of labor clusters together those poetic voices that participate in class struggle with those that participate in gender struggle. I suggest that Marvell adopts this logic of conjunction from contemporary gardens of rarities and explore its role within these social struggles. Although my reading is interested in Marvell's politics, I distance myself from critics who have construed those politics entirely in terms of his response to the events of the English Revolution. I assume rather that the war was one moment within larger, revolutionary changes in England's economy and that neither the war nor that larger revolution can account for all seventeenth-century social struggle.

In discussing the politics of Marvell's verse, I am indebted to a long tradition of criticism which has been committed to just that project.[2] Readings of the four mower poems most frequently link poetry and politics through the category of pastoral—relating the poems' generic stance to seventeenth-century intellectual and social history. Critics suggest, for example, that the Protestant Reformation, the English Revolution, and the rise of the new science precipitated a skepticism about the possibility of any correspondence between nature and artistry.

That skepticism, depending upon the individual critic's definition of pastoral, produced an attack against pastoral prelapsarian correspondence, a shift of pastoral conventions, or a pastoral last gasp from within a genre which was no longer relevant to the seventeenth-century mind. Others argue that Marvell's version of pastoral commonplaces is an allegory for seventeenth-century social events, that his version of pastoral was a response to contemporary political struggles, that pastoral's tradition of veiled political commentary made it an appropriate—and safe—vehicle for criticizing society, or, alternately, that pastoral actually inhibited political action.[3]

Although their assessments of pastoral politics vary, these readings generally share a larger preoccupation within political readings of Marvell; they attempt to map his literary career onto stages within a historical narrative whose centerpiece is the revolution. According to one paradigm, for example, his early work displays a Fairfacian pastoral or lyric retirement from the practical concerns of a political world, his later poetry a Cromwellian longer flight into a political engagement which neither pastoral nor lyric could support, and his final writing a Restoration prose flight from any belief in poetry's persuasive powers. Within these parameters, the mower poems fall either in Marvell's Fairfacian pastoral or lyric retirement or, alternately, within the poet's gradual realization that neither pastoral nor lyric could support his growing Cromwellian political engagement.[4]

The same assumptions about Marvell's career underpin discussions of the poems' thorny textual problems. Our only source for the mower poems is a folio volume of Marvell's verse which was printed in 1681, three years after the poet's death. The collection, entitled *Miscellaneous Poems*, was published by a woman who called herself "Mary Marvell" and claimed that "all these Poems . . . are Printed according to the exact Copies of my late dear Husband, under his own Hand-Writing, being found since his Death among his other Papers."[5] Scholars, kinder to the textual claims than to the marital claims of this volume's notorious sponsor, accept the authenticity of both the mower poems and their 1681 ordering. No other copies of or allusions to the four poems have been located, yet critics—citing both the poems' lyricism and their pastoral subject matter—generally assume that Marvell wrote them while tutoring Mary Fairfax at her father's country estate between 1650 and 1652.[6]

I would like to suggest not only that the actual date of the mower poems' composition remains undetermined but also, more importantly, that Marvell critics have accorded too prominent a role to the revolution as a punctual, midcentury event. My argument does not deny the cultural significance of the revolution but simply suggests that, although wage laborers at times may have supported the revolution, that revolution actually strengthened the structures which exploited those laborers. And, although revolutionary politics and seventeenth-century gender struggles at times reinforced one another, the revolution was not central to those struggles. I am sympathetic with critics who have insisted that poetry *is* political. Yet when they focus upon Marvell's allegiances during Charles I's reign, during the revolution and interregnum, and during the restoration, these critics tend to overlook his role within class and gender struggles which extended throughout the century.[7] Like Marvell critics, recent revisionist historians have analyzed the revolution as a punctual event. Their analyses challenge the marxist characterization of the war as a bourgeois revolution. Revisionists cite, for example, the mixed class-affiliations of both royalist and antiroyalist forces and the aristocratic solidarity which led antiroyalist landowners to hold in trust the estates confiscated from their royalist counterparts. By discussing the revolution as a punctual event, these accounts ignore marxists' insistence that the war marked one moment within a more general *structural* change in English society.[8] Both my stress upon the continuity of laborers' struggles and my comments about Marvell's depiction of seasonal wage labor remain indebted to that marxist paradigm.

## Wage Labor

In "Damon the Mower," Marvell participates in seventeenth-century class struggles by rejecting the conventional pastoral link between agricultural ease and poetic piping. In the poem's first stanza, the framing voice entwines Damon's mowing with those emotions which motivate his verse:

> Heark how the Mower Damon Sung,
> With love of Juliana stung! . . .
> Sharp like his Sythe his Sorrow was
> And wither'd like his Hopes the Grass.
> (st. i, ll. 1–2 and 7–8)

By alternating the priority of the agricultural and emotional terms, the paired similes in lines 7 and 8 suggest that Damon, like the pastoral shepherd, performs an agricultural task which is inseparable from his complaint. Yet the poem distances Damon from that shepherd when it stresses that his mowing is a difficult task. The sorrowful Damon is "stung" less by "love of Juliana" than by the shepherdess's silent refusal of his gifts—a snake "[d]isarmed of its teeth and sting," the "Chameleons changing-hue, / And Oak leaves tipt with hony due." He sings, "Yet Thou ungrateful hast not sought / Nor what they are, nor who them brought" (st. v, 11. 39–40). By implying that Juliana should have been more inquisitive and by ending his line with "brought," Damon alludes to the poem which prefaces Spenser's *The Shepheardes Calendar*. There the poet advises his book, "And asked, who thee forth did bring, / A shepheardes swaine saye did thee sing, / All as his straying flocke he fedde" (11. 8–10).[9] Unlike Spenser's inquisitive reader, the silent Juliana does not allow Damon to announce the pastoral link between his song and the ease of his task.

Instead, after he is rejected by Juliana, Damon reveals that his mowing was always a difficult labor but that nature, erasing all trace of that difficulty, once allowed him the pastoral appearance of leisure. In the parable told by his end-words, that leisure made "sweet" his "Sweat":

> I am the Mower Damon, known
> Through all the Meadows I have mown . . . .
> And, if at Noon my toil me heat,
> The Sun himself licks off my Sweat.
> While, going home, the Ev'ning sweet
> In cowslip-water bathes my feet.
> (st. vi, 11. 41–42, 45–48)

Rebuffed, Damon now distances himself from that pastoral appearance of leisure. He accepts the framing voice's equation between scythe and sorrow and looks "for Ease in vain." He gestures with each word he sings to his agricultural labor and joins that labor to the poetry of his complaint:

> How happy might I still have mow'd,
> Had not Love here his Thistles sow'd!
> But now I all the day complain,
> Joyning my Labour to my Pain;
> And with my Sythe cut down the Grass,
> Yet still my Grief is where it was:
> But, when the Iron blunter grows,
> Sighing I whet my Sythe and Woes.
> (st. ix, 11. 65–72)

In the seventeenth century, "whet" referred not only to the act of sharpening a scythe but also to the period of labor *between* sharpenings.[10] Damon's sorrow encompasses both meanings. Each period of his labor is a period of grief during which he mows down his withered hopes, leaving not new hopes but only that grief with which he endlessly resharpens his scythe. In *The Shepheardes Calendar,* Colin sings in his harvest years when "all my hoped gaine is turned to scathe. / Of all the seede, that in my youth was sowne, / Was nought but brakes and brambles to be mowne" (December eclogue, 11. 100–103). Unlike Colin, Damon links his poetic bemoaning of lost hope with the clearing of those brakes and brambles.

This emphasis upon labor distances Damon from the aristocratic shepherd who populates Elizabethan pastorals. It aligns him, instead, with the laboring plowman from an *earlier* sixteenth-century tradition which the Elizabethan pastoral later suppressed. That prior tradition had attacked aristocrats who were enclosing common land and had championed the impoverished and unemployed laborers who were displaced from that land. It depicted the aristocrat as an idle shepherd and the peasant as a laboring plowman. In Thomas More's *Utopia,* for example, Morus famously inveighs against "the nobility and gentility, yes, and even some abbots":

> Living in idleness and luxury without doing any good to society, no longer satisfies them; they have to do positive evil. For they leave no land free for the plow: they enclose every acre for pasture.

By celebrating aristocratic idleness as a form of courtly ease, the Elizabethan pastoral retained the link between aristocrat and shepherd while eliminating these references to the evils of enclosure.[11] Enclosure's removal of common land rights by the wealthy few began in the thirteenth century, provoked an outpouring of hostile literature in the fifteenth and sixteenth centuries, and ended with the parliamentary enclosures of the eighteenth and nineteenth centuries. The physical hedging in of common land generally was the final phase of a larger enclosing process which removed land rights from peasants and thus denied them control over their means of production. Without that control, both rural peasants and those forced into the city became wage-laborers who were increasingly dependent upon their employers. By the beginning of the seventeenth century, one-quarter to one-third of the English work force, now without land rights, had begun to hire themselves out.[12] The inequities of this arrangement were quite apparent to the seventeenth-century Digger, Gerrard Winstanley. "Israel shall neither take hire, nor give hire," he writes in *The True Levellers Standard Advanced.* "And if so, then certainly none shall say, This is my land, work for me, and I'll give you wages." In *A Letter to the Lord Fairfax and his Councell of War,* he adds that "[t]he poor that have no land are left still in the straits of beggary, and are shut out of all livelihood but what they shall pick out of sore bondage, by working for others as masters over them."[13] Plowing and mowing were two such occupations.

Yet plowing and mowing existed in very different relationships to the shifting practices of enclosure. Grazing never entirely displaced tillage, and most pastoral operations included some fields for arable crops; nonetheless, in the fifteenth century and first half of the sixteenth, a booming sheep industry and reduced demand for grain allowed an increased enclosing of arable common land for pastoral grazing. The early sixteenth-century plowman, then, was a worker who was not only newly displaced from the common land but also laboring within an increasingly obsolete occupation. "They would be glad to work," Morus says of these displaced agricultural laborers, "but they can find no one who will hire them. There is no need for farm labor, in which they have been trained, when there is no land left to be plowed." By the mid-seventeenth century, enclosers had begun to apply their large landholdings and lucrative profits to experiments which revealed how to rotate arable land with grassland and how to control the meadow species grown for fodder. A rising population's demand for grain and an increase in tenant rents combined with this rotation and control to promote extended enclosing for new mixed tillage and pastoral industries. Seventeenth-century mowers were exploited laborers because, like sixteenth-century plowmen, they had lost their common land rights and were dependent upon wages. Yet, unlike plowing, mowing was compatible with early pastoral enclosures. And, because mowers cut the hay used for fodder and the corn, oats, and barley grown for human consumption, their occupation actually was promoted by these later combined operations.[14]

Damon's labor alludes to the early literary plowman and, in this way, invokes the politics of enclosure. By replacing the laboring plowman with a laboring mower, however, the poem underscores *this* laborer's comparative success on the enclosed land. In the seventh stanza, Damon announces, in fact, that his strenuous labor earns him the wealth of the landowning shepherd—that early tradition's figure for an encloser:

> What, though the piping Shepherd stock
> The plains with an unnum'red Flock,
> This Sithe of mine discovers wide
> More ground than all his Sheep do hide.
> With this the golden fleece I shear
> Of all these Closes ev'ry Year.
> And though in Wooll more poor then they,
> Yet am I richer far in Hay.
>
> (ll. 49–56)

Although seventeenth-century writers never accorded the mower an elevated social status, they actually *did* acknowledge both the arduousness and the lucrativeness of his task. "[T]hough the labour of a smith be hard . . . [it is] little in comparison with threshing and reaping," writes Richard Baxter, "but as nothing in comparison with mowing which constantly puts forth a whole man's strength."[15] In a handbook describing the operation of his farm, Henry Best indicates that he pays his highest daily wages to mowers:

> Mowers have usually 10d. a day, and meate themselves; if they bee to take a peece of grownde to mowe they will scarce deale with it, unlesse they can allmost assure themselves that they shall come to 12d. a day.

In that same hay season, haymakers earned 4d., male wainfolk 6d., and female wainfolk 4d., each day.[16] The belief that mowing with a long-handled scythe demanded a man's strength and stature prompted a 53 percent increase in mowers' already high wages during the revolution. Despite the maintenance of a standing army and the consequent reduction of men in the labor force, mowing remained one of the only agricultural occupations in which women did not fill men's places.[17]

Within the lines above, the landowning shepherd overstocks his land "with an unnum'red Flock"; a few lines later, the laboring mower is "Depopulating all the Ground" with each stroke of his scythe. Seventeenth-century commentators associated both overstocking and depopulating with the evils of enclosure. By overstocking the common land with sheep, they claimed, large pastoral operations depopulated that land of its peasant inhabitants. In his 1662 *The History of the Worthies of England,* Thomas Fuller describes how the inhabitants of Warwickshire react to overstocking. "In this shire the complaint of J. rous continueth and increaseth," he writes, "that sheep turn cannibals, eating up men, houses, and towns; their pastures make such depopulation."[18] The connection between overstocking and depopulation suggests that the lucrative ground which Damon "discovers" resembles that which the enclosing shepherd's "Sheep do hide." According to the poem's logic, both the laboring mower and the landowning shepherd obtain their wealth from hide land—a measure which signified the amount of common land necessary to support one family.[19] In short, Damon claims that he is rich not only in the hay which he mows but also in the hay—or hedges[20]—of enclosure.

What is at stake, then, in Marvell's version of these agricultural practices? First, by suggesting that he is as wealthy as the shepherd, Damon ignores that very *structural* difference between wage-laborers and landowners which enclosure promoted; within that economic structure, wage-laborers—whatever their wages—are exploited. Second, when Damon announces the lucrativeness of his labor without admitting that his is a seasonal task, he elides one way in which enclosure not only forced both mowers and their fellow peasants into a wage-laboring dependence upon employers but also—within this system of exploitation—contributed to their *lack* of labor and low wages. Enclosure created an unemployed, reserve work-force which guaranteed that wages would remain low. The seventeenth-century mixed enclosures exacerbated these conditions. Their improved farming techniques, specialized crop production, large holdings, and tendency toward a division and specialization of labor made agricultural laborers even more dependent upon brief, seasonal employment during harvest on the arable land and haymaking on the pastoral. In the 1640s, one observer writes that "one quarter part of the inhabitants of most parishes of England are miserable poor people and (harvest time excepted) are without subsistence."[21] Mowing was one such seasonal occupation. For example, in 1622, Leonard Goodale—a mower on Best's farm—received his lucrative daily wage for two and a half weeks during the hay season; the following year, he received that wage for eleven days. Best also employed mowers during the oat and barley harvests; in 1641, he reports, laborers harvested the barley in six and a half days. Mowers were often villagers, migrant laborers, or cottagers who—whether employed or unemployed—were unable to subsist without this seasonal labor. In other words, mowers did not, as Best implies, have the luxury to "scarce deal with" mowing unless employers offered an exorbitant wage; instead, they scarcely could afford to "deal with it" without that wage.[22]

Finally, by featuring a laborer known for both the arduousness and the lucrativeness of his labor, Marvell reinforces seventeenth-century legislation which further impoverished wage-laborers. Not surprisingly, in spite of the mower's claim that his strenuous wage labor might offer him some sort of economic and social equality with the landowning shepherd, strenuous labor brought neither high wages nor social mobility to most workers. In 1563, for example, the Statute of Artificers compelled citizens without landholdings to labor in industry or agriculture, prevented the migration of those laborers from one employer to another, and attempted to establish both ceilings for their wages and minimum lengths for their working days. Throughout the seventeenth century, writers, pamphleteers, members of Parliament and representatives of public organizations—fearful of uprisings—reiterated that laborers must be employed but that their wages must be restricted. Justifying legislation to that effect, these commentators frequently calculated that workers' wages merely supplemented the subsistence they earned from the land. In other words, they denied that laborers were increasingly dependent not upon the land but upon their employers. In Damon's terms, they assumed that agricultural workers' "inflated" seasonal wages would translate into a lucrative subsistence. Average national wages did triple between 1500 and 1640, but that tripling coincided with both a six-fold increase in the cost of living and a widening distance between the incomes of laborers and those of their employers. Studies by Gregory King in the latter half of the century indicated that "laboring people and outservants," who comprised 23 percent of the national population, and "cottagers and paupers," who comprised another 24 percent, all received incomes which could not sustain them without the assistance of poor relief. Nor did the writers, pamphleteers, members of Parliament and representatives of public organizations accord a high social status to wage-laborers. Most coupled their championing of hard work with their scorn for the "mere hirelings" who performed that labor.[23]

"The Mower's Song" participates in seventeenth-century class struggles by twice alluding to the death of its mower—both during his arduous labor and during his pastoral idleness. The laboring mower promises to mow down himself, the flowers, and the grass:

> And thus, ye Meadows, which have been
> Companions of my thoughts more green,
> Shall now the Heraldry become
> With which I shall adorn my Tomb. . . .
>             (st. v, 11. 25–28)

The idle mower "lay trodden under" these meadows. By burying the mower during his labor, the poem elides his economic exploitation; by burying him during his idleness, it identifies the mower's fellow laborers as his true enemies. In this way, both images of the mower's death reinforce a growing urban economy and its method of exploiting laborers. I will begin by discussing the labored burial and its relationship to "Damon the Mower."

In "Damon the Mower," Marvell redescribes Damon's economic dependence upon the seasons as an emotional dependence upon that season's namesake shepherdess. In his farming handbook, Best describes the conditions which precede the mowing of hay:

> The cuttinge of grasse falleth not out allwayes alike, but sometimes sooner and sometimes later, accordingly as men can perceive it to beginne to turne and dye; for soe soone as the pennie-grasse beginne to welke and seeme dry, then is it time to beginne to mowe. . . . Wee beganne to mowe this 7th of July, 1641, beinge Wensday; for indeede it is most usuall to beginne aboute the middle of July.[24]

Within the poem, Juliana alone summons this parched scenario of Damon's labor:

> This heat the Sun could never raise,
> Nor Dog-star so inflame's the dayes.
> It from an higher Beauty grow'th,
> Which burns the Fields and Mower both: . . .
> Not July causeth these Extremes,
> But Juliana's scorching beams.
>                     (st. iii, ll. 17–20, 23–24)

In "The Mower's Song," Marvell reiterates Juliana's arrival within each stanza's refrain. In so doing, he once more collapses the mower's agricultural scythe with that temporal "sithe" which governs his lament for lost love. In the poem's first three stanzas, her arrival remains in the past tense as this mower sings, "When Juliana came, and She / What I do to the Grass, does to my Thoughts and Me." In the final two stanzas of the poem, however, the mower shifts the tense of his refrain, singing, "When Juliana comes, and She / What I do to the Grass, does to my Thoughts and Me." By shifting tenses, the mower more fully elides his economic dependence upon the seasons. Here the ever-returning Juliana replaces the July sun of the mowing season; in addition, her endless present-tense arrival stresses the inevitability not only of the mower's self-mowing but also of his rejuvenation.

In other words, the refrain describes the mower as a scythe-wielding herald not only of death but also of rebirth.[25] In so doing, it depicts his economic exploitation as one moment within a natural cycle of destruction and rejuvenation. In "Damon the Mower," Marvell narrates Damon's agricultural downfall:

> The edged Stele by careless chance
> Did into his own Ankle glance,
> And there among the Grass fell down;
> By his own Sythe, the Mower mown.
>                     (st. x, ll. 77–80)

Yet that downfall is followed by a rapid recovery. "With Shepherds-purse, and Clowns-all-heal," Damon sings, "The Blood I stanch, and Wound I seal" (st. xi, ll. 83–84). Similarly, in "The Mower's Song," deprived of Juliana's comfort, the mower accentuates the violence of what Juliana continually "does to my Thoughts and Me" when he resolves to join his mowing to his pain. "And Flow'rs, and Grass, and I and all," he vows, "Will in one common Ruine fall" (st. iv, ll. 21–22). And, although he plans to adorn his tomb with the products of his laborious mowing, Juliana's endless present-tense arrival guarantees that his self-interment is only one moment within a continuous cycle of burial and resurrection.

An earlier burial within the poem, however, suggests that the mower *is* oppressed—but by his fellow laborers rather than by his employers. Rejected by Juliana, the mower initially "with Sorrow pine[s]." Before he mows "the Flow'rs, and Grass, and I and all," this brief pastoral idleness allows the meadow to flower and escape the season of its mowing. "[N]ot one Blade of Grass you spy'd," he laments, "But had a Flower on either side" (st. ii, 11. 9–10). The mower compares these flowers surrounding each blade of grass to his fellow laborers circling a May pole. He chastises:

> Unthankful Medows, could you so
> A fellowship so true forgo,
> And in your gawdy May-games meet,
> While I lay trodden under feet?
> (st. iii, 11. 13–16)

The downtrodden mower stresses the fact that the feet of his initially idle versifying placed him beneath the feet of those games' players. By considering how invectives against idleness functioned within debates about agricultural practices and within debates about Sabbath and holy day observances, I argue that this image of trampling links the poem's support for enclosure with its support for Sabbatarianism.[26]

In More's *Utopia,* Morus describes enclosure as an economic evil with far-reaching moral consequences. Idle aristocrat enclosers seduce their servants into a "wanton luxury" and force unemployed laborers into thievery. "Let fewer people be brought up in idleness," he pleads. "Let agriculture be restored and the wool manufacture revived, so there will be useful work for the whole crowd of those now idle—whether those whom poverty has already made into thieves, or those whom vagabondage and habits of lazy service are converting, just as surely, into the robbers of the future."[27]

Although hostility to enclosure certainly persisted throughout the seventeenth century, its supporters appropriated the moral category of idleness and directed it against those peasants who worked the common land. In 1639, for example, John Smyth writes:

> Such common grounds, commons, or waste grounds, used as commonly as they are, and as here I know they are, yield not the fifth part of their true value, draw many poor people from other places, burden the township with beggarly cottages, inmates, and alehouses, and idle people; where the great part spend most of their days in a lazy idleness and petite thieveries and few or none in profitable labour.

The parceling of common land into large private holdings, he rhap-
sodizes, would breed "serviceable men and subjects, and of answerable
estates and abilities. Whereas now, not one of these beggars, lazy and
idle people, thus living and bred, are any ways useful or serviceable in
any kind." During the interregnum, one commentator, signing himself
"E. G.," warns the new authorities that "little or no consideration is had"
for the improvement of commons and waste lands "which as it is a
shame and reproach unto Irish, and other like lazy people, so much
more is it a shame to us English, because we bear the name and reputa-
tion of an ingenious and industrious people."[28]

Like debates about enclosure, debates about Sabbath and holy day
observances often turned on the "idleness" of the agricultural laborer.[29]
In 1618 James I issued the anti-Sabbatarian *Book of Sports,* declaring that,
on both Sundays and holy days, "after the end of Divine Service, Our
good people be not disturbed, letted, or discouraged from any lawful
recreation, such as Dancing (either men or women), Archery for men,
Leaping, Vaulting, or any other such harmless recreations, nor from hav-
ing of May Games, Whitsun Ales, and Morris Dances; and the setting up
of May Poles, and other sports therewith used." He claimed that Puritans,
who discouraged such rural festivities, were jeopardizing the nation and
its propertied citizens. Without this recreation, he warned, disgruntled
laborers might "set . . . up filthy tiplings and drunkenness, and
breed . . . a number of idle and discontented speeches in their ale-
houses."[30] Throughout the century, the recreation of rural peasants was
one battleground on which royalty and their adversaries fought to deter-
mine the nature of these idle speeches. Reissuing the *Book of Sports* in
1633, Charles—like his father—provoked an outcry among those who
continued to fear that the court might form a powerful alliance with rural
laborers. Because both James and Charles sanctioned not only rural Sab-
bath pastimes but also, implicitly, their own courts' Sunday masques and
recreations,[31] outraged commentators marshaled Morus's rhetoric about
an idle aristocracy. Unlike Morus's shepherds, however, aristocrats within
these seventeenth-century invectives do not merely seduce otherwise la-
boring peasants; instead, aristocratic excesses sanction already existing—
and already excessive—peasant pastimes.[32] This combination of anti-
royalist and antipeasant sentiment underpinned the increasingly vocal
Sabbatarian movement. Sabbatarianism attempted to enforce labor on
holy days and to restrict leisure to regular Sunday sabbaths; even that
respite from labor would be limited to a spiritual leisure which would
replace the piping and games which were most popular, and feared most
subversive, among the "idle" laborers.[33]

When "The Mower's Song" places the mower beneath the feet of his
May game companions during the poem's first burial, it emphasizes the

destructive—and self-destructive—nature of idle peasants and their rural pastimes. In so doing, the poem reinforces seventeenth-century invectives against idleness and endorses their calls for enclosure and for Sabbatarianism. What, then, are the politics of this dual endorsement? Throughout the seventeenth century, shifting forms of enclosure received support from royalists as well as from antiroyalists, and from aristocrats as well as from the "middling sort." Whatever the class allegiance of its actual supporters at any one time, enclosure separated peasants from their means of production and created a large wage-laboring work force. In this way, it contributed to the gradual urbanization and industrialization of an increasingly capitalist economy.[34] Although Fuller offers his remarks in defense of enclosure, he does suggest that the depopulation of rural England signals enclosure's tendency to create an industrial urban work force:

> [I]t is pleaded for these enclosures, that they make houses the fewer in this county, and the more in the kingdom. How come buildings in great towns every day to increase (so that commonly tenants are in before tenements are ended) but that the poor are generally maintained by clothing, the staple-trade of the nation?
> . . . [W]ool invisibly maintaineth people at many miles' distance, by carding, spinning, weaving, dressing, dyeing it.[35]

Unlike enclosure, the Sabbatarian movement was explicitly antiroyalist and associated with Puritanism. Yet, like enclosure, Sabbatarianism drew support from individuals who occupied very different class positions, and, again like enclosure, it structurally reinforced the growing urban economy and the bourgeoisie who benefited from it. Sunday leisure, rather than holy day leisure, favored the schedule of a working week over the less regular pattern of agricultural employment and even received intermittent support from urban wage-laborers who feared that, without Sabbath regulations, they might be forced into a seven-day workweek.[36] Moreover, the emphasis upon Sunday *spiritual* leisure was compatible with efforts by London merchants and, eventually, the Long Parliament, to fund religious instruction in the rural north and west of England. This instruction, offered as an antidote to the potentially subversive "idleness" of rural peasants, extended into the countryside a politics which was increasingly amenable to the interests of the urban "middling sort."[37]

By twice burying its mower, "The Mower's Song" reinforces England's new economy and its form of exploitation. Within the poem, the mower is trampled not by his employers during his wage labor on the enclosed land but, instead, by his fellow agricultural laborers during their idle May games. The wage-laborer's greatest enemy, Marvell suggests, is not the economy within which he labors but those threats to that economy which the mower must learn to "forgo" as, at best, anachronistic.

## Labor Pains

In "The Mower's Song" and "Damon the Mower," Marvell appropriates the voice of a wage-laborer and, in so doing, participates in seventeenth-century class struggles. I now turn to the seemingly voiceless Juliana in order to analyze the relationship between the poems' laborious, pain-filled voices and seventeenth-century gender struggles. Although struggles over wage labor certainly included and affected women, this section focuses on those struggles that were governed by gender concerns. Throughout the century, writing by and about women debated whether women deserved, if not equality with men, then at least a more productive form of subjugation. These limited demands were at times compatible with the intermittent challenges to male authority issued by recusant Catholic women, Protestant female preachers, and women affiliated with the Ranters and Levellers.[38] The rhetoric of these seventeenth-century debates often turned on the relationships of men and women to idleness and on the God-given enmity between women and serpents.

Joseph Swetnam, for example, writes his popular *The Araignment of lewde, idle, froward and unconstant women; Or the vanitie of them, choose you whether* while "[m]using with myself and being idle, and having little ease to pass the time." His composition depends upon indulging that sinful idleness which, he warns, emanates from "those most lascivious and crafty, whorish, thievish and knavish women." Afraid that his misogynist tract will open a Pandora's box of ungovernable female response, Swetnam promises to deal harshly with Eve's rebellious daughters. "For then," he says, "we will go upon those venomous adders, serpents and snakes and tread and trample them under our feet."[39] Ester Sowernam, responding to Swetnam in *Ester hath hang'd Haman,* reminds her readers that God granted Eve—more repentant than her mate—an enmity between the seed of the woman and that of the serpent:

> Woman supplanted by tasting of fruit, she is punished in bringing forth her own fruit. Yet what by fruit she lost, by fruit she shall recover. . . . Amongst the curses and punishments heaped upon the Serpent, what greater joy could she hear or what greater honor could be done unto her than to hear from the voice of God those words: "I will put enmity betwixt the woman and thee, betwixt thy seed and her seed," and that her

seed should break the Serpent's head? This must proof be an exceeding joy for the woman to hear and to be assured that her fruit should revenge her wrong.

Assuring his readers that he will crush women beneath his feet, Swetnam fulfills the vengeance promised to Eve but only by turning that vengeance upon her female progeny. Sowernam also reveals to unwary women the shape of contemporary serpents, warning that although "[t]he Serpent at first tempted woman, he dare assault her no more in that shape, now he employeth men to supply his part; and so they do: for as the Serpent began with Eve to delight her taste, so do his instruments. . . . First, they will extoll her beauty; what a paragon she is in their eyes; next, they will promise her such maintenance, as the best woman in the parish or country shall not have better."[40] When Swetnam promises women that "although in some part of this book I trip at your heels, yet I will stay you by the hand so that you shall not fall further than you are willing," he numbers among those serpent seducers.[41] As this tempter searches for the woman's Achilles' heel, he narrowly avoids being crushed under her feet.

The mowers in "Damon the Mower" and "The Mower's Song" also number among those contemporary serpents. Responding to Juliana's silent rejection of his snake "[d]isarmed of its teeth and sting," the first of these mowers—true to Sowernam's warning—praises the reluctant shepherdess's beauty, boasts of his wealth, and ultimately labels her as the only garden inhabitant still capable of stinging. The mower in "The Mower's Song" initially responds to Juliana's rejection by growing "more luxuriant still and fine." In turn, his neglect makes luxuriant the grass until, appropriately, he finds himself "trodden under feet."

Throughout the seventeenth century, women's more specific demands for social change shared Sowernam's—and Juliana's—moral rejection of idleness. Arguments which favored women's education, for example, stressed that women did not welcome idleness; when women *were* idle, the fault lay not with their moral inferiority but, instead, with society's corrupt practices. "I cannot but complain of, and must condemn the great negligence of parents," Hannah Woolley writes, "in letting the fertile ground of their daughters lie fallow, yet send the barren noddles of their sons to university." Such gardening metaphors were popular within these debates; women suffered, in Damaris Masham's words, from a "want of cultivating." In *An Essay to Revive the Antient Education of Gentlewomen,* Bathsua Pell Makin admits that women might be morally flawed but argues, with recourse to a gardening metaphor, that this sinfulness actually justifies support for women's education:

> As Plants in Gardens excel those, that grow wild; or as Brutes by due
> Management . . . are much altered: so Men; by liberal Education, are
> much betterid, as to intellectuals and morals. . . . But your doubt in your
> Letter is concerning the Females. I think the greater Care ought to be
> taken of Them: Because Evil seems to be begun here, as in Eve, and to be
> propogated by her Daughters. . . . Therefore without all Doubt great
> Care ought be taken, timely to season them with Piety and Virtue.

Not, like Makin, interested in asserting women's inferiority, Margaret
Cavendish nonetheless uses a similar metaphor in her *Sociable Letters,*
explaining, "[W]herefore those women are best bred, whose minds are
civilest, as being well taught and governed, for the mind will be wild
and barbarous, unless it be enclosed with study."[42] Although the meta-
phor of the enclosed garden does contain women within a sexualized
discourse which underscores their passivity, it also turns charges that
women are sinfully idle back upon the system which refuses to labor in
their education. Juliana—who rejects the idle offerings of Marvell's
contemporary serpents—is the gilliflor, the hybrid July flower which
epitomized the success of seventeenth-century garden experimentation.
The product of an enclosed garden, Juliana has obtained an education
and, "enclosed with study," has escaped the sinfulness of Eve.

It might seem, then, that Marvell's depiction of Juliana borrows from
contemporary commentators a particular version of virtuous wom-
anhood which—however problematic—often was deployed in limited
attempts to elevate women's social position. It might seem, in short, that
he appropriates a locally progressive gender paradigm in the service of a
less progressive class politics. Yet the mower in "Damon the Mower" is
mown "by his own Sythe." And the mower in "The Mower's Song" is
trodden under the feet of his own versifying. This self-mowing and
self-trampling suggest that Marvell's mowers perform not only as the
masculine serpents who besiege women but also as those virtuous wom-
en who feel enmity for their seducers and whose vengeance fulfills
God's promise to Eve.

In the "Mower to the Glo-Worms," the mower actually supplants a
popular seventeenth-century figure for the besieged but virtuous wom-
an—the nightingale. Here the mower addresses the glowworms which
traditionally "presage the Grasses fall"—the season of harvest and of
his laborious mowing:[43]

> Ye living Lamps, by whose dear light
> The Nightingale does sit so late,
> And studying all the Summer-night,
> Her matchless Songs does meditate. . . .
>                    (st. i, ll. 1–4)

Like the nightingale, this mower is "displac'd" and matchless without a mate. And, like her, he bemoans in his "matchless Songs" not his lack of a match but, instead, the lamentable results of that match's presence. He sings:

> Your courteous Lights in vain you wast,
> Since Juliana here is come,
> For She my Mind hath so displac'd
> That I shall never find my home.
> (st. iv, 11. 13–16)

Supplanting the nightingale's lament is not an idle choice. In so doing, the mowers sing not only as seductive contemporary serpents but also as their female victims. In addition, their laborious, pain-filled laments suggest that they must endure the postlapsarian pain meted out to women. By grafting aggressor to victim and Adam's labor to Eve's labor pains, these mowers sing Juliana's unvoiced song and claim for themselves the right to trample masculine serpents. Juliana is not the only hybrid gilliflor within Marvell's poetic garden. Within Marvell's mower poems, men co-opt the position from which seventeenth-century women conventionally figured their oppression and issued their demands for social change.

## Joining These Labors

By suggesting that the category of labor joins together those voices which exploit laborers and those which oppress women, I am drawing attention to one in a series of incongruous conjunctions within the poems. Critics have noted, for example, the odd coexistence of singing mowers with the poems' framing voices and ironic commentary, of laboring mowers with a pastoral shepherdess, and of the mower who utters a sophisticated diatribe in "The Mower Against Gardens" with those more comic mowers who sing simple laments in "Damon the Mower," "The Mower's Song," and "The Mower to the Glo-worms."[44] In the remainder of this essay, I suggest that "The Mower Against Gardens" offers a paradigm for understanding Marvell's hybrid verse.

During the seventeenth century, experiments within enclosed gardens were central to the success of larger enclosing practices. The gilliflor, for example, was one instance of that species-control which made possible the mixture of arable and pastoral industries. Contemporary commentators noted this link between enclosed gardens and the enclosure of common land. A 1660 sequel to Bacon's unfinished *New Atlantis* describes experiments with "grafting, inoculating, [and] melio-

rating the earth with several Composts." A guide to the College of
Agriculture explains, "All our study here is to improve a little ground
well with little pains and charges. . . . That we may do this in all places
alike and to the purpose, we use the means; and they are these: We buy
in all the Commons. . . . One such acre thus enclosed and improved
being now more beneficiall to the meanest of [the inhabitants], then
fower were before in Common."[45] As I have argued, enclosure actually
promoted economic structures which were beneficial not to the "mean-
est" but, instead, to the landowning inhabitants.

Not all descriptions of enclosed gardens addressed the dynamics of
agricultural communities. Yet, more generally, these descriptions fre-
quently were inflected with concerns about monitoring cultural hier-
archies. For example, John Ray, a seventeenth-century naturalist, de-
scribes the effects of garden enclosures by means of a parable about be-
neficent imperialism:

> [I]f you take the seed of the smallest and poorest plant in its kind, pro-
> vided it will admit culture, and sow it in a rich soil well watered, you
> shall soon get an offspring ten times as great as the mother-plant. Nay,
> take a root of a perennial and removeable plant, from off a cold barren
> mountain, and set it in a fat warm garden, it shall attain twice the stature
> and dimensions, which it would have been confined to, had it remained
> in its natural place.

He adds that one of those "plants, that are most apt to be thus diversified
by sowing, are julyflowers."[46] As I have explained, gardening also func-
tioned as a nexus for debates about women's education. In addition, it
was one terrain on which class status was negotiated. Perhaps the most
frequently cited instance of such negotiations is the scene in *The
Winter's Tale* in which Polixenes and Perdita debate the merits of the
streaked gilliflor "which some call nature's bastard."[47] And, in another
version of status negotiation, both Francis Bacon and Thomas Browne
correlate the power derived from wealth and conquest with an ability
actually to display enclosed gardens whose perfected natures approxi-
mate prelapsarian Eden; in their writings, enclosed gardens are both a
consequence and a guarantor of princely power.[48]

Critics have debated what sort of garden, what image of cultural hier-
archies, Marvell endorses within "The Mower Against Gardens."
Rather than endorsing a particular garden metaphor for cultural rela-
tions, I argue, "The Mower Against Gardens" endorses the *logic* which
organizes one popular version of enclosed gardens. These seventeenth-
century gardens of rarities included not only contemporary oddities
but, more importantly, the odd coexistence of disparate phenomena.[49]

Marvell adopts this logic of conjunction when he clusters together his four poems and their often divergent voices.

In the first half of "The Mower Against Gardens," the "Rarities" within the enclosed garden reproduce the progressive fall of the poem's luxurious man—first seduced and then the seducer.[50] "Luxurious Man, to bring his Vice in use, / Did after him the World seduce," the mower tells us in the poem's first two lines. Self-seduction precipitates a fall and, in turn, the effects of that fall prompt the luxurious man to lure "plain and pure" nature into the enclosed "Gardens square." There he kneads a "luscious" earth which simultaneously seduces the flowers and plants with promise of nutriment and wantonly[51] feeds upon them— offering, in return, only the stupefaction produced within the garden's "dead and standing pool of air." These seduced flowers and plants eventually display their own corrupted natures and their own seductiveness. The pink grows "double as his mind"; the rose adopts a "strange perfume"; and the flowers learn the self-painting which allows the naturally white tulip to interline its cheek. So successful is the tulip's seductive self-enhancement, in fact, that the value of one mere "Onion root" actually equals that of the entire meadow from which it was allured. In the first half of the poem, then, the mower bemoans the chain of seduction which corrupted postlapsarian nature.

Yet, in the central couplets of "The Mower Against Gardens," the mower draws a puzzling distinction between the first and second halves of the poem:

> And yet these Rarities might be allow'd,
>     To Man, that sov'raign thing and proud;
> Had he not dealt between the Bark and Tree,
>     Forbidden mixtures there to see.
>
> (11. 19–22)

The second half of the poem describes the products of those "forbidden mixtures." Critics generally ignore these lines or cite them when discussing the fallen world in both sections of the poem. In either case they never ask why Marvell distinguishes between these sections—why the mower might sanction the "Rarities" which populate a once "plain and pure" nature and yet *not* allow the "uncertain and adult'rate fruit" which the "forbidden mixtures" produce.[52] Seventeenth-century accounts of garden experimentation make this distinction even more curious. According to those accounts, the "Rarities" in the first half of the poem actually would have been produced by the unsanctionable mixtures which haunt the poem's second section. In Bacon's *New Atlantis,* for example, both the "strange perfume" of the rose and the

interlined cheek of the tulip arise from the same mixture of "Wild" and
"Tame" which produces "uncertain and adult'rate fruit." A citizen of
Bacon's new-science utopia describes a Bensalem laboratory to his Span-
ish visitors:

> In these we practice likewise all conclusions of grafting and inoculating,
> as well of wild-trees as fruit-trees, which produceth many effects. . . .
> We make them also by art greater much than their nature; and their fruit
> greater and sweeter and of differing taste, smell, colour, and figure, from
> their nature.[53]

In the poem's central couplets, then, the luxurious man oversteps his
bounds neither with a new corruption of nature nor with a newly artful
concocting of alluring if forbidden mixtures. His overstepping rests, in-
stead, in the new visibility of this Baconian concocting; his skillful
dealing is now "there to see." The mower might have sanctioned the
garden's "Rarities" had the luxurious man not made visible his artistry.

The second half of the poem enacts the luxurious man's forbidden
display by announcing the artistry which produces his enclosed garden:

> No Plant now knew the Stock from which it came;
> He grafts upon the Wild the Tame:
> That the uncertain and adult'rate fruit
> Might put the Palate in dispute.
> (ll. 23–26)

Here man's grafting adulterates the plants' essential natures by
enforcing adulterous couplings between them—an enforcing which
the mower elides in the first section of the poem with his metaphor of
luxurious seduction. Not new but newly visible in the poem's second
section, these mixings befuddle the plants who question "the Stock
from which they came" and the palate whose uncertain evaluation leaves
its authority "in dispute." Like the citizens of Bacon's Bensalem, whose
grafting of wild and tame allows "diverse plants [to] rise by mixture of
earths without seeds," the luxurious man concocts forbidden mixtures
which produce a eunuch cherry which, in turn, "procreates without a
sex."[54] In the second half of the poem, the alluring vice of the luxurious
man announces itself as an artistic vise which presses plants and flowers
into an "enforc'd" garden.

At the close of "The Mower Against Gardens," the mower claims
himself exempt from this garden where statues of fauns and fairies "to
adorn the Gardens stand"—not only "polish'd by some ancient hand"
but also announcing that artisan's skill. "But howso'ere the Figures do
excel," the mower writes of those garden statues, "The Gods themselves

with us do dwell" (11. 39–40). Claiming to dwell not with polished statues but, instead, with the fauns and fairies who "do the Meadows till,/More by their presence than their skill" (11. 35–36), the mower places himself outside of a world where "Tis all enforc'd" and within a world "Where willing Nature does all to dispence/A wild and fragrant Innocence" (11. 33–34).

Yet, even as the mower disavows the visible artistry of the luxurious man, "The Mower Against Gardens" announces its own author. When the luxurious man views the New World as a meadow from which might be seduced its alluring central wonder, "the Marvel of Peru," the poem highlights that poet whose artistry produces both the garden harem and the mower's seductive poetic voice. Like the statues of fauns and fairies which "to adorn the Gardens stand," the poem is "polish'd by some ancient hand" and announces that artistry.

Discussing "The Mower Against Gardens," critics have argued either that Marvell endorses the railing mower or, alternately, that he satirizes that railing by aligning himself with the poem's ironic commentary.[55] I am suggesting, instead, that these disparate positions coexist within the poem just as that product of imperialist expansion— the marvel of Peru—coexists with its English counterparts and just as the luxurious seductions in the first half of the poem coexist with the visible artistry in the second half. In short, the mower not only depicts, by means of his railing, a fairly standard enclosed garden of rarities but also—like Marvell—functions as a rarity within his own poetic garden.

The seventeenth-century diarist John Evelyn, who was devoted to the study of rarities, describes gardens which are organized according to vertiginous conjunctions of often incompatible phenomena. These gardens are most rare when organized according to one of the conjunctions that organizes "The Mower Against Gardens"—the conjunction of attempts to elide and attempts to advertise artistry. Walking through a garden at Cardinal Richelieu's castle, Evelyn passes, in turn, "Brasse statues, perpetualy spouting Water into a large Bason," "a Basilisk of Copper, which manag'd by the Fountanier cast water every way 60 foote, & dos of it-selfe move round so swiftly, that 'tis almost impossible to escape wetting," a grove with "that fruit-Tree & other raritys," "a Wall painted [with a] representation [of] the Arch of Constantine so rarely, as a man very Skillfull even in Perspective might mistake it for real stone & Sculpture: The Hills & Skye betweene the apertures of the Arches are so naturall, that Swallows & other Birds thinking to fly thro', have dash'd themselve[s] in pieces against it," "that exuberant, tho' artificial Cascade of Water, which rolls downe a very steepe declivity & steps of stone, with

a thundering noise & fury," "a showre as of raine from the Ceiling, as
from a Clowd," and, finally, "two extravagant Muscateers . . . who dis-
charge a full streame upon us from their musket barrells."[56]

Although the garden is often the "most considerable raritye" on the
estates which Evelyn visits, its organizing logic extends to other rare
collections. Adjoining a "Garden of Simples . . . well stor'd with exotic
Plants," for example, Evelyn finds:

> their Anatomy Schole, Theater & Repository adjoyning, which is very
> well furnish'd. . . . Here is the Sceletus of a Man on Horse-back, of a
> Tigar, and sundry other creatures: The Skinns of Men & Women tent-
> ur'd on frames & tann'd: Two faire and entire Mummies, Fishes,
> Serpents, Shells, divers Urnes; The figure of Isis cut in wood of a greate
> Proportion & Antiquity; a large Crocodile; The head of the Rynoceros;
> The Leomarinus, Torpedo, many Indian Weapons, Curiosities out of
> China, & of the Eastern Countries; so as it were altogether [impossible]
> to remember all, or take particular notice of them; though I could not
> forget that knife which they here shew'd us, newly taken out of a Drunk-
> en Dutch-mans gutts, by an incision in his side, after the sottish fellow
> had swallow'd it, when tempting to make himselfe vomit, by tickling his
> throat with the handle of it, he let it slip out of his fingers into his stomac,
> and had it taken out againe by the operation of that dextrous Chyrur-
> geon, whose Picture is together with his Patients preserv'd in this
> excellent Collection, and at my being in Holland both the Persons
> living.[57]

I cite this lengthy description in its entirety because it conjoins, without
distinction, the products of natural marvels, of imperialism, and of new
science. Although Evelyn's claim that it is "[impossible] to remember
all, or take particular notice of them" may seem disingenuous after his
staggering catalogue, seventeenth-century sketches of such rare displays
suggest that, in fact, he probably did remember only a fraction of the
exhibit. What he *does* remember and what he so memorably replicates,
however, is the insistent conjunction of these rare products. These
rarities are divorced from their histories and contextualized in terms of
their exuberant coexistence with one another.[58] Thus the struggles—in
this case frequently imperialist struggles—which produce them re-
main invisible. Evelyn adopts this depoliticizing strategy within his
own writing. During a visit to Paris, for example, he depicts an enclosed
garden "Paradice" in which persons of quality, citizens, strangers, gal-
lants, ladies, melancholy lovers, friars, studious scholars, and jolly
citizens coexist "without the least disturbance."[59] Evelyn's paradise de-
pends upon an exuberant conjunction of classes which renders class
struggle invisible.

In the mower poems, Marvell adopts the logic of conjunction which organizes Evelyn's rare gardens. When Marvell joins together those voices which exploit laborers with those which oppress women, he employs Evelyn's garden logic; that logic promised to suppress the fact that he is joining his poetic labor to their daily pain. This chapter has been interested in breaking that formal promise.

## Notes

I would like to thank Walter Cohen, Katharine Maus, Christopher Newfield, and Mary Ann Radzinowicz for their comments and criticisms.

1. All quotations of the mower poems are from *The Poems and Letters of Andrew Marvell*, ed. H. M. Margoliouth (Oxford: Oxford University Press, 1971), 1:43–48.

2. See, for example, Pierre Legouis, *Andrew Marvell: Poet, Puritan, Patriot* (Oxford: Oxford University Press, 1965); Harold E. Toliver, *Marvell's Ironic Vision* (New Haven: Yale University Press, 1965); John M. Wallace, *Destiny His Choice: The Loyalism of Andrew Marvell* (Cambridge: Cambridge University Press, 1968); Paul J. Korshin, *From Concord to Dissent: Major Themes in English Poetic Theory, 1640–1700* (Menston: The Scolar Press, 1973), 65–103; Isabel Rivers, *The Poetry of Conservatism, 1600–1745: A Study of Poets and Public Affairs from Jonson to Pope* (Cambridge: Rivers Press, 1973), 101–25; Joseph Summers, "Some Apocalyptic Strains in Marvell's Poetry," in *Tercentenary Essays in Honor of Andrew Marvell*, ed. Kenneth Friedenreich (Hamden: Archon Books, 1977), 180–203; John Carey, "Reversals Transposed: An Aspect of Marvell's Imagination," in *Approaches to Marvell*, ed. C. A. Patrides (London: Routledge and Kegan Paul, 1978), 153; Christopher Hill, "Milton and Marvell," in Patrides, *Approaches to Marvell*, 1–30; A. J. Smith, "Marvell's Metaphysical Wit," in Patrides, *Approaches to Marvell*, 56–86; J. D. Hunt, *Andrew Marvell: His Life and Writings* (Ithaca: Cornell University Press, 1978); R. I. V. Hodge, *Foreshortened Time: Andrew Marvell and Seventeenth Century Revolutions* (Cambridge: D. S. Brewer, 1978); Annabel M. Patterson, *Marvell and the Civic Crown* (Princeton: Princeton University Press, 1978); Barbara Everett, "The Shooting of the Bears: Poetry and Politics in Andrew Marvell," in *Andrew Marvell: Essays on the Tercentenary of His Death*, ed. R. L. Brett (Oxford: Oxford University Press, 1979), 62–103; Marion Meilaender, "Marvell's Pastoral Poetry: Fulfillment of a Tradition," *Genre* 12 (Summer 1979): 181–201; James G. Turner, *The Politics of Landscape: Rural Scenery and Society in English Poetry, 1630–1660* (Cambridge: Harvard University Press, 1979); Michael McKeon, "Pastoralism, Puritanism, Imperialism, Scientism: Andrew Marvell and the Problem of Mediation," *Yearbook of English Studies* 13 (1983): 46–65; Graham Parry, *Seventeenth-Century Poetry: The Social Context* (London: Hutchinson, 1985), 221–46; Leah Marcus, *The Politics of Mirth: Jonson, Herrick, Milton, Marvell and the Defense of Old Holiday Pastimes* (Chicago:

University of Chicago Press, 1986), 213–63; Charles Larson, "Fairfax's Wood: Marvell and Seventeenth Century Trees," *Durham University Journal* 80:1 (December 1987): 27–35; Margarita Stocker, "Remodeling Virgil: Marvell's New Astraea," *Studies in Philology* 84:2 (Spring 1987): 159–79; Michael Wilding, *Dragon's Teeth: Literature in the English Revolution* (Oxford: Oxford University Press, 1987), 138–72, and "Marvell's 'An Horation Ode upon Cromwell's Return from Ireland,' The Levellers, and the Junta," *Modern Language Review* 82:1 (January 1987): 1–14; and Steven N. Zwicker, "Lines of Authority: Politics and Literary Culture in the Restoration," *Politics of Discourse: The Literature and History of Seventeenth-Century England,* ed. Kevin Sharpe and Steven N. Zwicker (Berkeley: University of California Press, 1987), 237–46.

3. For discussions of pastoral and politics in the mower poems, see Legouis, *Marvell,* 50–52; Toliver, *Marvell's Vision,* 6, 88–95 and 103–13; Korshin, *From Concord to Dissent,* 69–71; Smith, "Marvell's Wit," 68–70; Everett, "Shooting of the Bears," 97–99; Meilaender, "Marvell's Pastoral Poetry," 181–94 and 200–01; Turner, *Politics of Landscape,* 153–85; McKeon, "Marvell and Mediation," 47–51; Parry, *Seventeenth-Century Poetry,* 221–30; and Marcus, *Politics of Mirth,* 233–40. Critics often invoke pastoral when discussing the politics not only of the mower poems but, more generally, of those poems which frequently are anthologized as "lyric poems."

4. See Patterson's discussion of variants upon the "three-phase theory," *Marvell and the Civic Crown,* 3–14. She distances herself from critics who have distinguished between Marvell's early lyric and later "political" verse. Although Patterson disagrees with these critics' specific claims, her work retains their impulse to chart Marvell's responses to "three radically different regimes."

5. Mary Marvell's note to readers of the *Miscellaneous Poems* is reprinted in *Andrew Marvell: Poet and Politician, 1621–78,* catalogue compiled by Hilton Kelliher (London: British Museum Publications, 1978), 121.

6. One exception is Carol Gilbertson, "'Many *Miltons* in this One Man': Marvell's Mower Poems and *Paradise Lost,*" *Milton Studies* 22 (1986): 152–54. Gilbertson discusses the similarities between the mower poems and *Paradise Lost,* concluding that the mower poems must have been composed after Marvell saw Milton's manuscript sometime between 1655 and 1665. This argument assumes, of course, that the similarities between the two authors can be explained only by a time frame which allows Milton to remain the literary master and Marvell the pupil.

7. For discussions of Marvell which do address more extensive struggles, see Turner, *Politics of Landscape,* McKeon, *Marvell and Mediation,* and Wilding, *Dragon's Teeth* and "Marvell's 'An Horation Ode.'" McKeon discusses mediation and its relationship to seventeenth-century secularization and imperialism. My argument questions Turner and Wilding's assessment that Marvell's mowers are theatrical "walking emblems" and also their related conclusions about the class politics of Marvell's verse (Turner, 177, 181 and 185, and Wilding, *Dragon's Teeth,* 159–63).

8. For Marxist responses to these revisionist historians, see, for example,

Hill, "A Bourgeois Revolution?" in *Three British Revolutions: 1641, 1688, 1776*, ed. J. G. A. Pocock (Princeton: Princeton University Press, 1980), 109–39, and Mary Fulbrook, "The English Revolution and the Revisionist Revolt," *Social History* 7:3 (1982): 249–64. See also, Lawrence Stone, "The Bourgeois Revolution of Seventeenth-Century England Revisited," *Past and Present* 109 (1985): 44–54.

9. All quotations are from Edmund Spenser, *The Shepheardes Calendar, Spenser: Poetical Works,* ed. J. C. Smith and E. de Selincourt (London: Oxford University Press, 1912), 415–67.

10. The *OED* defines "whet" as "1. An act of sharpening . . . the interval between two sharpenings of a scythe, etc."

11. For a discussion of the relationship between the Elizabethan pastoral and the earlier sixteenth-century tradition, see Louis Adrian Montrose, "Of Gentlemen and Shepherds: The Politics of Elizabethan Pastoral Form," *English Literary History* 50 (1983): 421–33. The quotation is from Thomas More, *Utopia,* trans. and ed. Robert M. Adams (New York: W. W. Norton, 1975), 14.

12. Karl Marx, *Capital,* trans. Ben Fowkes (New York: Vintage Books, 1976), 1:877–86; Alan Everitt, "Farm Labourers," *The Agrarian History of England and Wales,* vol. 4, *1500–1640,* ed. Joan Thirsk, series ed. H. P. R. Fineberg (Ithaca: Cornell University Press, 1967), 396–400, 406–9, and 424; Lawrence Stone, *The Causes of the English Revolution, 1529–1642* (New York: Harper and Row, 1972), 67–68; Raymond Williams, *The Country and the City* (New York: Oxford University Press, 1973), 96–97 and 101–3; Christopher Hill, *Change and Continuity in Seventeenth-Century England* (London: Weidenfield and Nicolson, 1974), 219–23; J. A. Yelling, *Common Field and Enclosure in England, 1450–1850* (Hamden: Archon Books, 1977), 1–29 and 214–32; Charles Tilly, "The Proletarianization and Rural Collective Action in East Anglia and Elsewhere, 1500–1900," *Peasant Studies* 10:1 (Fall 1982): 7–11 and 19–22.

13. Quoted by Hill, *Change and Continuity,* 232.

14. See Henry Best, *Rural Economy in Yorkshire in 1641, Being the Farming and Account Books of Henry Best,* Publications of the Surtees Society, vol. 33 (Durham: George Andrews, 1857), 31–42; Marx, *Capital,* I: 877–83; Joan Thirsk, *English Peasant Farming: The Agrarian History of Lincolnshire from Tudor to Recent Times* (London: Routledge and Kegan Paul, 1957), 159–67 and 180–86; Lord Ernle, "Obstacles to Progress," *Agricultural and Economic Growth in England, 1650–1815,* ed. E. L. Jones (London: Methuen, 1967), 49–65; Stone, *Causes of the English Revolution,* 68; Yelling, *Common Field,* 1–45, 58–63, 94–119, 174–92, 214–32; Michael Roberts, "Sickles and Scythes: Women's Work and Men's Work at Harvest Time," *History Workshop* 7 (Spring 1979): 14–19; Carolina Lane, "Development of Pasture and Meadows During the Sixteenth and Seventeenth Centuries," *Agricultural History Review* 28:1 (1980): 18–30; Ann Kussmaul, *Servants in Husbandry in Early Modern England* (Cambridge: Cambridge University Press, 1981), 107; and Tilly, *Proletarianization,* 7–11. The quotation is from More, *Utopia,* 14–15.

15. Quoted by Roberts, "Sickles and Scythes," 9.

16. Best, *Rural Economy,* 32 and 35–36. Best is also Roberts's source for a great many of his conclusions about seventeenth-century mowing.

17. Roberts, "Sickles and Scythes," 16–17. Roberts argues that, from the eleventh through the seventeenth century, mowing was one of the few agricultural tasks almost entirely carried out by men. By the end of the seventeenth century, the use of scythes rather than sickles to harvest corn would further expel women from the higher-paying agricultural occupations. K. D. M. Snell, "Agricultural Seasonal Unemployment, The Standard of Living, and Women's Work in the South and East, 1690–1860," *Economic History Review* 34:3 (August 1981): 425–30, also discusses the role of the corn scythe in increasing displacement of women from the more lucrative agricultural labor.

18. Thomas Fuller, *The History of the Worthies of England* (1662; rpt., London: Nuttal and Hodgson, 1840), 3:266. Fuller began to collect his data while traveling as a chaplain to royalist forces in 1643.

19. The *OED* defines "hide" as a "measure of land . . . primarily the amount considered adequate for the support of one free family with its dependents."

20. The *OED* lists, as a now-archaic definition of hay which *was* current in the seventeenth century, "1. A hedge, a fence. . . . 2. An enclosed space; an enclosure."

21. E. Lipson, *The Economic History of England* (London: Adam and Charles Black, 1931), 2:384, 386–89, and 392–95; D. C. Coleman, "Labour in the English Economy of the Seventeenth Century," *Economic History Review,* 2d ser., 8:3 (April 1956): 288–92; E. L. Jones, *Seasons and Prices: The Role of the Weather in English Agricultural History* (London: George Allen and Unwin, 1964), 63–66; Everitt, "Farm Labourers," 399 and 430–38; Kussmaul, *Servants,* 78–80; and Tilly, "Proletarianization," 17. The quotation appears in Coleman, 285. Everitt's at times cheerful account of wage labor must be balanced, first, by his own tendency to draw back and admit widespread hardship; second, by his approval of wage labor unless it causes visible hardship; and, third, by analyses cited elsewhere in this essay.

22. Best, *Rural Economy,* 32, 48, 53–54, and 156–57; Lipson, *Economic History,* 2:395; Everitt, "Farm Labourers," 430–34; and Kussmaul, *Servants,* 80–85.

23. For discussions of this paragraph's information, see Lipson, *Economic History,* 2:391, and 3:428–30, 454–62, and 469–77; Coleman, "Labour," 280–95; Everitt, "Farm Labourers," 435; C. H. Wilson, "Trade, Society and the State," *The Cambridge Economic History of Europe,* vol. 4, ed. E. E. Rich and C. H. Wilson, series ed. M. M. Postan and H. J. Habakkuk (Cambridge: Cambridge University Press, 1967), 515 and 539–40; Hill, *Change and Continuity,* 219–34; and F. G. Emmison, *Elizabethan Life: Home, Work and Land* (Saffron Walden: Hart-Talbot, 1976), 146–47. Coleman, "Labour," 283–84, quotes King and supports his findings.

When Hill reports a seventeenth-century scorn for the lack of freedom among laborers, he sometimes conflates people among whom contemporaries would have distinguished as either "servants" or "laborers." According to

Kussmaul, *Servants,* 3–85, servants were hired for the year, had only one master, resided with that master, and remained unmarried. Laborers were hired for the day, week, harvest month, or by the task; had several masters; and lived in their own residences with either their spouses or parents. Few seventeenth-century workers chose to be servants for a lifetime; most remained servants for an average of six years while in a transitional state between living with their parents and becoming wage-laborers with their own households. During their residence with their masters, servants were counted as politically invisible dependents of those employers' households.

24. Best, *Rural Economy,* 31–32.

25. See Erwin Panofsky, *Studies in Iconology: Humanistic Themes in the Art of the Renaissance* (New York: Oxford University Press, 1939), 69–93, for an account of similar mowers.

26. For a different assessment of the mower poems' relationship to seventeenth-century debates about holy day and Sabbath observances, see Marcus, *Politics of Mirth,* 233–40.

27. More, *Utopia,* 16.

28. John Smyth, III, *The Berkeley Manuscripts. A Description of the Hundred of Berkeley in the County of Gloucester and of Its Inhabitants,* and "Waste Land's Improvement, 31 October 1653," in *Seventeenth-Century Economic Documents,* ed. Joan Thirsk and J. P. Cooper (Oxford: Oxford University Press, 1972), 122–23 and 135.

29. Christopher Hill, *Society and Puritanism in Pre-Revolutionary England* (New York: Schocken Books, 1964), 146–53, 160–76, and 183–202.

30. James I, "The King's Majesty's Declaration to His Subjects, Concerning Lawful Sports to be Used, 24th May 1618," and Charles I's preface and conclusion to the 1633 edition of the declaration, in *Social England Illustrated: A Collection of Seventeenth Century Tracts,* ed. Edward Arber (Westminster: Archibald Constable, 1903), 313–14 and 316.

31. Maryann Cale McGuire, *Milton's Puritan Masque* (Athens: University of Georgia Press, 1983), 9–29, and Marcus, *Politics of Mirth,* 1–23.

32. See, for example, Lucy Hutchinson's remarks, cited in McGuire, *Masque,* 14.

33. Hill, *Society and Puritanism,* 153–59 and 168–76. Both supporters of enclosure and supporters of Sabbatarianism leveled charges of idleness against the displaced and unemployed; not surprisingly, then, such invectives often indicated a fear of peasant rebellion (Hill, *The World Turned Upside Down* [Harmondsworth: Penguin, 1975], 39–56, and Tilly, "Proletarianization," 13–22).

34. Marx, *Capital,* 1:877–86.

35. Fuller, *Worthies,* 3:266.

36. Hill, *Society and Puritanism,* 145–218.

37. Hill, *Change and Continuity,* 3–47.

38. For discussions of these groups, see Keith Thomas, "Women and the Civil War Sects," *Past and Present* 13 (1958): 42–62; Claire Cross, "'He-goats before the flocks': A Note on the Part Played by Women in the Founding of

Some Civil War Churches," *Studies in Church History* 8 (1972): 195–202; Christine Berg and Philippa Berry, "'Spiritual Whoredom': An Essay on Female Prophets in the Seventeenth Century," in *1642: Literature and Power in the Seventeenth Century,* ed. Francis Barker (Colchester: University of Essex, 1981), 37–54; Marie B. Rowlands, "Recusant Women, 1560–1640," in *Women in English Society, 1500–1800,* ed. Mary Prior (London: Methuen, 1985), 149–80; and Merry E. Weisner, "Women's Defense of Their Public Role," in *Women in the Middle Ages and the Renaissance: Literary and Historical Perspectives,* ed. Mary Beth Rose (Syracuse: Syracuse University Press, 1986), 17–21.

39. Joseph Swetnam, *The Araignment of lewde, idle, froward, and unconstant women,* in *Half Humankind: Contexts and Texts of the Controversy about Women in England, 1540–1640,* ed. Katherine Usher Henderson and Barbara F. McManus (Urbana: University of Illinois Press, 1985), 190, 193, and 192.

40. Ester Sowernam, *Esther Hath Hanged Haman,* in *Half Humankind,* 224–25 and 232.

41. Swetnam, "Araignment," 191. In addition to Swetnam and Sowernam's rhetoric, see the rhetoric of, for example, Jane Anger, *Her Protection for Women,* and Joane Sharp, "A Defence of Women," in *First Feminists: British Women Writers (1578–1799),* ed. Moira Ferguson (Bloomington: Indiana University Press, 1985), 64–70 and 80–83. For discussions of these misogynist debates, see Betty Travitsky, "The Lady Doth Protest: Protest in the Popular Writings of Renaissance Englishwomen," *English Literary Renaissance* 14:3 (Autumn 1984): 255–83; Linda Woodbridge, *Women and the English Renaissance: Literature and the Nature of Womankind, 1540–1620* (Urbana: University of Illinois Press, 1984), 74–113, 139–51, and 275–322; and Henderson and McManus, *Half Humankind,* 3–130. Later in the century, Margaret Askew Fell Fox argues that contemporary serpents include those who would deny women the right to preach. See Fox, *Women's Speaking Justified* (1667; rpt., Los Angeles: William Andrews Clark Memorial Library for The Augustan Reprint Society, Publication 194, 1979), 3–5.

42. Hannah Woolley, *The Gentlewomen's Companion; or A Guide to the Female Sex,* in *The Whole Duty of a Woman: Female Writers in Seventeenth-century England,* ed. Angeline Goreau (New York: Dial Press, 1985), 27; Lady Damaris Masham, *Occasional Thoughts in Reference to a Vertuous or Christian Life,* in Goreau, *The Whole Duty of a Woman,* 30; Bathsua Pell Makin, *An Essay to Revive the Antient Education of Gentlewomen* (1673; rpt., Los Angeles: William Andrews Clark Memorial Library for The Augustan Reprint Society, Publication 202, 1980), 7; and Margaret Cavendish, *Sociable Letters,* in Goreau, *The Whole Duty of a Woman,* 23.

43. Michael Craze, *The Life and Lyrics of Andrew Marvell* (New York: Barnes and Noble, 1979), 155.

44. See, for example, Legouis, *Marvell,* 43–44; Toliver, *Marvell's Vision,* 105–6, 107–9, 111, and 112; J. B. Leishman, *The Art of Marvell's Poetry* (London: Hutchinson, 1966), 130, 137, 141, and 153; Ann E. Berthoff, *The Resolved Soul: A Study of Marvell's Major Poems* (Princeton: Princeton University Press, 1970), 133–37 and 140; Rosalie L. Colie, *"My Ecchoing Song":*

*Andrew Marvell's Poetry of Criticism* (Princeton: Princeton University Press, 1970), 30–42; Patrick Cullen, *Spenser, Marvell, and Renaissance Pastoral* (Cambridge: Harvard University Press, 1970), 194–98; Donald M. Friedman, *Marvell's Pastoral Art* (Berkeley: University of California Press, 1970), 120, 129–30, and 132–36; Korshin, *From Concord to Dissent*, 67–68 and 71–72; Friedenreich, "The Mower Mown: Marvell's Dances of Death," in *Tercentenary Essays in Honor of Andrew Marvell*, 153; Bruce King, *Marvell's Allegorical Poetry* (Cambridge: The Oleander Press, 1977), 110–14, 119–20, 132, 137, 142, and 144; Carey, "Reversals," 142–43; Smith, "Marvell's Wit," 68–70; Hunt, *Marvell*, 95–96; Everett, "Shooting of the Bears," 97–98; Meilaender, "Marvell's Pastoral Poetry," 185–87; Turner, *Politics of Landscape*, 117, 177, and 181; Parry, *Seventeenth-Century Poetry*, 228; and Marcus, *Politics of Mirth*, 238–40.

45. [Francis Bacon] Lord Verulam and R. H. Esquire, *New Atlantis* (1660; rpt., New Haven: Yale Medical Library, 1988), 79–80.

46. John Ray, *Further Correspondence of John Ray*, ed. Robert W. T. Gunther (London: Dulau and Company, 1928), 80 and 82.

47. The quotation is from Shakespeare, *The Winter's Tale*, in *The Riverside Shakespeare*, ed. G. Blakemore Evans (Boston: Houghton Mifflin, 1974), 1569–603.

48. Francis Bacon, "Of Gardens," in *The Essays*, ed. John Pitcher (Harmondsworth: Penguin Books, 1985), 197–98 and 202, and Thomas Browne, "The Garden of Cyrus. Or, The Quincunciall, Lozenge, or Network Plantations of the Ancients, Artificially, Naturally, Mystically Considered," *The Prose of Sir Thomas Browne*, ed. Norman Endicott (New York: New York University Press, 1968), 295–96.

49. Margaret T. Hodgen, *Early Anthropology in the Sixteenth and Seventeenth Centuries* (Philadelphia: University of Pennsylvania Press, 1964), 111–206, and Hunt, *Marvell*, 26–56.

50. The *OED* defines "luxurious" as "1. Lascivious, lecherous, unchaste. 2. Outrageous, extravagant, excessive, also, passionately desirous *after* something. 3. a) Of persons, their habits, etc.: Given to luxury, or self-indulgence, voluptuous . . . ."

51. The *OED* defines "luscious" as "1. Of food, perfumes, etc.: Sweet and highly pleasant to taste or smell. 2. In a bad sense: Sweet to excess, cloying, sickly. . . . 4. Of tales, conversation, writing, etc.: Gratifying to lascivious tastes, voluptuous, wanton. . . . "

52. Legouis, *Marvell*, 43; Colie, "*Song*," 36–39; Cullen, *Renaissance Pastoral*, 167–68; C. A. Patrides, "'Til prepared for longer flight': The Sublunar Poetry of Andrew Marvell," in *Approaches to Marvell*, 42; Smith, "Marvell's Wit," 69; Hunt, *Marvell*, 95; Turner, *Politics of Landscape*, 117–18; and Marcus, *Politics of Mirth*, 238–39, neither quote these lines nor distinguish between the first and second halves of the poem. Toliver, *Marvell's Vision*, 104–5; Leishman, *Marvell's Poetry*, 133–34; and Meilaender, "Marvell's Pastoral Poetry," 185–86, quote these lines in their discussions of corruption in both sections of the poem yet do not distinguish between those sections. Friedman, *Marvell's Pastoral Art*, 126; Korshin, *From Concord to Dissent*, 66–67; King, *Marvell's Poetry*, 116; and

McKeon, "Marvell and Mediation," 60–61, do attempt to differentiate between the two sections yet do not address the curious way in which Marvell draws that distinction.

53. Bacon, *The New Atlantis,* vol. 5 in *The Works of Francis Bacon,* ed. James Spedding, Robert Leslie Ellis, and Douglas Denon Heath (New York: Hurd and Houghton, 1864), 401.

54. Ibid.

55. Legouis, *Marvell,* 43–44; Toliver, *Marvell's Vision,* 104–6; Leishman, *Marvell's Poetry,* 137; Berthoff, *Resolved Soul,* 141; Colie, "*Song,*" 38–39; Cullen, *Renaissance Pastoral,* 168; Friedman, *Marvell's Art,* 128–29; King, *Marvell's Poetry,* 119; Smith, 'Marvell's Wit," 69–70; Hunt, *Marvell,* 95 and 100; Meilaender, "Marvell's Pastoral Poetry," 185–87; Turner, *Politics of Landscape,* 117–18; McKeon, "Marvell and Mediation," 60–61; and Marcus, *Politics of Mirth,* 238–39.

56. John Evelyn, *De Vita Propria, The Diary of John Evelyn,* vol. 1, ed. E. S. De Beer (Oxford: Oxford University Press, 1955), 70–71.

57. Evelyn, *Kalendarium, The Diary of John Evelyn,* 2:53–54.

58. Ironically, the catalogue from an exhibition which commemorated the tercentenary of Marvell's death offers a less dramatic version of depoliticizing conjunctions. Exhibits 50–54, for example, were a miniature of Oliver Cromwell, a letter by James Scudamore which mentions Marvell in passing as "a notable English Italo-Machavillian," the manuscript of Marvell's "A Poem upon the Death of His late Highnesse the Lord Protector," Cromwell's wax death mask, and a sheet of paper which lists Marvell among those in the third section of Cromwell's funeral procession. Kelliher, *Andrew Marvell: Poet and Politician, 1621–78,* 61–65.

59. Evelyn, *De Vita Propria,* 83.

# 5

# Jonson and the Amazons

*Stephen Orgel*

When James I succeeded as king of England, he came to a throne that had been occupied for more than half a century by women. Both Henry VIII's daughters were legally illegitimate, and their claims to the crown were ambiguous at best; Elizabeth's was especially shaky, since Henry had argued at her mother's trial for adultery and incest that she was not even his daughter. She was queen because she was included in the line of succession established in her father's will, which overrode the earlier illegitimation, though it did not revoke it; but she made good her right to the throne through a combination of policy and extraordinary personal style.

An important component of that style was the chivalric mythology with which she surrounded herself. This had been introduced into the political life of the realm by her grandfather Henry VII, who used Burgundian models of knightly heroism to legitimate the de facto rule by conquest confirmed at Bosworth field. Henry VIII had extended the trope into lavish displays of Arthurian fantasy, asserting through spectacle a parity with Francis I and Charles V that he could not assert with arms. Elizabeth gradually redefined the family mythology, eventually placing herself at the center of a drama in which the essence of knighthood was not the performance of heroic deeds in battle but service to a lady. Chivalry became, in her hands, a myth that disarmed her heroes as it idealized her, and the language of heroism became the language of submissive love. This was not only a way of exerting her control over a large number of active and ambitious men who depended on the crown for employment; it was also a useful element of foreign policy. She supported privateers, not armies. The Armada victory was her one major military triumph, and she made the most of it. But she was resolved to keep England out of the European power struggles, and the

great cause that fired the enthusiasm of the most idealistic of her sub-
jects, a Protestant league and the freeing of the Netherlands from
Spanish domination, she wanted no part of. Despite the general un-
popularity of this position, her success for most of her long reign was
notable, though it was eclipsed during her last years by the uncertainty
of the succession, an issue that she carefully left unresolved until almost
the moment of her death. The popular adulation accorded to Sidney for
the most meager of military careers, the exaggerated hopes invested in
the disastrous Essex, are indices to how badly the realm yearned for
glory as Elizabeth's rule drew to an end.[1]

Despite her presentation of herself as a Petrarchan heroine and the
sovereign lady to a band of adoring knights, official representations of
her dealt warily with her womanhood. In portraits she appears in the
increasingly elaborate gowns that she loved, but the pose and the facial
expression tend always to be stylized, cool, impersonal. She herself was
distrustful of representations, and attempted to restrict their produc-
tion; the face in her portraits, indeed, was invariably based on one of a
small number of patterns supplied by her authority. Very few paintings
of her addressed the realities of her situation as a woman. The most
striking of these is the Sieve Portrait, probably painted around 1580 by
Cornelius Kettel, and now in Siena (fig. 1). She holds a sieve, the at-
tribute of the Roman vestal virgins, and stands before a column bearing
inset scenes from the story of Dido and Aeneas. The allusions have a
complex relevance: Elizabeth traced her descent from Aeneas, grand-
father of Brutus, the legendary founder of Britain; and Dido has a
double and contradictory history, as the chaste founder of Carthage
who committed suicide rather than give up her chastity to an importun-
ing suitor, and as the betrayed and abandoned mistress of the Trojan
hero. The allusion to the latter story invokes both her royal ancestry and
the dangers that threaten her peace and the realm's; the sieve assures us
that she is an incarnation of the the chaste Dido, not the fallen one.[2]
When the monarch was a woman, such reassurance was constantly
necessary.

But the language of love was a crucial part of her power. Lord
Thomas Howard in 1611 analyzed for Sir John Harington the dif-
ference in style between the old queen and her successor: "Your Queen
did talk of her subjects love and good affections, and in good truth she
aimed well; our King talketh of his subjects fear and subjection, and
herein I thinke he doth well too, as long as it holdeth good."[3] The new
king's ideology was as disarming as the queen's had been, and more
overtly so. James I was a pacifist; his motto, Beati Pacifici, blessed are the
peacemakers, appears inscribed over his head in the frontispiece to his

1. Cornelius Kettel (?), *Elizabeth I* (The Sieve Portrait), c. 1580. Pinacoteca di Siena.
Photo Soprintendenza B.A.S. Siena.

2. Penthisilea, Queen of the Amazons, costume design by Inigo Jones for *The Masque of Queens,* 1609. Devonshire Collection, Chatsworth. The Inigo Jones drawings are reproduced by permission of the Trustees of the Chatsworth Settlement.

works, published in 1616. The king's determination to keep his new realm clear of the European wars was as central an element in his foreign policy as it had been in his predecessor's. It was perhaps the only sensible part of the royal program; but to a nation longing for glory after the decline of Elizabeth's last years, it was again disappointing and unpopular. Eulogists could praise James's wisdom and learning, but the imagery of triumph was not easily applied to this autocratic, withdrawn, and uncharismatic monarch. Within a few years after the king's accession, Elizabeth was being recalled with a fervent nostalgia. Sir John Harington in 1606 had already anticipated Lord Thomas Howard, summing up what had passed from the royal style: "We all did love hir, for she said she loved us."[4]

To pursue the ideology of chivalry from Elizabeth's reign into James's is to confront a political dialectic that is almost occult in its complexity. It is also to confront a family drama: by the age of fourteen, James's elder son, Prince Henry, was already emerging as the focus of a militant Protestant opposition. Ben Jonson and Inigo Jones, poet and architect of the spectacles of the Jacobean state, were called on by both sides; here, as so often, we can see the conflicts of Jacobean politics expressed in the symbolic fables of royal theater.

The first explicitly heroic masque created for the Jacobean monarchy was Jonson's and Jones's *Masque of Queens,* performed at Whitehall in 1609. It celebrated, however, not King James but his queen, by whom it had been commissioned, and included a troupe of Amazonian heroines as supporting roles for her ladies (fig. 2). It was an unlikely part for Queen Anne, who studiously avoided politics and was unsympathetic to her son's ambitions—she was, indeed, a convert to Catholicism.[5] Nevertheless, through her patronage, Jonson here reconceived in heroic terms the form he had made peculiarly his own. In his earlier court masques Jonson had placed his performers in arcane symbolic fables, where they danced out philosophical arguments, recreated classical rituals, or participated in the creation of cosmic emblems. In 1609, for the first time, Jonson's ideal vision was expressed through a set of martial roles. The Jacobean court became the culmination and embodiment of two thousand years of militant female virtue. In this world of ancient examples, only Queen Anne, the living heroine, played a version of herself, Bel-Anna, Queen of the Ocean. If the epithet was intended to recall the triumphant Elizabeth of the Armada victory, it was the only allusion Jonson allowed himself to the dangerously successful model of the previous reign.

Jonson opens his masque on "a spectacle of strangeness," an ugly hell and a coven of witches, the opposites, he says, to fame and glory. This was his first fully realized antimasque, and he credits its inclusion to the queen, who,

> best knowing that a principal part of life in these spectacles lay in their variety, commanded me to think on some dance or show that might precede hers and have the place of a foil or false masque.[6]

But if it was the queen's idea to have an antimasque, the startling subject of the antimasque must have been determined by the king's interests. The royal treatise on witchcraft, *Daemonologie,* first published in Edinburgh in 1597, had been reissued in two separate London editions in 1603 upon James's accession to the English throne. It was a subject that was of passionate interest to him, and his expertise on the matter formed an important part of his scholarly and judicial credentials.

Jonson presents his own scholarly credentials in a set of elaborate marginalia composed at the request of Prince Henry—the masque in its final form appears as very much a family affair. Sources both classical and modern are adduced for the smallest details of the witches' performance, and the exhaustive citation of authorities naturally includes a reference to the king's book. This was doubtless intended as a compliment, but it displays a subtle antagonism as well. *Daemonologie* deals with general theological and philosophical issues rather than with specific cases or historical precedents; it is, granting its premises, a capable, economical, and intelligent discussion. Jonson invokes the royal expertise, however, on a specific point: to justify opening the performance with a dance, he contends on the king's authority that witches commonly begin their meetings in this way.[7] In fact, the matter is not touched on in *Daemonologie;* Jonson's real source appears to be, ironically, Reginald Scot's sceptical treatise *The Discoverie of Witches,* a tract James attacks in his own treatise.

But if Jonson thus marginalized the king's scholarship, usurping the royal authority with a rival expertise, the presentation of witches at court was anything but marginal. James was convinced that there had been, from his youth, a systematic and continuous conspiracy against his throne and his life; those responsible were not any of the multitude of political enemies that did in fact fill the early part of his reign, but witches under the direct control of the devil. He made it a point to be present at the interrogation of witches whenever possible, and the confessions invariably extracted from them under torture always confirmed his belief. English readers were offered an account of the conspiracy, and of the king's involvement in its detection, in a pamphlet published in London in 1591 entitled *Newes from Scotland.* One of the women interrogated, Agnis Tompson,[8] revealed that when James went to Denmark in 1589 to bring back his bride, the delays and extraordinary bad weather he experienced were the result of witchcraft; she herself had caused the storms, and had been designated by the devil to kill the king by sorcery. The latter project failed, she said, only because she was unable to persuade one of his loyal servants to provide her with the necessary piece of the king's soiled linen for her spells.

The king reportedly was initially skeptical of this story, and

> said they were all extreme liars, whereat she answered she would not wish his majesty to suppose her words to be false, but rather to believe them, in that she would discover such matter unto him as his majesty should not any way doubt of. And thereupon taking his majesty a little aside, she declared unto him the very words which passed between the king's majesty and his queen at Uppsala in Norway the first night of their marriage, with their answer to each other; whereat the king's majesty wondered greatly, and swore by the living God that he believed all the devils in hell could not have discovered the same, acknowledging her words to be most true. . . .[9]

If we are concerned with *The Masque of Queens* as a family drama, it is significant that the witchcraft in this account is specifically implicated in the king's marriage. It is designed to prevent his return with his bride, and the crucial evidence is a revelation of the secrets of his wedding night. The story, moreover, is authenticated by the king. James's intense interest in witchcraft is clearly related to his general distrust of women, and his compulsive and public attachment to young men.[10] For all the romance of his winter voyage across the North Sea to fetch his bride, he told his privy council that he was marrying simply to produce an heir; and he added that "as to my own nature, God is my witness, I could have abstained longer."[11] The defeat of the sorcery was a triumph not of true love but of the king's exceptional virtue, as Agnis Tompson testified, asserting that "his majesty had never come safely from the sea if his faith had not prevailed above their intentions."[12] But the battle was never to be won: she also reported that the witches "demanded of the devil why he did bear such hatred to the king, who answered, by reason the king is the greatest enemy he hath in the world."[13]

There are obvious cultural coordinates to these fantasies. James's own career was determined by his relation to two powerful and threatening women. His mother, the libidinous—and, to Protestants, diabolical—Mary, was the source of his power, but it was a power that depended on her absence: he was king of Scotland because she was not queen. She was also his link to the English succession, but she simultaneously represented the greatest danger to his achieving it. The claim she gave him through heredity she had rendered dubious by her sexual behavior: the charge that James was illegitimate, the child of his mother's secretary, David Rizzio, was widespread in the 1580s; James expressed fears that it would weaken his chances at the English throne, and he never felt entirely free of it. He undertook to replace Mary in his family line with the chaste and regal Elizabeth, whom he was regularly addressing by the mid-1580s as "madame and dearest mother."[14] She was a mother who could give him everything he wanted—safety, wealth, legitimacy: in short, the English throne—and he courted her tirelessly; but she made no promises, ever, and would not confirm him as her heir until the moment of her death; and it is not clear that she did so even then.

Out of these crucial, unreliable, powerful, dangerous, and—most important—absent women James's imagination constructed a world in which women were controlled by being incorporated. Upon his accession in 1603, he declared to Parliament that "I am the husband and the whole island is my lawful wife; I am the head, and it is my body."[15] The imagery derives from St. Paul on marriage, and the two statements are presented as synonymous. Mothers became unnecessary; he himself would be "a loving nourish-father" who would provide his subjects with "their own nourish-milk."[16] Psychologically, such a conception of his relation to the realm had obvious advantages. But as a political solution, James's patriarchy had a fatal weakness: it required Parliament to allow itself to be conceived as the monarch's children, or wife, or the body to his active mind, to be dictated to where it preferred to dictate. Queen Elizabeth's rhetoric with the men on whom her power and her purse depended had been shrewder, and much more effective: it represented them as her lovers. This was, for James, in every way an impossible act to follow. Jonson's witches and queens represent the limits of the Jacobean patriarchy.

2

The transition from witches to queens comes, in Jonson's masque, without even a confrontation:

> In the heat of their dance on the sudden was heard a sound of loud music, as if many instruments had made one blast; with which not only the hags themselves, but the hell into which they ran quite altered, scarce suffering the memory of such a thing. But in the place of it appeared a glorious and magnificent building figuring the House of Fame, in the top of which were discovered the twelve masquers sitting upon a throne triumphal erected in form of a pyramid and circled with all store of light. (334–41)

The new scene, like the hell it replaces, has its sources in poetry, schol-
arship, and a profoundly personal politics. The design of the House of
Fame is based, Jonson tells us, on Chaucer's poem, and as a spokesman
to moralize the spectacular transformation he introduces a classic figure
of heroic virtue, Perseus.

But Perseus as Jonson presents him is not simply heroic virtue, and
he does more than elucidate the antithesis of witches and queens. He
greatly complicates it as well. He represents, Jonson says, "a brave and
masculine virtue,"[17] and in the very moment of transition he preempts
the triumph of the masque's heroines:

> So should, at Fame's loud sound and Virtue's sight,
> All dark and envious witchcraft fly the light.
> I did not borrow Hermes' wings, nor ask
> His crooked sword, nor put on Pluto's casque,
> Nor on my arm advanced wise Pallas' shield
> (By which, my face aversed, in open field
> I slew the Gorgon) for an empty name.
> When Virtue cut off Terror, he gat Fame.
> And if when Fame was gotten Terror died,
> What black *Erinyes* or more hellish pride
> Durst arm these hags now she is grown and great,
> To think they could her glories once defeat:
> I was her parent and I am her strength.
>                     (344–56)

King James would have been pleased to find that the claims to heroic
responsibility were also patriarchal claims: the masque at its most clas-
sical is also most Jacobean. So it is again as Masculine Virtue introduces
the historic queens, naming them, and celebrating as their chief and
epitome Bel-Anna, who "alone / Possessed all virtues." But she wisely
keeps her eye on the king:

> She this embracing with a virtuous joy,
> Far from self-love, as humbling all her worth
> To him that gave it, hath again brought forth
> Their names to memory; and means this night
> To make them once more visible to light,
> And to that light from whence her truth of spirit
> Confesseth all the luster of her merit:
> To you, most royal and most happy king,
> Of whom Fame's house in every part doth ring
> For every virtue. . . .
>                     (401–10)

So much, in the Jacobean court, was no more than politic. Queen Anne was, to this extent, a sensible woman, and Jonson was a sensible poet.

But the moment, if we keep the pyramid of triumphant queens with Bel-Anna at its apex in view, is also a genuinely subversive one, and to evaluate it necessitates a look at Jonson's sources. Jonson says in a marginal note that the ancient authorities offer three possible figures symbolic of masculine virtue: Hercules, Bellerophon, and Perseus. His choice of Perseus, therefore, is in itself significant. He cites as his sources for information about the hero Hesiod and Apollodorus; but his unnamed intermediate sources are the sixteenth-century handbooks he so often consulted, of Cesare Ripa, Natalis Comes, and Vincenzo Cartari, and these are, for our purposes, more informative.[18] The rejected models, Hercules and Bellerophon, are the figures of Virtue elucidated in Ripa, who does not mention Perseus.[19] The passages about Perseus from Hesiod and Apollodorus appear only in Comes, in the expanded edition first published in 1581; this presumably was Jonson's primary reference work.[20] But to find his hero in it, he would have had to look not under Perseus, who is not listed in the index, but under *Medusa* and *Gorgones*—under feminine evil, not masculine virtue. He would have found Perseus directly only in Cartari, along with the general points about the relation of terror to heroic success.[21]

Something is significant here by its absence: for a Renaissance classicist, the major source for the story of Perseus would have been Ovid, in books 4 and 5 of the *Metamorphoses*. The fact that Jonson does not cite this account is probably the most revealing index to his interests. Ovid concentrates on the rescue of Andromeda, to which the Medusa story is ancillary, and relatively perfunctory. The Perseus Jonson wants is the victor over dangerous and destructive women, the hero who "cut off terror," that death-dealing female head, and made it an emblem of virtue. This is the Perseus of Comes, for whom Medusa is the embodiment of sensual temptation, lust, and illicit sexuality; but it is even more the quite different—and in certain ways more classical, and in every way more Jonsonian—Perseus of Cartari. Cartari's account of Perseus and Medusa is so germane to the masque, and so deeply embedded in its conception, that it will repay close attention. Here is a translation of the relevant section:

> Diodorus writes that the gorgons were warlike women in Africa who were overcome by Perseus, who also killed their queen Medusa; this may be historical. But the fables report, as Apollodorus writes, that the gorgons were three sisters, of whom only Medusa was mortal; the other two, Euriale and Sthenno, were immortal. Their heads were surrounded

and covered with scaly serpents; they had huge teeth like those of hogs, hands like branches, and wings of gold, with which they flew as they pleased; and they changed into stone whatever they looked at. Perseus, finding them asleep, cut off Medusa's head, took it away and gave it to Minerva, who had been of great assistance to him, because she furnished him with his shield, as Mercury had provided his sword and the wings for his heels, and Orcus [Pluto] the helmet that made him invisible. . . .

It is also said (and this is the most common fable) that the gorgons were three very beautiful sisters, called gorgons after the islands where they lived; Medusa was the most beautiful, with hair of gold. But when Neptune fell in love with her, he slept with her in the temple of Minerva, and the goddess, in her outrage, transformed Medusa from someone beautiful and lovely to see to someone terrible and frightening, and changed her golden hair to serpents. She wished whoever looked at her thereafter to be turned to stone; but since the world cannot endure so alien a monster, Perseus killed her, with the assistance I have described, and gave her head to Minerva, who always carried it on her shield or her cuirass. Thus, when Homer has this goddess arm herself for battle against the Trojans, he says she was surrounded with dreadful terror; and, along with the head of Medusa, she brought with her bold courage, confident valor, and a most threatening appearance—all things appropriate to the goddess of war, as is also victory. Therefore Pausanias says that the Athenians placed her on their breastplates with the head of Medusa. . . .

These things show the power of knowledge and prudence, which through wonderful works and wise counsels can astonish men and render them like stone with amazement, so that it can obtain whatever it wishes, provided it can suitably expound it: it is language that is expressed by that terrible head.[22]

This account, obviously, can be read many ways. As Cartari understands it, it is not primarily a story about the dangers of lust and illicit sex: Medusa is punished for attracting the attentions of Neptune, but the concluding moralization ignores this in favor of quite other points. It is also not simply, or even primarily, a story about male valor—Perseus is furnished by the war-goddess Pallas with the crucial mirror-shield that enables him to kill Medusa without looking at her, and he acts as Pallas's agent. The gorgon head is brought to her, and it is she who wears it on her armor to betoken martial courage and certain victory—hers, not his: the power of Medusa is quintessentially female power.[23] Cartari gives no support to Jonson's claims for the genetic and functional relationship of Perseus and Fame, "I was her parent, and I am her strength"; Perseus's strength, on the contrary, depends on Pallas. In fact, if one were starting from this account of Perseus, the logical figure for Heroic Virtue would be Pallas, the goddess of both war and wisdom.

Why then is Pallas not the guide from antimasque to masque for this celebration of heroic queens?

A simple answer might be that Jonson's focus at this point is on the defeat of the witches; he wants a martial hero whose triumph over evil is a triumph over hideous women, and Medusa is an obvious prototype for feminine evil. Still, as we read Cartari's account, even this assumption grows increasingly problematic. The gorgons prefigure the queens as much as they prefigure the witches: they are, in Cartari's historical allegory, martial women. They were, to begin with, beautiful, and the Medusa head becomes the emblem of Pallas because of its association specifically with militant female power, courage, and victory. A very different answer is suggested by the final allegorization. Here Medusa is "knowledge and prudence," "wonderful works and wise counsels"— the emblem now of Pallas as wisdom, not as war; and the emblem as well of the poet and adviser to kings: "it is language that is expressed by that terrible head."

None of this, of course, is original with Cartari. Giovanni Pierio Valeriano in the *Hieroglyphica* allegorizes the Medusa head as prudence, and reports that the Athenians took it as their civic emblem because it was the sign of a strong and prudent city.[24] Coluccio Salutati made Medusa embody "artful eloquence," and the allegory ultimately derives, as Nancy Vickers points out, from

> a privileged classical source. During still another lighthearted male contest of both drinking and oratory, the *Symposium,* a flattering Socrates tells Agathon, the speaker who immediately precedes him, that he was held spellbound by the dazzling display of Agathon's speech. He compares Agathon to the master rhetorician Gorgias, and then permits himself a witty play on words: "I was afraid that when Agathon got near the end he would arm his speech against mine with the Gorgon's head of Gorgias' eloquence, and strike me as dumb as a stone."[25]

Given this context, Jonson's attraction to Perseus looks more and more marginal, his attraction to Medusa more and more central. Perseus is there because he confers—on the poet—the power of women, the power of the gorgon.

If Jonson's preference for Cartari's Perseus over Comes's subverts the queen's interests, it fully supports the king's. We might observe, to begin with, that for James the defeat and decapitation of the primary sensual and beautiful woman in his life was the crucial act of empowerment. But Jonson's mythography also points to an essential aspect of the poet's sense of himself. For Comes, the story is about the defeat of erotic temptation and illicit sexuality, and the finding of true love in the faithful wife Andromeda. This was not a Jonsonian model. "In his youth," he told William Drummond in 1619, he was "given to venery. He thought the use of a maid nothing in comparison to the wantonness of a wife, and would never have another mistress." His own wife "was a shrew yet honest; five years he had not bedded with her."[26] He was lavish in adulation of his noble patronesses, but printed a poem in praise of the countess of Bedford immediately after an epigram asserting that the words "woman" and "whore" were synonyms;[27] by 1610 he had at least two illegitimate children.[28] The play he wrote directly after *The Masque of Queens* was the openly misogynistic *Epicoene*. Explaining " Why I Write Not of Love," it is Cupid, not Venus, that he seeks to bind in his verse;[29] in another poem, attempting to find a subject, he banishes Venus to "invent new sports" with the Graces, "thy tribade trine," a lesbian trio (and thereby apparently introduced into the language this first English adjective for female homosexuality),[30] concluding,

> Nor all the ladies of the Thespian lake
> (Though they were crushed into one form) could make
> A beauty of that merit that should take
> My muse up by commission. . . .[31]

His own fantasy of heroic self-sufficiency is fed by a parallel fantasy of the misanthropic self-sufficiency of beautiful women.[32]

## 3

The triumph of heroic virtue is the triumph of Jonson and the word, and *The Masque of Queens,* whatever else it says and unsays, unconditionally asserts the power of poetry. The House of Fame realizes a Chaucerian allegory, but its implications are characteristically Jonsonian (fig. 3). Architecturally, the building is an amalgam of classical and English elements: the Roman arch below supports the Gothic trefoil above. Within the trefoil is a turning machine, bearing the twelve queens on one side and the winged figure of Fame on the other. The facade, Jonson tells us, is adorned with statues: on the lower tier are Homer, Virgil, and Lucan, on the upper Achilles, Aeneas, and Caesar—the heroes' fame is supported and preserved by the immortal poets; heroism (says this architectural emblem) depends on the ordering, transforming, and preserving power of poetry. Jonson's text, however, maintains a discreet distance from its performance: the witches of the antimasque are "twelve women in the habit of hags or witches" (14–15); Perseus is "a person . . . in the furniture of Perseus" (341–42)—these, like the triumphant queens, are all impersonations. But his

3. The House of Fame, Inigo Jones's setting for the transformation scene of *The Masque of Queens*. Devonshire Collection, Chatsworth.

own invention is authenticated, he writes, by "the all-daring power of poetry."[33]

And where is the king in this Jacobean triumph? Jonson's claims for himself are royal claims too: poet and king in this text assert the same authority. Outside the fiction, but at the center of the courtly spectacle, sits the monarch, declaring by his presence that in this masque of queens, heroism may be personified in the royal consort, but the highest virtue is that of the Rex Pacificus, scholar and poet. We confront again both Jacobean politics and the family drama; it is the royal pacificism that has compelled the witches' presence, and that they deplore:

> I hate to see these fruits of a soft peace,
> And curse the piety gives it such increase;
>                 (132–33)

It is not the martial glory of Perseus and the Amazons—and the ambitious and popular Prince Henry—that Fame's trumpet sounds, but the king's peace (l. 410). It was as a scholar that James had himself represented on the tower of Oxford's Bodleian Library, to commemorate his gift to the university of the folio of his works, published (like Jonson's own folio) in 1616 (fig. 4). The masque, for all its spectacle and martial imagery, celebrates the sovereign word.

### 4

It is clear that Jonson's fable of heroic queens is less straightforward than it appears, and if we look further beneath its rhetoric it will reveal a good deal about the complexities of Jacobean ideology. On one level, it expresses erotic idealization through martial metaphors—an expansion of the sort of praise Othello gives Desdemona when he calls her his fair warrior. There is a perennial male fantasy behind this; its modern counterpart, at its crudest, idealizes women dressed in leather and spike heels. But the queen's masque, I have also been suggesting, embodies a political fantasy too, and is more a mirror of the king's mind than of the queen's. As such, it may be taken as a good example of absolutist mystification.

Jacobean chivalry is only superficially a revival of the Elizabethan mystique; beneath the surface the two are crucially different. In 1609, the royal ideology is no longer that of courtly love. For all the military chic of Inigo Jones's costumes, there is no suggestion in *The Masque of Queens* that the power of Bel-Anna and her Amazons derives in any way from their erotic attractions. Jonson's reformulation of the chivalric myth is, in its way, far more radically disarming than Elizabeth's had been. Elizabeth's version expressed a truth: much of the queen's power lay in her desirability as a wife, and for a good part of her reign her control over political factions derived significantly from her ability to treat their leaders as her suitors. Chivalry under King James was quite a different matter; for none of the power of the Jacobean monarchy inhered in the queen, and Jonson's chivalric metaphor in effect deprived Anne and her ladies of the only real source of authority they possessed—their status as desirable consorts. Female chivalry, in this new formulation, leaves male power unaffected: unmoved, unthreatened, uncompromised. As such, the mythology was ideally suited to the purposes of the king, by nature withdrawn and secretive, by ideology absolutist and patriarchal, programmatically pacifist, and far more attracted to men than to women.

Prince Henry too was interested in *The Masque of Queens,* but for different reasons. He asked Jonson for an annotated copy of the text, with detailed information about the poet's authorities. *Evidence* concerned this young man; he saw through the courtly compliment of his mother's masque to the historical reality of heroic examples. Jonson presented the prince with a beautiful manuscript in his own hand, anatomizing, in a way that is all but unique in English, the relation of a Renaissance poet to the sources of his invention. Jonson was as deeply concerned as the prince to establish the authority of his poetic fictions.

And when the chivalric ideology was adopted by Prince Henry, its implications were suddenly disturbing and subversive. Two years after *The Masque of Queens,* at New Year's 1611, he commissioned the masque of *Oberon* from Jonson and Inigo Jones. They presented him as a romantic hero, in a costume adapted from imperial Roman armor (fig. 5). James's heir had serious military ambitions, and the chivalric mode had now to do not with courtly love but with jousts and tilts, and ultimately with training and leading armies. By the age of fourteen, Henry's military interests were being noted throughout the country with excitement and admiration, making him in effect a powerful rival to the withdrawn and pacifist king. The prince's militant Protestantism was something that James, like Elizabeth before him, wanted no part of. The heroic persona that Jonson and Inigo Jones devised for Henry thus expressed not only ideals but intentions. If Elizabethan chivalry had been disarming, the chivalry of *Oberon* was a declaration of war, and King James did his best to counteract it. The prince had wanted his masque to culminate in barriers, martial games in which he could distinguish himself. But the king vetoed this proposal, and insisted that *Oberon* conclude instead with the dances and songs of courtly society. And as in *The Masque of Queens,* Jonson finally served the king: at the

4. King James presenting his *Works* to the University of Oxford, 1619; sculpture on
the Tower of the Five Orders in the Old Schools Quadrangle, Bodleian Library.

crucial moment of revelation, when Oberon at last appears in a chariot
drawn by two white bears, a chorus celebrates the prince's heroic ambi-
tion,

> Oberon's desire,
> Than which there nothing can be higher,
> Save James, to whom it flies:
> But he the wonder is of tongues, of ears, of eyes.
>
> (223–26)

The focus of admiration remains the king in the audience. *Oberon* is
thus a curiously double-edged work, creating for its ambitious young
protagonist an imperial persona, but disarming him at the same time.
James and Jonson contrive to transform the heroic assertions of *Oberon*
into the the subverted claims of *The Masque of Queens.* Henry, denied
his triumph on stage, pursued it in the political world, supporting his
sister's marriage to the Elector Palatine and proposing to follow her and
her husband to Bohemia at the head of a Protestant army. It was only his
sudden death in 1612, probably of typhoid fever, that ensured that the
heroic persona of his masque would never be translated into reality.
Queen Anne asserted till her dying day that her son had been poisoned.

## Notes

For references and valuable suggestions, I am indebted to David Riggs, to the
general editors, to an anonymous reader for the University of Chicago Press,
and, as always, to Jonathan Goldberg.

1. For a fuller discussion, see my "The Spectacles of State," in *Persons in
Groups,* ed. Richard Trexler (Binghampton, N.Y., 1985), pp. 109–21; for gener-
al accounts of the development of Elizabethan chivalry, see Roy Strong, *The
Cult of Elizabeth* (London: Thames and Hudson, 1977), and Frances Yates,
*Astraea* (London: Routledge, 1975).

2. The context of the painting is discussed in my "Shakespeare and the
Cannibals," in *Cannibals, Witches and Divorce,* ed. Marjorie Garber (Baltimore:
Johns Hopkins University Press, 1987), pp. 58–62. Roy Strong's indispensable
discussion elucidates the contemporary political dimensions of the painting,
which includes allusions to Sir Christopher Hatton and English imperial am-
bitions, but he sees Elizabeth as a new Aeneas, and is apparently unaware of the
tradition of the chaste Dido. See *Gloriana* (London: Thames and Hudson,
1987), pp. 95–107.

3. *Nugae Antiquae,* ed. Henry Harington and Thomas Park (London: J.
Wright, 1804), 1:395; the passage, with an enlightening discussion, is cited in
Jonathan Goldberg, *James I and the Politics of Literature* (Baltimore: Johns
Hopkins University Press, 1983), pp. 28ff.

5. Inigo Jones, Prince Henry's costume for *Oberon,* 1611.
Devonshire Collection, Chatsworth.

4. *Nugae Antiquae,* p. 360.

5. It is not known when Queen Anne formally converted, but whenever it was, it was done very quietly. To have become a Catholic before James was securely settled on the English throne would have been politically dangerous; nevertheless, she may have done so. In any case, her sympathies were always well known, and she refused to take the Anglican communion when she came to London as queen in 1603.

6. Lines 9–12; quotations are from *Ben Jonson: The Complete Masques,* ed. Stephen Orgel (Yale University Press, 1969).

7. Gloss on l. 36 (*Complete Masques,* p. 526).

8. Her name appears once as Agnis Sampson, apparently a misprint, though the association of witchcraft with the hero whose downfall came from his attraction to heathen and emasculating women is worth remarking.

9. Bodley Head Quarto (also including *Daemonologie*) ed. G. B. Harrison (London: John Lane, 1924), p. 15; the text has been modernized.

10. For a discussion of James's attacks on women as an index both to his relations with his mother and his sense of himself, see Jonathan Goldberg, *James I and the Politics of Literature* (Baltimore: Johns Hopkins University Press, 1983), pp. 24–25.

11. Cited in G. P. Akrigg, *Jacobean Pageant* (Cambridge, Mass.: Harvard University Press, 1963), p. 13.

12. *Newes from Scotland,* p. 17.

13. Ibid., p. 15.

14. Goldberg, *James I,* p. 16.

15. *Political Works of James I,* ed. C. H. McIlwain (Cambridge, Mass.: Harvard University Press, 1918), p. 272.

16. Ibid., p. 24.

17. Gloss on l. 346.

18. These were the three most influential iconologies and mythographies of the period; they are sometimes cited by Jonson, but were more often used by him simply as reference works, without acknowledgment. Cesare Ripa's *Iconologia* was first published in 1593 without illustrations; the first illustrated edition appeared in 1603. It appeared in innumerable editions and mutations thereafter, and was an essential resource until well into the eighteenth century. The *Mythologia* of Natalis Comes (or Conti) was issued first in 1551, in an enlarged edition in 1581, and frequently thereafter. Vincenzo Cartari's *Imagini,* the most popular of the Renaissance mythographies, appeared first in 1556, and in two dozen editions by the late seventeenth century.

19. Padua, 1611, pp. 537–40.

20. The story of Perseus appears in book 7, chapters 11 and 12 (Padua, 1616, pp. 390–95).

21. Padua, 1571, pp. 383ff.

22. Pp. 383–84.

23. The point is made in John Freccero's "Medusa: the Letter and the Spirit," *Yearbook of Italian Studies* 2 (1972): 1–18; see esp. p. 7.

24. G. P. Valeriano, *Hieroglyphica* 16.32 (Lyons, 1610, p. 165).

25. Nancy Vickers, "'The blazon of sweet beauty's best': Shakespeare's *Lucrece*," in *Shakespeare and the Question of Theory*, ed. Patricia Parker and Geoffrey Hartman (London: Methuen, 1985), p. 110. John Freccero's detailed and enlightening discussion of the figure in "Medusa: the Letter and the Spirit" has already been cited; see also Jonathan Goldberg's powerful and suggestive remarks in *Voice Terminal Echo* (London: Methuen, 1986), pp. 150–51, and Tobin Sievers, *The Mirror of Medusa* (Berkley: University of California Press, 1983), passim.

26. *Conversations with Drummond*, in C. H. Herford and P. Simpson, *Ben Jonson* (Oxford: Oxford University Press, 1925) 1:140, 139.

27. *Epigrams* 83, 84.

28. The documentary evidence is analyzed in Mark Eccles, "Jonson's Marriage," *Review of English Studies* 12, no. 47 (July 1936): 268.

29. *The Forest*, 1.

30. This is the earliest usage cited in the *OED;* "tribadree" appears in a MS poem addressed to Donne by "T. W." (Thomas Woodward?) dating from the mid-1590s (not recorded in the *OED*), printed in Milgate's edition of Donne's *Satires, Epigrams and Verse Letters* (Oxford: Oxford University Press, 1967), p. 212.

31. *The Forest* 10, lines 17, 25–29.

32. A classic version of this fantasy may be the source of Perseus's claim to be Fame's parent, "When Virtue cut off Terror he gat Fame." The mother of Fama in Virgil is *Terra*, the earth, who conceives Fama (i.e., rumor, spreading truth and falsehood indiscriminately), "monstrum horrendum, ingens," a horrible huge monster, in anger at the gods (*Aeneid* 4.174ff.).

33. *Complete Masques*, p. 547.

# II

# LITERARY THEORY AND THE TRANSMISSION OF THE TEXT

# 6

# Shakespeare's Sonnets as Literary Property

*Arthur F. Marotti*

In England prior to 1709 authors' property rights to the texts they produced were insecure. Official statutes and the regulations governing the Company of Stationers defined printers' or publishers' "copyright"—i.e. the right to print or reprint particular texts—and royal patents were granted to some printers to produce specific kinds of books (Common-Law texts, for example, being assigned to Richard Tottel). Authors, however, were left largely unprotected, having to rely upon their own (limited) abilities to control the dissemination of their writings and to derive direct or indirect economic benefits from them.[1]

In a system of manuscript circulation of literature, those into whose hands texts came could, in a real sense, "own" them: they could collect, alter, and transmit them. Recipients could treat lyric poems, for example, as prized possessions, could revise, expand, or answer them with poems of their own, and could decide to share them with friends and acquaintances. The large number of variants among the manuscript versions of some widely circulated poems testifies to the textual instability implicit in such circumstances. When a printer got hold of a work or a collection, he was free to enter it in the Stationer's Register for a small fee and thereafter claim the exclusive right to publish it (at least until such time as it went of print). *With or without authorial consent,* printers could take possession of literary property. Despite authors' sometimes disingenuous charges that printers were greedy and underhanded in acquiring texts for the press, social custom and the regulations governing the profession gave publishers wide latitude. Theirs were the financial risk *and* the economic rewards of publication. Authors might sell texts for modest sums and/or for complimentary copies of their books, but they were more likely to benefit economically from dedicating their works to patrons and patronesses than from any direct payments from publishers for their texts.[2] Thus writers tended to view print as a technology facilitating their exploitation of a patronage system to which they already had access than as a direct route to financial rewards. In publishing his sonnet sequence *Licia,* Giles Fletcher, for example, made it clear that the "favours" he hoped for from his dedicatee were his main object. He left the publisher to protect his own interests within the economics of the profession: "let the Printer look he grow not a begger by such bargaynes."[3]

Despite the decision to publish two narrative poems early in his career, *Venus and Adonis* and *Lucrece,* and despite their obvious market value—ten editions of the former by 1612—Shakespeare was not fundamentally a publishing professional poet; he was a professional actor, playwright, and theatrical shareholder. The published narrative poems happened to fall in a period in which theatrical activity was curtailed by the plague, a time when Shakespeare might have been hard pressed for money. He apparently cared little, however, about the production of accurate published texts: bibliographical evidence indicates that he failed to take the opportunity usually afforded to authors to check proofs at the printer's.[4] His attitude toward publication, therefore, differed sharply from that of his more scrupulous dramatist-contemporary, Ben Jonson, who saw some of the ways that print could give authors greater control over the texts they produced and enhance their own sociocultural status.

This study will concentrate on the status of Shakespeare's *Sonnets* as literary property from the time of their original composition through the first two-thirds of the seventeenth century. My larger purpose is to use the poems as a focus for a discussion of some of the ways literature itself was being institutionalized in the early modern era as print technology gradually redefined authorship, the roles of readers, and the character of texts. I emphasize the importance of the material means of their transmission in order to delineate sociocultural issues, for, as poems subjected to the processes of both manuscript circulation and publication in print, the sonnets have a revealing history. If we examine their status from the point of their initial (and subsequent) manuscript circulation, through their partial or complete publication in Jaggard's *The Passionate Pilgrim,* Thorpe's 1609 Quarto, and Benson's 1640 edition, we can see some of the ways that their shifting status as literary property implied changing conceptions of authorship, readership, and literary texts.

### The *Sonnets* and the Poetry of Patronage

The major portion of Shakespeare's sonnet collection consists of poems written to a younger man who is clearly treated as a patron. The context in which these sonnets should first be read is that of manuscript-circulated patronage poetry, a set of circumstances in which literary property was conceived of in different ways than it was in the culture of the book.

As I have argued elsewhere, the major crisis of the young-man sonnets occurs in those poems dealing with the favoring of a rival poet, an act the speaker of the sonnets treats as a serious betrayal that threatens to destroy the poetry's enabling conditions.[5] This episode highlights the terms of the patronage relationship, including the question of the sonnets' ownership. In contrast to the poems in the "dark lady" section of the 1609 Quarto (127–54), the poems to the young man constantly refer to themselves as commodities—texts in which the poet has a proprietary interest but which are offered as gifts and tribute to a patron who becomes, in effect, their owner. In dedicating *Lucrece* to the Earl of Southampton, Shakespeare had written: "What I have done is yours, what I have to do is yours, being part in all I have devoted yours."[6] In the literature of patronage, this statement is conventional—in fact, sometimes poets portray themselves as owned by their patrons:[7] the speaker in the young-man poems refers to himself as the "slave" (57.1), "servant" (57.8), and "vassal" (58.4) of the young man.[8]

Ceding property rights of texts to a patron, however, probably stimulated the poet to assert his own literary or creative ownership. In the young-man sonnets, he repeatedly refers to "my verse" (17.1, 19.4, 38.2, 60.13, 76.1, 78.2, 79.2, 81.9, 86.8, 105.7), asserting the quality and efficacy of his poetry. Revealingly, such assertions of proprietorship are virtually absent from the "dark lady" subsequence. Shakespeare does strike a pose of humility in denigrating his verse as literarily unremarkable: he refers to "my barren rhyme" (16.4), "These poor rude lines" (32.4), "my blunt invention" (103.7), "this poor rhyme" (107.11), characterizing his work as inferior to the virtuoso productions of an (aureate) poetical rival that make him into a "tongue-tied" (80.4, 85.1) competitor. But he alludes, with obvious pride, to his "muse" (38.1, 82.1, 85.1, 101.1, 103.1) and to "this powerful rhyme" (55.2), the verse that has the ability to immortalize the person he is complimenting: "to times in hope my verse shall stand, / Praising thy worth" (60.13–14); "Your monument shall be my gentle verse, / Which eyes not yet created shall o'er-read. . . . You still shall live—such virtue hath my pen" (81.9–10, 13); "thou in this shalt find thy monument, / When tyrants' crests and tombs of brass are spent" (107.13–14). All these statements underscore the value of his poems as objects worthy of being presented as gifts to a patron, even though (contradictorily) they depict the verse as a classical monument, as an artifact that has become public property.

Shakespeare characterizes the sonnets to the young man as "The barren tender of a poet's debt" (83.4), pieces to be sent to their addressee to maintain the patron-client relationship. When the poet apologizes in Sonnets 83, 100, 101, 102, and 103 for a drop in the rate of composing and sending such encomiastic pieces, chiding his "truant muse" (101.1) for the "poverty" it "brings forth" (103.1), he assumes that he owes his patron regular poetic tributes, having enjoyed his favor, as Sonnet 104 indicates, for some three years.[9] Sonnet 26, an epistolary poem, assumes that the patron's receptivity to such tributary verse is a precondition for its production:

> Lord of my love, to whom in vassalage
> Thy merit hath my duty strongly knit,
> To thee I send this written ambassage,
> To witness duty, not to show my wit.
> Duty so great, which wit so poor as mine
> May make seem bare, in wanting words to show it,
> But that I hope some good conceit of thine
> In thy soul's thought, all naked, will bestow it;
> Till whatsoever star that guides my moving
> Points on me graciously with fair aspect,
> And puts apparel on my tottered loving
> To show me worthy of thy sweet respect.
>     Then may I dare to boast how I do love thee;
>     Till then, not show my head where thou mayst prove me.

Unable to "show" his "head," that is, to appear in person before the addressee, because of his embarrassing status as a man "in disgrace with fortune" (29.1), the speaker of this poem sends "this written ambassage" or sonnet-epistle as the expression of "duty." Within its immediate socioliterary context, the poem is presented as literarily incomplete until it is perfected by the patron, who clothes its nakedness with the "good conceit" of a receptive reading, an act resembling a feudal lord's literal clothing of his vassal. This trope, which characterizes the primary reader as a poetic collaborator, is, of course, one of the features of the poetry of patronage, part of the deferential stance of the poet-client. By connecting the clothing metaphor of the addressee's "good conceit" with the "apparel" the speaker hopes to be put on his "tottered loving," he suggests that it is not merely from a "star that guides [his] moving" that he hopes for prosperity but from the patron himself. In the *quid pro quo* of such a relationship, compliments are offered to the addressee, but there are benefits expected in return. Such a poem, presented to a patron or patroness in either manuscript or printed form was conventionally portrayed as the property of the addressee.[10]

This sonnet-epistle calls attention to an original manuscript transmission of the sonnets to the young man. Although transcribed on separate sheets that may or may not have been kept in the poet's possession—Shakespeare refers to "my papers, yellow'd with their age" (17.9)[11]—the sonnets are presumed to be handwritten documents: "if you read this line, remember not / The hand that writ it" (71.5–6). It should be noted that the normal practice of English Renaissance poets writing verse on unbound sheets of paper was to compose on bifolia, in either quired or unquired form. This means that, instead of using separate small sheets, one per poem, it was likely that a poem had to share the space of a particular bifolium with other writing, perhaps other poems.[12] If, like Sidney and Donne, Shakespeare used bifolia in correspondence and sent poems along with letters or within letters to a patron, it is quite likely that more than one poem was sent at a time, given the amount of space available on the four sides of each folded sheet. Exercises in reordering Shakespeare's *Sonnets,* such as that undertaken by Brents Stirling, though probably futile as attempts to create aesthetically more convincing structures for the whole collection, highlight the obvious linking of a number of the sonnets in small subgroups.[13] This method of composition would certainly have suited epistolary transmission of such verse—and, interestingly, would have formed some legitimate basis for what John Benson did in his 1640 edition when he habitually conflated sonnets into units larger than the quatorzain.

However originally transmitted, the sonnets were collectible, of course, in the kind of table-book Sonnet 77 suggests was sent by the poet as a gift, a bound volume of blank pages to be used as a commonplace book by its owner:

> Thy glass will show thee how thy beauties wear,
> Thy dial how thy precious minutes waste;
> The vacant leaves thy mind's imprint will bear,
> And of this book this learning mayst thou taste.
> The wrinkles which thy glass will truly show,
> Of mouthed graves will give thee memory;
> Thou by thy dial's shady stealth mayst know
> Time's thievish progress to eternity.
> Look what thy memory cannot contain,
> Commit to these waste blanks, and thou shalt find

> Those children nursed, delivered from thy brain,
> To take a new acquaintance of thy mind.
> These offices, so oft as thou wilt look,
> Shall profit thee, and much enrich thy book.

In offering a "book" with "vacant leaves" or "waste blanks" to his patron, the poet hopes that the volume might be used as a help to "memory," that is, as the repository of valuable texts the owner might want to recall, normally prose sententiae and other writing of importance.[14] Of course, such a book also served as the collection point of verse in the system of manuscript transmission of poetry and Shakespeare might have been hinting that some of the texts he composed might be preserved in such a format. Perhaps if the sonnet itself were transcribed on the flyleaf of this table-book, such a use might have been encouraged. Certainly in Sonnet 122 the table-book the poet speaks of having received from his patron is presented as a convenient place in which to record the sonnets written to him:

> Thy gift, thy tables, are within my brain
> Full charactered with lasting memory,
> Which shall above that idle rank remain
> Beyond all date even to eternity,—
> Or at the least, so long as brain and heart
> Have faculty by nature to subsist—
> Till each to razed oblivion yield his part
> Of thee, thy record never can be missed.
> That poor retention could not so much hold,
> Nor need I tallies thy dear love to score.
> Therefore to give them from me was I bold,
> To trust those tables that receive thee more.
> To keep an adjunct to remember thee
> Were to import forgetfulness in me.
> (Sonnet 122)

Affirming that the "tables" of the poet's brain are a better place in which to preserve the young man's "lasting memory" than the physical pages of a book, the poem cleverly makes an excuse for lending out the patron's valued present, a volume into which, it suggests, was transcribed a "record" of him. This would have been just the sort of manuscript in which a holograph copy of part or all of the sonnet collection might have been made.

In one of the few manuscripts in which the text of a Shakespearean sonnet is preserved, we can detect what might have been a textual vicissitude following an initial stage of manuscript transmission. In a seventeenth-century commonplace book found in the Rosenbach Library, there is a version of Shakespeare's Sonnet 106 that begins "When in the Annales of all-wasting time" (instead of "When in the chronicle of wasted time") an alternate version that appears, as well, in at least one other manuscript.[15] Here, however, the poem is conflated with the text of a lyric that is found also, in slightly different form, in the 1660 poetical anthology pretending to be an edition of the poems of Pembroke and Rudyerd:

> When mine eyes first admiring of your beauty
> Secretly stole the picture of your face
> They fearing they might erre, with humble duty
> Through vnknowne pathes convayd it to that place
> Where reason & true judgment hand in hand
> Sate, and each workmanship of sences scand:
> Reason could find noe reason but to loue it
> Soe rich of beauty was it, full of grace
> True iudgment scand each part & did approue it
> To be the modell of some heauenly face
> And both agreed to place it in my hart
> Where they decreed it neuer should depart,
> Then since I was not borne to be soe blest
> Your reall selfe faire mistris to obtaine
> Yet must your image dwele within my brest
> And in that secrett closett still remaine,
> Where all alone retyrde, Ile sit and view
> Your picture Mistress, since I may not you.[16]

Although ascriptions in the 1660 Pembroke and Rudyerd edition are unreliable and the lyric, unlike many of the others in the collection, is not preceded by a "P." or "R." identifying those two authors, it is quite possible that the poem was written by William Herbert, Earl of Pembroke, who is, of course, one of the two main candidates proposed as Shakespeare's young patron.[17] If so, this piece may be that author's competitive handling of the same topic as Sonnet 106—perhaps a lyric sent in response to Shakespeare's poem.[18] Even if the manuscript addition were not composed in such circumstances, it is interesting that the Pembroke poem came to be conflated with Sonnet 106. The two separate lyrics could have been combined either deliberately or accidentally at almost any point in the transmission process. If deliberately, this would have been a typical expression of the freedom that collectors of verse had in a system of manuscript transmission. In such circumstances, Shakespeare's sonnet was not being treated like a sacred text, but as a found-object capable of being put to a number of rhetorical uses. Even if the poems were conflated accidentally, through a copyist's error, they might have been contiguous in the source-text. However tantalizing the Pembroke connection, the important thing to note is the way in which this particular act of textual manipulation was not at all unusual outside the environment of print.[19]

Within the circumstances of manuscript-circulated poetry, the young-man sonnets, then, had complex status as literary property: they belonged properly to the poet, to the patron, and as well to anyone into whose hands the poems fell. The lyrics could have existed in several forms in manuscript—in the bifolia " foul papers" of the author, either separately quired or bound in multiple quires into a larger volume, in letters, or as bifolia sheets of verse sent along with correspondence to an addressee, in table-books or commonplace books owned by the patron and by the poet himself, the poet's volume perhaps having been loaned to others. In addition, poems such as the first seventeen sonnets, which it has been plausibly suggested might have been verse commissioned for an occasion such as a young aristocrat's seventeenth birthday, would have been transcribed in fair copy by either the poet himself, or, more likely, by a professional scribe.

## The Passionate Pilgrim and the Circulation
## of the Sonnets in Manuscript

If some of the 154 sonnets of the 1609 Quarto circulated in manuscript in the 1590s among Shakespeare's "priuate friends," as Francis Meres stated,[20] they were more likely to have been those from the "dark lady" section of the collection than from the young-man one. It is not surprising that Jaggard's *The Passionate Pilgrim* (1599) contains versions of two poems from the "dark lady" subsequence and no poem from the young-man section of the sonnet collection. The "dark lady" poems, as verse lacking the social exclusiveness of the more private encomiastic sonnets to the young man, might well have circulated more freely in a social milieu in which an opportunistic printer like William Jaggard would have been hunting for poems to print that were written by the author of the popular *Venus and Adonis* and *Lucrece*.

The difference between the Jaggard versions of Sonnets 138 and 144 and the texts of these poems in the Quarto raises the issue that has received so much recent attention, that of Shakespeare's practices of revision.[21] Gary Taylor has argued that the (admittedly skimpy) manuscript evidence points to Shakespeare's having revised some of the sonnets. In his interesting study of the texts of Sonnet 2 found in various seventeenth-century commonplace books, Taylor claims that the large number of variants between the two major versions of the poem most likely results from Shakespeare's having changed the text between the time of its original composition and the publication of the 1609 Quarto version. Although only a few Shakespearean sonnets found their way into seventeenth-century commonplace books—a situation that contrasts with that of the poetry of Ralegh, Jonson, Donne, and most other contemporaries—Taylor argues that the manuscript variants from the 1609 Quarto texts are not simply the result of errors introduced in the transmission process but derive from different authorial versions of poems that circulated separately in manuscript.[22] But, although we may never know whether Shakespeare actually revised particular poems, it is quite likely that some textual variants were produced by the process of transmission to which they were subjected.

The sonnets printed in *The Passionate Pilgrim,* for example, show signs of having passed through some of the forms of unconscious revision J. B. Leishman has associated with the custom of transcribing poems from memory.[23] It is revealing to compare the text of Sonnet 138 in *The Passionate Pilgrim* and the 1609 Quarto text with the possibility of memorial transcription in mind.[24] In the practice of transcribing poems from memory, several marks of the process distinguish the resulting texts from those affected by copyist errors. Foremost among these are the substitution of common expressions or clichés for unusual verbiage, the replacement of syntactic convolutions by simpler structures, and the regularization of meter. Interestingly, these very features mark the adaptation of poems for song-settings. Phrases like "false forgeries" (4) and "a soothing toung" (11) in Jaggard's edition (for "false subtilties" and "in seeming trust" in the 1609 Quarto) look like formulaic expressions substituted for forgotten original language. The end rhyme "toung" in the Jaggard version, of course, dictates the rhyme change in line 9, where the phrase "my Loue that she is young" is found instead of "she not she is vnjust" of the Quarto, a nonsensical version, since the mistress's age is not at issue in the poem, but rather her honesty. In line 7 of the Jaggard version, the words "I smiling" for "Simply I" syntactically regularize the poetically inverted formulation found in the Quarto version. A comparison of the two versions of line 13 of Sonnet 144 reveals a similar syntactical smoothing: "The truth I shall not know" (Jaggard) instead of "Yet this shal I nere know" (Quarto). The final couplet of Jaggard's version of Sonnet 138 may have been the result of the repression of the more sexually explicit and morally sharper language of the text that appears in the Quarto. "Therefore I'le lye with Loue, and loue with me" is generalized, while "Therefore I lye with her, and she with me" is unmistakably specific, the latter fully exploiting the pun on the word "lie." The final line of the text in *The Passionate Pilgrim,* "Since that our faults in Loue thus smother'd be," is much less morally forceful a way of ending the poem than is "And in our faults by lies we flatter'd be." Hallett Smith says of the last two lines of the *Passionate Pilgrim* version of Sonnet 138: "I think this is clearly a memorial reconstruction and that it is absurd to suppose that this is an early draft which Shakespeare later revised."[25]

If some of the expressions in *The Passionate Pilgrim* sonnets are the result of alterations made in the transmission process rather than Shakespearean originals later revised to produce the text that was published in the 1609 Quarto and if, specifically, these variations are best accounted for by the transcription of texts from memory, then the question of authorship of the Jaggard versions of Sonnets 138 and 144 is a vexed one. These poems, like folk ballads, might have had a kind of composite or communal authorship, creatively appropriated by someone or some persons other than Shakespeare, traveling through the memories and pens of others. The transformation of Sonnet 116 into a song-text by Henry Lawes is an analogous phenomenon, but it is an example of conscious alteration of a Shakespearean text.[26] Nonetheless, it is odd that, in the case of an author whose plays were presumed to have passed through the unreliable memories of actors into "bad quartos" produced by unscrupulous printers, the possibility that these two Jaggard sonnets could have been similarly "corrupted" has not been seriously entertained. Before the Quarto, before Jaggard's book, at least some of Shakespeare's *Sonnets* were in the system of literary transmission, their texts open to deliberate and accidental alteration by those with access to them.

Despite the association of his and his son Isaac's name with the First Folio of Shakespeare's plays, William Jaggard has hardly enjoyed a favorable reputation among bibliographers and textual critics for publishing *The Passionate Pilgrim,* a work presented in the 1599 edition and through one of the two title pages of the 1612 edition as a collection of poems by William Shakespeare. Jaggard has been the target of criticism not only for the economic opportunism that led him to pirate authentic Shakespearean lyrics but also for the fraudulent presentation of the whole volume as Shakespeare's work. He was, thus, guilty of the deception practiced by Richard Jones, who presented another poetical miscellany under the guise of a single-author collection, *Britton's Bowre of Delights,* a work to which the wronged Nicholas Breton publicly objected.[27] After Jaggard added poems to the original thin miscellany in the edition of 1612 and persisted in using a title page ascribing all the contents of the collection to Shakespeare, Thomas Heywood, nine of whose poems from *Troia Britanica* (1609) were appropriated by Jaggard, vehemently objected in the epistle to the printer appended to the contemporary publication of *An Apology for Actors* to the inclusion of two of his heroical epistles in the volume, an act that left him vulnerable to the charge of plagiarism. Referring to the 1612 edition of *The Passionate Pilgrim,* he wrote: "I must necessarily insert a manifest injury done me in that worke, by taking the two Epistles of *Paris* to *Helen,* and *Helen* to *Paris,* and printing them in a lesse volume, vnder the name of another, which may put the world in opinion I might steale them from him: and hee to doe himself right, hath since published them in his owne name: but as I must acknowledge my lines not worthy his patronage, vnder whom he hath publisht them, so the Author I know much offended with M. Jaggard that (altogether vnknowne to him) presumed to make so bold with his name."[28] In complaining about the misattribution of his work, Heywood goes out of his way to pay tribute to Shakespeare as a superior poet whose "name" or reputation deserved respect. Whether or not Heywood was accurate in reporting Shakespeare's own annoyance at Jaggard, it appears that the objection had at least the effect of forcing the substitution of a new title page that omits Shakespeare's name. Hyder Rollins speculates that "Shakespeare or his friends" brought the pressure that forced the cancellation of the original title page and the production of the new one. If so, this reveals Shakespeare's sensitivity not to the literary pirating of his works but to the misattribution of the work of others to him that left either him or Heywood open to the charge of plagiarism, that is, to a violation of an author's creative proprietorship.[29]

If we look beyond the issues of piracy and fraud to examine the text of *The Passionate Pilgrim* as evidence concerning Shakespeare's activities as a sonneteer before the publication of the 1609 Quarto, several facts stand out. First, some Shakespearean sonnets were circulating in the mid-to-late 1590s, at least two of which were in texts differing from the 1609 versions. Second, aside from the sonnets from the plays (two from *Loves Labour's Lost* reproduced in Jaggard's volume), Shakespeare might have composed sonnets other than those appearing in the Quarto collection—for example those Venus and Adonis sonnets in Jaggard that some scholars have identified as Shakespeare's, pieces that might have contributed to contemporary impressions of him as an Ovidian poet.[30] Third (and this is a point crucial to this discussion), the sonnets were easily able to be incorporated in the context of a miscellany or poetical anthology. Fourth, Shakespeare's name as a author was becoming important as a cultural phenomenon and *The Passionate Pilgrim* was thus an important text in terms of the literary institutionalization of Shakespeare's works.

Although, like Richard Jones, Jaggard deceptively presents the whole collection of verse as the work of a single author, what he was doing in printing the Shakespeare poems and mixing them with the verse of other writers was quite legitimate. He might have found the pieces, in fact, in a manuscript commonplace-book miscellany and mistakenly believed the whole collection to be a Shakespearen one. Such manuscript-circulated verse was ready to be appropriated by enterprising publishers and it is a historical mistake for modern critics to express outrage for such a publishing practice as the printing of works without an author's permission. There was absolutely no legal or moral need for Jaggard to have sought Shakespeare's cooperation in printing the texts he obtained. Jaggard had property rights to the texts he printed even though he did not enter his publication in the Stationers' Register. The misrepresentation of the whole collection as Shakespearean is another issue, a question, first, of truth in advertising (a concept one could not comfortably apply in the early era of print), and, second, of the status of authorship as a cultural sign.

In a period in which personal authorship was taking on new meaning and there was some cultural, though not strict legal, acknowledgment of authors' creative ownership of the texts they produced—one of the effects of the Gutenberg revolution[31]—identifying Shakespeare as the author of all the poems of *The Passionate Pilgrim* was a strategy to invest the works with a special value the publisher hoped to exploit economically even as he acknowledged the importance of a living author. It would seem to be no mere coincidence that Jaggard's 1599 publication came shortly after the first appearance of Shakespeare's name on the title pages of play quartos, the 1598 editions of *Richard II* and *Richard III*. Whereas earlier quartos of the same plays as well as those of plays such as *Titus Andronicus* and *Romeo and Juliet* did not call attention to authorship—and, we should also note, Shakespeare's name was missing from the title pages of *Venus and Adonis* and *Lucrece*—his name began to have commercial value about the time that Jaggard produced his anthology: in the same year, the quarto of *Henry IV, Part I* alleged that this previously published play was "Newly corrected by W. Shakespeare." Obviously, Shakespeare's reputation as both dramatist and poet made his identity as author economically valuable: but, more to the point of this discussion, the name itself, within the medium of print, began to take on a cultural authority that authors began more deliberately to seek in the early modern period,[32] an improving status that gradually strengthened the authorial property rights that the 1709 statute belatedly acknowledged in law.

## Thomas Thorpe's 1609 Quarto of *Shake-speares Sonnets*

Thomas Thorpe called his 1609 Quarto *Shake-speares Sonnets* rather than giving it a title alluding to a love object (*Laura* or *Diana*, for example) or to a fictional amorous relationship (*Astrophil and Stella, Parthenophil and Parthenophe*). The poems seem to have been presented as texts that were in demand but, until Thorpe was able to lay hold of them for publication, unavailable to a general readership. By contrast, the authorized (1592) edition of Daniel's sonnets has a title page without the author's name, "*Delia. Contayning certayne Sonnets: with the complaint of Rosamond.*" Conversely, Newman's 1591 unauthorized edition of Sidney's sonnet sequence used that poet's easily understood initials for promotion purposes, "*Syr P. S. his Astrophel and Stella.*" Given the fact that title pages of books were used by publishers as advertising posters,[33] it is understandable that a publisher wishing to promote the sale of a text whose potential popularity rested on the reputation of a particular writer would want to call attention to authorship.

I agree with the majority of bibliographers that Thorpe's Quarto was an unauthorized publication. Were it, as Katherine Duncan-Jones argues,[34] an authorially sanctioned edition of the *Sonnets,* it would probably have had, like *Venus and Adonis* and *Lucrece,* an author's dedicatory epistle or perhaps, instead, his letter to readers. The printer's cryptic epigraphal dedication to "Mr. W. H." makes it appear that, as happened in earlier examples of printers' publishing works without authorial consent, the printer, not the author, was the one who intended to benefit from the typographical presentation of this body of poetry.

The whole collection of poems in Thorpe's 1609 Quarto does not really constitute a sonnet sequence in the way that, say, the poems of Sidney's *Astrophil and Stella* and Spenser's *Amoretti* do.[35] They do not, like most other contemporary sonnet collections, tell a love story, but seem, in fact, to resist doing so.[36] Like Greville's *Caelica,* the separate poems of which were evidently designed for coterie manuscript circulation rather than print, Shakespeare's sonnets are a heterogeneous collection. It is obvious that the poems written in the context of patronage belonged to a socioliterary situation distinct from that of the miscellaneous poems found in the "dark lady" section of the collection. As sonnets presented as gifts or tributes, they would have fit within the social conditions of an ongoing relationship with a benefactor, but such a situation is conceived as a timeless one, changed only by being broken or altered significantly by the patron himself, as the rival-poet crisis indicates. The only potentially narrative aspects of the young-man sonnets are the addressee's affair with the poet's mistress and the rival-poet episode, the former portrayed as doing no real damage to the patronage relationship. Significantly, in the sonnets following the rival-poet poems in the Quarto, the poet resumes the strategy of praise (albeit with a stronger sense of the young man's imperfections): it is as though there is only a status quo to be maintained and one either repeats the same encomiastic gestures indefinitely or ceases writing to the addressee.

The collection of 126 poems to the young man seem distinct structurally as well as socioliterarily from the more miscellaneous poems that fill out the collection. However, the "dark lady" poems, which might have dramatized the stages of a courtship or affair, also seem narratively stagnant. They seem as stuck in the poetics of blame as the other poems are in the poetics of praise. Like other manuscript-circulated verse in this period, they appear to have relied upon the social context in which they were composed and transmitted, if not specifically upon their primary audience's knowledge of the particular circumstances that generated them. Though some 17 of the poems of this section define the "dark lady" as addressee, 9 others, including the thematically general Sonnets 129 and 146, exist outside this rhetorical framework.[37] In addition, the Anacreontic final two poems, which look like alternate renditions of the same material, contrast tonally with the harsh realism with which the preceding poems treat heterosexual love. They look like pieces composed (and possibly circulated) in circumstances other than the ones surrounding the affair with the "dark lady." Finally, because the young man's involvement with the "dark lady" is also treated in this section of the sequence, Sonnets 126–54 obviously overlap chronologically with Sonnets 1–126, rather than following these poems, even though they were probably directed to another audience.

If Thorpe published Shakespeare's *Sonnets* without the cooperation of their author, there is a strong probability that the arrangement of the poems is, to some extent, his. It looks like someone made the effort to comply with the conventions of published sonnet sequences in setting forth the collection. Most obviously, the Anacreontic tailpieces and the appended "A Lover's Complaint" bring the edition into line with some of the sonnet collections of the 1590s. Consecutive numbering of the sonnets hides the fact that the young-man lyrics are a poor fit with the more miscellaneous verse of the "dark lady" section of the collection. As scholars have noted, Sonnet 126 marks a boundary in the work: this six-couplet lyric, to which Thorpe added paired parentheses probably because he thought it lacked the final two lines that would have made it a sonnet, serves as an envoy to the first 125-poem unit, after which the rest of the poems look like a separate, if related, collection.

Thorpe was free, of course, to print any poetical texts he obtained and to arrange them as he saw fit. Once Shakespeare's *Sonnets* were in the hands of a publisher, however, they were affected in their typographical presentation by printing-house practices. The sonnets were subjected, as MacDonald P. Jackson has shown, to the differing spelling and punctuation habits of the two compositors involved in the production of the 1609 Quarto.[38] In addition, Jackson offers good evidence that one of the compositors was prone to errors of "memorial substitution," a situation which produced, as he notes, "the notorious crux in 146.2, 'My sinfull earth these rebell powres that thee array.' "[39] Judging from the errors introduced in Benson's later edition, whose type was set from printed texts, the Thorpe edition of the *Sonnets,* which was typeset from a manuscript (or manuscripts), probably has even more errors than the obvious ones detected by textual scholars. Its text is a product of the vicissitudes of the printing-house, not a magical typographical translation of Shakespeare's handwritten papers.

Thorpe's Quarto, as the two surviving forms of the title page indicate, was meant to have been sold by two different booksellers, William Aspley and John Wright. It was released at a time in which new editions of *Venus and Adonis* and *Lucrece* were on the market and good and bad quartos of plays were for sale with the dramatist's name conspicuously on the title pages—for example, "*Mr. William Shak-speare his true chronicle historie of the life and death of king Lear and his three daughters*" (1608), "*The late, and much admired play, called Pericles, prince of Tyre.* By William Shakespeare" (1609), a new edition of *Romeo and Juliet* (1607), and even the apocryphal "*The London prodigall.* As it was plaide by the kings maiesties seruants. By W. Shakespeare" (1605). In this commercial context, "*Shake-speares Sonnets* . . . Neuer before Imprinted" should have been hot literary property.

Only in the eyes of modern critics who assume that Shakespeare's contemporaries would have treasured a publication like Thorpe's enough to preserve it carefully for posterity is it strange that only about a dozen copies of the 1609 Quarto would have survived. Thus the speculation that somehow the edition must have been called in after the author, with the help of powerful friends, took steps to have it suppressed. But it is obvious that, in comparison with other poetical pamphlets appearing in quarto form, the disappearance of all but a few copies of this edition is far from atypical: in fact, twelve surviving copies is, by some measures, an unusually large number.[40] The STC lists considerably fewer copies of Newman's first 1591 edition of Sidney's *Astrophil and Stella,* of the 1595 edition of Spenser's *Amoretti and Epithalamion,* and of the 1592 edition of Daniel's *Delia.* The fact of the matter is that "*Shake-speares Sonnets*" was a poetical pamphlet whose status as a book was ephemeral, given the casual manner in which short quartos were treated. However many copies were printed—and chances are that they numbered no more than 800 to 1,000[41]—their survival rate was not apt to be very high.

We need to recognize the difference between both folio and octavo publication of literary works, on the one hand, and quarto publication of poetical pamphlets or play texts, on the other. To take the latter first, one needs to recall that small-scale publications of poetry and drama in quarto, sold usually unbound by booksellers, were not very durable. Whereas obviously folio publication was reserved for serious and important works meant to be preserved in personal libraries or collections, and whereas substantial octavo publications were, even in bound form, both portable and preservable, short quartos, often apt to remain unbound, were peculiarly perishable. Hence the loss of so many copies of quarto publications, many of which, like the poetical miscellanies of which Hyder Rollins writes, were "literally read out of existence."[42] As T. A. Birrell remarks in an interesting article on some of the effects of book size on the presentation and preservation of literature, "The text of a play in quarto averages out at about thirty or forty leaves. Not only is it unsuitable for the pocket, it will not stand up by itself on the bookshelf, for it was issued unbound, probably not even stiched, but roughly stabbed with string or thread. After it was read it lay around, the top leaf and the bottom leaf got dirty and torn, then the string broke, and it distintegrated and was thrown away. It was, to coin a phrase, a self-destructing artefact."[43] Thorpe's quarto of *"Shake-speares Sonnets"* was evidently such a "self-destructing artefact"—an idea that is difficult for us to accept, given our archaeological affection for this volume.

## Benson's 1640 Edition of Shakespeare's Poems

Because of the modern tendency to treat printed poetical texts as sacred objects, John Benson has been condemned for disturbing the order of the 1609 Quarto and the integrity of the individual sonnets in his 1640 augmented edition of "POEMS: / WRITTEN / BY / WIL. SHAKE-SPEARE. / Gent." He has been criticized for reordering the poems, for freely conflating sonnets into larger poetic units, for omitting poems that appeared in the 1609 Quarto, for reproducing verse from the 1612 edition of *The Passionate Pilgrim* he should have known was written by other authors, and for mixing Shakespeare's work with that of other writers. If we look at what Benson did, however, in the context of the more liberal practices of the early stages of the print era, his edition looks less like a felonious assault on the Shakespearean canon. In the context of contemporary social and professional practices, Benson was free to take possession of the text of Shakespeare's *Sonnets* for publication and to arrange the poems as he saw fit. Not only was he well within his rights as a publisher, but also he was exercising the kind of creative control over acquired texts that collectors, editors, and printers had in this period.[44]

Benson's edition is presented within the context of making all of Shakespeare's works available to the book-buying public. In the publisher's letter to the reader, Benson assumes that literary consumers who had access through the First (1623) and Second (1632) Folios to Shakespeare's plays and through the continuing editions of *Venus and Adonis* and *Lucrece* to some of his poetry, would be grateful for the opportunity to purchase an edition of the remaining verse not currently in print:

> I Here presume (under favour) to present to your view, some excellent and sweetely composed Poems, of Master William Shakespeare, Which in themselves appeare of the same purity, the Authour himselfe then living avouched; they had not the fortune by reason of their Infancie in his death, to have the due accommodatio[n] of proportionable glory, with the rest of his everliving Workes, yet the lines of themselves will afford you a more authentick approbation than my assurance any way can, to invite your allowance, in your perusall you shall fine them Seren, cleere, and eligantly plaine, such gentle straines as shall recreate and not perplexe your braine, no intricate or cloudy stuffe to puzzell intellect, but perfect eloquence, such as will raise your admiration to his praise: this assurance I know will not differ from your acknowledgement. And certaine I am, my opinion will be seconded by the sufficiency of these ensuing lines; I have been somewhat solicitus to bring this forth to the perfect view of all men; and in so doing, glad to be serviceable for the continuance of glory to the deserved Author in these his Poems.[45]

Benson bardolatrously offers his volume as the completion of *The Complete Works of William Shakespeare,* as it were. Despite what critics have assumed, he did not actually say that the *Sonnets* had never been published—after all, Thorpe's quarto was evidently one of his copy-texts—but that they lacked the "due accommodatio[n] of proportionable glory, with the rest of his everliving Workes," that is they were not in print in a format that was suitable for preserving the poems for succeeding generations.[46] Benson would have regarded neither the quartos of the plays ("good" or "bad"), nor the quarto of the *Sonnets,* nor the relatively skimpy editions of Jaggard's *The Passionate Pilgrim* as a fit medium in which to present the works of so respected an author as Shakespeare. He probably believed that, in producing an octavo of considerable bulk, he was doing for the poetry what the First and Second Folios did for the drama, presenting Shakespearean texts (whether or not published previously) in a form worthy of that author, one able to be esteemed by a book-buying public.

As part of the strategy of attracting a clientele for his edition of the poetry, Benson portrays Shakespeare as an eloquent but plain, and therefore accessible, author—not the polyvocal poet of the carnivalesque notes to Stephen Booth's edition. He contrasts him with those writers who "perplexe [the] braine" or "puzzell [the] intellect," a poet like Donne, for example, the 1633 edition of whose poetry contains an elegiac poem emphasizing his complexity and difficulty.[47] Benson asserts the same claim the editors of the Folio made about the text of their publication, that it was the corrected authentic version of the works, "of the same purity, the Authour himselfe then living avouched." Just as Heminge and Condell maintained they took play-texts that had been "maimed, and deformed by the frauds and stealthes by iniurious imposters" and presented them to readers "cur'd, and perfect of their limbes,"[48] so Benson seems to assert, when he says he was "somewhat solicitus to bring this [edition of the poetry] forth to the perfect view of all men," that he is offering readers the best texts of Shakespeare's verse. Finally, and it has direct bearing on the changing relationship of authors and publishers, he adopts a role of subservience to the deceased author, presenting himself as "serviceable for the continuance of glory to the deserved Author in these his Poems," a role analogous to the poet's in immortalizing the young man of the *Sonnets.*

Despite the pose of humility, Benson aggressively exercised his rights as an editor-publisher. And, despite the negative response to his actions on the part of modern scholars, we must recognize that he was not violating accepted norms in doing what he did. He made an honest effort to gather as much of Shakespeare's poetry as he could find (with the exception of the two narrative poems). Thus, he took the (expanded) 1612 edition of Jaggard's *The Passionate Pilgrim,* Thorpe's 1609 Quarto of *Shake-speares Sonnets* (including "A Lover's Complaint"), and Chester's *Loves Martyr* (containing "The Phoenix and the Turtle") as the main copy-texts for his collected edition of the verse, either uncritically accepting the non-Shakespearean poems in Jaggard as Shakespeare's or following that editor in deliberately supplementing authentically Shakespearean works with the work of other poets.[49] Benson concluded the Shakespearean part of his anthology with a lyric from Fletcher's *The Bloody Brother,* the first stanza of which appears in *Measure for Measure* ("Take, O take those lippes away"), "The Phoenix and the Turtle" and "Threnes" from *Loves Martyr,* a song from *As You Like It* ("Why should this Desart be"), Milton's epitaph on Shakespeare from the 1632 Folio, William Basse's popular epitaph on Shakespeare, and an anonymous elegy on Shakespeare. The last part of the volume, which Benson entered separately in the Stationers' Register,[50] is headed "An Addition of some Excellent Poems, to those precedent, of Renowned *Shakespeare,* By other Gentlemen," twenty-one pages of verse by such authors as Jonson, Beaumont, Herrick, Strode, Cartwright, and Carew.

But Benson did not merely collect verse for his volume. He creatively exercised his prerogatives as an editor to produce a poetical anthology that was, in effect, a new literary artifact. In the body of Benson's edition, 146 of the sonnets that appear in the Quarto are conflated into 72 poems, ranging from one to five sonnets each. Each of these is presented with a title presumably invented by the editor. Some of the conflations obviously work well thematically, as in the case of the two composite poems with which the Shakespearean collection begins, "The glory of beautie" (Sonnets 67, 68, 69) and "Injurious Time" (Sonnets 60, 63, 64, 65, 66). Since, for example, Sonnets 61 and 62 do not merge well with the adjacent poems incorporated in this second lyric, Benson did well to print them separately.[51] Some conflated poems, however, make less sense. In "The benefit of Friendship," Benson includes Sonnets 30, 31, and 32, even though the last of these is a poor thematic fit with the first two. Similarly, "A Congratulation" awkwardly fuses Sonnet 40 with the more obviously related Sonnets 38 and 39. Margreta De Grazia is right to note that Benson conceives of the sonnets as *typical* renditions of amorous experience, fine rhetorical examples of how one might handle traditional poetic themes. Thus Benson did what other English publisher-editors did back to the time of Richard Tottel's famous miscellany: he took verse that originally had specific social coordinates and handled it as conventional lyric utterances within the context of the usual literary depiction of amorous experience. The titles of many of the poems reveal this generalizing process—e.g. "The glorie of beautie," "True admiration," "Loves crueltie," "Happiness in content," and "In prayse of his Love." Other titles designate familiar lyric topics and kinds: "A Valediction" (Sonnets 71, 72, 74), "A Resignation" (Sonnets 86 and 87), "Complaint for his Loves absence" (Sonnets 97, 98, 99), "An Invocation to his Muse" (Sonnets 100, 101). Poems are treated as lyric models in a literary history in which Shakespeare participated, not as language bound to actual social occasions or issuing directly from the emotional depths of their author.[52] Their typicality, not their uniqueness, installs them in the institution of literature, despite the special reverence accorded their author.

Benson, as is well known, felt free to change a number of the gender references in the sonnets to make it appear that most of the young-man poems were addressed to a woman. Clearly he freely appropriated the texts to rewrite them in this way just as he created new conflated poems out of separately numbered sonnets from Thorpe's quarto. But, he did not have to do much to the texts of the sonnets themselves to create the impression that most of the poems were heterosexual love poems. Some of the juxtapositions in the reordered collection did this work for him. For example, after printing the *The Passionate Pilgrim* versions of Sonnets 138 and 144 (poems from the "dark lady" section of the *Sonnets*), he sandwiched in three separately printed sonnets (21, 23, 22) before returning to *The Passionate Pilgrim* to pick up two more poems obviously addressed to a female beloved. In context, the three sonnets, entitled "True content," "A bashfull Lover," and "Strong conceite," look like heterosexual love poems. Titles also identify a female beloved for some of the young-man sonnets: for example, "Selfe flattery of her beautie" (Sonnets 113, 114, 115), "Vpon the receit of a Table Booke from his Mistris" (Sonnet 122), and "An intreatie for her acceptance" (Sonnet 125). After the last of these poems, Benson omits the envoy poem (Sonnet 126) and continues with "Vpon her playing on the Virginalls" (Sonnet 128), "Immoderate Lust" (Sonnet 129), and "In prayse of her beautie though black" (Sonnets 127, 130, 131, 132), creating the impression that the female referent of the pronouns is the same in each case. The very typicality of some of the other titles, which evokes the context of traditional amorous verse, is enough to maintain the fiction of a female addressee of most of the poems.

Although Benson's arrangement of the poems in his edition makes less aesthetic sense than that found in Thorpe's quarto, the very fact of reordering bespeaks this editor's free manipulatation of the literary property in his hands. Especially since Benson's text became the standard form in which Shakespeare's *Sonnets* were printed until Malone's edition some century and a half later, this arrangement of the sonnets and the interspersing of the poems from *The Passionate Pilgrim* should not be dismissed as a momentary aberration. Although at certain points Benson's procedure of alternating between Thorpe's and Jaggards' texts caused him to omit some poems unintentionally,[53] some of the sections of the collection work well as groups of poems—for example, the 30 sonnets presented in the 11 poems at the start. In the absence of reader expectations for the types of aesthetic order found in the sonnet sequences published in the 1590s, Benson could adopt the looser plan of the collector-anthologizer, even to the point of deciding to augment the main Shakespearean (and pseudo-Shakespearean) part of the volume with the poems of other authors. In this kind of publication, Shakespeare's versatility as a poet stood out.

What is happening in Benson's text is that Shakespeare's *Sonnets* are being incorporated in a developing literary institution within which authorship, texts, and the role of readers are being redefined. The process of literary institutionalization in which Benson's text participated is one in which authorship took on new meaning in the context of print culture, particularly in those editions that presented the collected works of individual authors as cultural monuments. Benson was out for profit, of course, to exploit the market for works by an author whose name guaranteed sales—but the project he undertook was of a piece with other late sixteenth- and early seventeenth-century projects such as the 1598 Sidney Folio, the 1616 and 1640 Jonson Folios, the 1623 edition of Daniel's collected works, the posthumous publication of Donne's and Herbert's poetry in 1633, and the 1632 edition of Greville. Clearly, in the context of such monumental publishing projects, the 1609 Quarto of the sonnets was not a book worthy of Shakespeare. It was not available for purchase in the 1630s, so Benson's augmented text could lay claim to providing readers access to Shakespearean works they could not buy. It was accepted on the literary market and established the text of the *Sonnets* that was read through the seventeenth and most of the eighteenth century.

## From Print to Manuscript: Excerpting Benson's Edition

Long before nineteenth-century editors produced their poetical treasuries and golden anthologies, the practices of excerpting and anthologizing verse were well established in both manuscript and print cultures. Fraunce's and Puttenham's literary excerpts in their rhetorical treatises constitute one method by which this was done. Another is exemplified by the collection of verse quotations published as *Belvedere* (1600), a book that includes short (sometimes two-line) poetical passages as illustrations of commonplace-book subject headings.[54] The publication of poetical miscellanies and songbooks, along with the growth in the number of serious, rather than ephemeral, publications of lyric poetry, certainly encouraged the anthologizing and collecting mentality that became a feature of the modern institution of literature. Shakespearean scholars are familiar with the collection of excerpts from Shakespeare's plays that was apparently transcribed from memory by Edward Pudsey after their performances[55] and the enormous mid-seventeenth-century compilation of quotations that came into the possession of James Halliwell-Phillipps. Peter Beal has calculated that the original manuscript of the latter contained some 1,028 pages with quotes from 302 works, among them 36 of Shakespeare's plays, the excerpts all arranged alphabetically under commonplace-book headings.[56] Certainly the practice of isolating poetical gems, which flourished in the nineteenth century, began quite early.

There is an interesting, small mid-seventeenth-century manuscript in the Folger Library containing miscellaneous material including several pages of poetry excerpted from Benson's volume.[57] On folios 22r–24r, beginning with the notation "Shakespeare" at the top right of the page, followed by two lines from the Jonson poem on Shakespeare found on the Benson page containing a sketch based on the Droeshout engraving of Shakespeare from the First Folio of the plays, there are some fifty-one poetical excerpts from Benson's book, thirty-one of which are from the Shakespearean poems. These run in length from the phrase "Summers front" from Sonnet 102 to whole poems: Sonnet 107 (entitled "A Monument")[58] and the untitled Sonnets 33 and 68. It would seem that the transcriber-collector leafed through Benson's text, following its page order, selecting those poems and parts of poems that struck his fancy, usually excerpts one quatrain in length or shorter. Sometimes he rewrote an excerpt to convert it to a memorable phrase or to have it stand grammatically independent of the poem from which it came: for example, he took lines 10–12 of Sonnet 29—"Haply I thinke on thee, and then my state,/ (Like to the lark at break of day arising) / From sullen earth sings himns at Heavens gate"—and reduced it to the phrase "To sing from sullen earth hymnes at heavens gate" (fol. 23r). Beginning a six-line excerpt from Sonnet 65, he changed the first line from "How with this rage shall beautie hold a plea" to "O how shall beauty with this rage hold plea" to make it parallel to "O how shall Summers hungry breath hold out" (itself a corruption of the Quarto's "O how shall summers hunny breath hold out"). Language from lines 9 and 10 of Sonnet 82—"yet when they have devis'd, / What strained touches Rhetorick can lend"—became "Devise what strained touches rhetoric can lend" (fol. 23r); the phrase "the pleasure of the fleeting yeare" from the second line of Sonnet 97 got expanded grammatically into "Thou art the Pleasure of the fleeting yeare" (fol. 23r). Language from ll. 5–7 in Sonnet 142 ("Or if it doe, not from those lips of thine, / That have prophan'd their scarlet ornaments, / And seal'd false bonds of love as oft as mine") was condensed to the two-line unit, "Thy lips Profane their scarlet ornaments / And seald fals bonds of love" (fol. 23v). In all of these cases, Shakespearean passages were being converted into memorable and treasured poetical excerpts. The whole is a personal collection shaped by the taste, judgment, and arbitrariness of an individual who exercised the collector-transcriber's prerogatives, even when copying from a printed text—a practice, incidentally, that was not at all uncommon in the era in which the two systems of literary transmission continued to overlap. The anonymous collector, in one sense, was free to make Benson's Thorpe's Shakespeare's words his own. Literary texts remained in the public domain, despite the official rights of publishers.

## Conclusion

It is important to recognize that Shakespeare produced sonnets that continued to be reproduced, with accidental and deliberate modifications, by the poet himself, by recipients and collectors in the system of manuscript transmission, by editors, by printing-house compositors, and by modern textual scholars. There is *no* text of the *Sonnets,* in either manuscript or print, that can be shown to represent the ideal of old-fashioned textual critics, the "author's final intentions."[59] In addition, from the time of their composition to the present, certain institutional constraints have operated to define the character of the texts being read—the results being quite varied in the course of the history of their reception. Jaggard's *The Passionate Pilgrim* presents two of the sonnets as works of the dramatist whose play-texts were marketable under his name and who was also the author of the popular *Venus and Adonis.* The few manuscript miscellanies in which individual Shakespearean sonnets appear treat the poems as lyrics that are collectible, but of a piece with a large body of manuscript-circulated verse, much of which was unascribed. Thorpe's *"Shake-speares Sonnets . . .* Neuer before Imprinted" presents the poems as having been procured for a general readership from an environment of restricted circulation, just as Sidney's *Astrophil and Stella* sonnets had been. Benson's edition of Shakespeare's poetry pretends to round out the publication project(s) that had been presenting this author's complete works: the First and Second Folios, the continuing editions of *Venus and Adonis* and *Lucrece.* The same centripetal forces drawing non-Shakespearean plays into the body of work recognized as canonical also operated, both consciously and unconsciously, in Benson's project, marking the new valuation of authorship implicit in the emerging institution of Literature. On a smaller scale, the same thing happened in the case of Donne, whose name became associated with poems by other poets. Finally, as Margreta De Grazia has explained, Malone's late-eighteenth-century edition and the romantic interpretation of Shakespeare's work set the terms by which the *Sonnets* were received by modern readers as the heartfelt utterances of an eloquently self-expressive master-poet.[60]

Now we are able to undo some of the idealizations of the New Bibliography and traditional humanist criticism in order to perceive in the poems the kind of fascinating textual instability that appeals to a postmodern sensibility. By examining Shakespeare's *Sonnets* as literary property passing through the different, but overlapping, systems of transmission in manuscript and print, we can not only rediscover some of the unusual ways literary texts were treated by readers and collectors in the early modern era, but we can also begin to understand how literature itself was being redefined socioculturally, a process that shaped and was shaped by these very texts.[61]

## Notes

1. W. W. Greg, *Some Aspects and Problems of London Publishing Between 1550 and 1650* (Oxford: Clarendon Press, 1956), p. 63, remarks: "What an Elizabethan would have understood by 'copyright', and what he did understand by rights in a copy, had nothing to do with the author, but was the right of a stationer to the exclusive enjoyment of a copy which he had been the first to publish or had lawfully acquired from a former owner. This was essentially an affair of the Stationers' Company and part of the discipline it exercised over its members." For a discussion of copyright in relation to larger cultural issues, see Alvin Kernan, *Printing Technology, Letters & Samuel Johnson* (Princeton: Princeton University Press, 1987); Martha Woodmansee, "The Genius and Copyright: Economic and Legal Conditions of the Emergence of the 'Author,' " *Eighteenth-Century Studies* 17 (1983–84): 425–48; and Mark Rose, "The Author as Proprietor: *Donaldson v. Becket* and the Genealogy of Modern Authorship," *Representations* no. 23 (Summer 1988): 51–85.

2. Generally, authors who sold their manuscripts to publishers were paid relatively little for them. For example, as Majorie Plant has noted, "For John Stow's great life-work, the *Survey of London,* which John Wolfe published in 1598, the payment was only £3 and forty copies of the work; for his *Brief Chronicle* he received £1 and fifty copies" (*The English Book Trade: An Economic History of the Making and Sale of Books,* 2d ed. [London: Allen & Unwin, 1965], p. 74). Authors could, of course, either sell their complimentary copies or use them as presentation copies to patrons and friends. For a discussion of the economics of patronage in relation to publication, see H. S. Bennett, *English Books & Readers 1558 to 1603: Being a Study in the History of the Book Trade in the Reign of Elizabeth I* (Cambridge: Cambridge University Press, 1965), pp. 30–55.

3. *The English Works of Giles Fletcher, the Elder,* ed. Lloyd E. Berry (Madison: University of Wisconsin Press, 1964), p. 76.

4. Although most textual scholars believe Shakespeare did not bother to read proofs at the printers for the two narrative poems, George Walton Williams (*The Craft of Printing and the Publication of Shakespeare's Works* [Washington: Folger Shakespeare Library and London and Toronto: Associated University Presses, 1985], pp. 73, 75) remarks: "It cannot be said confidently that Shakespeare saw these two volumes [*Venus and Adonis* and *Lucrece*] through the press or corrected the 'printer's proofs' of them, but they are both cleanly printed, and it is not unlikely that Shakespeare was attentive to

their publication and anxious that the poems should appear in decent dress. Such a statement can be made of none of the plays or of the other poems."

5. Arthur F. Marotti, "'Love is not love': Elizabethan Sonnet Sequences and the Social Order," *ELH* 49 (1982): 410–12.

6. William Shakespeare, *The Poems*, ed. F. T. Prince (London: Methuen, 1960), p. 64.

7. John Donne, for example, defined just such an exclusive relationship with Lucy, countess of Bedford in his prose and verse letters to her. See my discussion of this relationship in *John Donne, Coterie Poet* (Madison and London: University of Wisconsin Press, 1986), pp. 202–32. In a 1613 letter to Viscount Rochester (later earl of Somerset), Donne declared his political and social clientage to this patron in a revealing way: "After I was grown to be your Lordships, by all the titles that I could thinke upon, it hath pleased your Lordship to make another title to me, by buying me" (*Letters to Several Persons of Honour* [1651], a facsimile reproduction with an introduction by M. Thomas Hester [Delmar, N.Y.: Scholars' Facsimiles and Reprints, 1977], p. 290). I am grateful to Heather Dubrow for this reference.

8. All quotations from the sonnets are from *Shakespeare's Sonnets*, edited with analytic commentary by Stephen Booth (New Haven and London: Yale University Press, 1977). I refer to sonnet and line numbers.

9. Furthermore, he accuses himself of having wasted his creative energies "on some worthless song, / Dark'ning [his Muse's] power to lend base subjects light" (100.3–4) when he should have been entirely attentive to the person praised as the very source of his poetry. The verse he sends to the patron, Sonnet 32 assumes, would be in the possession of the addressee after the poet's death:

> If thou survive my well-contented day,
> When that churl Death my bones with dust shall cover,
> And shalt by fortune once more re-survey
> These poor rude lines of thy deceased lover,
> Compare them with the bett'ring of the time,
> And though they be outstripped by every pen
> Reserve them for my love, not for their rhyme. . . .
>                          (32.1–7)

Sonnets 71 and 74 describe a similar situation.

10. Booth notes that "This sonnet uses language and conceits traditional in Elizabethan literary dedications. Shakespeare used some of the same ones in dedicating *Lucrece* to Southampton" (p. 175).

11. Daniel, in *Delia*, refers to "these my papers" (36.1), "my papers" (48.5), and the "ill accepted papers" (49.2) sent to the beloved. I cite the texts from Samuel Daniel, *Poems and A Defense of Ryme*, ed. Arthur Colby Sprague (Chicago: University of Chicago Press, 1930).

12. See Germaine Warkentin, "Sidney's *Certain Sonnets:* Speculations on the Evolution of the Text," *The Library*, 6th ser., 2 (1980): 430–44. Warkentin states: "Sidney and his contemporaries did not write on pre-cut single sheets as

we do today, but on folded folio sheets or bifolia. Single sheets or quarto writing-paper first appeared in the early seventeenth century. . . . Thus, the 'papers' of a writer in the sixteenth century would only exceptionally have consisted of single pages in a folder, or quantities of single poems one to a bifolium. Much more likely would have been bifolia fairly heavily written over, and quired paper books or vellum-bound notebooks in which material had been drafted or recopied" (pp. 434–35). Warkentin notes that "surviving fragments in the hands of Skelton, Raleigh, Southwell, and Browne all show signs of composition on bifolia" (p. 436n).

13. Brents Stirling, *The Shakespeare Sonnet Order: Poems & Groups* (Berkeley and Los Angeles: University of California Press, 1968). Cf. John Padel, *New Poems by Shakespeare: Order and Meaning Restored to the Sonnets* (London: The Herbert Press, 1981).

14. Booth (p. 267), following George Stevens, notes that Shakespeare puts just this sort of book in Hamlet's possession (*Hamlet* 1.5.98–107).

15. Peter Beal, *Index of English Literary Manuscripts* (London: Mansell, 1980), 1: 454, calls attention as well to the version in the Pierpont Morgan Library MS MA 1057.

16. Rosenbach MS 1083/16 (formerly Phillips MS 9549), p. 256. Cf. *Poems, Written by the Right Honorable William Earl of Pembroke . . . Whereof Many of which are answered by way of Repartee, by Sᵣ Benjamin Ruddier, Knight. With several Distinct Poems, Written by them Occasionally, and Apart* (London, 1660), pp. 54–55. The published version of the poem is broken into three stanzas in the form used in Shakespeare's *Venus and Adonis*. It has some significant variants from the manuscript text, including "your rare beauty" for "of your beauty" (1), "stand" for "scand" (6), and "Whence" for "Where" (12). Of these, the second looks like a copyist's or compositor's error.

17. See, for example, the discussion in William Shakespeare, *The Sonnets,* ed. John Dover Wilson (Cambridge: Cambridge University Press, 1969), pp. lxxxvii–cxxii.

18. H. W. Piper argues that the poem found in the 1660 edition of Pembroke and Rudyerd, the earl of Pembroke's "Yet was her Beauty as the Blushing Rose," is connected with his meeting the "dark lady" ("A Herbert Sonnet," *TLS,* 21 October 1983, p. 1161). This might be additional evidence of a connection between William Herbert and the circumstances surrounding the sonnets.

19. Margaret Crum, "Notes on the Physical Characteristics of Some Manuscripts of the Poems of Donne and Henry King," *The Library,* 4th ser., 16 (1961): 121, quotes from the Henry King poem inscribed in the table-book given to a lady in which the poet invited her to become "both the Scribe and Author"—that is, both to copy verse into the volume and to compose her own in it.

20. In *Palladis Tamia,* cited in E. K. Chambers, *William Shakespeare: A Study of Facts and Problems,* 2 vols. (Oxford: Clarendon Press, 1930), 2: 194.

21. See, for example, Ernest A. J. Honigmann, "Shakespeare as a Reviser," and Michael J. Warren, "Textual Problems, Editorial Assertions in Editions of

Shakespeare," in *Textual Criticism and Literary Interpretation,* ed. Jerome J. McGann (Chicago: University of Chicago Press, 1985), pp. 1–23 and 23–37, and the papers in Gary Taylor and Michael J. Warren, eds., *The Division of the Kingdoms: Shakespeare's Two Versions of "King Lear"* (Oxford: Clarendon Press, 1983).

22. Gary Taylor, "Some Manuscripts of Shakespeare's Sonnets," *BJRL* 68 (1985–86): 210–46. Taylor remarks (pp. 224–25): "Altogether, 10 of the sonnets survive in a total of 19 manuscripts. Only two manuscripts . . . contain more than one sonnet, and both clearly derive from the 1609 or 1640 edition. In fact, ignoring temporarily the texts of [Sonnet 2], only three sonnets survive in manuscripts which are not demonstrably derivative of the printed texts: Sonnets 6 . . . 106 . . . and 128. . . . In total, then, we possess 16 texts of individual Sonnets which may be independent of the printed tradition, and these 16 texts occur in 16 different miscellanies. This pattern of distribution would be difficult to explain if the sonnets had circulated in manuscript as a sequence; it strongly suggests, instead, that they circulated as individual poems." While agreeing with Taylor's contention that the sonnets circulated in manuscript in a form other than that of the whole collection found in the 1609 Quarto, I think it unlikely that *single* poems were passed about, given, as I have noted, the ways that paper was used in this period. Unless they were included in letters composed in bifolia or coupled with other verse filling out the individual bifolia sheets that were the standard paper size, the uncollected sonnets were either circulated in small sets or groups of poems, passed about in commonplace-book collections, or transmitted through memorization.

23. See J. B. Leishman, "'You Meaner Beauties of the Night,' A Study in Transmission and Transmogrification," *The Library,* 4th ser., 26 (1945): 99–121. Cf. Suzanne Woods, "'The Passionate Sheepheard' and 'The Nimphs Reply': A Study of Transmission," *HLQ* 34 (1970): 25–33.

24. I cite the text from *The Passionate Pilgrim* by William Shakespeare, facsimile edition, with Introduction by Joseph Quincy Adams (New York and London: Scribner's, 1939).

25. Hallett Smith, *The Tension in the Lyre: Poetry in Shakespeare's Sonnets* (San Marino, Calif.: Huntington Library, 1981), p. 56. The most substantive variant in the poem, however, is in the eighth line: in Jaggard, "Outfacing faults in loue, with loues ill rest"; in the Quarto, "On both sides thus is simple truth supprest. . . ." This is a more difficult case for speculation: it may, in fact, signal an actual Shakespearean revision rather than a change introduced beyond authorial control in the processes of transmission.

26. See Willa McClung Evans, *Henry Lawes: Musician and Friend of Poets* (New York London: Oxford University Press, 1941), pp. 42–45.

27. See *Brittons Bowre of Delights, 1591,* ed. Hyder Edward Rollins (Cambridge, Mass.: Harvard University Press, 1933), pp. xiv–xv.

28. Chambers, *Shakespeare,* 2: 218.

29. *The Passionate Pilgrim* by William Shakespeare, 3d ed. (1612), facsimile ed. with Introduction by Hyder Edward Rollins (New York and London: Scribner's, 1940), p. xxviii.

30. In their separate editions of the 1599 and 1612 editions of *The Passionate Pilgrim,* J. Q. Adams and Hyder Rollins are reluctant to assign more than five poems of the total in each collection to Shakespeare: the two sonnets that appeared later in the Quarto, and two sonnets and one song from *Love's Labour's Lost.* There are, of course, a number of other poems in the collection whose authorship is unknown, but, given the suspicions about Jaggard's reliability, few textual scholars have been willing to call them Shakespeare's. Among these are several sonnets on the Venus and Adonis theme, poems that Jaggard obviously had in mind when, in attempting to capitalize on the popularity of Shakespeare's narrative poem, he expanded the title of the 1612 edition to read *The Passionate Pilgrim. Or Certaine Amorous Sonnets, Between Venus and Adonis.* Hyder Rollins, ed., *A New Variorum Edition of Shakespeare: The Poems,* (Philadelphia and London: Lippincott, 1938), pp. 539–41, notes that Edmund Malone and a number of later critics have been willing to consider the Venus and Adonis poems (other than the one attributable to Bartholomew Griffin) as relics of Shakespeare's early attempt to handle the Venus and Adonis story before he settled upon the stanza form and narrative progression of the poem he finally produced. More recently, C. H. Hobday, "Shakespeare's Venus and Adonis Sonnets," *Shakespeare Survey* 26 (1973): 103–9, makes a good case for their canonicity. He suggests that they "circulated in manuscript among Southampton's circle and Shakespeare's literary friends, with whom their eroticism made them popular. These Ovidian sonnets, and perhaps others of a similar character now lost, rather than the more personal sonnets published in 1609, may have been the 'sugared sonnets among his private friends' which, together with *Venus and Adonis* and *Lucrece,* helped to persuade Francis Meres that 'the sweet witty soul of Ovid lives in mellifluous and honey-tongued Shakespeare' " (p. 108). Meres's comments, it is important to remember, occur in a passage dealing with the classical affiliations of particular English poets and, specifically, of Shakespeare's identity as an Ovidian writer: "As the soule of *Euphorbus* was thought to liue in *Pythagoras:* so the sweete wittie soul of *Ouid* liues in mellifluous & hony-tongued *Shakespeare,* witness his *Venus* and *Adonis,* his *Lucrece,* his sugred Sonnets among his priuate friends, &c." (Chambers, *Shakespeare,* 2: 194). Looking for whatever miscellaneous Shakespearean lyrics he could find in the late 1590s, Jaggard might have come upon these "sugard" Ovidian poems and grabbed them for publication.

31. See Elizabeth Eisenstein, *The Printing Press as an Agent of Change: Communications and Cultural Transformations in Early Modern Europe,* 2 vols. (Cambridge: Cambridge University Press, 1979), 1: 121.

32. This topic has become an important issue in current scholarship. See, particularly, Richard Helgerson, *Self-Crowned Laureates: Spenser, Jonson, Milton, and the Literary System* (Berkeley: University of California Press, 1983).

33. Marjorie Plant, *The English Book Trade,* remarks (p. 248): "the title-page came to be nailed up on the whipping-posts in the streets, on the pillars of St. Paul's, and on the walls of the Inns of Court. . . . it was an established custom for bookbinders' servants every Saturday night to post up the titles of those works which were to be be bound during the coming week."

34. Katherine Duncan-Jones, "Was the 1609 *Shake-speares Sonnets* Really Unauthorized?" *RES*, n.s. 34 (1983): 151–71. Although Duncan-Jones makes a good attempt to prove that Thorpe's edition of Shakespeare's sonnets was an authorized publication, there are several key points in her argument with which I disagree. She believes that Shakespeare wouldn't have been careless about releasing his poems into circulation, but, of course, this ignores the comment of Meres and plays down the evidence of the separate appearance of Sonnets 138 and 144 in *The Passionate Pilgrim*. She notes the absence of contemporary manuscripts including them, but, as Sonnet 122 suggests, Shakespeare might very well have loaned a table-book containing the sonnets, even a complete collection of them, to others and a text such as this might have been copied or itself shown to a printer. Her comments about the respectability of Thorpe have little to do with the possibility that he followed a quite ordinary practice of printers in publishing a valuable and interesting manuscript or manuscripts without seeking authorial permission. The argument that Shakespeare might have sold his sonnets to Thorpe in 1609 to earn money, once again at a time the theaters were closed due to the plague, ignores the facts that the dramatist was undoubtedly more prosperous in 1609 than he was in 1592–94, that the publisher's payment for the text would not have been very great, and that there is no evidence in the presentation of the text that the author was appealing to a patron for economic assistance. Without the sort of appeal for help from a patron found in the dedicatory letters to *Venus and Adonis* and *Lucrece,* it would have made little sense to sell the poems to a printer and, furthermore, as Peter Blayney has suggested to me in conversation, if Shakespeare had deliberately looked for a printer for the sonnets, he would probably have selected the former Stratfordian who printed his two narrative poems, Richard Field. Finally, although textual scholars and bibliographers have concluded that Shakespeare did not follow the usual practice of authorial correction of printer's proofs in the course of the printing process in either the clearly deliberate publication of the two narrative poems or in the case of the 1609 Quarto, it would seem that his neglect in the latter case would have been much more damaging to the final result, given the obvious misprints and problems in that edition.

35. Although it is not surprising to find Anacreontic lyrics at the conclusion of printed sonnet collections, it looks as though Thorpe chose to print what might have been an original and a revised poem as though they were independent pieces. The traditional unwillingness on the part of critics and editors to think of Shakespeare as a reviser of his work has probably predisposed readers to view the lyrics as independent works.

36. Heather Dubrow, *Captive Victors: Shakespeare's Narrative Poems and Sonnets* (Ithaca: Cornell University Press, 1987), pp. 171–90, intelligently discusses Shakespeare's apparently deliberate avoidance of both the narrative and the dramatic in his *Sonnets.*

37. By contrast, of the first 126 sonnets, the vast majority, some 112 poems, seem clearly addressed to the young man. Five poems have a problematic addressee: 21, 25, 94, 116, 121. Nine others refer to the young man in the third person: 19, 63, 64, 65, 66, 67, 68, 100, and 101.

38. MacDonald P. Jackson, "Punctuation and the Compositors of Shakespeare's *Sonnets,* 1609," *The Library,* 5th ser., 30 (1975): 1–24.

39. Ibid., p. 10.

40. Duncan-Jones, *Shake-speares Sonnets,* p. 51, makes a similar point.

41. The regulations governing printing normally limited the number of copies that could be printed from one setting of type to between 1,250 and 1,500. It is not likely that the Thorpe Quarto would have approached either limit.

42. Hyder Rollins, *Brittons Bowre,* pp. xxiv–xxv.

43. T. A. Birrell, "The Influence of Seventeenth-Century Publishers on the Presentation of English Literature," in *Historical & Editorial Studies in Medieval & Early Modern English,* ed. Mary-Jo Arn and Hanneke Wirtjes (Groningen: Wolters-Noordhoff, 1985), p. 166.

44. For a defense of Benson's practices, see Josephine Waters Bennett, "Benson's Alleged Piracy of *Shake-speares Sonnets* and of Some of Jonson's Works," *Studies in Bibliography* 21 (1968): 235–48. Cf. Hallett Smith, *The Tension in the Lyre,* pp. 140–44.

45. Benson, Unsig. pp. 2r–v.

46. Bennett, *English Books & Readers,* points out that the copyright of Thorpe's book had lapsed to the Stationers' Company (p. 238) and that William Aspley, one of the two booksellers through whom Thorpe's Quarto was originally sold, probably provided Benson with a copy for him to use (p. 240).

47. Jasper Mayne's poem, "On Dʳ Donnes death," reprinted in *The Poems of John Donne,* ed. with introductions and commentary by Herbert J. C. Grierson, 2 vols. (Oxford: Oxford University Press, 1912), 2: 382–84.

48. *The Norton Facsimile: The First Folio of Shakespeare,* prepared by Charlton Hinman (New York: Norton, 1968), p. 7.

49. See the discussion of the Benson edition in Shakespeare, *Poems,* ed. Rollins, pp. 604–9. Bennett points out that Benson probably thought the Marlowe and Ralegh poems he found in *The Passionate Pilgrim* could be included in a Shakespeare collection, but he chose to reprint the longer versions of the lyrics found in *England's Helicon* (p. 246).

50. Bennett, *English Books and Readers,* pp. 237–40, argues that the care Benson took to follow the publishing rules indicates that he was hardly acting like a pirate in the whole venture. Both Thorpe's text and *The Passionate Pilgrim,* the basis for the major portion of the edition, belonged to the Stationers' Company and he probably did what was necessary to secure the right to reprint them.

51. Sonnet 62 is printed as a separate poem, "Sat fuisse" (sig. D1r), and Sonnet 61 becomes "Patiens Armatus" (sigs. D1v–D2r).

52. Margreta De Grazia argues convincingly that the effect of Benson's edition is to offer a new context of interpretation for Shakespeare's *Sonnets,* one differing sharply from that of Malone's and modern scholarship's author-centered one. Instead of encouraging the reader to think of the lyrics as uniquely self-expressive utterances, Benson arranges his edition in a way that makes the

"subject of the poems . . . a representative lover, not an individuated one." For him, *love* was the subject, and the poems were to be read philosophically—as definitions, occasions, and accidents of love" ("Locating and Dislocating the 'I' of Shakespeare's Sonnets," in *William Shakespeare: His World, His Work, His Influence,* ed. John F. Andrews, 3 vols. [New York: Charles Scribner's Sons, 1985], 3: 441). Hallett Smith, *The Tension in the Lyre,* p. 144, calls Benson a "thematic reader" of the sonnets.

53. For example, Sonnet 43 dropped out of the edition when Benson shifted from two poems incorporating Sonnets 38–42 to three *Passionate Pilgrim* poems back to Sonnets 44 and 45 (conflated in one poem entitled "Melancholy Thoughts"). The lost sonnet was not picked up at the end of the section of the volume in which some sonnets missed earlier are printed (such as Sonnets 73, 77, 78, 79, 107, and 108).

54. Cf. also *England's Parnassus* (1600), ed. Charles Crawford (Oxford: Clarendon Press, 1913), a dictionary of quotations derived from both manuscript and printed sources.

55. Beal, *Index,* 1: 449.

56. Ibid., 450.

57. Folger MS V.a.148.

58. This is distinguished from "A monument to fame" found in Benson over the composite poem made from this and Sonnet 108.

59. See Jerome McGann's revisionist textual approach in *A Critique of Modern Textual Criticism* (Chicago: University of Chicago Press, 1983). Cf. Randall McLeod, "UnEditing Shakespeare," *Sub-Stance* 33 /34 (1982): 26–55; Jonathan Goldberg, "Textual Properties," *SQ* 37 (1986): 213–17; and Margreta De Grazia, "The Essential Shakespeare and the Material Book," *Textual Practice* 2.1 (Spring 1988): 69–86.

60. De Grazia, "Locating and Dislocating the 'I' of Shakespeare's Sonnets," 3: 435–37.

61. I am grateful to Margreta De Grazia and Heather Dubrow for helpful comments made on an earlier version of this essay.

# 7

# Jacobean Poetry and Lyric Disappointment

*Jane Tylus*

One of Michael Drayton's many bones of contention in his massive blend of fantasy and scholarship called *Poly-Olbion* is Julius Caesar's characterization of the ancient Britons in his *Gallic Wars* as barbarians without a history. Such "desecration," according to Drayton, has produced a series of "fictive ornaments" about Britain, all the result of Caesar's incomprehension "of our former state, beginning, our descent[;] / The warres we had at home, the conquests where we went, / He never understood" (4:119).[1] This failure of interpretation and the subsequent erasure of Britain's great past with its "noble Trophies [rear'd] long 'ere [the Romans] arriv'd," made the isle an easy prey for invaders, who virtually on Caesar's heels descended upon Britain:

> The *Roman,* next the *Pict,* the *Saxon,* then the *Dane,*
> All landing in this Ile, each like a horrid raine
> Deforming her; besides the sacrilegious wrack
> Of many a noble Booke, as impious hands should sack
> The Center, to extirp all knowledge, and exile
> All brave and ancient things, for ever from this Ile.

It is not people but books which the invaders attack; it is not London but Britain's spiritual "Center," represented by Wales and its honored bards,[2] which constitutes the key to the island's survival. Cultural artifacts constitute a defense against alien conquerors who are all too ready to substitute their *own* version of history and legitimation for that which they efface—or, as in Caesar's case, purport to be nonexistent in the first place.[3] Without a past, Britain can have no present.

Addressed not to the Scottish monarch who liked to associate himself with Rome's emperors but to his two sons, *Poly-Olbion* precariously straddles an uncertain present in order to look hopefully to the future and back to a recent past which had been all but silenced since Elizabeth's death. Like other poets who professed loyalty to the Elizabethan age, many of whom were lawyers attempting to uphold England's common law against the potentially arbitrary will of their most recent "conqueror,"[4] Drayton refused such silence in the course of his journeys to the margins of the island where he imagined the old Druidic bards, entrusted with the preservation of their precious pasts, to be living still. Precisely such a refusal, however, has resulted in the characterization of Drayton and his fellow poets such as William Browne, Christopher Brooke, George Wither, and Phineas Fletcher as figures who wallowed in a nostalgia that makes them a tragic curiosity at best and at worst a negligible "remnant of another time."[5] Yet these writers were far from turning to the past merely as a "refuge" from or "antidote" to the "degeneracy of the present."[6] Rather, their work reflects both the desire to resituate England's cultural community in a domain outside of the Jacobean court,[7] and a hostility to an absolutism which no longer acknowledged its dependence on the English *country*.[8] Writing history became an ultimately political action for those who felt that their new king, like Caesar, was prepared to disown their past.

Such emphasis on the communal contexts of cultural production had as a necessary consequence a mistrust of the emerging subject representative of a different but not completely alien kind of self-sufficiency from that of James.[9] The Spenserians' two communal collections of eclogues of 1614–15, *The Shepheards Pipe* and *Shepheards Hunting,* and the dedications to Browne's *Britannia's Pastorals* and Drayton's *Poly-Olbion* reflect a reluctance to embrace the often strident independence of seventeenth-century lyric and a desire to locate poetry within a plurality of poetic voices. George Wither would flee the "Chambers of Kings" for the open "Fieldes" where false intimacy might give way to public voices,[10] and Drayton derided "this lunatique Age" when nothing is "esteem'd . . . but what is kept in Cabinets" and "wholly deduc't to Chambers" (4:v*). Poets such as Donne or Jonson, to be sure, were quite as cynical as Drayton and Wither about courtly politics, and frequently turned to "lyric sites" notable for their remoteness from earlier centers of poetic production such as the court.[11] But while the regionalism of a Herrick has something in common with that of *Poly-Olbion,* Herrick looks ultimately toward self-authorization, a "place" which will eventually become, in Harold Toliver's phrase, that of "personal empire."[12] Drayton and his fellow Spenserians for the most part refuse the temptations of such an empire. Even Drayton's odes of 1606, characteristic of the most "sublime and therefore dangerous form of the lyric,"[13] almost compulsively situate themselves in relationship to a prior literary community.

It is, however, the Spenserians' and particularly Drayton's consistently explorative use of pastoral that registers most acutely this belief in communal voices and its attendant crises. It was also pastoral, of course, which provided Drayton and his cohorts with one of their strongest links to the Elizabethan age, a moment which served as a touchstone throughout their careers. Yet what may seem an almost compulsive return to an era and a genre was not so much an unthinking act of homage or commemoration as an attempt to recover those clearly subversive elements of Virgilian pastoral perhaps too readily silenced or ignored during Elizabeth's reign. If Virgil celebrates the fruitful relationship between monarch and grateful subject, as well as the vision of a new community made possible through empire, he is also careful to preserve the traces of a prior community to which the subject, however reluctantly, must renounce his allegiance. The Spenserians' pastoral becomes a return to that prior community stifled by empire—an empire created not only by a James who had little taste for the subtle cultural dynamics at work in Elizabethan pastoral, but by an Elizabeth who had obscured critical issues such as agricultural crisis and who had sought to disempower her courtier-shepherds by alienating them from every community *but* the court.[14] To this process of alienation, and the extent to which the Spenserians succeeded in exposing and redressing it, I now wish to turn.[15]

George Puttenham's *Arte of English Poesie* has emerged in recent years as crucial for understanding the complex mediations of a pastoral genre in which, to cite a by-now familiar phrase, the poet "under the vaile of homely persons, and in rude speeches insinuate[s] and glaunce[s] at greater matters, and such as perchance had not bene safe to have beene disclosed in any other sort."[16] Especially for Louis Adrian Montrose, such indirection as practiced by the courtier-shepherd has extraordinary potential in a society which undermines and discredits *openly* ambitious aspirants to power. By creating an ideology that mediates the glaring differences in Elizabethan society so that the queen might become its "natural" center, the shrewd writer uses social poetics as a vehicle for his own desires. Pastoral becomes for Montrose a genre with explicitly lyric pretensions: the *real* purpose of a poem such as Spenser's "Aprill" is to construct "a recognizably modern mode of subjectivity" first articulated in the literary conventions of Petrarchism.[17] The "resistance" Spenser felt regarding "the perhaps not consciously articulated contradiction between [his] exalted self-representation as an Author and his subjection to the authority of an other" results in the "refashioning of an Elizabethan subject as laureate poet" as well as the "refashioning of the queen as the author's subject" (323). Such resistance attests to the modernity of Montrose's Spenser, functioning as the sign of a fragmented, inevitably isolated identity turned relentlessly in upon itself in its quest for "uncertain mastery."

What seems most striking about Montrose's largely persuasive reading is its characterization of Spenser as someone operating in collusion with a queen desirous of obfuscating social and political relationships. Spenser's focus on the *subject,* on the ultimately isolated—and isolatable—relationship between subject and queen, that is, ensures that the very social displacements which Montrose claims are so central to the way that pastoral "works," *must,* perforce, take place. If Spenser and Puttenham indeed are symptomatic of the strategies and crises of modernism, the costs of that investment and the removal of the subject from political and social concerns which extend beyond the court—all issues of concern to the Spenserians—need to be more deeply addressed.

At the same time, it is possible that Spenser *was* suggesting that the poet is responsible for determining what is wrong with the system.[18] If Elizabethan pastoral depends on the mediation and obfuscation of actual economic and social realities and on the protection of those in power from opposition, then the eloquent silences throughout *The Shepheardes Calender* would seem to record, indeed, a greater "resistance" than Montrose implies: a resistance both to the project of pastoral as it seems to be defined in "Aprill" and to the project of a "subjectivity" that can only exist in terms of royal sovereignty. Colin's own, eloquent silence referred to on the margins of Hobbinol's repeated song[19] becomes, perhaps, symptomatic of the larger, more disturbing process of silencing at work in the eclogue as a whole. Moreover, *The Shepheardes Calender* can be said to register not only the poet's perhaps symbolic silence[20] but that of others, more threatening in that it is the result of censorship and political exile. The poem is dedicated to Sidney, only recently chastened by Elizabeth for his protests over her marriage negotiations with Alencon; "Julye" is balanced delicately on the figure of Algrind, alias Archbishop Grindal, asked to leave his ecclesiastical post for disagreeing with Elizabeth on matters of religious prophesying; and finally, in the "Envoy" the poet asks his calendar to follow the "ploughman" who is perhaps Robert Crowley, who had lost some of his benefices in the 1560s because of his trenchant satire of the Elizabethan Compromise.[21] To take note of such suppression is to begin to criticize, if in extremely subtle fashion, the very ideologies one is purportedly championing. In the case of *The Shep-*

*heardes Calender,* such criticism surfaces by way of a poorly defined but decidedly *non*courtly community of militant Protestantism, the community otherwise marginalized in the poet's putative attempts to create himself as subject.

It would be beyond the scope of this essay to demonstrate that Spenser's first published work exhibits more tension than Montrose might allow between a subjectivity dependent on the subject's relation to his queen and an identity that may inhere within a communal body critical of courtly celebration. But it is possible to suggest that one of the victims of "silence" addressed on the margins of *The Shepheardes Calender* propounded a definition of pastoral that takes stock of such a dialectic by grounding it in one of the few models of the genre which the Renaissance had: Virgil's *Eclogues*. In the *Apology for Poetry,* written within a few years of Spenser's poem, Sidney suggests that one of the projects of pastoral—at which, perhaps, Spenser had only, tactfully, hinted—was to take note of precisely what the ideology in power was attempting to silence. Focusing on the oppositions developed in the first Eclogue, Sidney writes, "Is the poor pipe disdained, which sometimes out of Meliboeus' mouth can show the misery of people under hard lords or ravening soldiers? and again, by Tityrus, what blessedness is derived to them that lie lowest from the goodness of them that sit highest."[22] Sidney's critical conjunction, "and again," links Tityrus's acquisition of his farm and the ascendancy of the new order, which he celebrates in honoring Octavian as his liberator and god, with Meliboeus's exile (to, among other places, the *divissos orbe Britannos* which Virgil, following Julius Caesar's lead, perceived as barbarous). Coexisting with Octavian's appropriation of power and his elevation of certain figures in his realm to the rank of *fortunatus* is the often brutal story of his rise to power, which includes massive dispossessions and the bloody civil wars in villages such as Perugia—wars which Propertius, for one, would condemn at the eloquent close of his *Monobiblos*.[23]

Sidney's interpretation is all the more important given what often seems to be in the *Eclogues* a program for the self-legitimation of poets *and* emperors: a program that would involve the necessary silencing of Meliboeus, with his reminders of war and republican Rome, and thus a past offering a pattern of legitimation which is not that of Octavian. The *Eclogues* are based on Theocritus's *Idylls;* the bucolic poems, Virgil's first major work, enact a process of *translatio* of an influential and sophisticated Hellenistic body of poetry into Roman garb. This is a body of poetry, moreover, which performs eloquent homage to originating "voices" from which younger, obeisant poets derive their own authority: hence Thyrsis's careful imitation of Daphnis's last verses in Theocritus's first verse, Idyll 1; and the elegant rite of passage in the seventh idyll as the mysterious goatherd Lykidas hands the olive branch to Simichidas after their poetic contest. Yet as John Van Sickle has observed, Virgil proceeds to disguise or efface this process of *translatio* which is "canonized" in the Theocritan corpus and bucolic poets after Theocritus, an effacement which would make Virgil the "original" pastoralist.[24] Such effacement is projected most convincingly in the fourth Eclogue, in which a new babe is praised as the originator of a golden age which will obliterate the history that has gone before. In this unabashed celebration of empire—and as centuries of Christian commentators would read it, of the new dispensation ushered in by Christ—Virgil holds out the political equivalent of poetic self-legitimation.

The pastoral experience in Virgil is thus potentially disquieting, insofar as it offers an ideological program of effacing the past and thereby disguising the manner through which power has often brutally triumphed. Meliboeus's presence in Eclogue 1, like that of the forgetful old poets in Eclogue 9 whose lives have been disrupted by the barbarity of civil war, is an altogether necessary counterpart to Tityrus's invocation of the "deus [qui] nobis haec otia fecit." Meliboeus exists as the reminder of a history Octavian and his propagandist Tityrus would seek to obscure: a history that attests to the recognition that "possession" and "sovereignty" always require another's *dis*possession, another's dethroning. In order to legitimize the new order, it is helpful to claim—as the fourth Eclogue (almost) does—that one is beginning a new era; that the barbarity of history and the history of barbarousness are at an end. To silence Meliboeus, a silence that is virtually assured in his imminent exile, would be to produce only the radiant but false surface of a present that has disowned its past; a present that depends on the words of the "sovereign" and his sovereign poet, and on the exile of the republican community of which Meliboeus and his fellows ("*nos* patriam fugimus: *tu*, Tityre, lentus in umbra . . ."—the distinction between the one and the many could not be clearer) are representative.

To create one community, figured in the beneficent shade beneath which Tityrus sings his hyperbolic praises of the "god" in Rome, is to disturb, even to efface, another; to write one version of history is to silence another. This is the realization that compels Virgil to create a Meliboeus in Eclogue 1 and, perhaps, the anonymous persona at the end of Eclogue 10 who insists that he must leave the shade and travel elsewhere.[25] This realization is also behind what would appear to be the recovery of Virgil's explicit (as opposed to Spenser's implicit) criticism of sovereignty and shade in Christopher Brooke's lines of 1614—lines which echo Sidney's paraphrase of Virgil in the *Defense:*

And to this Mount thou [shepheard] dost translate thine Essence
Although the plaines containe thy corporal presence,
Where though poore peoples misery thou shewe
That under g[r]iping Lords they undergoe,
And what content they (that do lowest lye)
Receive from Good-men; that do sit on hye.[26]

Brooke's "plaines" hardly reveal the "apolitical bias" of much
Elizabethan pastoral, a bias effected through the insistence on subjec-
tivity discerned by Montrose.[27] Rather, Brooke's "new" Jacobean
pastoralist must recuperate what his namesake was partially responsible
for obscuring: the process through which the poet had become a neu-
tralized force in English society, a trajectory charted by Puttenham,
who had boldly begun his treatise recalling the ancient days when poets
were "the first Priests, the first Prophets, the first Legislators and Poli-
tiens in the world." Puttenham's antidote, however, to the decline of
humanist values was the pastoral "glaunce" at greater matters, a policy
of indirection which is "safe" only because shepherds themselves play a
putatively neutral, ahistorical, and above all, apolitical role in society.[28]
But once this community becomes conscious, like Meliboeus, of unset-
tling histories; once the "shepherd" becomes intent on disclosing the
political relationships and exploitation inherent in the countryside;
once, in short, the country no longer functions as a mirror for the court
and the desire for lyric subjectivity is relegated to a desire for a more
communal identity, then the assumed "safety" of shepherds must be
qualified. In the verses of the Spenserians, as in the verses of Meliboeus,
this communality is asserted in the potentially dangerous form of re-
membrance: a remembering of shared histories which a new sovereign
is attempting to take away. The "golden age" slogans which James ex-
ploited throughout the early years of his reign certainly necessitated this
drive to remember and to cultivate histories that were properly British.
Significantly, however, this work of communal assertion began before
James ascended the English throne, suggesting some dissatisfaction even
during Elizabeth's reign with Spenser's overly subtle silences.

Unless one considers the half-hearted elegies written for Elizabeth's
death in 1603, the miscellany *Englands Helicon* represents the last burst
during Elizabeth's reign of the pastoral genre that had largely come to
be shaped for and around the English queen. Or at least the editor of
*Englands Helicon*, Nicholas Ling, saw pastoral as such a hallmark; for of
the 150 poems and fragments of poems in his collection, there are sever-
al dozen which—like Astrophel's fourth song to Stella—were not
originally pastoral poems but only became so under Ling's forced guid-

ance and the addition of suitable titles and several shepherds and nymphs.[29] As in the awkward elegies of 1603, there is something almost desperate about this belated invocation of pastoral deities, although the elegies breathe an unstifled sigh of relief that this is the last time such posturing would have to take place. Evoking the principle of Elizabeth's chastity for what it really had meant to at least one male poet—barrenness and the uncertainty of English succession—the elegist John Fenton announces the apparent collapse of Elizabethan pastoral mythology when, at the crucial peripeteia, he moves abruptly from Elizabeth's funeral to James's coronation and announces

> Eliza died in Winter, left the Spring
> To entertaine (with greater ioy) a King.
> At whose arrivall, loe the trees do bud,
> Saying our fruites in harvest will proove good:
> The Nightingale doth sing, so chirps the Larke,
> The aged Oakes put on a fresher barke,
> The day growes longer-ag'd, the night growes old,
> Withering by flourishing is now contrould.[30]

Yet if Fenton celebrates the "potent" King James and an almost georgic fertility implicit in the very word *steward*—and in so doing, liberates England from the sterility obscured by the "springtime" metaphors that dominated Elizabethan pastoral—*Englands Helicon,* for all its apparent homage to Elizabethan convention, also enacts a kind of liberation. For it liberates pastoral verse, and in the case of Sidney, Astrophel's "songs," from the innumerable contexts that had determined their original moments of production: the sonnet sequence, the pastoral novel, the pastoral drama, the eclogue "book" such as *The Shepheardes Calender* and Drayton's *Idea: A Shepheards Garland.* In placing or displacing poetic fragments into a realm of almost exaggerated autonomy, insofar as each verse was bracketed off from others with a heavy border and an authoritative *Finis,* Ling creates a radically new version of pastoral which neither depends on nor is called into question by the contextual matrices which had previously defined it—such as Elizabeth's court. Indeed, while Elizabeth's centrality is studiously observed at the beginning of the collection with the song from Spenser's "Aprill," Drayton's praise of "Beta," and Edmund Bolton's "A Canzon Pastorall in honour of her Maiestie," by the time one has reached the end of the volume there is little sign of the queen.[31] Two verses sung for her progress to Elvetham are now assigned to their respective authors, Thomas Watson and Nicholas Breton, with no mention of their "original" moment of production; two fragments from George Peele's

*Arraignment of Paris* appear towards the close of *Englands Helicon* with no allusion to Elizabeth's necessary presence in that play.[32] Moreover, the work which claims most attention in the volume, much to the ire of most modern commentators, is Jorge de Montemayor's *Diana,* translated by (and attributed to) Bartholomew Yong. Thus a very different Diana than that "embodied" by Elizabeth occupies the center of the text—a Spanish Diana, no less, who is neither chaste nor tyrannical. The aging Elizabeth becomes one shepherdess among many shepherdesses, and her court stands to lose its privilege as the domain where and for which pastoral discourse is produced.

In progressing from the " historical" Elizabeth to "Flora" and the "wanton lasses" of Morley's " Sheepheards Consort" who close the miscellany—and in thus enacting a fall out of history similar to that manifested in the final cantos of Spenser's *Faerie Queene*[33]—*Englands Helicon* may appear to be documenting a fall into literature and an aesthetic, only gradually emerging in the early seventeenth century, which devalued the social and political contexts of the written word. Arguably, such devaluation is the result of all anthologies and commonplace books, which disrupt original contexts and pretend to create a realm of "pure" literature completely divorced from its moment of production. And yet, both the *re*contextualization of pastoral and nonpastoral fragments from Surrey to Shakespeare as well as the Jacobean reception of the volume belie this divorce. In silencing originating moments dominated by the queen, Ling enables those moments to be reconstituted by those who *sing* them, heralding the singers as members of a shepherdly community of poets. Thus, for example, the praise which Colin wrote for Elizabeth in "Aprill" now becomes "Hobbinols Dittie in prayse of Eliza Queene of the Sheepheards." Ironically, Ling brings to fruition what Hobbinol himself had feared: Colin's permament "foreswearing" of his song. In so doing he appropriates Colin's song *not* for the queen but for the community from which Colin had alienated himself—a community which Ling defines in his preface "to the reader, if indifferent":

> if any man whatsoeuer, in prizing of his owne birth or fortune, shall take in scorne, that a far meaner man in the eye of the world, shal be placed by him: I tell him plainly whatsoeuer so excepting, that, that mans wit is set by his, not that man by him.[34]

The "great and sacred Name[s]" of poets, Ling goes on to add, "haue beene placed with the names of the greatest Princes of the world, by the most autentike and worthiest iudgements, without disparagement to their soueraigne titles: which if any man taking exception thereat, in ignorance know not, I hold him unworthy to be placed by the meanest that is but graced with the title of a Poet." On the one hand, the dictum may seem to proclaim an elitist notion of poetry divorced from "far meaner" concerns; yet on the other, it effaces social rank to create a distinctly *anti*hierarchical community of poets indifferent to the concerns of privilege. In focusing on "names" rather than on "men," on the ideal of the "poet" rather than on the often courtly contexts which compromise that ideal, Ling enables the creation of a text whose authors need no longer be submissive to their readers—or to each other.

But it is the second edition of *Englands Helicon* in 1614 which subtly insists on the autonomy of the "great and sacred" poet and the community to which he putatively belongs. Whereas the original title page of *Englands Helicon* was graced with four Latin lines from Tibullus attesting to the act of "purification" performed within the miscellany's covers,[35] the 1614 edition, now in octavo form rather than the more expensive quarto, has on its cover the simple couplet "The Courts of Kings have no such straines, / As daily lull the Rusticke Swaines."[36] While nothing is known of the new editor, Richard More, the fact that of nine poems added to the second edition, the only two which had been previously unprinted were by William Browne and Christopher Brooke,[37] suggests that the Spenserians may have had a hand in the publication.[38] In returning *Englands Helicon* and thus Elizabethan pastoral to print with the proviso that the voices of Spenser, Sidney, and others belonged to a community that existed outside of the court, More, and perhaps Browne and Brooke, attempted to rewrite Elizabethan and define Jacobean cultural history by *de*centering the court.

Some such decentering had already begun in Drayton's collection of pastoral poetry of 1593. Like *The Shepheardes Calender, Idea: A Shepheardes Garland* enacts the hopes and despairs of a lovesick shepherd, here named Rowland, perhaps in memory of the epic hero of medieval and Renaissance romance. And like *The Shepheardes Calender,* Drayton's first pastoral collection does homage to its queen; Eglog 3 enacts the performance by Rowland of a panegyric to "Beta." But whereas Spenser's "Eliza" is situated in the midst of a countryside, Beta is placed securely in London, along the "fayre silver Thames"; and whereas Eliza's shepherds praised her during the moment of song, Drayton's shepherds will honor Beta in the future: "Wee'l straw the shore with pearle where Beta walks alone, / And we wil pave her princely Bower with richest Indian stone" (1:58). Performed, reluctantly, while "Collin" is "to fayrie gone a Pilgrimage: / the more our mone" (1:57), Rowland's song does not so much usurp Spenser's role of panegyrist as displace it. For if Beta is elaborately distanced from the shepherdly community of

Drayton's collection, two other figures, praised, respectively, as "the God of Poesie" and "the Muse of Britanye" are brought into its center: Philip and Mary Sidney. The one has, of course, retreated to the Elysian fields where he reassumes a distinctly pastoral posture of "Feeding his flocke on yonder heavenly playne" (1:64); the other has become the sole retreat for "Vertue," who "is fled" to "Pandora"'s "sweete bosome" where "from the world . . . she lives at rest" (1:73). Two years before Spenser's "Astrophel" appeared in print, Drayton places the Sidneys *not* at the margins of his collection but at its center.

Yet it is precisely this center which kings threaten to plunder in Drayton's massive 1606 revision of the eclogues. If Rowland's reticence and "endles griefe" (1:94) in the 1593 collection came as a result of his failures in love—failures which may imply anticipated rejection, as in Colin's case, by the shepherdess at court[39]—the despair of Drayton's arch-poet in 1606 has to do neither with the melancholy of love nor the fickleness of a queen, but with a monarch's betrayal of the entire pastoral community: "So did great OLCON, which a PHOEBUS seem'd, / Whom all good Shepheards gladly flock'd about, / And as a God of ROWLAND was esteem'd, / Which to his prayse drew all the rurall rout" (2:561). James himself had taken Apollo as his "patron" god, a figure who symbolizes both the sun-god and the god of poetry, particularly of "Th'old *Lyrick* kind," as Drayton implies in his ode "To Himselfe, and the Harpe," also of 1606. More important, Drayton had celebrated James as the consummate poet-king in a sonnet appended to *Englands Heroicall Epistles* three years before James took the English throne:

> Others in vaine doe but historifie,
> Whene thine owne glory from thy selfe doth spring,
> As though thou did'st, all meaner prayses scorne:
> Of Kings a Poet, and the Poets King . . . .
> And Kings can but with Diadems be crown'd,
> But with thy Laurell, thou doo'st crowne thy Crowne.[40]

Highlighted in these verses is the myth of self-sustenance, of a king who needs neither poets to "historifie" him nor history itself as validation and legitimacy. But already in Drayton's "To the Maiestie of King James: A Gratulatorie Poem," written three years later for James's accession, there is some hesitancy regarding this mythical self-sufficiency. Invoking the much-maligned figure of the future *Poly-Olbion,* Drayton writes, "*If* in thy grace thou deigne to favour us /, And to the Muses be propitious, / *Caesar* himself, Roomes [sic] glorious wits among, / Was not so highly, nor divinely sung" (2:475; emphasis mine).[41] This leap into the future which suggests that James has *already* surpassed Caesar does not disguise Drayton's uncertainties. By the time of the pastoral eclogues of 1606, Sidney, once a quiescent shepherd miraculously translated into peaceful Elysium, is now protesting "false" deifications: he "Laughs even kings and their delights to scorne, / And all those Sots that them doe Deifie" (2:549). This later Sidney is now portrayed demystifying the golden age premisses of both James's reign and, for that matter, Elizabethan pastoral. Yet Sidney's voice emerges in the 1606 revision only through the concerted efforts of two older shepherds, one of whom takes the name of one of the first English publishers of Virgil's *Eclogues,* Wynken de Worde.[42] Wynken complains that Rowland, who composed the elegy to Sidney in 1593, has now betrayed a shepherdly community invested with the project of *memory.* Lured to the "Southerne Fields" of London by "thriftless vaine delight," and "scorning well-neere a Shepheards simple Name" (2:550), Rowland is simply the latest victim of a false "Phoebus" who threatens to obliterate the past and Sidney's now bitter voice. With the last two eclogues of the collection, however, Rowland "returns" from London, lamenting in Eclog 10 not love's melancholic consequences but the fact that he was tempted by "Fortune and Time" into that greater world where his efforts to embrace a greater "Name" and to "incourag' [his] desire" (2:572) for a subjectivity more sovereign than an "anonymous" shepherd's, came to nought.

Yet Drayton balances this closing and despondent eclogue with a more collective vision found in an eclogue completely new to the 1606 collection, the ninth. A celebration of a sheep-shearing festival, the poem is the only one of the ten eclogues, as Kathleen Tillotson has remarked, "to specify date and place—'late 'twas in June,' on Cotswold" (5:186). This new *placement* of pastoral in the heart of England's wool industry, the insistence on communal labors, "common flocks," and the "ancient Statutes of the Field" which determine that "He that his Flocks the earlyest Lambe should bring / . . . Always for that yeere was the Shepheards King" (2:564–65), situate the eclogue within a context scorned by "proud Courts": "For Countrey toyes become the Countrey best, / And please poore Shepheards, and become them well" (2:564). Yet such initial assurance seems to diminish in the course of the poem. While "Kingship" is boldly claimed to be dependent on both the land's "ancient Statutes" and on the sexual reproduction and "labors" of one's flocks, and while the shepherds' king is both obeyed by his "subjects" and "Bound as the rest" by his commands, the fact that this king is none other than Rowland back from London complicates matters, as does the manner in which Rowland himself is described. In the few stanzas before Rowland dutifully performs his *own* song, he is characterized as "the Clownish King" and a swayne "unworthy" of his Nymph Idea, and his Roundelay is glossed by his chorus as only a "poore Shepheard's Song" (4:569–70). Such deflation of—or vacillation regarding—the posture of sovereignty in passages of which the famous fourth act of *The Winter's Tale,* with its pastoral community openly branded as *traitors* by the Bohemian king, will be reminiscent,[43] raises certain, perhaps un-answerable, questions. Does Rowland's sovereignty "bound" by the land constitute a model for James's kingship; or does it, rather, suggest a *dis*-empowering, given his community's distance from England's politi-cal center? What kind of authority does Drayton's Cotswold commu-nity *have,* thus engaged in the preservation of ancient custom and, in effect, the *re*writing of the pastoral mystifications of the queen's prog-ress of 1591?[44] No longer an abstract community of poets anxious to assert the independence of their pastoral powers from the queen, Dray-ton's gathering of Cotswold shepherds takes on an ambivalent function which arises from the very perils of attempting to decenter the court as the primary focus of pastoral—perils which the "dying" and despon-dent Rowland articulates in his closing eclogue.

*Poly-Olbion,* already begun during Elizabeth's reign and the first part of which was published in 1612, becomes a partial solution to the prob-lem which Drayton staged around Rowland's desire to leave a noncourtly community that cannot give him a "Name." In the four-teenth song of *Poly-Olbion,* which celebrates the region of the Cotswolds and "the Sheepe our *Wold* doth breed," Drayton resituates, almost ver-batim, eight lines from the ninth eclogue praising the custom that determines each year's "Sheepheards King" and the feast over which he presides. With its sheep-shearing festival and coronation of the "shep-heard-king," Eglogue 9 is recuperated as a rare, positive image of the present in a poem which both labors to recreate England's past and to expose the failings of the present. Whereas the eclogue had ended with Rowland's "roundelay" and the collection as a whole with his dejection, the festival in *Poly-Olbion* closes with an apostrophe to "Mount Cotswold": "be this spoke to th'onely praise of thee, / That thou of all the rest, the chosen soyle should'st bee,/ Faire *Isis* to bring-forth (the Mother of great *Tames*) / With those delicious Brooks, by whose im-mortall streames / Her greatnesse is begunne" (4:298). The locus of the pastoral community becomes the point of origination of the tributary that will eventually produce the Thames—"our Rivers King"—who "derive[s] his stem by thee, / From kingly *Cotswolds* selfe" (4:298).

The allusion to Isis and her son, moreover, prepares Drayton for the celebration of Isis's wedding to Tames, to be described in the following song in an epithalamion that derives from and arguably competes with Spenser's epithalamion for Thames and Medway in Book IV of the *Faerie Queene*. But whereas in Spenser, as Richard Helgerson has observed, rivers "rise up" from their actual sites in obeisance to a "sovereign will," in Drayton's poem, waters stay in their natural riverbeds, attending "only the marriages to which the course of nature . . . invite[s] them."[45] Moreover, rather than celebrate the merging-point of England's great rivers and the city to which they lead, Drayton focuses on the rivers' *source:* on their origins in a productive countryside which freely recalls the past; on the crucial tributaries which do not automatically obey "sovereign will" but respect and maintain their natural paths. If Spenser's epithalamion had epitomized the *translatio* of empire from the continent to Tudor England[46]—and, by implication, the Spenserian *translatio* of epic—then Drayton articulates another kind of "translation" of authority altogether: one which happens *within* Britain, from its margins to its "center," from its early writers, historiographers, and heralds epitomized in the Welsh bards to those of the present age. Henry II's voyage to "Penbrooke" in Song 6 where an anonymous "Musician, Herault, Bard" commands his "powerfull Harpe" (4:118) to sing of Arthur, the first British king, exemplifies a king's necessary deference to "marginal" communities which are the repositories of a history that alone is capable of legitimizing Henry's own claims to the throne. Those who "now . . . scarce beleeve that *Arthur* ever was" challenge and disrupt—or completely ignore—such patterns of authorization.

This present failure of belief makes itself felt most keenly in the song dedicated to England's political center, London, suggesting that Drayton's—and Henry's—idealized version of *translatio* has broken down. Once the river which originates in England's pastoral communities comes, finally, to London, it discovers only a locus in which are gathered "foolish foraine things/ Which upstart Gentry still into our Country brings," sapping "the publique wealth" (4:321–22). It is just this failure of *translatio* that Drayton registers in his preface, where he indicts those who will inevitably refuse "to take paines to search into ancient and noble things" and to

> walke forth into the *Tempe* and Feelds of the Muses, where through most delightfull Groves the Angellique harmony of Birds shall steale thee to the top of an easie hill, where . . . thou maist fully view the dainty Nymphes in their simple naked bewties . . . [and] harmlesse Shepheards . . . some exercising their pipes, some singing roundelais, to their gazing flocks. (4.v*)

"If," Drayton concludes, "thou hadst rather, (because it asks thy labour) remaine, where thou wert . . . the fault proceeds from thy idlenesse, not from any want in my industrie." A process of *labor*, the rejection of "idle" London and the decision to engage in, as Drayton defines it in his final song, his "strange *Herculean* toyle" (4:579), reveals not only Drayton's epic pretensions but an insistence, only partially evident in the eclogues, on the shared labors of memory. Not content with the potentially insulated community of poets "created" by *Englands Helicon*, Drayton appeals to a community of *readers* who exemplify none of the "idlenesse" associated with England's center—and by implication, with the court, controlled by a monarch who, unlike Henry II, does not venture to Pembroke to hear a bard sing of Arthur.

James's isolation is emphasized by the notable omission of his name in the following song, where "Tames" launches into a far from uncritical appraisal of British monarchs since William[47] and stops abruptly with Elizabeth's triumphs: she was "Rude *Ireland's* deadly scourge; who sent her Navies hence / Unto the either *Inde*, and to that shore so greene, / *Virginia* which we call, of her a Virgin Queen" (4:338). With this praise, " Here suddainly he staid"; James is promptly, "suddainly," left *out* of the account of monarchs who have occupied Brut's city, as Tames is interrupted by the "Tide . . . which thrust him rudely out." Yet despite the interruption and Tames's retreat to the countryside outside of London where the woods protest their deforestation (another symptom of a rudely interrupted history), Drayton hardly removes his poem from the realm of royalty, and it is in this refusal to do so that the Virgilian dialectics of the first Eclogue are most fully felt— and transformed. The first part of *Poly-Olbion* was dedicated to Prince Henry,[48] whose portrait follows the frontispiece of Albion surrounded by four conquerors of the past—Brut, Caesar, Hengist, and William. Together, the frontispiece and the famous engraving of Henry by William Hole situate *Poly-Olbion* in a vacuum—in a moment of interruption, of *silenced* history—between a past which was often threatened with erasure and a future which Henry, shown wielding a lance in blatant opposition to his father's dangerous "peacetime" policies, theoretically represents. The decentering effected by the poem, by the sudden halt of Tames's monologue, by the arrival of Cotswold's tributaries at London only to find there the importation of foreign goods and nothing else, is thus only, the poet hopes, temporary. Removing James from the poem, creating around him an eloquent silence, suggests that he is *not* a part of English history; it places him in the posture of the alien whom Selden's original Angles, "homines integri," refused to "mirari."[49] Silencing James becomes the poet's reaction to a synonomous act of silencing: that invoked by a Caesar who, with his claims to a golden age which eradicates Britain's honorable past, uproots Meliboeus, and replaces him with a Tityrus who forges "suppos'd Gentillitie" (1:65), threatens to displace the body of the poem with his own. But another "body," that of Henry, takes over in the second engraving, as though to return Meliboeus to his rightful place. Prince of Wales and bearer of a name which suggests continuity with Elizabeth's own father, Henry opposed the politics of a golden age which heralded only enervation and idleness and a disguised but threatening antagonism to the wishes of Drayton's putative readers.

But as the opening letter to *Poly-Olbion*'s second part of 1622 attests, Henry's early death deprived the poem's Virgilian dialectic of its force, and the community which Drayton had hoped for and of which he had imagined himself spokesperson did not materialize. The faithful group of Browne, Wither, and John Reynolds voices its support and mutual bitterness in the dedicatory verses, but the readers on whom Drayton had counted are condemned to the worst possible fate the poet can imagine: forgetfulness and self-sufficiency: "I wish it may be hereditary from them to their posteritie, that their children may bee beg'd for Fooles to the fift Generation, untill it may be beyond the memory of man to know that there was ever any other of their Families" (4:391). It is precisely this isolation that Drayton so consistently fought against in the pages of his Jacobean writings, as is evidenced most clearly—and most painfully—in those moments when he is most aware of the uncertainty of his mission, the nebulous status of a community which has only the possible fictiveness of history with which to unite itself against an unsympathetic king. The first lines of *Poly-Olbion* are not declarative but indecisive; no "arma virumque cano" but "Of Albions glorious Ile the Wonders *whilst* I write / . . . What helpe shall I invoke to ayde my Muse the while?"(4:1). Soon thereafter the poet makes a promising but ultimately pathetic invocation to the "original" British poets, the bards:

> Yee sacred Bards, that to your Harps melodious strings
> Sung th'ancient Heroes deeds (the monuments of Kings)
> And in your dreadfull verse ingrav'd the prophecies,
> The aged worlds descents, and Genealogies;
> If, as those *Druides* taught, which kept the British rites . . .
> When these our soules by death our bodies doe forsake,
> They instantlie again doe other bodies take;
> I could have wisht your spirits redoubled in my breast,
> To give my verse applause, to times eternall rest.
>                          (4:2)

"If"; "I could have wisht": subjunctives and expressions of hesitancy, qualifications, regret, to be found also in the second line of Drayton's first ode: "And why not I, as hee / That's greatest, if as free, / . . . Th'old *Lyrick* kind revive?" (2:347). But revival and redoubling are consistently negated by Drayton's own, always tentative grammar. The *option,* of course, is not to follow anyone: to take on for himself the primacy—one might argue, the sovereignty—of poetic voice. But in his perhaps most celebrated ode, "To the Virginian Voyage," where Drayton does explicitly entertain such thoughts of primacy in the "virgin" territory of the New World, such conjecture is mercilessly silenced. Only *after* "laurell" has been discovered by the heroes of the Virginia expedition, Drayton explains, can it be used "A poets browes / To crowne, that may sing there" (2:364). Note the hesitant "may": even, especially in prophecy, the solitary voice can only be tentative, never assertive. Acts of heroism, of *others'* sovereignty, must precede poetic creation; Drayton can exhort his fellow countrymen to victory only after they have embarked.[50]

But it is another embarcation, described in the second half of *Poly-Olbion,* which ultimately reveals both Drayton's sensitivity to a poetics of history and the limitations of his refusal to declare him*self* as sovereign. Significantly, it is a passage in which the golden-age politics he entertained both skeptically and hopefully throughout his writing play no uncertain part. In 1622, when Henry had been dead for nine years and it was becoming increasingly apparent that Charles would no more protect British "history" than his father, Drayton turned to surrogate leaders who had to find their legitimacy by turning *outward:* Raleigh, Drake, Hakluyt, praised for their overseas expeditions in Song 19. Drayton's verses on Raleigh's recent, unsuccessful trip to Guiana and the promises of "El Dorado"—the mysterious Golden Man—are particularly compelling:

> *Rawleigh,* whose reading made him skil'd in all the Seas,
> Imbarqu'd his worthy selfe, and his adventurous crue,
> And with a prosperous Sayle to those faire Countries flew,
> Where *Orenoque,* as he, on in his course doth roule,
> Seems as his greatnes meant, grim *Neptune* to controule;
> Like to a puisant King, whose Realmes extend so farre,
> That many a potent Prince his Tributaries are.
> So are his Branches Seas, and in the rich *Guiana,*
> A Flood as proud as he, the broad-brim'd *Orellana:*
> And on the spacious firme *Manoas* mightie seat,
> The land (by Natures power) with wonders most repleat.
>
> (4:406)

Manoa was the legendary Venezuelan city whose streets were paved with gold; the Orinoco the river that had flooded the first time Raleigh attempted to discover El Dorado and that on the third try had carried Raleigh's son, his old captain, and numerous colleagues to death in a bitter battle with the Spaniards—after which Raleigh was sentenced to death.[51] But it is not the Spaniards who defeat Raleigh and his troops. Rather, the "puisant King" *Orenoque* and his princely tributaries, and thus "Natures power" confirmed in the sovereignty of her rivers, represent the insurmountable hurdle to England's boldest conqueror. Rebuffed by the monarchy of the land and unwilling, unlike Julius Caesar, to efface that sovereignty and its history, Raleigh had to turn back to his own sovereign and to certain death at the Tower.

Two visions of monarchy put themselves forth in the allegory of Raleigh's tragic venture: one inheres in the land; the other in the person. Raleigh's vulnerability to the one forces him to become vulnerable to the other; true conquerors and absolutists, like James, simply refuse to respect what is indigenous to a land and to its communities. Drayton spent his entire career articulating a cultural divide between James and the nation—a nation that attempted, in Raleigh's person, to go elsewhere but which was not yet convinced of its own "sovereignty."[52] Drayton's lack of certainty that he spoke *for* a nation and that the community's "labors" and his own were one and the same makes his Jacobean poetry, finally, a poetry of disappointment. Only with figures such as Milton did the connection between voice and national community become, if only temporarily, assured. It is thus not as a poet of belatedness that Drayton must be read, but as a poet who had the misfortune of writing too early.[53]

## Notes

1. *The Works of Michael Drayton,* ed. J. William Hebel, Kathleen Tillotson, and Bernard H. Newdigate (Oxford: Shakespeare Head Press, 1931–61), 4:119. All references to Drayton's work will be from this edition; volume and page numbers will be cited parenthetically in the text.

2. See Carol Maddison, *Apollo and the Nine: A History of the Ode* (London: Routledge and Kegan Paul, 1960), pp. 292–94; and Geoffrey Hiller, "'Sacred Bards' and 'Wise Druides': Drayton and his Archetype of the Poet," *ELH* 51 (1984): 1–15.

3. See Selden's somewhat more judicious remarks on the Romans' ignorance in his commentary published with Drayton's poem: "For indeed many are which the author here impugnes, that dare beleeve nothing of our storie, or antiquities of more ancient times; but only *Julius Caesar,* and other about or since him. And surely his ignorance of this Isle was great, time forbidding him

language or conversation with the *British*. Nor was any before him of his country, that knew or medled in relation of us. . . . In the somewhat later Poets that liv'd about *Augustus*, as *Catullus, Virgil*, and *Horace*, some passages of the name have you, but nothing that discovers any monument of this Island proper to her inhabitants" (4:124–55). Elsewhere in his commentary, Selden observes that Caesar's knowledge of Britain was limited because he went only as far as London—which is clearly not (either in the past or present) exemplary of Britain itself (4:217–18).

4. Drayton's (and Selden's) "historicizing" in *Poly-Olbion* is in many ways reminiscent of the efforts of Coke and others to validate the origins of England's customs in a "time immemorial" that rejects attempts by monarchs to claim their authorship of English law and institutions such as Parliament; on which, see J. G. A. Pocock, *The Ancient Constitution and the Feudal Law* (1957; rev. ed., Cambridge University Press, 1986), esp. chaps. 2 and 3. On the "circle" with which Drayton was loosely connected, see B. H. Newdigate, *Michael Drayton and His Circle* (Oxford: Basil Blackwell, 1941); and Richard Hardin, *Michael Drayton and the Passing of Elizabethan England* (Lawrence: University Press of Kansas, 1973), esp. pp. 88–92.

5. As Samuel Daniel said of himself in 1605; cited in Richard Helgerson, *Self-Crowned Laureates: Spenser, Jonson, Milton, and the Literary System* (Berkeley: University of California Press, 1983), p. 35.

6. This is Gary Waller's characterization of those who turned to Sir Philip Sidney in the early seventeenth century as a "model" poet and courtier; in *English Poetry of the Sixteenth Century* (London: Longman, 1986), p. 172. For more sympathetic views, see Joan Grundy, *The Spenserian Poets* (London: Edward Arnold, 1969), Hardin, *Michael Drayton and the Passing of Elizabethan England*, and David Norbrook, *Poetry and Politics in the English Renaissance* (London: Routledge and Kegan Paul, 1984).

7. In calling attention to the etymological roots of "culture" in cultivation and possession, Edward Said discusses cultural definition as a "proprietary process," the establishment of a boundary through which principles of inclusion and exclusion—and ultimately "an elevated or superior position to authorize"—come into play; see his *The World, the Text, and the Critic* (Cambridge: Harvard University Press, 1983), pp. 8–16.

8. See, among other works, Hugh Trever-Roper, "The General Crisis of the Seventeenth Century," in his *Religion, the Reformation and Social Change* (London: Macmillan, 1967); Perez Zagorin, *The Court and the Country* (New York: Atheneum, 1970); and most recently, Leah Marcus, *The Politics of Mirth: Jonson, Herrick, Marvell, and the Defense of Old Holiday Pastimes* (Chicago: University of Chicago Press, 1986). For the argument that in *Poly-Olbion*, Drayton turns to the "country" as a "rival source of authority," see Richard Helgerson, "The Land Speaks: Cartography, Chorography, and Subversion in Renaissance England," in *Representing the English Renaissance*, ed. Stephen Greenblatt (Berkeley: University of California Press, 1988), pp. 327–61.

9. For a general discussion of the significance of "sovereignty" and the

"sovereign subject" in seventeenth-century England, see Catherine Belsey, *The Subject of Tragedy: Identity and Difference in Renaissance Drama* (London: Methuen, 1985), chap. 4.

10. "See, if any *Palace* yeelds/ Ought more glorious, then the *Fields,*/ And consider well, if we/ May not as high-flying be/ In our thoughts, as you that sing/ In the Chambers of a King" (*Faire-Virtue* [London, 1622], fol. B8ᵛ).

11. Harold Toliver, *Lyric Provinces in the English Renaissance* (Columbus: Ohio State University Press, 1985), contains one of the most sensitive treatments in recent years of seventeenth-century lyric and its "placement" in domains exclusive of the court; the phrase "lyric sites" is from p. ix.

12. Ibid., p. 14. See also Gordon Braden, "Herrick's Classical Quotations," in *Trust to Good Verses: Herrick Tercentenary Essays,* ed. Roger B. Rollin and J. Max Patrick (Pittsburgh: University of Pittsburgh Press, 1978), for the argument that the lyric fragments of *Hesperides* "integrate . . . a life by treating thematically its emotional dynamics and by providing a career and title appropriate to both the writer's ambition and his place" (p. 140).

13. The phrase is that of Mary Jacobus, in "Apostrophe and Lyric Voice in *The Prelude,*" in *Lyric Poetry: Beyond New Criticism,* ed. Chaviva Hosek and Patricia Parker (Ithaca: Cornell University Press, 1985), p. 169. Drayton's own definition of the ode in "To the Reader" of the 1606 collection is, admittedly, remarkably eclectic, although he tends to privilege the sublime ode of Pindar: "[Odes] are (as the Learned say) divers: Some transcendently loftie, and farre more high then the Epick (commonly called the Heroique Poeme) witnesse those of the inimitable Pindarus, consecrated to the glorie and renowne of such as returned in triumph from Olympus, Elis, Isthmus, or the like: Others, among the Greekes, are amorous, soft, and made for Chambers, as other for Theaters; as were Anacreon's, the very Delicacies of the Grecian Erato. . . . Of a mixed kinde were Horaces, and may truely therefore be called his mixed; whatsoever else are mine, little partaking of the high Dialect of the first: 'Though we be all to seeke / Of *Pindar,* that great Greeke'" (*Works of Michael Drayton,* 2:345).

14. The articles of Louis Adrian Montrose are primarily responsible for this renewed attentiveness to Elizabethan pastoral's topical relevance; see, for example, "Gifts and Reasons: The Contexts of Peele's *Arraignment of Paris,*" *ELH* 47 (1980): 433–61; "'Eliza, Queene of shepheardes', and the Pastoral of Power," *English Literary Renaissance* 10 (1980): 153–82; "Of Gentlemen and Shepherds: The Politics of Elizabethan Pastoral Form," *ELH* 50 (1983): 415–89; and most recently, "The Elizabethan Subject and the Spenserian Text," in *Literary Theory/Renaissance Texts,* ed. Patricia Parker and David Quint (Baltimore: Johns Hopkins University Press, 1986), pp. 303–40. But see also Annabel Patterson's exemplary *Pastoral and Ideology* (Berkeley: University of California Press, 1988).

15. One might hazard the suggestion that, paradoxically, Ben Jonson, for whom Spenser had "writ no language," rather than the "Spenserians," becomes the genuine heir of "Aprill" in his reinforcement of the courtly aspirations and

concessions of Elizabeth's chief poet. For an excellent discussion of the dif-
ferences between Jonson and the Spenserians, see Norbrook, *Poetry and Politics
in the English Renaissance,* chaps. 8–10.

16. George Puttenham, *The Arte of English Poesie* ([1589] Kent, Ohio: Kent
State University Press, 1970), p. 53. Daniel Javitch's *Poetry and Courtliness in
Renaissance England* (Princeton: Princeton University Press, 1978) effectively
reintroduced Puttenham to contemporary criticism.

17. Montrose, "The Elizabethan Subject and the Spenserian Text," p. 323.

18. Annabel Patterson makes this important point in reference to
Montrose's reading in *Pastoral and Ideology,* pp. 130–31.

19. According to Hobbinoll, "Shepheards delights [Colin] dooth them all
forsweare, / Hys pleasaunt Pipe, whych made us meriment, / He wylfully
hath broke, and doth forbeare / His wonted songs, wherein he all out-
went" ("Aprill," ll. 13–16; in *Spenser's Minor Poems,* ed. Ernest de Sélincourt
[Oxford: Clarendon, 1910], p. 37).

20. See Jonathan Goldberg's important comments on Spenser's "fantasy of
having by not giving" in *Endlesse Worke* (Baltimore: Johns Hopkins University
Press, 1981), p. 173; and my "Spenser, Virgil, and the Politics of Poetic Labor,"
*ELH* 55 (1988): 53–77.

21. On the topicality of *The Shepheardes Calender,* see Paul McLane,
*Spenser's Shepheardes Calender: A Study in Elizabethan Allegory* (Notre Dame:
University of Notre Dame Press, 1961); for Crowley, see John N. King, *English
Reformation Literature* (Princeton: Princeton University Press, 1982), esp. p.
432. On Spenser's Protestantism, see Althea Hume, *Edmund Spenser: Protestant
Poet* (Cambridge: Cambridge University Press, 1984); John N. King,
"Spenser's *Shepheardes Calender* and Protestant Pastoral Satire," in *Renaissance
Genres: Essays on Theory, History, and Interpretation,* ed. Barbara Lewalski
(Cambridge: Harvard University Press, 1986), pp. 369–98; and Andrew
Weiner's paper, "Spenser and the Myth of Pastoral," presented at the Sixteenth-
Century Studies Conference, Tempe, Arizona; October 1987, and now in
*Studies in Philology* 85 (1988): 390–406.

22. Philip Sidney, *An Apology for Poetry,* ed. Geoffrey Shepherd (London,
1965), p. 116. Annabel Patterson notes that Sidney's account "was not only Vir-
gilian in focus and political in inference but peculiarly limited to the first
eclogue and its dialectical nature" (*Pastoral and Ideology,* p. 127).

23. "Tullus, over and over you ask me, for friendship's sake, / to tell of my
rank, my family, my home. / Rome's dead lie in Perugia; Rome's heartbreak /
began in Perugia, darkening all of Rome / with the madness of civil war" (*The
Poems of Propertius,* trans. Constance Carrier [Bloomington: Indiana Univer-
sity Press, 1963], I: xxii; p. 55).

24. John van Sickle, *The Design of Virgil's Bucolics* (Rome: Ateneo, 1978),
esp. pp. 187–205.

25. The repetition of "umbra" in the last few lines of Eclogue 10 is striking,
particularly given its positive implications in the first eclogue: "surgamus; solet
esse gravis cantantibus umbra, / iuniperi gravis umbra; nocent et frugibus um-

brae" (in Vergil, *Eclogues,* ed. Robert Coleman [Cambridge University Press, 1977], p. 70). Virgil's spokesperson's final phrase—"Ite capellæ"—echoes, as Coleman observes, Meliboeus's farewell to his Arcady in Eclogue I.74 (p. 294), suggesting a possible connection between the Virgilian persona and the exile who will *not* be silenced.

26. In William Browne, *The Shepheards Pipe* (London, 1614), n.p. See also Drayton, *The Owl* (1604), in which he protests against the "grip and hunger of [the] ravenous Lord" and the "cruell *Castrell,* which . . . [by] / Raising new Fines, redoubling ancient Rent; / And by th'inclosure of old Common Land, / Rackes the deare sweat from his [Tenant's] laborious hand" (2.501).

27. The phrase is Jane Hedley's, in *Power in Verse: Metaphor and Metonymy in the Renaissance Lyric* (University Park: Pennsylvania State University Press, 1988), p. 23. For the important thesis that the apolitical nature of lyric in fact only perpetuates the social domination of the subject, see Theodor W. Adorno, "Lyric Poetry and Society," *Telos* 20 (1974): 56–71.

28. The citation is from *The Arte of English Poesie,* p. 22. Puttenham has read Aristotle's *Politics,* as he mentions in the chapter on pastoral (p. 53)–a text where Aristotle writes "There are great differences in human ways of life. The laziest are shepherds; for they get their food without labor from tame animals and have leisure" (*Politics* 1256a30). As Hannah Arendt notes, the word for leisure (*Skholazousin*) is derived from *skhole,* abstention from certain activities which constitute the condition for political life; see *The Human Condition* (Garden City: Doubleday, 1959), p. 323n.

29. For the involvement of John Bodenham—who was also behind "encyclopedic" texts of the late 1590s such as *Wits Commonwealth* (1597), *Wits Theater of the Little World* (1599), and *Belvedere: the Garden of the Muses* (1600)—and Anthony Munday in *Englands Helicon,* see Celeste Turner Wright, "Anthony Mundy and the Bodenham Miscellanies," *Philological Quarterly* 40 (1961): 449–61. See also F. B. Williams, Jr., "John Bodenham, 'Art's Lover, Learning's Friend'," *Studies in Philology* 31 (1934), and H. E. Rollins's introduction to his two-volume edition of *Englands Helicon* (Cambridge: Harvard University Press, 1935), 2: 41–63. On Drayton's possible involvement in the 1600 *Englands Helicon,* see J. W. Hebel, "Nicholas Ling and *Englands Helicon,*" *Library,* 4th series, 5 (1924): 153–60.

30. *King James his Welcome to London. With Elizaes Tomb and Epitaph* (London, 1603), fol. Cʳ. On the elegies for Elizabeth, see Barbara Keifer Lewalski, *Donne's Anniversaries and the Poetry of Praise* (Princeton: Princeton University Press, 1973), pp. 19–29.

31. *Englands Helicon* (London, 1600), fols. Cᵛ, C4ᵛ, and D4ʳ, respectively.

32. It must at the same time be noted that the practice of applying songs to authors and thus dismantling them of their courtly contexts does not occur where the author's name is unknown; thus the song entitled "Ceres Song in emulation of Cinthia" (a poem rather fainthearted in its rejection of fertility for chastity) is followed by the explanation, "This Song was sung before her Maiestie, at Bissam, the Lady Russels, in prograce. The Authors name unknowne to

me." One has the impression, however, that were the "Authors name" known to Ling, the prefatory material alluding to the progress would have been unnecessary.

33. See David Quint's insightful comments on the *Mutabilitie Cantos* and the "retreat" of Elizabeth /Diana from Spenser's poem, in his *Origin and Originality in Renaissance Literature: Versions of the Source* (New Haven: Yale University Press, 1983), esp. p. 166: "The *Mutabilitie Cantos* acknowledge the precariousness of an allegory founded on a historical moment that is bound to pass away."

34. *Englands Helicon*, fol. A4ᵛ.

35. Ling appeared to be interested in propagating a concept of "purity" that would make his volume pleasing to the "superis" or powers above; on the work's lavish title page, appear the lines "Casta placent superis / pura cum veste venite, / Et manibus puris / sumite fontis aquam" (Chaste things please the powers above, / [thus] come with pure garments, / and with clean hands/ approach the waters of the fountain).

36. This separation of country from court, of pastoral from kings, will be stressed much more explicitly in the anthology's next edition almost two centuries later. Writing in an era still obsessed with the bogus Ossian and a poetics of the common "folk" initially championed by Herder and opposed to the polite and civilized society of the courts, the editors of the 1812 *Englands Helicon* claim that the Elizabethan miscellany is a testament to the concerns of those

> bearded chiefs, whose portraits adorn the pannels of our halls and galleries, still bearing witness to the same natural and eternal truths; still inveighing against the pomp, the fickleness, and the treachery of courts; and uttering the songs of the shepherd and the woodman, in language that defies the changes of time, and speaks to all ages the touching effusions of the heart.

What in 1614 was simply *a*-courtly has now become defiantly *anti*-courtly, a point the editor makes abundantly clear when he contrasts the "far-fetched subtlety of metaphysical verses" favored by the "vile taste of King James, and his court" to the "healthy" pastoralism of an earlier era. From *Englands Helicon*, ed. S. E. Brydges and Joseph Haselwood (London: T. Bensley, 1812), pp. xx–xxi.

37. The remaining seven poems were all from Francis Davison's popular *A Poeticall Rhapsody*, first published in 1602. The poem that closes the 1614 *Englands Helicon*, Brooke's "Epithalamion; or a Nuptiall Song, applied to the Ceremonies of Marriage," vividly suggests the extent to which pastoral had become de-centered from Elizabeth's mythology of chastity.

38. David Norbrook is alone among recent critics to underscore the ideological importance of *Englands Helicon*'s re-edition in 1614; see his *Poetry and Politics in the English Renaissance*, p. 207.

39. On the connection between the sonnet sequence and social ambition, see Arthur Marotti, "Love Is not Love," *ELH* 49 (1982): 396–429.

40. In Sonnet 62 from *Idea,* dedicated "To the high and mighty Prince, James, King of Scots," and appended to *Englands Heroicall Epistles* in 1600 (in *Works,* 1:488). Significantly, the poem is omitted in most later editions. On James's willingness to cultivate the image of the "poet-king," see Jonathan Goldberg, *James I and the Politics of Literature* (Baltimore: Johns Hopkins University Press, 1983), pp. 17–28.

41. Rushing James's earlier "welcome" into print, Drayton neglected to write an elegy for Elizabeth—a choice he regretted years later; in the elegy to George Sandys, probably of 1621, Drayton would write, "It was my hap before all other men / To suffer shipwrack by my forward pen: / When King JAMES entred; at which joyfull time / I taught his title to this Ile in rime" (*Works* 3:210).

42. See Kathleen Tillotson's note on the original version of Sidney's elegy in *The Shepheardes Garland,* where she observes that Wynken de Worde was active in London from roughly 1476 to 1534; "Drayton no doubt possessed books bearing his imprint; perhaps his edition of Virgil's *Bucolics,* his Chaucer, his *Guy of Warwick*" (*Works* 5:8). Annabel Patterson also notes Drayton's use of Wynken de Worde in her *Pastoral and Ideology,* p. 134n.

43. See IV.iv, in which Polixenes calls Florizel " too base / To be acknowledged," and brands Camillo "an old traitor" and Perdita a witch, undoing both the *a*political nature of the countryside and the Jonsonian premise that pastoral functioned to protect its monarch from opposition. On Jonson, see Stephen Orgel, *The Illusion of Power* (Berkeley: University of California Press, 1975), pp. 49–58.

44. The Sudely entertainments of 1591 can be found in *The Dramatic Works of John Lilly,* ed. F. W. Fairholt (London, 1892), vol. 1. Montrose discusses the numerous "strategies" of the progress designed to unify the crown and commons against a baronial threat, and the elite against a popular threat, in "'Eliza, Queene of shepheardes' and the Pastoral of Power," esp. pp. 172–80.

45. "Sovereign will . . . assembles rivers whose waters would otherwise meet only in the great oceanic annihilation of fluvial identity" (Helgerson, "The Land Speaks," pp. 354–55).

46. See David Quint, *Origin and Originality in Renaissance Literature,* pp. 156–61.

47. See, for example, the comments on William's "ill-gotten gains" and on Henry's "enslavement" of the English people; of Edward II (in a covert reference to James?), the poet says "Faire *Ganimeds* and Fools [he] rais'd to Princely places; / And chose not men for wit, but only for their faces" (*Works* 4:334).

48. Drayton was one of the prince's poets, with a salary of ten pounds per year; see Roy Strong, *Henry, Prince of Wales and England's Lost Renaissance* (New York: Thames and Hudson, 1986), p. 157, who also observes that "Henry was deliberately employing an author who was disliked by his father."

49. See Selden's comments on Song 10: "the *Angles* hither traduc'd, being *homines integri,* and using, *naturali simplicitate sua defensare, aliena non mirari,* did now learn from the *stranger-Saxons* an uncivill kind of fiercenes, of the *Flemings* effeminacy, of the *Danes* drunkennes, and such other"; in the margins

is the translation of the Latin and a credit to Malmesbury: "Honest men, by simplicity of nature, looking onely to their own, neglecting others" (*Works* 4:213).

50. On the failure of lyric voice in the odes, see Paul Fry, *The Poet's Calling in the English Ode* (New Haven: Yale University Press, 1980), pp. 30–36.

51. For details of the search for El Dorado, see Boies Penrose, *Travel and Discovery in the Renaissance, 1420–1620* (New York: Atheneum, 1962), pp. 141–49.

52. See Christopher Hill's comments on George Wither's similar endeavor, in "George Wither and John Milton," in *The Collected Essays of Christopher Hill* (Sussex: Harvester Press, 1985), 1:133–56. On Milton's Christian community and its relationship to a pastoral voice that is ultimately incorporated within it, see Stanley Fish, "*Lycidas:* A Poem Finally Anonymous," *Glyph* 8 (1982): 1–17.

53. My thanks to the Folger Shakespeare Library for funding initial research on this essay, done in summer 1987; and to William Klein, Arthur Marotti, Leah Marcus, and the anonymous readers at the University of Chicago Press for their invaluable suggestions and encouragement.

# 8

# Dating Milton

*Jonathan Goldberg*

In a footnote to his biography of Milton, William Riley Parker pauses to make a confession: "In this entire book there is no question of dating on which I have changed my mind so many times as that of *When I consider.*"[1] Confession is Parker's word: "this chapter, I confess, was the last to be typed in its final form." As a glance at the commentaries gathered in the Milton Variorum or at the footnotes in Merritt Hughes's edition would show, Parker is hardly alone in his guilty irresolution in the face of the conflicting evidence about the date of the poem. Thanks to one phrase in the sonnet, "ere half my days," the poem apparently dates itself some time before Milton reached the age of thirty-five (in 1643); but because the poem did not appear in the 1645 *Poems,* and because the poem is assumed to refer to Milton's blindness (complete in 1651–52), it is presumed to be later (and much ingenuity has been spent to explain away the troubling self-dating the poem offers). Yet, when the poem was published (in 1673), it was placed after the sonnet on the Piedmont massacre of 1655. Like "half my days," this placement of the poem also appears to date it, but the 1655 date (for which Parker finally opted), disturbs scholars who, like Parker earlier, assign the poem to 1651–52, and read (and date) it as a record of, as Parker puts it, Milton's "fresh reaction to blindness."

When was sonnet 19 written? What impels historical scholarship to resolve the multiple and contradictory pieces of evidence about "When I consider" into a single and determinate moment of composition, a moment remarkable for its "freshness" and for the presumed presence of Milton writing at that very moment? To ask the question that way begins to suggest some answers, and in the pages that follow, the question of dating is engaged in order to raise some fundamental questions about the kinds of narrativizations that produce conventional literary history.

We may believe that we go to Parker or to the Variorum for facts, but what we encounter instead are narratives of value that need to be read historically. In the reading I propose (which is *not* a reading of the sonnet), a different sense of history from that which informs historical scholarship (or, it will be suggested, a variety of kinds of new historicisms) will be advanced. It calls into question the self-presence of the moment.

Rather than seeking the single, determinate, present moment of composition of the sonnet, the argument here depends upon the irresolvability of the evidence sketched above. In place of a narrative which imagines a Milton who was always the same, always himself (and in which the dating of the poem is part of that self-unfolding), I would offer a different account, one that refuses self-sameness either to "Milton" or to the supposed regularities of a temporal progression. Opening itself to chance, contingency, and revision, the narrative I would offer can scarcely be contained by the economies of a conventional historical account; indeed, as much as this essay seeks to disrupt standard ways of reading the sonnet, so too it opens the possibility of a different way of engaging history. The irresolvable temporalities which mark the poem are, I will argue, legible through acts of intercalation, situating the poem and its speaker (neither of which, however, are assumed to be self-unified, self-identical, or immediately present) against a range of Miltonic self-productions. Thus, most of this essay reads Milton's prose, to find there the subjects, the various Miltons, whose traces remain to disturb the possibility of determining a single Miltonic "I" or a single moment of its writing in sonnet 19.

The Wordsworthian title of Mary Ann Radzinowicz's *Toward Samson Agonistes: The Growth of Milton's Mind* conveniently summarizes the informing narrative of historical scholarship. For all the arguments about dating sonnet 19 recorded in the Variorum, no matter which date of composition is advanced, depend upon the shared supposition that the "correct" single date of the poem will best explain how Milton became (and therefore always was) himself. When Parker, for example, changed his mind, it was to show the "biographical *rightness*" of his new dating; the poem revealed Milton ready to write *Paradise Lost,* and the expended light of sonnet 19 referred back to the years when "the poet" (for Parker, the essential Milton) had been writing prose. The poet, however, within the same essentializing construction, is no less the subject of the sonnet in the reading that A. S. P. Woodhouse offers (against the later Parker) in support of a 1651–52 dating of the poem in the Variorum. From an initial "mood of depression, frustration, even impatience," in the initial lines, the sonnet, Woodhouse contends, "is not so much resolved as lifted to a plane where self-regarding thoughts become irrelevant."[2] Woodhouse's *Aufhebung* is explicitly transcendental; to date the poem properly enables it to be "lifted" out of history.

"The main argument for dating *Sonnet 19* in 1652 has always been the state of mind it expresses" (449), the Variorum editors contend. So saying, they point to the shared suppositions of historical scholarship; "always" here (like Woodhouse's higher plane) reveals the teleological imperatives that produce "biographical *rightness*." Whatever date is argued for the poem, it is always in the service of this same story. Radzinowicz's account makes this perfectly clear; she dates the poem 1652, but considers it along with sonnets written in 1655 and later because, she argues, with them it "records calm of mind," "spiritual progress."[3] The "growth of Milton's mind" is "a dialectic leading to resolution, internal drama leading to integration, conflict leading to harmony" (4).

This "dialectic" serves a double dating; chronology submits not only to higher designs, the poet is imagined as always "growing" into himself, never changed, or split, by historical experience. There is another way to read the conflicting evidence, however, one that would not efface the tension between "ere half my days" and the placement of the poem in the 1673 volume by resolving the contradictory evidence in the transcendental "rightness" of a life whose every moment is part of some transhistorical schema. It is that reading I would advance here. In that account, "When I consider" would have been written and rewritten over a number of years, and could not be resolved into a singular chronological placement. Closest to this argument is E. A. J. Honigmann's willingness to make a case for dating the poem either in 1644 or 1651–52 or 1655. To admit the possibility of any of these dates, however, is nonetheless not to admit the possibility that I am imagining, of revision and rewriting across these dozen years. That is resisted because it would involve denying that the poem dates from a single and fully saturated moment in the Miltonic career. (Revision is generally accepted when it can be shown as part of the process of growth towards self-sameness.) But if the poem was written well before, at the same time, and several years after Milton became totally blind—during years, too, in which plans for what became *Paradise Lost* varied enormously, and in which Milton's political engagement moved from Presbyterian to Independent and beyond party identification—it will hardly deliver the "always" that historical critics desire, nor that single "state of mind" that would accompany it. Revision of this sort would deny the author his transcendental status. It would imbed the lyric in a history that refuses the teleological imperatives of historicism. For in such accounts, as the complicities between teleological narrativization and transcendental identification suggest, the attempt to date and place a poem definitively does not aim at putting the poem in history but in removing it from history. The self-realization of the author, the translation of the events of life into texts, produces texts which have been delivered from the conditions of their production.

It was precisely the conditions in his own production of the life of Milton that provoked Parker's guilty confession: "this chapter, I confess, was the last to be typed in its final form." Indecisiveness is shameful, and perhaps even more shameful the admission that the biography was not written straight through, in chronological order. Guilt attaches itself to second thoughts and to revisions. And, I would argue, what is guilty in the practice of the biographer (committed, after all, to the truth of chronological unfolding), is, given a commitment to Milton's growth towards dialectical resolution, simply unthinkable when the question of dating Milton arises. These narratives of artistic transcendence tell the story of the timeless subjectivity of the modern subject: in his Wordsworthian "growth," Milton grows into, is always already, a modern poet.

If traditional historical scholarship has this story to tell, it is one that more recent historicist analysis has uncovered in Milton's poem. Whereas traditional historical accounts claim to be finding the historical Milton, but instead produce the timeless modern Milton, Anthony Easthope, for instance, argues that Milton attempts to efface history in his sonnet in order to produce the illusory effect of the modern subject. For Easthope, the sonnet does not make present Milton-the-man in the throes of a devastating experience, nor does it offer an instance of Milton-the-transcendental-author behind the text; rather, the only Milton there is arises as an effect of textualization; "the subject," Easthope writes, "is constituted as an effect of discourse."[4] Looking at relations between signifier and signified, in terms of polysemy as well as syntactic deployment, and considering, especially, the relationship between enunciation and enounced in Milton's sonnet, Easthope charts Milton's position between Shakespeare and Dryden, concluding that the sonnet on his blindness— because of its controlled polysemy, its resolution of any disturbance in its syntax and, especially, because of its movement towards a resolution of the "I" of the text into a structure of enunciation that has effaced the "I"—is a "transitional" (311) text within a history of modern poetry. Quoting Christopher Caudwell's dictum, "Modern poetry is *capitalist* poetry" (302), Easthope argues that Milton's poem delivers a recognizable bourgeois subject. The mark of that subject-position lies in the effacement of the materiality of the signifier, producing the effect of the transparence and autonomy of the speaking-subject.

From Easthope's perspective, then, what both Parker and Radzino-wicz respond to is a particular discursive effect, a certain mode of constructing the subject that is recognizable from the vantage point of their modernity because Milton's is a relatively early version of the modern subject. In Easthope's view, which I share, to historicize historical scholarship would necessitate a recognition of historical difference and distance even within modernity. Historical scholarship would not seek to repeat the ideological effects of the earlier text but to locate them within a history that attended to the materiality of writing. Parker, guiltily, admits his use of a typewriter, acts of revision, even a change of mind, in his practice; less openly, Radzinowicz attempts to date the poem twice, thereby revealing the refusal to admit change that might not be assimilated to a pattern of growth and self-sameness.

Easthope is committed to a reading of the poem within a history of the subject. Nonetheless, his account confirms the traditional historicist reading of the poem. Although he demystifies that reading, he offers one that still depends entirely on it. He finds it "convincing" (301), for instance, that Milton's sonnets offer a chronological sequence charting Milton's growth from youth to maturity and retirement. Proving that the poem's polysemy is not radical, he repeats New Critical readings of the poem that show, of course, that its ambiguities do not go beyond resolvable double meanings. These resolutions, that narrative of growth, may be writing-effects produced in the service of a suspect bourgeois ideology. Nonetheless the difference between Easthope and a traditional historicist account has to do with whether the designs of the poem are repudiated or embraced.

Easthope places Milton's text in a "transitional" position, and the narrative he produces, with Shakespeare's radical polysemy on one side and Dryden's transparency on the other, is another version of the Hegelian "dialectic" that also informs traditional historicists, although here inflected with a Marxist critique, as well as through a Lacanian account of the subject. In this history of the emergence of the capitalist subject in modern poetry, Easthope charts a movement from desire to demand, from a poetry inextricably connected to the body to a poetry that registers the split that signals entrance into the Symbolic. Although its terms are different, this is a very familiar history of English poetry in the seventeenth century; it is T. S. Eliot's modernist account of the dissociation of sensibility, now translated into a narrative of the development of the subject from Imaginary unity to Symbolic division.[5]

To tell the vital story that impels him, Easthope cannot be bothered with the finicky questions that trouble traditional historical scholarship. "Milton's sonnet 'On his Blindness' (the title added by Newton) is usually dated 1652 or 1655" (307), he begins. Dating is apparently inconsequential and an eighteenth-century title for the poem is acceptable too. From these indications, there would appear to be no history of modernity. Nor could the poem betray signs of the compositional history that I have been suggesting. Of the poem itself, Easthope writes, "Any dislocation is temporary, is fully resolved, and only confirms the decisive and unequivocal closure of the syntagmatic chain strung across these fourteen lines and two sentences" (308). One might be reading Woodhouse. Closure, resolution, and the like, there exalted, here exposed, are nonetheless in the service of narratives which share the same teleological imperatives.

The poem, I am suggesting—and this hypothesis is no more acceptable to traditional historicists than it is to Marxist historiography—can neither be determinately dated, nor can it be an instance in a history that seems to have no need of dates. The counterevidence of "ere half my days" and the seemingly chronological placement of the poem after the one about the 1655 Piedmont massacre is evidence nonetheless even if it cannot be easily homogenized. So, too, within the poem. It records a voice which is allowed articulation only to be silenced, retrospectively, by another voice which is, only afterwards, said to have come before the first voice speaking:

> Doth God exact day-labor, light denied,
> I fondly ask; but patience, to prevent
> That murmur, soon replies . . . .

The temporality of such voicing not only refuses an empiricist chronology, ownership of voices in the poem is also thrown into question. The line before the ones just quoted could prepare for the entrance of the divine voice into the text, "lest he returning chide," while the voice marked as that of "patience" does not only retrospectively supervene in this doubly marked voice-within-quotation; there is also no mark that makes clear whether that voice ever stops speaking in the poem or whether the "I" of the first line of the poem ever recurs. The poem remains unresolved, resisting those designs which would lift it out of history.[6]

Like Easthope, I have no desire to repeat the claims of traditional historical criticism; but I believe that an ideological critique must resist the complicities revealed in Easthope's essay. If a history of the subject is to be written, I would argue, it will need to take into account the irresolvable temporality that affects the dating of Milton's sonnet and the complex temporality of projection and retrospection that marks, and remarks, its voices. These do not merely produce the split subject; they make resolution the illusory effects of a reading that has moved too quickly in its historicization. To let history into this poem—to let this poem be in history—a history that acknowledged difference would have to be practiced. It would be based on quite different assumptions about the text—positing, for instance, its lack of empirical unity, its refusal to situate itself in a moment that submits to the concept of self-sameness; hence it would be impossible to describe the poem as the utterance of a subject-position characterized by its ability to own a moment, own itself, or transform self and moment into a linguistic object of transcendental value. These assumptions are not opposed to Easthope's, but they also refuse the possibility that one could misrecognize a putatively 'autonomous' subject-position in sonnet 19.

The ungroundedness of this position (the position outlined above, which informs this essay) may help to identify the false grounds of traditional historical scholarship or the too easy assumption that one can demystify such accounts while, at the same time, accepting their premises. As such, this notion of dating also would be anathema to the New Historicism, whose great strength in showing the imbeddedness of artistic production within its cultural situation nonetheless rests upon the same empiricist ground as traditional historical accounts. From the position of any of the historicisms, new or old, that I have outlined here, the dating of the sonnet that I have suggested would be unacceptable, since the temporality it claims has eschewed the a priori truth of teleological chronology or the possibility that the historic moment is present-to-itself, that it is outside of subsequent narrativization. (The temporality sketched here could be called, after Freud, Nachträglichkeit, and would insist that what is retrospectively constructed is not necessarily, is necessarily *not* what was; rather, in Derrida's elegant phrase, it would be "a past that has never been present,"[7] nor would it be present in its rewriting.)

The vexed relationship to a linear or teleological temporality in "When I consider" and its dating will not quite produce an "autonomous" subject. Nor will it support an account that reifies the notion of a ruptured history against which a new subjectivity takes shape. Undeniably, there is a history of the subject and of textuality, but to tell it and to situate this sonnet, its numerous dislocations and incompatibilities must be taken into account.[8] In "When I consider," one must recognize that the temporality of that text is riddled and redoubled in the relationship between the "I" and the buried talent, that the economics of self-representation and self-effacement is, explicitly, an economics that registers a relationship to a market economy of use-value and a feudal economics of a lord-servant relationship, a relationship problematized through questions of use and uselessness, and of an expenditure that seems, at once, complete and in process, and not yet to have occurred.

From such a perspective, one could never read Milton's lyric as the

display of a subject that registers its relationship to the social and histor-
ical as its negation or its effaced internalization. The subject-position in
the poem cannot be a refuge for bourgeois ideology, but neither will it
simply submit to Marxist exposures of the "autonomous" bourgeois sub-
ject which, I have been arguing, are, for many practitioners, the effect of
a historical narrative that unknowingly rewrites the narrative of mod-
ernism and creates, thereby, a spurious modernity as its object of attack.
To begin to situate historically the subject-positions in "When I consid-
er," I propose, instead, to read Milton's autobiographical practices
through the period during which, I have argued, the poem may be
thought to have been (re)written. Three passages from the prose, always
anthologized, are my texts here, and I read them with an eye to the
subject-positions in the lyric. They provide a way to pursue the discon-
tinuous modes of self-production which, I have argued, can be read in
"When I consider." Thus, I will read the autobiographical passage in
*Reason of Church-Government* against the "prevention" of the sonnet,
the autobiographical passage in the *Apology* against the open quotations
of the lyric, and the autobiographical passage in the *Second Defense*
against the thematization of blindness. I make no claims that these are
the only loci for those concerns (indeed, much that I have to say here
would not have been possible without Christopher Kendrick's reading
of *Areopagitica* or Francis Barker's incisive remarks on that tract); I
choose them because they are, in these texts, applied to self-representa-
tion. Moreover, two of these texts date from the earliest possible date for
"When I consider"—1642, when Milton would have been thirty-four,
just short of half his biblical lifespan of seventy—while the last is from
1654, close to the latest date proposed in conventional accounts of its
composition. I will argue that these passages do not deliver the "same"
Milton, neither a Milton who is identical to himself nor the transcen-
dental author of *Paradise Lost*.

These three moments (and to call them that is already to have mis-
named them, since they are not moments of presence or moments of
self-identification, that is, moments that are identical to themselves) will
not easily submit to a narrative of growth or development. Even to say, as
I have, that they are autobiographical passages in which Milton speaks
of himself is also to misstate them, for if their temporality refuses to
deliver an undivided present, the self writing and being written cannot
be assumed as self-identical. Nor, except for the sake of convenience,
does the name "Milton" secure them. To speak of "Milton" this way
may seem to make a mockery of the notion of the historical Milton or of
Milton's authoring. Yet the aim here could not be further from such
goals. I attempt to write a history of the subject whose very historicity

can best be registered in a refusal to construct the unified subject of twentieth-century Miltonists. I offer no "autonomous" subject here, but a subject of chance living towards the retrospective determination of inevitability and, by the *Second Defense,* actively reconstructing a self in retrospect. That Milton may come closest to the "autonomous" Milton of twentieth-century criticism, but the story I want to tell in no way necessitates that moment, nor sees it as the arrival of self-realization, rather, as the chance coincidence which might as easily never have occurred. Yet, by chance, I do not mean to reduce history to mere randomness. It is Milton's chance I am talking about, the chance delivery of the retrospectively recognizable Miltonic "I," the chance, in short, that lets itself be called Milton's chance; a story that only retrospectively, if then, could be called a story.

## Prevention

The second book of *The Reason of Church-Government* opens with an autobiographical account that is, in the opening phrase of the chapter following it, called a "digression" (1:823).[9] Within that "digression," the writing of the tract is itself a digression: "if I were wise only to mine own ends, I would certainly take such a subject as of it self might catch applause, whereas this hath all the disadvantages on the contrary" (807). The tract is a digression from "mine own ends," a telos that might be regarded as self-owned or self-directed. Yet, as this line of thought is developed, it turns around on itself. The tract must be written straight through, it brooks no delay, and the true writing that would be owned would be a writing of delay and digression: "in this argument the not deferring is of great moment to the good speeding" (807). What he would write would be elaborated, "delayed at pleasure" in a temporality that gave "time enough to pencill it over" (807), a text whose revisionary status might also render it one that never could come to the "perfection" towards which such elaboration aims. The temporality of such composition, as "pencill it over" might suggest, involves writing, rewriting, unwriting. The pleasure of delay seems to entail the failure of delivery.

The space of such true—and in *Reason of Church-Government*—deferred and delayed writing is replaced by the undeferred writing of the tract—undeferred, and yet, a writing of, and as, digression, divagation. True writing, as defined, would not only always be yet to come, at any moment it could not be true writing (true writing is perfect only at the end of the process of elaboration); at any moment it would virtually not be at all. So, in *Reason of Church-Government,* digressing within a digression, writing is as true as it might be were it to be called a version of the real thing. As it is. For if, on the one hand, the autobiographical digression takes the occasion to "covnant with any knowing reader" (820) towards a future delivery, it also writes itself as that futurity, "an abortive and foredated discovery" (820), whether what is being described is the text that is yet to come ("those intentions which have lived within me") or the one that is delivered here. For *Reason of Church-Government* is written within a "preventive fear" (806) that is represented as the heeding of a voice of the future that will look back at Milton in 1642 and ask, how did you advance the Revolution? To that voice, in that voice, *Reason of Church-Government* is written, within a future which *prevents* him, literally comes before him so that the present of writing is after this future and yet this future is blocking him from the future he would have as his own, and towards which, and in which, he writes when he covenants with the knowing reader towards the future which he has delivered and aborted by writing within the future that cuts him off, prevents him and yet, by standing in his way, opens the way towards writing.

As this rather tangled description hopes to suggest, the place of the writing of the self in *Reason of Church-Government* is the place of a present that appears only to exist retroactively through a projected future which works to prevent that future ever from coming. This space of writing is the desired space of a pleasurable writing that takes its pleasure precisely from this structure of an enabling denial. Within this structure, the discrimination of what is one's own from digression is disabled, and the present of writing is a nonexistent moment, "abortive and foredated," on the one hand, "prevented" on the other. In a much-quoted remark about Milton's prose,[10] K. G. Hamilton describes it as "jumping up and down in one place";[11] that place of writing in *Reason of Church-Government* is a space of digression. It is not proper, self-owned, self-directed; in every way, it is not.

Such a space could be said to be "autonomous" only insofar as it has been loosed from a self-owning "auto"; it cannot submit to linearity even as it is written. Hence, the digression in which the self is produced is also the space in which "all" of the tract is written and retracted. Thus, having opened with an introductory section, it is withdrawn in order for the first chapter proper to begin—"I shall no longer deferre" (750). No sooner begun, with "the first and greatest reason of Church-government," (750) the discussion is blocked, the first reason incapable of delivery "untill I have said what is meet to some who do not think it for the ease of their inconsequent opinions to grant that Church discipline is platform'd in the Bible" (ibid). Thus, the second chapter proceeds to take up the first reason deferred in the first chapter, only to "passe over"

(758) any biblical texts that would define the reason of church govern-
ment. Instead, citations of St. Paul are offered, in which he declares the
authoritative nature of what he says, but what he says remains uncited:
" And thus we find here that the rules of Church-discipline are not only
commanded, but hedg'd about with such a terrible impalement of com-
mands" (760). The hedges and impalements are cited, but not what is
within them, which has been passed over. The text is in parentheses,
undelivered; digressive marks around that space appear instead. "We
may returne now from this interposing difficulty thus remov'd" (761),
the next chapter begins, as if it had removed what it had erected.

These terms continue to the end of the tract. Thus, the penultimate
chapter finds the subject of writing "almost in suspense betwixt yea and
no" (830), almost ready to "relinquish that which is to follow" (831), and
relinquishing it—"anon more fully" (834) is how the tract moves for-
ward, yet the concluding section opens as an addition ("I adde one thing
more" [850]) to a conclusion that has concluded by not concluding—"I
do not conclude that Prelaty is Antichristian, for what need I? the
things themselves conclude it" (850). Yet it has been the "things them-
selves" that the tract has yet to offer, delivering its preventive, digressive,
and dilatory hedges. The autonomous truth of things is this dilatory
space. For the text, however much it would present the self-evident, un-
arguable difference between true church government (presbyterianism)
and false prelatry, stumbles over a "thing" that defines the space of writ-
ing as the impossibility of the delivery of differences: "both the names
and offices of Bishops and Presbyters at first were the same" (776). The
text cannot go back to recover the original truth and first reason of
things without coming up against this founding duplicity. No text sup-
ports this text, no citations are needed to present what is evident ("the
plainnesse thereof a matter of eye sight rather then of disquisition, I vol-
untarily omit" [775]—hence, no citations support the arguments, no
arguments are offered). And no evidence: for what "we see . . . with
our own eyes" is that those who see "persist in . . . blindnesse" (766).

Where can one write a self in this position, where locate it? The tract
opens with a declaration of invisibility, and an invitation to a visibility
within that invisibility: "For my yeares, be they few or many, what im-
ports it? so they bring reason, let that be lookt on" (749). To see what?
An invisible text, produced only as it is bracketed with delay and defer-
ral, so that the writing-subject is undistinguished and yet not identical
to what is written. The text is to "be lookt on" in a mirror scene that is
also the scene, or so it is later described, of the founding of the subject in
a blind gaze: "the reflection of his own severe and modest eye upon
himselfe" (842), a self-eyeing that is the reading of a text legible (but only

in a mirror or in the eyes of an other) like the mark of Cain, "the price of his redemption . . . visibly markt upon his forehead" (842). The price of those wares (the parable that Milton records in a letter written in the 1630s and in "When I consider" also figures the preventive economy of the autobiographical in the *Reason of Church-Government*—"those few talents which God at that present had lent me" [804]), is the sacrifice of this present, written here as a past, elsewhere as a future, a present without presence in which self-presence and self-presentation is also withdrawal and illegibility. "God even to a strictnesse requires the improvment of these his entrusted gifts" (801), but such "improvment" would only be a straying from an origin that remains unrecorded and effaced in this "improving" discourse that situates the act of writing and the self written in these dilatory, secondary maneuvers.

> And if the love of God, as a fire sent from Heaven . . . , be the first principle of all godly and vertuous actions in men, this pious and just honouring of ourselves is the second, and may be thought as the radical moisture and fountain head, whence every laudable and worthy enterprize issues forth. (841)

Human being is this original ("radical") secondarity, a water that puts out the first fire (a water described a bit later as not only flowing but also "restraining" itself to "glob[e] itself upward" [842]). Turning around upon itself, it achieves the radical autonomy of being a digression, a set of parentheses, hedges, around nothing save the retroactive possibility of a present emerging from the self-divided, schismatic, and self-canceling moment.

To conclude: St. Paul's discovery conditions the movement of this text: "there fell scales from his eyes that were not perceav'd before" (796). Sight, the very visibility of the self-evident, is a secondary phenomenon in which what was there is there only as it is no longer. Seeing is to see what one did not see before; it is to see what kept one from seeing. It is to see what blocks and prevents, and the moment of such seeing is the moment when the scales, which before were not evident, only are, then, retroactively present. This is what the tract offers to be seen, how it offers its wares in an economy of difference deferred, the economy that Derrida calls *differance*. Only a later chance will make this passage on blindness a piece of autobiographical evidence; retrospectivity will make it a true instance of self-recording.

## Quotations

Only a few months separates the publication of *The Reason of Church-Government* from *An Apology against a Pamphlet call'd A Modest Con-*

*futation of the Animadversions of the Remonstrant against Smectymnuus*
and its autobiographical account. The earlier tract delivers the author's
name on its cover and is the first publication of Milton's to do so. The
*Apology* appears anonymously and, as John Guillory has brilliantly ar-
gued, its task is "the vindication of a private name" without ever
delivering that name.[12] As Guillory argues, the tract invests the author
metonomyically, figuratively; he becomes the force of a rhetoric that
speaks beyond him and towards a futurity in which his name could
come to be registered. That rhetoric has the force of the "autonomy" of
the differential space in which *The Reason of Church-Government* is
written, and one could perhaps construct a sequential narrative, or a
narrative of the same, in which "Milton" is produced and reproduced
from the earlier tract to the later one.

Yet, however compelling that story might be as a description of the
representation of the autobiographical "I" of the treatise, it would have
accepted what this reading of the autobiographical "moment" in Milton
seeks to investigate. For Guillory writes of Milton-the-poet and of his
self-realization in *Paradise Lost*. However much (and it is much) he rec-
ognizes that there is a history of the Miltonic subject, and that the
strategies of writing are not simply the same from the beginning to the
end of the career, Guillory is interested in tracing Milton's emergence
into the Miltonic; his narrative succumbs to a teleological imperative.
What I would offer instead here is a narrative which, however much it
recognizes "the same" in the production of the Miltonic subject, would
also seek to recover a multiplicity that is not simply reducible to the
"same." I would speak then of modes of self-marking that will not nec-
essarily produce the Milton of *Reason of Church-Government* or "the"
Milton of *Paradise Lost*. My point is not only that there are different
Miltons from "moment" to "moment," but that any "moment" might
offer a multiplicity which the name "Milton" will not reduce to unity or
identity without a remainder. Moreover, even within a narrative of the
same "autonomous" Milton from *The Reason of Church-Government* to
the *Apology,* what one would recognize (and here, I imagine, Guillory
would agree) would not be Milton per se so much as strategies of writing
that situate an "I" that is yet-to-be- "Milton."

Indeed, the "autonomy" of textual excess is thematized throughout the
*Apology* in its concern with its style and rhetorical strategies. If "Milton" is
produced within a rhetorical excess that goes beyond the possibility of
self-naming, rhetorical autonomy exceeds a capacity for ownership. This
is not merely a rhetorical situation; it is also political. For the excessive
rhetoric is not merely not one's own; it is another's, the prelatical oppo-
nent's (Joseph Hall and / or his son, Milton supposes). It is only several
pages into the autobiographical passage near the beginning of the

*Apology* that it is labeled a digression (888); the passage is not, as in *Reason of Church-Government,* bracketed afterwards, but internally. Before, "the just vindication of my selfe" he "yet . . . could deferre" (883), he writes, yet no deferral follows, nor could this autobiographical passage be described as a writing within deferral. For, whereas in *Reason of Church-Government* a fantasized futurity had demanded a present account, here the account has already been made. The Confuter (as Milton names "Hall" in an act as metonymical and figurative as any self-naming in the tract) has already written Milton's autobiography and the autobiography of the *Apology* is circumscribed by that prior textualization and can only "digresse" within its confines. Thus, even within the "autonomous" autobiographical digression Milton submits to textual models: he tells of a life spent wandering in books, a discovery of "natures part in me" (889; the word "nature" recurs) that is the discovery of other authors. Thus the famous sentence, "that he who would not be frustrate of his hope to write well hereafter in laudable things, ought him selfe to be a true Poem" (890).

Futurity depends upon prior textualization. But so, insistently, does the present instance of writing. The author of *A Modest Confutation* (as anonymous as the author of the *Apology*) had characterized Milton's *Animadversions* as "*a mime thrust forth upon the stage*" (879). "But in an ill houre hath this unfortunate rashness stumbl'd upon the mention of miming," Milton answers, for Hall's *Mundus alter et idem* is "the idlest and paltriest Mime that ever mounted upon bank" (880). Milton claims that the Confuter does not know what a mime is (is not the form, properly defined, acclaimed by Plato? he asks [879], and might not Plato himself, to such a "player" as the Confuter, seem merely risible? he continues, with the last question putting himself in the position of the Confuter), and that Hall (if he is the author of the *Confutation*) is self-confuted by what he has already written to misname what he reads.

Yet, so, too, is the equally anonymous Milton, for self-justification lies in the ability to trade citations, not in some escape from prior textualization:

> But when I discern'd his intent was not so much to smite at me, as through me to render odious the truth which I had written . . . I conceav'd my selfe to be now not as mine own person, but as a member incorporate into that truth whereof I was perswaded, and whereof I had declar'd openly to be a partaker. (871)

Having already delivered himself in his writing, delivered himself, that is, to his writing, that textualization refuses stabilization. He can recover himself from the Confuter only by reclaiming himself within citation. Writing has its "being," the writer is, within the act of citation. "And whereas he tels us that *Scurrilous Mime was a personated grim lowring foole,* his foolish language unwittingly writes foole upon his owne friend, for he who was there *personated,* was only the *Remonstrant;* the author is ever distinguisht from the person he introduces" (880). The Confuter has mistaken Milton's ventriloquizing of the Remonstrant for Milton's own voice. Yet such a "distinction" of person from the personated, as quotation-within-quotation suggests, with its ability to slide away from the stabilization of the referent, is a virtual impossibility. "I" writes "I" within a prior textualization of open quotations whose end is unmarked (like the voices in "When I consider how my light is spent"). Self-representation is confined within a hall (a Hall) of mimic mirrors, and self-nomination is only possible within the division of the citation. As Milton writes, Hall, having written a book of characters, characters the writer of the *Animadversions* from the book he has written. But so, too, does Milton, citing scripture for his scriptive efforts, "we may safely imitate the method that God uses; *with the froward to be froward, and to throw scorne upon the scorner*" (875). The Confuter can be confuted only by one who does "that over againe" (872), returning citations, clubbing quotations.

The autobiography is written within the already written, Cambridge "*vomited out*" Milton (884), the Confuter charges, as Milton begins to write "his" autobiography; Milton attempts to thrust the vomit back into the gorge that has discharged it (and he is still doing that in the final sentences of the tract, attacking those that "have their voice in their bellies" [953]), but he also takes "apt occasion" (884) to rewrite his relationship to the university. The vomit is also his food, the words of the other give him words (just as the other was given words by what *he* had already written—his mime and his book of characters; his *toothlesse Satyres* are also charged against him). Two nameless authors are named and unnamed in the shared terrain of the re-citable, a ground as unstable as the nothing within parentheses of *Reason of Church-Government;* but here it is not an empty text but an already written one that must be rewritten and erased. Such erasure serves, however, not only to answer Hall—for Hall is repeatedly "named" in the tract through what he has written—but also to produce Milton. He has, he says, been "stained" (871) by what has been written already—covered with ink and made to appear, covered over with ink and made to disappear; to produce himself he must write clean what has already been written: "I thought it my duty, if not to my selfe, yet to the religious cause I had in hand, not to leave on my garment the least spot, or blemish in good name so long as God should give me to say that which might wipe it off" (871). Yet, it is not God that gives him his text so often

as it is the Confuter; "content with such reasons as my confuter him-
selfe affords me" (912), the Confuter confuted provides the space of
autobiography, a space of traces and retracings, mutually constitutive
and annihilative:

> *and where my morning haunts are he wisses not* . . . . (885). These are the
> morning practices; proceed now to the afternoone; *in Playhouses,* he
> sayes, *and the Bordelloes.* Your evidence, unfaithfull Spie of Canaan? he
> gives in his evidence, that *there he hath trac't me.* Take him at his word
> Readers . . . : he concludes against himselfe . . . hamper'd in his owne
> hempe (886). I turn his *Anti-strephon* upon his owne hed; the Confuter
> knows that these things are the furniture of Playhouses and Bordelloes,
> therefore by the same reason, *the Confuter himselfe hath been trac't in
> those places* (886).

Citation is turned against citation; the citation is split, and the auto-
biographical "I" is written within citation. The end of the argument,
marked with the italics of the other's script, rewrites that script as one's
"own." The effect is the same as that of the open and unmarked citations
in "When I consider how my light is spent," for here too voices cannot
be distinguished and the mark of propriety (the italic) is moveable: the
italicized citations are *emphatically* incorporated into Milton's "own"
story—and he tells his own in an other's words that have intervened in
and shaped and spaced his own. As the words are thrown back upon the
Confuter they also rebound upon the writer, taken "at his word."

Milton claims to reveal his internality against the besmirched exteri-
ority of his defamation and misnomination. Yet, as should be apparent
by now, it is in a text-within-citation (a text whose value lies in its iter-
ability) that the path is traced. It is a textuality that knows no names but
only refiguration. It cannot secure the inside against the outside.

> With me it fares now, as with him whose outward garment hath bin
> injur'd and ill bedighted; for having no other shift, what help but to turn
> the inside outwards, especially if the lining be of the same, or, as it is
> sometimes, much better. (888–89)

This garment of style knows no difference between inside and outside.
It is always a matter of quotations, and there is no end to them. Where
these "younger feet wander'd" (890) are the paths of prior and inescap-
able textualization. Were he to claim more as his own, he would claim
too much: if

> it be lawfull to attribute somewhat to guifts of Gods imparting, which I
> boast not of, but thankfully acknowledge, and feare also lest at my cer-
> taine account they be reckon'd to me many rather than few . . . (869)

Once again, the parable of the talents is alluded to; here, unlike *Reason of Church-Government,* disowned expenditure is cast in the light of its circulation rather than its prevention; sonnet 19 does not decide these readings. What has written him cannot be called his own; yet the textual autonomy to which he submits is also how the Confuter is produced in an economy of figuration that will not deliver a proper name.

## Blindness

The defenses of the 1650s are, insistently, self-defenses, but it is the *Second Defense* of 1654 that offers an autobiographical account. Here, too, one could point to supposed continuities from the self-presentations of 1642; notably that the narrative of the life is constructed within the citations of another, anonymous as the Confuter in the *Apology* (here, Milton takes him to be Alexander More): "Shall I then always contend with those who are nameless?" (4,1:560). Here, too, such naming of the other also reflects the "self": until the 1650s, Milton's tracts tended to be anonymous productions. And although this pamphlet proclaims its author's name, the attack on More (who Milton persisted in believing was his opponent, even when presented with evidence to the contrary) proceeds in a manner recognizable from the *Apology,* although the change in positions implicit there in its citational mode is even more apparent here. More is charged with the bordello visiting (and worse) that had been the Confuter's allegation, and Milton, one might suppose, continued to believe that More was his opponent because of this alter-identity. The presentation of the self here, as in the *Apology,* is dictated by the tract being cited and answered; rather than a single autobiographical passage (or digression), however, autobiography is produced entirely by the chance organization of the *Clamor Regis.* Autobiography is produced discontinuously in the *Second Defense;* neither the bracketing of *Reason of Church-Government* nor the citationality of the *Apology* will account for it.

So much is all but admitted in a passage that also rationalizes the delay of Milton's answer (two years elapsed between the tract of "More" and Milton's reply), and serves to introduce the most extended of the autobiographical passages. The combination of discontinuous self-production and rationalization is the most noteworthy feature of this autobiography. " 'A certain John Milton'" (607) appears, reluctantly, in quotation marks, produced only as the *Clamor Regis* dictates. "Who I am and whence I come is uncertain, you say; so once it was uncertain who Homer was, and who Demosthenes."

> I was not greedy for fame, whose gait is slow, nor did I intend to publish
> even this, unless a fitting opportunity presented itself. It made no dif-
> ference to me even if others did not realize that I knew whatever I knew,
> for it was not fame, but the opportune moment for each thing that I
> awaited. (608)

The " prevention" of *Reason of Church-Government* has been replaced
by "opportunity"; no internalized fantasmic figure speaks in a futurity
to compel a deferred writing. Yet this passage of self-production
through the text of another comes several pages after a fantasy of univer-
sal fame, Milton's name and writing known throughout Europe. And
the fantasy includes another about writing. For two years, Milton says,
he has been waiting for a tract by Salmasius to appear ("By these tactics
he achieved but one result—that of postponing for a little while the pay-
ment of the penalty for slander, for I thought it better to wait" [558]),
but now Salmasius is dead. That chance apparently allows the writing
of the *Second Defense*. That chance, retrospectively, in a fantasy affirmed
and denied at once, is the product of (not) writing: "there are those who
even place the responsibility of his death on me and on those barbs of
mine, too keenly sharpened" (559).

Everything has been externalized here so that desiring fame, or not
desiring it, writing or not writing, all seem to wait upon chance, and
chance dictates the discontinuities of self-assertion and self-negation. "I
had learned to hold my peace, I had mastered the art of not writing, a
lesson that Salmasius could never learn" (608)—and, being dead, has
learned thanks to Milton's (un)written shafts. "The art of not writing"
might almost describe the "writing" of the 1642 tracts, but here it
makes a present in which real events (not only writing events) take
place, have taken place. Not only is a Salmasius dead; a new Homer or
Demosthenes has killed him. That figurative self-nomination makes
claims to an equally real status.

So doing, extraordinarily, the subject of writing is "Milton," the rec-
ognizable Milton of *Paradise Lost*. For the surrender of writing to
occasion, the entirely occasional and fully discontinuous nature of the
autobiographical within the *Second Defense,* is coupled with such famil-
iar epic self-identifications (lists are produced, prophets, including
Tiresias and Phineus, classical heroes and modern ones). By the end of
the *Second Defense* Milton in fact claims that its oratory is epic; in him,
Demosthenes is Homer. That self, however much it may be related to
the citational and preventive modes of writing in the 1642 autobiogra-
phies, cannot simply be derived from them.

Chance delivers "Milton" (the "real" Milton). "Is there anything in
my life or character which he could criticize?" (582), the first auto-

biographical passage begins. "Nothing, certainly. What then? He does what no one but a brute and barbarian would have done—he casts up to me my appearance and my blindness." Blindness is his (mis)fortune; the body now (and only now) has been divided from the subject of writing so that writing is allied to this self-division; his eyes proclaim it externally: "They [his eyes] have as much the appearance of being uninjured, and are as clear and bright, without a cloud, as the eyes of men who see most keenly. In this respect alone, against my will, do I deceive" (583). "Simulator sum," the Latin original reads. Milton sees himself with others' eyes; no glance in a mirror would deliver this vision of himself deceiving the truth of his blindness, yet the sentence of self-reporting is written within this deceit (writing as if he saw himself). The lie of the body is the truth of the writing. "Although I am past forty, there is scarcely anyone to whom I do not seem younger by about ten years" (583). Or, perhaps, writing has overcome the body. So chance is mastered, discontinuity renamed as liberty, autonomy, self-direction, self-control, self-assertion. The trope of prevention is lived in the "evidence" to (others') senses that Milton is not living within chronological time. Aging and blindness refuse to make their mark upon him; the body has been delivered for the sake of the writer.

"Simulator sum"; the role call of the blind prophets and bards in which Milton continues, investing his identity, keeps insisting, even as citations refuse to deliver this story, that blindness is a mark of favor and no punishment. The quotation about Phineus from the *Argonautica* and the invocation of Tiresias record divine punishment. "But God himself is truth!" (585), Milton continues: the truth of simulation. And blindness is, ultimately, heroic choice, like Achilleus choosing a short and glorious life rather than a long and undistinguished one (588). Milton has chosen both: to wait for time to overcome him, to live and not to age, to grow perfect in (not) writing, taking his chances and claiming to have made them; seeing blind. "There is a certain road which leads through weakness, as the apostle teaches, to the greatest strength" (589). Milton "chooses" that over which there can have been no choice: to go blind. The chance of a lifetime: it realizes the strength of (not) writing: "I had mastered the art of not writing" (608).

Thus, pages later, submitting to chance, the life can be told, rationally, sequentially, as a series of choices. Discontinuity is rationalized. "If I had been expelled from Cambridge, why should I travel to Italy?" (609); the two events, as Milton tells them, are logically related within the unfolding of his *"humanitas"* (ibid.). Chronology has its reasons. "'Returning, he wrote his book on divorce'" (609). No, Milton insists; he wrote only what others did; charges of lying about *Eikonoklastes* follow. More's chronology is wrong, and Milton tells it straight: "Who I am, then, and whence I come, I shall now disclose" (612). The ordered disclosure and the ordering of its chances into choices is everywhere displayed; discontinuity is recast as Liberty, the making of choices, and Liberty is unfolded as a rational life:

> Since, then, I observed that there are, in all, three varieties of liberty without which civilized life is scarcely possible, namely ecclesiastical liberty, domestic or personal liberty, and civil liberty, and since I had already written about the first, while I saw that the magistrates were vigorously attending to the third, I took as my province the remaining one, the second or domestic kind. This too seemed to be concerned with three problems: the nature of marriage itself, the education of children, and finally the existence of freedom to express oneself.(624)

An instrumental rationality governs the deployment of the autobiography. Writing follows a chronological path from which all chance has been removed, a sequential unfolding governed by a rational logic. Such is the simulated truth that Milton offers as his truth.

And such has been the Miltonic truth in biographies written subsequent to the *Second Defense,* starting with the early life by Edward Phillips and continuing to Parker. This is the Milton that has been delivered over to history and, especially, to those who regard Miltonic history as coincident with the author's self-realization in *Paradise Lost.*

It is important, then, to register the economy of this self-presentation, the chances upon which it capitalizes and the discontinuities which it suppresses in order to make this construct. If here we see what Christopher Kendrick calls "self-validating ethos," the self as a series of autonomous, rational choices, that rationality suppresses the chances of Milton's arrival. He writes himself, John Milton, Englishman, in Latin, as the instrument of a government whose Independency is Milton's independence (the rationality of this ordering is the political rationale which allows the *Second Defense* to find its true heroic subject in a panegyric of Cromwell and the author's assumption of his governing position, dictating to the nation its own good). It is, in short, a rationality that is allied to power, and which displays that power as weakness: blindness, writing in a foreign tongue ("which I must of necesity use, and often to my dissatisfaction" [554]); even the rationalized account of the trip to Italy (as proof that he had never been rusticated) also conjures up the image of Saturn exiled by Jupiter (609), a castrating admission akin to the double accounts of the prophetic models of Phineus and Tiresias. Keith Stavely describes the stance: "Milton presumes in his prose, as the ruling-class leaders of the Revolution did in reality, to orchestrate and control the behavior of newly awakened social groups."[13] Stavely calls this "idealism" (knowing others' interests better than they do), although he also recognizes the propertied interests from which the Independents spoke. Herman Rapaport, perhaps as extremely (from the opposite direction) as Stavely, calls this position proto-fascistic in its alliance of dictatorial violence to "Liberty": "The Third Reich speaks *avant la lettre*."[14] Perhaps the phrase to be supplied instead (it will cover what both Stavely and Rapaport see) is "bourgeois liberalism." Milton is the state's secretary, or scrivener (to recall his father's trade). Heroism is the rule of the army.

Although the *Second Defense* offers a final autobiographical passage, I would add the caution that the identification that it offers is not the "end" for Milton, although it may mark Milton's arrival at the subject-position of *Paradise Lost* or the "moment" of the final rewriting of "When I consider how my light is spent." Retrospectively, one could construct *a* Milton from these passages—or from the lyric. The scales that retrospectively fell from St. Paul's eyes have now fallen from Milton's; and they are there, invisible. The marriage that does not defile (and that would secure a self-against-citation in the *Apology* against its promiscuous besmirching) is now accomplished: Mary Powell Milton is, by chance, dead as Milton writes the *Second Defense*. Prevention is realized in the weakness of blindness, the ruin (denied) of the body, the perfection of writing as not-writing. But this story needs to be recast in the recognition that nothing necessitates this secondary revision, this falling into place of the pieces. To say otherwise would mean accepting the rationalization of the *Second Defense* as truth. He did not write knowing he would be blind. Or that he would survive. The revolution need not have occurred. He did not, in short, make his history, neither his own nor that of his nation. And when the two coincided by chance in 1654, "Milton" appeared. Not the truth of Milton but the simulation that retrospectively shaped such chances as his chance.

If we were to go on "dating Milton" (and making good on the pun that titles this essay), we would want to turn to the last sonnet and its vexed question of dating and identification (which wife is the "late es-poused Saint," the critics ask and argue, and I would, again, answer: both wives dead by 1658), and to pursue the construction of the auto-biographical into the field of the Other inevitably also constructed in a history of the discontinuities of the subject. The autobiographical in the divorce tracts would have to be read. The vexed dating of *Samson Ago-nistes* (immediate response to the first marriage? final poem?) would have to be raised, and the production of yet other Miltons would be implicated in these questions of temporality and writing. These must remain for another date. So, perhaps this essay ought, retrospectively, to be retitled. We could call it "Blind Dating."

## Notes

1. William Riley Parker, *Milton: A Biography,* 2 vols. (Oxford: Clarendon Press 1968), 2:1042.

2. A. S. P. Woodhouse and Douglas Bush, *A Variorum Commentary on the Poems of John Milton* (New York: Columbia University Press), 2:2:469.

3. Mary Ann Radzinowicz, *Toward Samson Agonistes: The Growth of Milton's Mind* (Princeton: Princeton University Press, 1978), pp. 142, 144.

4. Anthony Easthope, "Towards the Autonomous Subject in Poetry: *Milton On his Blindness,*" in *1642: Literature and Power in the Seventeenth Century,* ed. Francis Barker (University of Essex, 1981), p. 301.

5. This is the version of literary history that is repeated, too, in Francis Barker's otherwise compelling *The Tremulous Private Body* (London: Methuen, 1984).

6. The reader who wishes a reading of the poem based on these premises may turn to my *Voice Terminal Echo: Postmodernism and English Renaissance Texts* (London: Methuen, 1986), pp. 130ff.

7. Jacques Derrida, "Différance," in *Margins of Philosophy,* trans. Alan Bass (Chicago: University of Chicago Press, 1982), p. 21.

8. The position I am taking here could be compared to Christopher Kendrick's in *Milton: A Study in Ideology and Form* (London: Methuen, 1986).

9. Prose citations from *Complete Prose Works of John Milton,* 10 vols. (New Haven: Yale University Press, 1953–83).

10. For example, in Stanley Fish's "Reason in *The Reason of Church Government,*" in *Self-Consuming Artifacts* (Berkeley: University of California Press, 1972), to which this discussion is indebted.

11. K. G. Hamilton, "The Structure of Milton's Prose," in *Language and Style in Milton,* ed. R. D. Emma and J. T. Shawcross (New York: Frederick Ungar, 1967), p. 329.

12. John Guillory, *Poetic Authority* (New York: Columbia University Press, 1983), pp. 95–103.

13. Keith W. Stavely, *The Politics of Milton's Prose Style* (New Haven: Yale University Press, 1975), p. 24.

14. Herman Rapaport, *Milton and the Postmodern* (University of Nebraska Press, 1983), p. 177.

# III

# POETIC SUBJECTIVITY AND THE
# LANGUAGE OF DESIRE

# 9

# Masculine Persuasive Force:
# Donne and Verbal Power

*Stanley Fish*

### "My Feigned Page"

For a very long time I was unable to teach Donne's poetry. I never had anything good to say about the poems, and would always find myself rereading with approval C. S. Lewis's now fifty-year-old judgment on Donne as the "saddest" and "most uncomfortable of our poets" whose verse "exercises the same dreadful fascination that we feel in the grip of the worst kind of bore—the hot eyed, unescapable kind."[1] Indeed my own response to the poetry was even more negative than Lewis's: I found it sick, and thought that I must be missing the point so readily seen by others. I now believe that to *be* the point: Donne is sick and his poetry is sick; but he and it are sick in ways that are interestingly related to the contemporary critical scene. In short, the pleasures of diagnosis have replaced the pleasure I was unable to derive from the verse.

Let's get the diagnosis out of the way immediately: Donne is bulimic, someone who gorges himself to a point beyond satiety, and then sticks his finger down his throat and throws up. The object of his desire and of his abhorrence is not food, but words, and more specifically, the power words can exert. Whatever else Donne's poems are, they are preeminently occasions on which this power can be exercised; they report on its exercise and stage it again in the reporting, and when one asks about a moment in the poetry, "Why is it thus?" the answer will always be "in order further to secure the control and domination the poet and his surrogates continually seek." This is, I think, what Judith Herz is getting at in a recent fine essay when she remarks that "Donne . . . will say anything if the poem seems to need it,"[2] an observation I would amend by

insisting that the need to be satisfied is not the poem's but the poet's, and
that it is the need first to create a world and then endlessly to manipulate
those who are made to inhabit it.

In more than a few of the poems Donne not only performs in this
way but provides a theoretical explanation of his performance. Such a
poem is the elegy usually entitled "The Anagram," a variation on the
topos of the praise of ugliness. What Donne adds to the tradition is an
account of what makes it possible, the capacity of words to make con-
nection with one another rather than with some external referent that
constrains them to accuracy. Four lines teach the lesson and exemplify it:

> She's fair as any, if all be like her,
> And if none be, then she is singular.
> All love is wonder; if we justly do
> Account her wonderful, why not lovely too?
>                    (23–26)[3]

That is, if your mistress is indistinguishable from the indifferent
mass of women, then say "she's fair as any," and if she is distinguished by
the oddness of her features, then say, "she is singular," i.e., a rarity. In
either case you will be telling the truth, not as it exists in some realm
independent of your verbal dexterity, but as it has been established in
the context *created* by that dexterity. This is even truer (if I can use that
word) of the second couplet in which we are first invited to assent to an
unexceptionable assertion ("All love is wonder") and then told that by
assenting we have assented also to the infinite conclusions that might be
reached by playing with the two words and their cognates. It is as if the
copula operated not to form a proposition, but simply to establish an
equivalence between two sounds that can then be related in any way that
serves the interpreter's purpose. If love equals wonder, the so-called ar-
gument goes, the condition of being full of wonder should equal the
condition of being full of love, but since loveful is not a proper word,
let's make it lovely.

The obvious objection to this self-propelling logic of schematic fig-
ures is that it knows no constraints and is wholly unstable; meaning can
be pulled out of a suffix or out of thin air, and the linear constraints of
syntax and consecutive sense are simply overwhelmed. But Donne fore-
stalls the objection by putting it into the poem, not however, *as* an
objection but as a rationale for the interpretive fecundity of his "meth-
od": "If we might put letters but one way, / In the lean dearth of words,
what could we say?" (17–18). The answer is that we could say only one
thing at a time, and that the one thing we could say would be formed in
relation to some prior and independent referent. By refusing to be con-

fined by the lean dearth of words Donne becomes able to say anything
or many things as he combines and recombines words and letters into
whatever figurative, and momentarily real, pattern he desires. As
Thomas Docherty has recently observed, in this poem "anything we
choose to call a stable essence is always already on its way to becoming
something else."[4] The result is an experience in which the reader is al-
ways a step behind the gymnastic contortions of the poet's rhetorical
logic, straining to understand a point that has already been abandoned,
striving to maintain a focus on a scene whose configurations refuse to
stand still.

The case is even worse (or better) with another of the elegies, "The
Comparison"; for if the lesson of "The Anagram" is that the "lean
dearth of words" is to be avoided, the lesson of this poem is that the lean
dearth of words—the sequential fixing of meaning—can't be achieved.
Structurally, the "plot" of the poem couldn't be simpler: the poet's mis-
tress is compared feature by feature to the mistress of his rival and
declared to be superior; but this simplest of plots soon becomes radically
unstable because the reader is often in doubt as to which pole of the
comparison he presently inhabits. The trouble begins immediately, in
the first line: "As the sweet sweat of roses in a still"; the key words in this
line could go in either direction; in classical and Italian epic the sweat of
nymphs and goddesses is routinely and without irony regarded as
sweet, but in other poems such as Skelton's "Elynour Rummyng" (the
scene of which not incidentally is a still), sweat is fetid and redolent of
moral and physical decay. The matter isn't helped very much by the sec-
ond line, "As that which from chafed musk cat's pores doth trill"
(solemnly glossed by Helen Gardner and other editors), and it is only
with the third line—"As the almighty balm of th' early east"—that the
reader is sure of the verse's direction and knows that the subject of these
lines is the object of praise. This stability lasts for several lines and into
the first of the poem's turns, a turn that is carefully marked for unmis-
takable difference: "Rank sweaty froth thy mistress' brow defiles" (7). In
what follows the poet warms to his task, as "menstruous boils" give way
to "scum" and then to "parboiled shoes" and "warts" and "weals" as ve-
hicles of an extended negative comparison.

It would seem that the comparison is being extended further in the
couplet that begins "Round as the world's her head," and ends with a
reference to "the fatal ball which fell on Ide" (15–16). True, the circle is
often invoked as a symbol of perfection in several philosophical, astro-
nomical, and symbolic contexts; but there is something more than a
little grotesque in the image of a hugely spherical head, and it is hardly
flattering to be linked with the apple of discord that led to Paris's disas-

trous choice, a choice that reenacts the scene of original sin of which the poem immediately reminds us by adding the forbidden apple to the items of which "her head" is a simulacrum: "Or that whereof God had such jealousy, / As for the ravishing thereof we die" (17–18). It is only with the next line—"Thy head is like a rough-hewn statue of jet"— that we realize, after the fact, that the affective direction of the verse has already changed, and then we only know because the lines we are now reading are *relatively* less attractive than the lines we have just read: "Where marks for eyes, nose, mouth, are yet scarce set; / Like the first Chaos, or flat seeming face" (20–21). In place of the absolute scale promised by the initial act of comparison, we have a sliding or analog scale in which the same quantity bears different values depending on its place in the sequence of the reading experience.

When the flat-seeming face of line 21 is identified as belonging to Cynthia (22), everything begins to shift again. On the one hand Cynthia, in her role as controller of tides and bringer-in of storms, is a proper figure to bring up the rear of a list that includes Chaos; but on the other hand, Cynthia is also the figure of female chastity. Like everything and everyone else in the poem, she participates in both of the directions that are supposedly being distinguished, and her multivalence reaches out to infect Persephone, who arrives in the next line: "Like Proserpine's white beauty-keeping chest." The question is just whom is Proserpine supposed to be "like." The structure of the syntax links her strongly to chaos ("Like the first Chaos"); but the whiteness of her beauty associates her just as strongly with pale Cynthia in her more positive aspects. The doubt is removed in line 24 with the adjective "fair," but needless to say it will be reintroduced at later moments when we again discover that we have been in the wrong relation of judgment to a woman who keeps changing into her opposite.

It is an amazing performance, a high-wire act complete with twists, flips, double reverses, and above all, triumphs, triumphs at the expense of the two women who become indistinguishably monstrous when the poet makes it impossible for us to tell the difference between them ("the language of vilification contaminates that of praise")[5]; and triumphs, of course, at our expense, as we are pushed and pulled and finally mocked by the incapacity he makes us repeatedly feel. But it is a triumph that has its cost, as the last half line of the poem makes clear:

. . . comparisons are odious.

(54)

This is a moment of revulsion, not from the women for whose features he is, after all, responsible, but from the act by which he makes of them (and us) whatever he wills. Comparisons are odious because they are too easy. Given the requisite verbal skill, it is impossible for them *not* to succeed, and their success carries with it a lesson that turns back on itself, the lesson of a plasticity in nature so pervasive that it renders victory meaningless. What pleasure can be taken in the exercise of a skill if it meets no resistance? And what security attends an achievement that can be undone or redone in a moment, either by the verbal artificer himself, or by the very next person who comes along?

It is a lesson that has just been learned by the speaker of *Elegy 7,* a complaint-of-Pygmalion poem in which the first-person voice discovers to his distress that the woman he has fashioned has detached herself from him and is now free to go either her own way or the way of another. He begins by recalling her as she was before they met, and remembers her exclusively in terms of the languages she did not then understand: "thou didst not understand / The mystic language of the eye nor hand / . . . I had not taught thee then, the alphabet / Of flowers, how they devisefully being set / . . . might with speechless secrecy, / Deliver errands mutely" (3–4,9–12). The point is not only that these were languages unknown to her, but that independently of them she was herself not known because she was as yet unformed. What she now understands now understands—in the sense of supporting or providing a foundation for—her; she is the sum of the signifying systems whose coded meanings and gestures now fill her consciousness and that is why her previous state is characterized as the *absence* of signification: "ill arrayed / In broken proverbs, and torn sentences" (18–19). "Arrayed" means both "clothed" and "set into order": by being clothed in *his* words she attains an order where before there was only linguistic—and therefore substantive—chaos, *broken* proverbs, *torn* sentences. Quite literally, his words give her life: "Thy graces and good words my creatures be: / I planted knowledge and life's tree in thee" (25–26).

The horror is that after having in-formed her, he finds that she is no less malleable than she was when she was nothing but verbal bits and pieces waiting for someone who might make her into something intelligible. The two stages of creation—from incoherent fragments into sequenced discourse—are finally not so different from one another if the configuration achieved in the second stage is only temporary, if once having been planted, knowledge and sense can be *sup*planted by another gardener who brings new knowledge and an alternative sense. The poet cries out in dismay: "Must I alas / Frame and enamel plate, and drink in glass? / Chafe wax for others' seals?" (27–29). In short, must others now "write" you, inscribe you, as I have done? Cannot the work of signification be frozen once it has been accomplished? What the speaker here discovers, three hundred and seventy-five years before Derrida writes "Signature Event Context," is the "essential drift" of language, the capacity of any signifier to "break with every given context, engendering an infinity of new contexts in a manner which is absolutely illimitable."[6] Once an intelligible sign has been produced, one can always "recognize other possibilities in it by inscribing it or *grafting* it onto other chains." "No context can . . . enclose it," a truth the speaker of *Elegy 7* now ruefully acknowledges as the poem ends: "Must I . . . / . . . break a colt's force, / And leave him then, being made a ready horse?" This final line and a half could not be more precise: the shaping power he exerted before the poem began is given its precise name—force—but, once given, the name declares its own problematic; he who lives by force is precariously at the mercy of force wielded by others, by strangers. The grafting of signifiers—and, remember, that is all she is, a chain of signifiers—onto other chains cannot be stopped; and it cannot be stopped because there is nothing to stop it, no extralinguistic resistance to its inscribing power, a power the speaker once again displays when he un-creates what he has made by de-gendering it. He leaves his rival not with a "her" but a "him," a ready-made horse in place of the previously ready-made woman. It is as if he were attempting to forestall the reinscription of his creation by performing it himself and thus removing from the world the graces his words have placed there. It is a particularly nasty instance of someone saying, "if I can't have her, no one will," with a decided emphasis on the will.

It should be obvious by now that in these poems the act of writing is gendered in ways that have been made familiar to us by recent feminist criticism. The male author, like God, stands erect before the blank page of a female passivity and covers that page with whatever meanings he chooses to inscribe. This is how the speaker of the elegies *always* imagines himself, as a center of stability and control in a world where everyone else is plastic and malleable. But this self-dramatization of an independent authority can be sustained only if the speaker is himself untouched by the force he exerts on others. Were that force to turn back and claim him for its own by revealing itself to be the very source of *his* identity (which would then be no longer his) he would be indistinguishable from those he manipulates and scorns; he would be like a woman and become the object rather than the origin of his own performance, worked on, ploughed, appropriated, violated. (This is in fact the posture Donne will assume in many of the *Holy Sonnets*.) The suspicion that this may indeed be his situation is continually surfacing in these poems, as when in "The Comparison" the despised mistress is said to be "like the first Chaos," an image that seems to place the poet in the preferred position of shaping creator, the bringer of order; but he cannot occupy that position unless chaos—the feminine principle—precedes him and provides him with the occasion of *self*-assertion. Chaos is thus *first* in a sense infinitely less comfortable than the one he allows himself to recognize;[7] for it is necessary both to the emergence of his being—such as it is—and to the illusion of his mastery, a mastery that is never more fragile than at those moments when it is most loudly proclaimed.

That proclamation and its fragility are the double subject of *Elegy 3*, "Change." This poem is built on a supposed contrast between the speaker and a woman whose constancy he doubts even though the firmness of her love has been "sealed" by "hand and faith, and good works too" (1). The key word is "sealed" because it names his desire, that things be settled once and for all in a way that precludes change and variation. He is prepared to do his part and agrees even to interpret her occasional lapses as proof of her fidelity ("though thou fall back, that apostasy / Confirm thy love" [3–4]), but he finds nevertheless that he fears her, and for a reason we have already met in *Elegy 7*:

> Women are like the arts, forced unto none,
> Open to all searchers, unprized, if unknown.
> If I have caught a bird, and let him fly,
> Another fowler using these means, as I,
> May catch the same bird; and, as these things be,
> Women are made for men, not him, nor me.
> (5–10)

The fear is not of one woman, or even of women in general, but of the condition that women seem particularly to embody, the condition of being open to interpretation, and therefore to change. Like poems and paintings, women are always receiving the seal of some new appropriative interpretive gesture and so refuse to remain "sealed" in the comforting sense of line 2. But even this is not the true fear; it is rather a displacement of it onto a convenient other. As Wilbur Sanders observes, the poem is "shot through with incompatible worries and aggressions."[8] The aggression is, as so often is the case, against women, but the worry is about his own identity, which he here shores up by defining himself as the fixed pole in relation to which women stray and wander: "if a man be / Chained to a galley, yet the galley is free; / Who hath a ploughland, casts all his seed corn there / And yet allows his ground more corn should bear" (15–18). "Chained" reaches back to "sealed" and indicates that there is at least one person whose word is his bond; that person then casts himself in the role of the honest plowman (another figure of the masculine inscriber), thereby incorporating himself into the tradition of Piers Plowman and other plain speaking heroes.

At this point the images and their attendant arguments are coming so quickly and forcefully that we may forget to ask an obvious question: at whom are they directed? The original audience is the lady herself addressed in complaint, but she has long since been left behind. Arthur Marotti thinks that the poet now turns to his fellow libertines,[9] but the more likely addressee is the poet himself. That is, the poem at this point becomes an attempt at *self*-persuasion, but by falling into this mode the poet courts the very danger he sees in his defining other, the danger of change; for if his effort of self-persuasion is successful he will no longer believe what he professed to believe at the beginning of the poem; he will no longer be in the same place and he will no longer be the same person. In fact, the change is already occurring in the ambivalence of words like "chained" and "bound," which suggest both a desired stability and an uncomfortable confinement. The speaker's own vocabulary is surreptitiously preparing the ground for the moment when he will do an about-face. But when that moment comes, that is, when he changes, he attributes the change to the pressure exerted by the woman, who now returns in order once again to provide the necessary vehicle of displacement. He asks of her, "canst thou love [liberty] *and* me" (my emphasis), a question that answers itself. Of course she cannot. There remains only one alternative: given the rule that love depends on likeness between the lovers ("Likeness glues love"), he decides that if their love is to survive he must become as she, although even as he reaches this conclusion he rebels against it: "Likeness glues love: then if so thou do, / To make us like and love, must I change too? / More than thy hate, I hate it" (23–25). Here the speaker portrays as a crisis yet to be confronted an alteration he is already undergoing, and as he moves inexorably in the direction of the feared Other, he proliferates personal pronouns, as if his failing sense of identity could be restored by language, the very medium that refuses to leave him a space. "I-hate-it" is a textbook example of an utterance that insists on the independence of the subject from the forces (the "it") that threaten it, and that subject makes one last-ditch attempt to keep itself from being swept away: "rather let me / Allow *her* change, than change as oft as she, / And so not teach, but force my opinion" (25–27; emphasis added). Helen Gardner comments that "'force' would seem to be used in the sense in which we 'force' a text of Scripture, making it bear a sense beyond its own."[10] The speaker wants to bear his *own* sense, wants to be inscribed by convictions to which his will has assented; he doesn't want to be someone else's text. What he fails to see is that the condition of being his own text, of persuading himself, is no different from the condition he fears; for insofar as he is the object-audience of his own arguments, he is quite literally talking himself into something, into something *other* than he was.

That is precisely what happens at the end of the poem when he makes a perfect revolution from the stance of the opening lines to conclude "change is the nursery / Of music, joy, life and eternity" (35–36). Critics complain that this conclusion seems inauthentic, that the "work seems to come apart intellectually and emotionally,"[11] but the complaint assumes the survival of a first-person voice of whom unity and integrity might be predicated. But that voice has been the casualty of its own poem, undone by the gymnastic virtuosity that impels both it and the poem forward. All that remains is what Sanders calls "the serene beatitude of these lines," a beatitude that might mark an achieved coherence in a poem like Spenser's *Mutabilitie Cantos,* whose conclusion it resembles, but here marks only the dislodgement of the centered self by the fragmentary, ecphrastic discourse it presumed to control.[12] As Docherty puts it, there remains "no identifiable 'Donne', no identifiable or self-identical source or authority. . . . Donne is that which is always the Other [to] himself."[13]

The continual reproduction of a self that can never be the same, that can never be "its own" is at once reported and repeatedly performed in the last of the elegies I shall consider, *Elegy 16,* "On His Mistress." The poem is an address to a woman who has offered to accompany the speaker on a journey disguised as his page, and commentary has foundered on the biographical speculation that the woman in question may have been Donne's wife. But the fact of the dramatic occasion is not revealed until line 15, and before that line the poem is focused neither on the woman nor on her proposed stratagem but on itself and on the other verbal actions that have preceded it.

> By our first strange and fatal interview,
> By all desires which thereof did ensue,
> By our long starving hopes, by that remorse
> Which my words' masculine persuasive force
> Begot in thee, and by the memory
> Of hurts, which spies and rivals threaten'd me,
> I calmly beg: but by thy fathers wrath,
> By all pains, which want and divorcement hath,
> I conjure thee. . . .
>
> (1–9)

This long syntactic unit is an extended oath, but while oaths typically invoke some extraverbal power or abstraction, this oath invokes previous oaths. Even when the verse names emotions that would seem to be prior to words, they turn out to have been produced by words: desires that proceed from interviews (exchanges of talk), hurts that flow from threats, pains fathered by the expressions of wrath. The lines call up a familiar Ovidian world of plots, dangers, crises, but the principal actors in that world are not the speaker or his mistress or her father, but the various speech acts in relation to which they have roles to play and meanings to declare. A phrase like "fathers wrath" names a conventional linguistic practice, not a person, and when the speaker swears by it, indeed *conjures* by it, he acknowledges the extent to which the energy he displays is borrowed from a storehouse of verbal formulas that belong to no one and precede everyone.

Yet even as that acknowledgment is made, the speaker resists it by claiming that the power that is working in this scene has its source in him, or, more precisely, in the "masculine persuasive force" by means of which he produces (begets) his mistress's character. The three words that make up this phrase are mutually defining and redundant. The masculinity he asserts is inseparable from his ability to persuade—that is, to control—and "force" is just a name for the exercise of that control, an exercise that validates his independence and thereby confirms his masculinity. But even as the power of masculine persuasive force is asserted the line itself assigns that power to the *words*—"my words' masculine persuasive force"—which thereby reserve for themselves everything the speaker would mark as his own, including his own identity. In the guise of telling a story about a man, a woman, and a proposed journey, the poem stages a struggle between its own medium and the first-person voice that presumes to control it. That struggle is enacted again in the next line and a half when the speaker declares that his words are subordinate to the inner reality of which they are the mere expressions: "all the oaths which I / And thou have sworn to seal joint constancy" (9–10). The assertion is that the constancy is a feature of his character and is prior to the oaths that serve only as its outward sign; but no sooner has that assertion been made than it is flatly contradicted by the (speech) action of the next line: "Here I unswear, and overswear them thus." "Overswear" means "swear over," both in the sense of "again" and in the sense of *re*inscribing, of writing over what has been written previously. Not only does this overswearing undermine the constancy that has just been claimed, it also renders empty the personal pronoun that stood as the sign of the claimant. A consciousness that can rewrite its own grounds in the twinkling of an eye is not a consciousness at all, but a succession of refigurings no different finally from the refigurings it boasts to have produced in others.

The speaker, however, cannot let that difference disappear lest he disappear with it, and in the lines that follow he attempts to reaffirm it by insisting that his mistress remain firmly identifiable. In response to her suggestion that she accompany him disguised as a page, he says, "Be my true mistress still, not my feigned page," but given his earlier claim to have begotten her, to have fashioned her through the power of his words, the plea is incoherent. What he asks from her—stability of identity—he has already taken away. She cannot be the wax tablet on which he inscribes his will—indeed his "feigned page"—and yet be the fixed pole in relation to which other fixities, including his will, can be defined. He can't have it both ways.

Nevertheless he presses on and tries again: "Dissemble nothing, not a boy, nor change / Thy body's habit, nor mind's" (27–28). Again the plea is undercut by everything that precedes it. How can she be herself, if the self she presents is made up of the words he would put in her mouth? How can something characterized as a "habit"—a style, or form, inherently changeable—be asked to maintain its essence? These questions answer themselves, but they also point to the speaker's desperation and to the fear that stands behind it, fear not for her safety or person, but for himself; for he knows that unless her body and mind have an integrity that repels assaults, his own integrity is disastrously compromised. Masculine authority can be asserted only in relation to a firmly defined opposite; were the opposition to blur in either direction, the fixity of *both* poles would be immediately compromised. In order for him to be a man she must be unmistakably and essentially a woman.[14] When he says "be yourself," a command that follows ludicrously upon his injunction that she "feed on this flattery," he is really saying, "be yourself because if you are not, I cannot be *my*self, and I can no longer claim to be exerting masculine persuasive force." That is why the truly threatening prospect is the prospect of her metamorphosing into a boy, for if that were to happen, he would either have to assume the role of a woman, or, what is worse, betray his masculinity by entering with her/him into an unnatural relationship. So threatening is this prospect that he cannot confront it directly but instead displaces it onto an imagined scenario in which she is pursued throughout Europe by a succession of indiscriminate seducers: "Men of France, changeable chameleons, / . . . Will quickly know thee, and know thee; and alas / Th' indifferent Italian, as we pass / . . . well content to think thee page, / Will hunt thee with such lust, and hideous rage, / As Lot's fair guests were vexed" (33–41). The ploy is obvious: it will not be he, but the French and Italians, the traditional figures in England of everything transitory and variable, who will force her; it is they who are changeable, purveyors of mere fashion, devisers of theatrical scenes (this accusation in the midst of a scene he is even now devising); it is they, not he, who blur distinctions and threaten even the boundaries of gender in their (and how precise this is) "indifferent lust." It is they, not he, who by giving reign to that lust lose their own identities even as they seek to corrupt hers. But of course the ploy will not work; the activities he projects onto them are too transparently his own; the chameleon-like behavior he excoriates is the behavior he has already displayed when he blithely overswears the oaths of the previous moment. The fierce appropriativeness against which he warns her is even now directed at her as he twice implores her to "stay here," that is both in England and here on the page where he would fix her so that he himself could be fixed in relation to her. In the end the independence of which he so often boasts can only take form on the stages he sets. In short, it isn't independence at all, but one more fragile creation of a power that undoes him even as he exercises it.

He exercises it for the last time in a virtuoso performance. First he imagines her asleep, that is, in the perfect passive posture; and then he inscribes a scene on the blank tablet of her consciousness, a scene in which *he* dies a death that is triply screened, first by its occurrence in a dream and second by its status as something *reported* by her to a nurse when she awakens, and third by the fact that the dream is one he is warning her *not* to have: Do not, he says, fright thy nurse by crying out, "Oh, oh / Nurse, O my love is slain, I saw him go / O'er the white Alps alone; I saw him, I / Assailed, fight, taken, stabbed, bleed, fall, and die" (51–54). It is a tribute to the poet's powers that this passage is often praised by commentators for its immediacy and sincerity of feeling, but in fact it is a triumph of illusionistic art. No small part of that art is the figure of the Nurse who, as the audience to the dreamer's cries, establishes a role, a textual place, that we as readers can occupy, indeed *must* occupy; as we occupy it we forget what we have just been told, not only that none of this is happening, but that the speaker is forbidding it to happen. The power of the Nurse to draw us in is a function in part of her late appearance; she seems to be independent of the issues and concerns that have possessed the poem to this point. In fact, however, she is, like everything else in the poem, a rewriting of a previously written form, for although we may not recognize her, we have met her before in line 16: "Thee only worthy to nurse in my mind." The line has two readings: (1) only the memory of you will nurse in me a desire to return, and (2) you are worthy, i.e. substantial, only when my mind nurses you and gives you form. In this second reading the verb is a muted equivalent of everything that masculine persuasive force stands for, and when the verb turns up in the dream, now transformed into its noun, it/she is the representative *in* the scene of the force that is conjuring it up. That force, that impetuous rage, that indifferent interpretive lust, occupies every role, plays all the parts, sets the scene, lights it, frames it, and then glosses it with a commentary. But, of course, that is just the trouble. By playing *all* the parts, the practitioner of masculine persuasive force denies himself a part of *his own;* by filling every space, he leaves himself with no place to stand, no place that is not already occupied by the theatrics that have become his essence. In a final irony this moment of spectacular illusion does in fact enact his death, his disappearance as anything but a continually changing figure on a succession of illusionistic stages.

## "All Signs of Loathing"

That irony is the subject of the *Satires,* despite the still influential account of them as spoken in the voice of one who "consistently defends the spiritual values of simplicity, peace, constancy, and truth."[15] Certainly there is much talk of these virtues in the poems, but they are invoked at the very moments at which the speaker is displaying their opposites; rather than naming his achievements, they name the states from which he is always and already distant, the state of being one thing (simplicity), of being that thing without conflict (in peace), and of being that thing forever and truly. The satires record the desperate and always failing effort of the first-person voice to distinguish himself from the variability and corruption—alteration from an original—he sees around him. The basic and (literally) self-defeating gesture of these poems is enacted in the very first lines of *Satire I:*

> Away thou fondling motley humourist,
> Leave me . . .

The phrase "fondling motley humourist" is made up of words that point to the same quality, instability; a humorist is a person of irregular behavior, "a fantastical or whimsical person" (*OED*); a fondling is a fool, someone dazed, incapable of focusing (in an earlier manuscript Donne wrote "changeling"); and motley is what a fool wears because a cloth "composed of elements of diverse or varied character" (*OED*) perfectly suits one who is without a center. It also suits the traditional figure of the satirist, the writer of a random discourse who moves from one topic to another in ways that display no abiding rationale; the linking definition of satire as "*satura* medley"—a full dish of mixed fruit indiscriminately heaped up—was a standard one in the period and linked the satirist both with the court fool (as he appears, for example, in *King Lear*), and with the "mirror" or recorder figure who reflects the disorder of a world without coherence and has no coherence of his own. (Here one might cite Skelton's Parrot). In short, what the first-person voice pushes away or tries (in an impossible effort) to push away is himself; rather than saying, as he would like to, "Get thee behind me Satan," he is saying (in perfect *self-*contradiction), "Get thee behind me me." From the beginning he is protecting and defending an identity—a separateness from flux and surface—that he never really has.

In what follows, each declaration of distance and isolation is undermined even as it is produced. In line 11 he vows *not* to leave the "constant company" of his library; but in the previous line that company is said to include "Giddy fantastic poets," an acknowledgment that at once belies the claim of constancy and points once again to the giddiness (absence of stability) of the speaker, who is after all practicing poetry at this very moment. In line 12 he is betrayed even by his own syntax:

> Shall I leave all this constant company,
> And follow headlong, wild uncertain thee?

Who is "headlong"—that is, madly impetuous—the motley humorist or the speaker who (at least rhetorically) disdains him? Since "headlong" can either be an adverb modifying "I" or an adjective modifying "thee" it is impossible to tell, and this impossibility faithfully reflects the absence of the difference the speaker repeatedly invokes.

The claim of difference is further (and fatally) undermined when the speaker without any explanation decides that he will follow along after all. As if to reaffirm his self-respect (and his self) he asks for assurances that he will not be left alone in the street ("First swear . . . / Thou wilt not leave me" [13–15]), but this weak (and, as he himself knows, futile) gesture only underlines the extent of his capitulation: the distance between "leave me" and "don't leave" has been traveled in only fifteen lines; the stutter rhythm of push away/embrace is now instantiated in the poem's narrative as the now indistinguishable pair prepares to exit together. Before they do, the speaker rehearses the dangers he hopes to avoid, but his recital of them is so detailed and knowledgeable that he seems already to have fallen to them, and when he once again reasserts his difference from the world he is about to enter—"With God, and with the Muses I confer" (48)—one cannot take him seriously. Immediately after uttering this line he says "But" and performs the action he vowed never to perform in line 1:

> I shut my chamber door, and come, let's go.
> (52)

Yet even here he hesitates, pausing on the threshold (which he has long since crossed) to analyze an action that he himself finds inexplicable; after all he knows his man too well to believe that he will be faithful, and he knows too that any fickleness will be accomplished by a justification for "why, when, or with whom thou wouldst go" (65). The real question, however, is why the *speaker* would go in the face of such knowledge, and he poses the question himself in the very act of going:

> But how shall I be pardoned my offence
> That thus have sinned against my conscience.
> (66–67)

There is no answer, merely the report that, finally, "we are in the street" (67), but the answer is all too obvious: if by conscience he means an inner integrity—an identity that holds itself aloof against all external temptations and assaults—then conscience is what he has not had ever since his first words revealed a mind divided against itself. Ironically, that mind is now unified (if that is the right word) when it accepts (certainly not the right word) its implication in the giddy and the variable, and ventures out into the world to encounter other versions of himself, others who, like him, are "many-colored" and forever on the move. The fiction that it is not he but his fickle companion who refuses to stand still (86) is rhetorically maintained by the distinction of pronouns, but even that distinction is collapsed in the final lines:

> He quarreled, fought, bled; and turned out of door
> Directly came to me hanging the head,
> And constantly a while must keep his bed.
> (110–12)

That is, he comes *home,* where he lives, to the speaker, and he comes "directly," as if by instinct, and as he comes he shares with the speaker the pronoun "me"—is it "comes to me while hanging his head" or "comes to me who am hanging my head"? The attribution of "constancy" is mocked not only by the immediate qualification of "a while," but by everything that has transpired in a poem where inconstancy rules and most spectacularly rules the voice who would thrust it from him ("Away . . .").

In *Satire 2* the spectacle of a self-divided being continuing to claim a spurious independence is even more pronounced. Here the speaker begins by firmly distinguishing himself from the town which he does "hate / Perfectly" (1–2). The perfection of his hatred and the distance it implies are compromised, however, when he specifies it more precisely: he hates those who wield words, and he hates especially poets, and among poets he hates those who have transferred their verbal arts to the public sphere in order to manipulate the law. "Words, words, which would tear / The tender labyrinth of a soft maid's ear" (57–58), perform their

seductions in a much wider field—in the court, the courts, the manage-
ment of estates—until they threaten to "compass all our land" (77).

The question, of course, is that of the speaker's place in this dark
vision. What is the status of *his* words? The answer is given with perfect
ambiguity in the poem's last lines:

> . . . but my words none draws
> Within the vast reach of the huge statute laws.
>                (111–12)

Does this mean, as A. J. Smith takes it to, that the satirist's words alone
escape the reach of a corrupted law?[16] Or is Wesley Milgate right to see
this as another declaration (and claim) of a difference between the
speaker and those he indicts?[17] And if that is at least a possible reading,
isn't it, as John Lauritsen insists, an instance of protesting too much:
"the satirist . . . attempts to exculpate himself from a charge that no one
has made . . . assuring no one so much as himself that he . . . is one
person and Coscus quite another, that his dread of Coscus is not in fact a
mirror image of his own guilt, that his fear of Coscus is not ultimately a
fear of . . . his own perversion of the word."[18] Or could these lines (as
Arthur Marotti suggests) be a complaint that no one is paying attention
to him, that his words, unlike Coscus's, are ineffectual, and that his
vaunted independence is something he would gladly lose if he could
only gain a portion of the spoils won by others?[19] There is no answer to
these questions—this is another of those poems which, as Herz says,
"simply will not resolve"[20]—and in the absence of an answer (or in the
presence of too many) the speaker's claim not to have been compassed
by what encompasses everyone and everything else in the land is with-
out firm support.

Moreover, insofar as the speaker's relationship to the world he scorns
is precarious, so is Donne's, for nothing in the poem authorizes us to
perform the saving and stabilizing move of formalist criticism in which
a sharp distinction between the poet and his persona allows the former
to stand outside the predicament of the latter. In Donne's poems, as
Herz observes, "inside and outside are no longer clearly fixed points,"[21]
and therefore we cannot with any confidence locate a place in which the
poet is securely established as a controlling presence. This is particularly
true of *Satire 4,* a poem in which the speaker plays with the dangers of
displaying Catholic sympathies in a way that cannot be separated from
the danger Donne—the Catholic-in-the-course-of-becoming-an-An-
glican—risks in presenting such a speaker. Is it the satiric voice who
begins by declaring "Well; I may now receive" and then labors to render
the suggestion of a forbidden ceremony metaphorical and jesting, or is

it Donne? One simply cannot tell in a poem in which, as Thomas Hester observes, the "consistent glances at the predicament of the Catholic in Elizabethan England" are always "equivocal."[22] That equivocality is not only a feature of the relationships *within* the poem, but characterizes the relationship between the poem and its maker; just as we don't know whether the speaker intends something serious by his references to Jesuitical practices or is merely producing them in order to frighten away his importunate interlocutors, so we don't know whether Donne, in the same references, is alluding to "his own situation"[23] or merely fleshing out the situation of a fictive drama.

What we do know is that once again a Donne poem presents a speaker who refuses to recognize himself in the indictment he makes of others. In this case the indictment is of those who go to court, which is the very first thing the speaker does in an action he finds as inexplicable as we do:

> My mind, neither with pride's itch, nor yet hath been
> Poisoned with love to see, or be seen.
> I had no suit there, nor new suit to show,
> Yet went to Court.
>
> (5–8)

The claim is, as in the earlier poems, a claim of interiority—he need not show himself in order to acquire value; he is content with what he is in himself—and in order to maintain the claim, he at once minimizes his sin and renders it something external by calling it "my sin of going" (12). Characterized that way, the sin seems accidental to an inner being it does not touch, something that "happens" to that being before it is even aware. Of course he knows what the commission of this little sin will suggest to some, that he is "As prone to all ill, and of good as forget- / ful, as proud, as lustful, and as much in debt, / As vain, as witless, and as false as they / Which dwell at Court, for once going that way" (13–16); but by insisting on the "once," on the anomalous nature of the event, he pushes the accusation away and reaffirms his status as something apart from the scene he unwillingly enters.

It is in the service of the same affirmation that he labels everything and everyone he meets "strange" and a "stranger," indeed "Stranger than strangers" (23). That is to say, nothing I saw is like *me*, an assertion belied by the very first person he encounters; that person wears coarse clothes which leave him bare (30); he "speaks all tongues" (35) and has none of his own; rather he is "Made of th' accents" (37), a confection of "pedant's motley" (40). He is, in short, a satirist, affectedly coarse, deliberately ill-attired, a mirror of everything around him, an indiscriminate mixture. The speaker has met himself, and he responds in language that at once admits the kinship and disclaims it:

> He names me, and comes to me; I whisper, "God!
> How have I sinned, that thy wrath's furious rod,
> This fellow, chooseth me?"
>                           (49–51)

"He names me" is literal in its identification of the two, but of course in so exclaiming the speaker intends only wonder at so unlikely an act of recognition; but then he performs (unknowingly) the same recognition when he "names" the stranger "thy wrath's furious rod," for this is still another standard description of the satirist and his purpose. Unable to free himself from this unwelcome companion, he has recourse to behavior that will he hopes drive the wretch away: "I belch, spew, spit, / Look pale, and sickly" (109–10); but this is precisely the aspect the "stranger" already bears, and it is no wonder that upon meeting it in the speaker "he thrusts on more" (111). The "more" he produces is a compendium of stock satiric themes—"He names a price for every office paid; / He saith, our laws thrive ill, because delayed; / That offices are entailed" (121–23)—and as he listens to this version of himself even the speaker is close to seeing the truth:

> . . . hearing him, I found
> That as burnt venomed lechers do grow sound
> By giving others their sores, I might grow
> Guilty. . . .
>                (133–36)

Guilty, that is, not simply of going, but of being, or rather of nonbeing.

The thought is too horrible and he thrusts it away with a gesture that is its own allegory:

> . . . I did show
> All signs of loathing.
>           (136–37)

"All signs of loathing" is a formulation that definitively begs the question both for the speaker and for Donne. "Signs" of loathing are precisely external indications of something that may be otherwise; whether the speaker *really* loathes is something we don't know and something *he* doesn't know either. The same holds for Donne: the entire poem constitutes *his* sign of loathing, *his* declaration of distance from the world he delineates and from the voice he projects: "this is not me but my creature; this is not my world, but the world in which my creature is implicated in ways that he does not know; I, like you, know; I am in control." But the only evidence he might cite in support of this declaration and its claim (the claim to be in possession of himself in contrast to his creature who is not) are his signs of loathing, his production of words, his *show;* but whether or not anything lies behind the show, whether the *signs* of loathing stand in for an authentic loathing or whether they constitute a ruse by which the true nature of Donne's impure being is concealed from us and from himself in exactly the manner of his fictional (or is it true?) surrogate, is something we cannot determine. *And neither can he.* As in the elegies, the foregrounding of the power of signs and of their tendency to "compass all the land" catches the foregrounder in its backwash, depriving him of any independence of the forces he (supposedly) commands. The more persuasive is his account and exercise of verbal power the less able is he to situate himself in a space it does not fill, and he is left as we are, wondering if there is or could be anything real—anything other than artifice—in his performance (a word that perfectly captures the dilemma).

## "True Griefe"

The relationship between the exercise of power and the claims to independence and sincerity continues to be thematized in the *Holy Sonnets* although in these poems Donne occupies (or tries to occupy) the position of the creature and yields the role of the shaper to God. That difference, however, is finally less significant than one might suppose since the God Donne imagines is remarkably like the protagonist he presents (and I would say *is*) in the elegies, a jealous and overbearing master who brooks no rivals and will go to any lengths (even to the extent of depriving Donne of his wife) in order to secure his rights. It is as if Donne could only imagine a God in his own image, and therefore a God who acts in relation to him as he acts in relation to others, as a self-aggrandizing bully. To be sure, in the sonnets the speaker rather than exerting masculine persuasive force begs to be its object ("Batter my heart, three person'd God"), but this rearrangement of roles only emphasizes the durability of the basic Donnean situation and gives it an odd and unpleasant twist: the woman is now asking for it ("enthrall me," "ravish me"). One might almost think that the purpose of the sonnets, in Donne's mind, is retroactively to justify (by baptizing) the impulses to cruelty and violence (not to say misogyny) he displays so lavishly in his earlier poetry. In an important sense "Thou hast made me and shall thy work decay" is simply a rewriting of "Nature's lay idiot," which might itself be titled "I have made you, and shall *my* work decay?" The plot is the same, an original artificer now threatened by a rival artisan ("our old subtle foe so tempteth me"), and a complaint against change in the name of a control that would be absolute. Of course in the "sacred" version the complaint is uttered not by the about to be supplanted creator, but by the creature eager to remain subject to his power ("not one houre I can myself sustaine"); nevertheless the relational structure of the scene is the same, a structure in which masochism (and now sado-masochism) is elevated to a principle and glorified, earlier in the name of a frankly secular power, here in the name of a power that is (supposedly) divine. The fact that Donne now assumes the posture of a woman and like the church of "Show me deare Christ thy spouse" spreads his legs (or cheeks) is worthy of note, but to note it is not to indicate a significant (and praiseworthy) change in his attitude toward women and power; it is rather to indicate how strongly that attitude informs a poetry whose center is supposedly elsewhere.

Moreover, even as Donne casts himself in the female role, he betrays an inability to maintain that role in the face of a fierce and familiar desire to be master of his self, even of a self whose creaturely nature he is in the process of acknowledging. In a poem like "As due by many titles I resigne / My selfe to thee," the gesture of resignation is at the same time a reaffirmation of the resigner's independence: considering well the situation, it seems proper that I choose to be subservient to you. As Hester has observed, this is not so much a resigning, but a re-signing, the production of a signature and therefore of a claim of ownership, if not of the self that was, as he says, "made" (1.2), then of the act by which that self is laid down (a distinction without a difference).[24] Ostensibly the poem is an extended plea to be possessed (in every sense) by God, but in fact it is a desperate attempt to leave something that will say, like Kilroy, "Donne was here."

That desperation is the explicit subject of "If faithfull soules be alike glorifi'd," a first line that enacts in miniature everything that follows it.[25] As it is first read, the question seems to be whether or not all faithful souls are glorified in the same way (are they alike?), but then the first two words of the second line—"As Angels"—reveal that the likeness being put into question is between all faithful souls (now assumed to be glorified alike, but without any content specified for that likeness) and angels who are themselves glorified alike but perhaps not in the same manner (alike) as are faithful souls. If the pressure of interrogation falls on the notion of likeness and therefore on the issue of identity (one must know what something or someone uniquely is before one can say for certain whether or not it or he or she is like or unlike something or someone else), then the interrogation is from the very first in deep trouble when the word "alike," meaning "not different," turns out to be different from itself in the passage from line 1 to line 2.

The trouble is compounded as line 2 further unfolds:

> As Angels, then my fathers soule doth see

Whether or not his father's soul sees is still in doubt since the entire construction remains ruled by "If"; and the fact of his father's being a Catholic reinvigorates the question that had been left behind in the turn of the second line: are faithful souls glorified alike even if they are faithful to papism? As a result, the status of his father's vision is doubly obscure; we don't know whether it is like the vision of other, more safely, faithful souls, and we don't know, should it pass that test, whether it is as perspicuous as the vision of angels.

It is in the context of that unsure vision that we meet the sight it may or may not see: "That valiantly I hels wide mouth o'erstride" (4). The line presents itself as an assertion of the way things really are—despite appearances I stand firm against the temptations of the world, flesh, and devil—but in the context of what precedes it, the assertion remains only a claim until it is confirmed by one who sees *through* appearances to the inner reality they obscure. Since, however, the question of whether his father is one who sees in that penetrating way has been left conspicuously open, neither he nor we can be sure of that confirmation, and there remains the suspicion that behind the sign of purity, behind the verbal report of spiritual valor, there is nothing; the suspicion that the truth about him is no deeper or more stable than his surface representation of it. It is this dreadful possibility that Donne (one could say "the speaker," but it will come down to Donne in the end) raises explicitly in the next four lines:

> But if our mindes to these soules be descry'd
> By circumstances, and by signes that be
> Apparent in us, not immediately,
> How shall my mindes white truth to them be try'd?
> (5–8)

That is, if my father and other glorified souls (if he is, in fact, glorified and if all faithful souls are glorified alike) descry just as we on earth do, through a variety of glasses darkly, by means of signs, of representations, of what shows (is "Apparent"), then there is no way that anyone will ever know what's inside me or indeed if there *is* anything inside me. A "white truth" is a truth without color, without coverings, without commentary, but if colored, covered, and textualized truth are all anyone can see, then the white truth of his mind will continue to be an untried

claim, and one moreover that is suspect, given the innumerable ex-
amples of those who feign commitments they do not have:

> They see idolatrous lovers weepe and mourne,
> And vile blasphemous Conjurers to call
> On Jesus name, and Pharisaicall
> Dissemblers feigne devotion.
> (9–12)

Anyone can *say* they are faithful or sincere or "white," but such sayings,
proffered as evidence of a truth beyond (or behind) signs, are themselves
signs and never more suspicious than when they present the trappings
of holiness. It is at this point (if not before) that the precarious situation
of the poem becomes obvious; as a structure of signs it has done all
the things it itself identifies as strategies of dissembling: it has wept,
mourned, dramatized devotion; and then, as if it were following its own
script, the poem closes by performing the most reprehensible of these
strategies; it calls on Jesus' name:

> . . . Then turne
> O pensive soule, to God, for he knowes best
> Thy true griefe, for he put it in my breast.
> (12–14)

There are at least two levels on which this is an unsatisfactory conclusion.
First, there is no reason to believe that the turn to God is anything but
one more instance of feigned devotion, one more *performance* of a piety
for which the evidence remains circumstantial (that is, theatrical) and
apparent, a matter of signs and show. To be sure, the structure of the
sonnet lends these lines the aura of a final summing up, of a pronounce-
ment ("Then") detached from the gestures that precede it; but nothing
prevents us from reading the pronouncement itself as one more gesture,
and therefore as a claim no more supported than the claim (that he val-
iantly o'erstrides hell's mouth) it is brought in to support. And even if
we were to credit the sincerity of these lines and regard them not as
dramatic projections but as spontaneous ejaculations, they would not
provide what the poem has been seeking, a perspective from which we
could discern once and for all what, if anything, was inside him; for all
the lines say is that whatever there is in his breast, God knows it, which
means of course that we don't, and that we are left at the end with the
same doubt that his "true griefe" (here just one more "untry'd" claim)
may be false, a confection of signs and appearances. As in the elegies and
the satires, the relentless assertion and demonstration of the power of
signs to bring their own referents into being—to counterfeit love and
grief and piety—undermines the implicit claim of *this* producer of

signs to be real, to be anything more than an effect of the resources he purports to control.

Again, the large question is, does Donne *know* this? Does he stand apart from the corrosive forces his speakers fail to escape? An affirmative answer to this question has always been the strategy of choice in Donne criticism. One argues, as Roger Rollin recently has done, that while the sonnets are "sick poems," poems infected by spiritual malaise, confusions, and unacknowledged rationalizations, they are intended by Donne to be both diagnostic and salutary, "preventive medicine . . . meant to be exemplary to disease-prone readers."[26] In other words, the poems are diseased, the speakers are diseased, and the readers are diseased, but Donne is not. What aside from the tradition in which authors are always accorded an extraordinary measure of control and awareness authorizes this claimed exemption? What the poems show us is theatricality triumphant, and it is hard to see how one can move from the repeated dramatization of that triumph to the identification of a consciousness that is not itself dramaturgic (and thus suspect in all the ways it records) but real, purely present, valiantly o'erstriding the abyss of textuality. It is easy to see why readers might desire to identify such a consciousness, for there would then be a state (of awareness, control, and self-possession) to which they could at least aspire; but the desire can only be realized in an act of construction that is no less fragile than the constructions it would transcend. The reader in short must engage in an act of self-persuasion, which will, if he performs it, replicate and extend the act Donne himself performs in writing the poem. Far from being the distant and calm physician to readers that Rollin projects, Donne is his poem's first reader, the desperate audience of its hoped-for effect. Not only is he trying to convince readers of his ultimate sincerity—of his mind's white truth—he is trying to convince himself.

This is spectacularly the case in "What if this present were the worlds last night?" This first line might well open one of the sermons Donne was later to write; it is obviously theatrical and invites us to imagine (or to be) an audience before whom this proposition will be elaborated in the service of some homiletic point. But in the second line everything changes abruptly. The theatricalism is continued, but the stage has shrunk from one on which Donne speaks to many of a (literally) cosmic question to a wholly interior setting populated only by versions of Donne:

> Marke in my heart, O Soule, where thou dost dwell,
> The picture of Christ crucified, and tell
> Whether that countenance can thee affright?
> (2–4)

Donne addresses his own soul and asks it to look in his heart, where will
be found a picture he has put there, either for purposes of meditation or
in the manner of a lover who hangs portraits of his lady in a mental
gallery. But the meditation is curious in the way we have already noted:
Donne does not direct it at his beloved, whether secular or spiritual, but
to another part of himself. Although Christ's picture is foregrounded,
especially in the lines (5–7) that rehearse its beauties in a sacred parody
of the traditional blazon, in the context of the poem's communicative
scene, the picture—not to mention the person it portrays—is off to the
side as everything transpires between the speaker and his soul. The ges-
ture is a familiar one in Donne's poetry; it is the contraction into one
space of everything in the world ("All here in one bed lay"), which is
simultaneously the exclusion of everything in the world ("I could eclipse
and cloud them with a wink");[27] but here it seems prideful and perhaps
worse, for it recharacterizes the Last Judgment as a moment staged and
performed entirely by himself: produced by Donne, interior design by
Donne, case pled by Donne, decision rendered by Donne. Again, as in
the elegies, Donne occupies every role on his poem's stage, and since the
stage is interior, it is insulated from any correcting reference other than
the one it allows. Thus protected from any outside perspective and from
the intrusion of any voice he has not ventriloquized, Donne can confi-
dently ask the poem's urgent question:

> And can that tongue adjudge thee unto hell,
> Which pray'd forgivenesse for his foes fierce spight?
> (7–8)

The question's logic assumes a distinction between "that tongue" and
"thee" (i.e., me), but since Donne is here all tongues, the distinction is
merely verbal and cannot be the basis of any real suspense. The answer
is inevitable and it immediately arrives: "No, no" (9). But as John
Stachniewski acutely observes, "the argument of Donne's poems is often
so strained that it alerts us to its opposite, the emotion or mental
state in defiance of which the argumentative process was set to work."[28]
Here the mental state the poem tries to avoid is uncertainty, but its pres-
sure is felt in the exaggerated intensity with which the "No, no" denies
it. Uncertainty and instability return with a vengeance in the final lines:

> . . . but as in my idolatrie
> I said to all my profane mistresses,
> Beauty, of pitty, foulnesse onely is
> A signe of rigour: so I say to thee,
> To wicked spirits are horrid shapes assign'd,
> This beauteous forme assures a pitious minde.
> (9–14)

In the rhetoric of this complex statement, Donne's idolatry is in the past, but his words also point to the idolatry he has been committing in the poem, the idolatry of passing judgment on himself in a court whose furniture he has carefully arranged. The assertion that he is *not* now in his idolatry is undermined by the fact that he here says the very same things he used to say when he was. As he himself acknowledges, what he says is part of a seductive strategy, more or less on the level recommended in "The Anagram": if your beloved's countenance is forbidding and harsh, impute to her a benign interior; and if her aspect is "pitious," impute to her a consistency of form and content. In this poem, the suspect logic is even more suspect because it is directed at himself: the referent of "thee" is his own soul, the addressee since line 2. The soul is asked to read from the signifying surface of Christ's picture to his intention, but since that surface is one that Donne himself has as-signed, the confident assertion of the last line has no support other than itself.

Indeed the line says as much in either of its two textual versions, "This beauteous forme *assures* a pitious minde" or "This beauteous forme *assumes* a pitious minde."[29] In either variant "This beauteous for-me" refers not only to the form Donne has assigned to Christ's picture, but to the form of the poem itself; it is the poem's verbal felicity and nothing else that is doing either the assuring (which thus is no more than whistling in the dark) or the assuming (which as a word at least has the grace to name the weakness of the action it performs). The poem ends in the bravado that marks some of the other sonnets (e.g., "Death be not proud"), but the triumph of the rhetorical flourish (so reminiscent of the ending of every one of the *Songs and Sonnets*) only calls attention to its insubstantiality. Once again, the strong demonstration of verbal power—of the ability to make any proposition seem plausible so long as one doesn't examine it too closely—undermines its own effects. In the end the poet always pulls it off but that only means that he could have pulled it off in the opposite direction, and *that* only means that the conclusion he forces is good only for the theatrical moment of its production. This is true not only for his readers but for himself; as the poem concludes, he is no more assured of what he assumes than anyone else, neither of the "pitious minde" of his savior, nor of the spiritual stability he looks to infer from the savior's picture. The effort of self-persuasion—which is also at bottom the effort to confirm to himself that he is a self, someone who exceeds the theatrical production of signs and shows—fails in exactly the measure that his rhetorical effort succeeds. The better he is at what he does with words, the less able he is to claim (or believe) that behind the words—o'erstriding the abyss—stands a self-possessed being.

The realization of radical instability ("the horror, the horror") is given full expression in "Oh, to vex me, contraryes meete in one," a poem that desires to face the specter down, but in the end is overwhelmed by it. The problem is succinctly enacted in the first line: if contraries meet in one, then one is not one—an entity that survives the passing of time—but two or many. This would-be-one looks back on its history and sees only a succession of poses—contrition, devotion, fear—no one of which is sufficiently sustained to serve as the center he would like to be able to claim:

> . . . to day
> In prayers, and flattering speaches I court God:
> To morrow I quake with true feare of his rod.
> (9–11)

These lines at once report on and reproduce the dilemma: "prayers" seems innocent enough until "flattering speaches" retroactively questions the sincerity of the gesture; and the same phrase spreads forward to infect the assertion of line 11; when he quakes with "true fear," is the adjective a tribute to his artistry, to his ability to simulate an emotion in a way that convinces spectators (including himself) of its truth; or is the fear true in a deeper sense, one that would allow us to posit a moment (however fleeting) of authenticity in the midst of so many performances? The question is of course unanswerable, although as the poem ends (both with a bang and a whimper) there is one last attempt to draw the kind of line that would make an answer possible:

> So my devout fitts come and go away
> Like a fantastique Ague: save that here
> Those are my best dayes, when I shake with feare.
> (12–14)

"Devout fitts" recapitulates the problem: can devotion be genuine—heartfelt—if it comes and goes like the ever-changing scene of a fever? In the continual alternation of contradictory spiritual states, no one moment seems any more securely "true" than any other. Nevertheless the poem proceeds to declare an exception with "save that. . . ." On one level the exception is to the comparison between spiritual and physical health: while in the illness of the body the best days are the days when convulsions subside, in spiritual matters the best days are marked by fearful agitation.[30] But the exception Donne here tries to smuggle in is one that would attribute authenticity to the fits he displays on some days as opposed to others: my life may be characterized by changeful humors, but among those humors one speaks the genuine me. In order for that claim to be strongly received, however, the last line must be disen-

gaged from everything that has preceded it and be marked in some way
with the difference it attempts so boldly to declare. But no such mark is
available, and as we read it the line is drawn into the pattern from which
it would distinguish itself. Either it refers backward to the "true fear" of
line 11, already identified as a theatrical production, or, if we give the
word "here" full force, it refers to itself—I am at this very moment of
writing shaking with true fear—and asks us to accept as unperformed
and spontaneous the obviously artful conclusion to a sonnet. In either
case, one cannot rule out a reading in which the best days are the days
when he best simulates the appropriate emotion ("look at how good I
am at shaking with fear"), and we are as far from an emotion that is not
simulated—from an emotion produced other than theatrically by
someone other than a wholly theatrical being—than we were when he
uttered the first self-pitying line, "Oh, to vex me. . . ."

Reading this same poem, Anne Ferry makes observations similar to
mine but reaches a different conclusion. She takes the poem's lesson to
be "that what is grounded inward in [the speaker's] heart is at a distance
from language used to describe it, which cannot render it truly," and she
generalizes this lesson into a Donnean theory of sincerity:

> . . . what is in the heart cannot be interpreted or judged by outward
> signs, among which language is included, even when they are sincere.
> Inward states cannot therefore be truly shown, even by the speaker's own
> utterance in prayers or poems, cannot be defined by them, even to
> himself.[31]

Ferry assumes what it seems to me these poems put continually into
question, that the "inward experience" or "*real self*" is in fact there and
the deficiency lies with the medium that cannot faithfully transcribe it. I
have argued that the problem with language in these poems is not that it
is too weak to do something, but that it is so strong that it does every-
thing, exercising its power to such an extent that nothing, including the
agent of that exercise, is left outside its sphere. I am not offering *this* as
the insight Donne wishes to convey as opposed to the insight Ferry
urges, but, rather, saying that it is not an insight at all—in the sense of
something Donne commands—but the problematic in which he re-
mains caught even when he (or especially when he) is able to name it as
he does in this passage from a sermon delivered during his final illness:

> The way of Rhetorique in working upon weake men, . . . is to empty
> [the understanding] of former apprehensions and opinions, and to shape
> that beliefe, with which it had possessed it self before, and then when it is
> thus melted, to powre it into new molds, . . . to stamp and imprint new
> formes, new images, new opinions in it.[32]

Once again Donne identifies, this time by its proper name, the activity he has practiced all his life, an activity propelled by a force that knows no resistance and simply writes over (overswears) whatever meanings and forms some previous, equally unstoppable, force has inscribed. Once again, he attempts to assert his distance from that force even as he exercises it and reports on its exercise, attempts to possess it without being possessed by it. And once again the attempt takes the form of an act of displacement by means of which his fears are pushed onto others, not this time onto women or Frenchmen or Italians, but onto "weake men." Weak men are men whose convictions are so malleable, so weakly founded, that they can be shaped and reshaped by the skilled rhetorician who becomes, in an implied opposition, the very type of the strong man. But as we have seen, in the story that Donne's poems repeatedly enact, the skillful rhetorician always ends up becoming the victim/casualty of his own skill, and no more so than at those moments when his powers are at their height. The stronger he is, the more force-full, the more taken up by the desire for mastery, the less he is anything like "himself." The lesson of masculine persuasive force is that it can only be deployed at the cost of everything it purports to incarnate—domination, independence, assertion, masculinity itself.

In much of Donne criticism that lesson has been lost or at least obscured by a concerted effort to put Donne in possession of his poetry and therefore of himself. The result has been a series of critical romances of which Donne is the hero (valiantly o'erstriding the abyss). Ferry gives us one romance: the poet, ahead of his times, labors to realize a modern conception of the inner life. An older criticism gave us the romance of immediacy and the unified sensibility: the felt particulars of lived experience are conveyed by a verse that is at once tactilely sensuous and intellectually bracing. Often this romance was folded into another, the romance of voice in which a singular and distinctive Donne breaks through convention to achieve a hitherto unknown authenticity of expression. At mid-century the invention of the persona produced the romance of craft: Donne surveys the range of psychological experience and creates for our edification and delight a succession of flawed speakers. And the most recent scholarship, vigorously rejecting immediacy, voice, authenticity, and craft as lures and alibis, tempts us instead with the romance of postmodernism, of a Donne who is "rigorously skeptical, endlessly self-critical, posing more questions than he answers."[33] (This last is particularly attractive insofar as it transforms obsessive behavior into existential heroism of the kind academics like to celebrate because they think, mistakenly, that they exemplify it.) As different as they are, these romances all make the mistake of placing Donne outside the (verbal) forces he sets in motion and thus making him a figure of control. In the reading offered here, Donne is always folded back into the dilemmas he articulates, and indeed it is the very articulation of those dilemmas—the supposed bringing of them to self-consciousness—that gives them renewed and devouring life.

## Notes

1. C. S. Lewis, "Donne and Love Poetry in the Seventeenth Century," in *Seventeenth Century English Poetry: Modern Essays in Criticism,* ed. William Keast (New York: Oxford University Press, 1962), pp. 98, 96.

2. Judith Herz, " 'An Excellent Exercise of Wit that Speaks So Well of Ill': Donne and the Poetics of Concealment," in *The Eagle and the Dove: Reassessing John Donne,* ed. Claude J. Summers and Ted-Larry Pebworth (Columbia, Mo.: University of Missouri Press, 1986), p. 5.

3. *John Donne: The Complete English Poems,* ed. A. J. Smith (Baltimore: Penguin Books, 1971). All further citations of the elegies and the satires are taken from this text.

4. Thomas Docherty, *John Donne, Undone* (New York: Methuen, 1986), p. 68.

5. Arthur F. Marotti, *John Donne, Coterie Poet* (Madison: University of Wisconsin Press, 1986), p. 48.

6. Jacques Derrida, "Signature Event Context," trans. Samuel Weber and Jeffrey Mehlman, *Glyph* 1 (1977): 182, 185.

7. For a brilliant discussion of chaos as it operates in Renaissance literature in general and in Milton's *Paradise Lost* in particular, see Regina Schwartz, "Milton's Hostile Chaos: '. . . And the Sea Was No More'," *ELH* 52 (1985): 337–74.

8. Wilbur Sanders, *Donne's Poetry* (Cambridge University Press, 1971), p. 41.

9. Marotti, *John Donne,* p. 308.

10. Helen Gardner, ed., *The Elegies and the Songs and Sonnets* (Oxford: Clarendon Press, 1965), p. 137.

11. Marotti, *John Donne,* p. 308.

12. Sanders, *Donne's Poetry,* p. 41.

13. Docherty, *John Donne,* p. 60.

14. See on this point ibid., pp. 200–201. Docherty writes, "Male lovers look into the mirror of their lover's eye, or womb, and see the reflection of themselves (or of their sons, as representations of themselves), thus supposedly guaranteeing a stable, transhistorical male identity; and such eternal 'sameness', identity, slips into 'truth'," (p. 200).

15. N. J. C. Andreason, "Theme and Structure in Donne's *Satyres,*" in *Essential Articles: Donne's Poetry,* ed. John R. Roberts (Hamden, Conn.: Archon Books, 1975), p. 412.

16. A. J. Smith, *The English Poems,* p. 479.

17. Wesley Milgate, ed., *The Satires, Epigrams and Verse Letters* (Oxford: Clarendon Press, 1967), p. 139.

18. John Lauritsen, "Donne's *Satyres:* The Drama of Self-Discovery," *SEL* 16 (Winter 1976): 125.

19. Marotti, *John Donne,* p. 40.

20. Herz, "Poetics of Concealment," p. 5.

21. Ibid., p. 6.

22. Thomas Hester, *Kinde Pitty and Brave Scorn: John Donne's Satyres* (Durham: Duke University Press, 1982), p. 74.

23. Ibid., p. 74.

24. M. Thomas Hester, "Re-Signing the Text of the Self: Donne's 'As due by many titles'," in *"Bright Shootes of Everlastingnesse": The Seventeenth-Century Religious Lyric,* ed. Claude J. Summers and Ted-Larry Pebworth (Columbia, Mo.: University of Missouri Press, 1987), p. 69. See also Docherty, *John Donne,* p. 139.

25. All citations from the *Holy Sonnets* are taken from *John Donne: The Divine Poems,* ed. Helen Gardner (Oxford: Clarendon Press, 1964).

26. Roger Rollin, "'Fantastic Ague': The *Holy Sonnets* and Religious Melancholy," in *The Eagle and the Dove: Reassessing John Donne,* ed. Claude Summers and Ted-Larry Pebworth (Columbia, Mo.: University of Missouri Press, 1986), p. 131.

27. "The Sun Rising," 11.20, 13.

28. John Stachniewski, "John Donne: The Despair of the 'Holy Sonnets'," *ELH* 48 (1981): 691.

29. All manuscripts read *assures,* but the 1633 edition reads *assumes.*

30. Anne Ferry, *The "Inward" Language* (Chicago: University of Chicago Press, 1983), pp. 242–43.

31. Ibid., pp. 243, 249.

32. *Sermons,* ed. George R. Potter and Evelyn M. Simpson, 10 vols. (Berkeley: University of California Press, 1953–62), 2: 282–83.

33. Docherty, *John Donne,* p. 29.

# Unspeakable Love: Petrarch
# to Herbert

*Gordon Braden*

I wish to mourn perpetually the absence of what I love or might love.
Isn't that what religious people call the love of God?
George Santayana[1]

Among the familiar commonplaces about love in the Renaissance is its
power as a source of persuasive speech: "Love alwaies makes those elo-
quent that have it" (Marlowe, *Hero and Leander* 2.72). Woven in with
this conviction, however, is the contrary proposition that in the very in-
tensity of his feeling the lover may in fact not be able to say anything at
all. The definitive instance is Petrarch's:

> Pien d'un vago penser che me desvia
> da tutti gli altri e fammi al mondo ir solo,
> ad or ad ora a me stesso m'involo,
> pur lei cercando che fuggir devria,
>     e veggiola passar sì dolce e ria
> che l'alma trema per levarsi a volo,
> tal d'armati sospir conduce stuolo
> questa bella d'Amor nemica e mia!
>     Ben, s'i' non erro, di pietate un raggio
> scorgo fra 'l nubiloso altero ciglio,
> che 'n parte rasserena il cor doglioso;
>     allor raccolgo l'alma, e poi ch'i' aggio
> di scovrirle il mio mal preso consiglio
> tanto gli ò a dir che 'ncominciar non oso.

Full of a yearning thought that makes me stray away from all others and go alone in the world, from time to time I steal myself away from myself, still seeking only her whom I should flee; and I see her pass so sweet and cruel that my soul trembles to rise in flight, such a crowd of armed sighs she leads, this lovely enemy of Love and me. If I do not err, I do perceive a gleam of pity on her cloudy, proud brow, which partly clears my sorrowing heart: then I collect my soul, and, when I have decided to discover my ills to her, I have so much to say to her that I dare not begin. (*Canzoniere* 169)[2]

The topic is not original with Petrarch. It has famous classical precedent in Sappho and Catullus. It is well established in medieval lore about love, and in a form very close to Petrarch's. Among the questions asked in the anonymous *De uero amore* is, "Why, before he speaks to his beloved with the secret discourse of love, can the true lover scarcely bring forth the first words?" The answer is that "before it expresses the first words of love, the heart is extremely full of longing . . . like a very full jar from which, unless a little is emptied, nothing comes out if it is opened."[3] Petrarch's phrasing suggests that he had an immediate source in Arnaut Daniel, who graphs the paradox with special concision:

> c'ades ses lieis dic a lieis cochos motz;
> pois qand la vei, non sai—tant l'ai—que dire.

For still, without her, I speak to her heated words; then when I see her, I don't know—so much I have—what to say. (15.6–7)[4]

We may well guess that, as a human experience, such haplessness is a transhistorical constant of courtship.

Petrarch's treatment of the theme, however, has unusual force for being of a piece with a larger configuration of his work, a configuration that itself looms significantly in the immense influence of that work throughout the European Renaissance. Local frustration of speech rhymes with the larger frustrations of a desire essentially hopeless. Petrarch's love for his Laura is never consummated, and the Petrarchan mistress of subsequent tradition is similarly expected to be unwinnable. That expectation becomes in the course of that tradition a target of increasing impatience and eventual mockery. By the end of the sixteenth century the frustration of male sexuality looks like a mere convention that only narrows the range of serious love poetry, and we welcome the liberating influence of Ovid and Donne. But the tenacity of the convention makes its rationale worth meditating on. The bluntest gloss is that women are naturally cruel and actively enjoy torturing their devotees; the outcome can be misogynistic rage:

> Venir tipossa el diavolo allo letto
>> da poi che io non viposso venir io
>> et rompidi due chostole delpetto
>> elaltre membra che tefatto idio
>> et titiri permonti epervalli
>> et spichati elchapo dalle spalle.

May the devil go to bed with you, since I'm not welcome there; may he break a couple of your ribs, and the rest of your body, made by God; may he drag you over mountains and through valleys, and chop your head clean off.[5]

A soberer understanding sees the problem as a more complicated sort of knot: what causes the woman to reject her lover is her virtue, which is a major part of what makes her so attractive. Many poets take the woman's refusal as an act not only of admirable self-control but also of unrecognized generosity toward the man, an important event in his moral education. Petrarch himself affirms such a perspective in his *Trionfi* when he has the spirit of Laura tell him from beyond the grave that her disdain was in fact an expression of reciprocal love:

> Mai diviso
>> da te non fu 'l mio cor, né già mai fia;
>> ma temprai la tua fiamma col mio viso,
>> perché a salvar te e me null'altra via
>> era, e la nostra giovenetta fama;
>> né per ferza è però madre men pia.

My heart was never divided from you, and never will be. But I tempered your flame with my look because there was no other way to save you and me and our youthful fame. A mother is no less loving for using the rod. (*Triumphus mortis* 2.88–93)

With the aid of Neoplatonic philosophy and a glance back at Petrarch's stilnovist predecessors, sixteenth-century theorists systematize a model of sexual frustration as the first step in an expansive process of moral and intellectual enlightenment. In many circles—such as that of Castiglione's courtiers—this becomes the prevailing interpretation of what the Petrarchan experience means.

We need not lose touch with any of those possibilities; but within the *Canzoniere* there are other, stranger currents at work as well.[6] "Pien d'un vago penser," despite appearances, actually dramatizes one of the most aggressive moments in Petrarch's courtship. The tongue-tied lover of *De uero amore* is only temporarily incommoded: "after he has spoken three words [it is] easy for him to say what he wants," and presumably he takes further action according to the response he receives. In the *Canzoniere,* though, the failure to speak shows signs of being final; usually Petrarch does not even try. We miss in the sequence most of the overt efforts which other love poets, even other Petrarchan love poets, make in their attempts to undo their frustration. There is no clear evidence within the fictional world of the poems that Petrarch ever—to draw a specific contrast with Sidney's Astrophil—directly propositions Laura, or kisses her, or even sends her any of his poems.[7] He usually does not progress as far as even the attempt to speak:

> Quel vago impallidir, che 'l dolce riso
> d'un'amorosa nebbia ricoperse,
> con tanta maiestade al cor s'offerse
> che li si fece incontr'a mezzo 'l viso.

That lovely pallor, which covered her sweet smile with a cloud of love, with so much majesty presented itself to my heart that he went to meet it in the midst of my face. (123.1–4)

Wordless expression meets wordless expression. The allure of such restraint is indeed probably connected to the fact that Petrarch's greatest intimations of reciprocity come at just these moments:

> Chinava a terra il bel guardo gentile
> e tacendo dicea, come a me parve:
> Chi m'allontana il mio fedele amico?

She bent to earth her lovely noble glance and in her silence said, as it seemed to me: "Who sends away from me my faithful friend?" (12–14)

Yet the silence also makes the reciprocity ambiguous. Laura's *pietoso penser,* her "merciful thought," is one "which no one else perceived" (*ch'altri non scerse* [l. 7]). We cannot be sure that it is not simply generated by the lover's obsessive need to see it. The "gleam of pity" that he thinks he detects in "Pien d'un vago penser" is similarly attested largely by his own imagination. His failure to speak keeps him—and us—from finding out. Actual conversations with Laura are characteristically anticipated in some distant future (*Canzoniere* 12), or—like that in the *Trionfi*—come in dream visions after her death. So consistent is the avoidance of direct exchange of speech between the two that we are not greatly surprised to be told in the last poem in the sequence that, while alive, Laura "of my thousand sufferings did not know one" (*di mille miei mali un non sapea* [366.94]). Petrarch's passion might as well never have been revealed to her, and the failure of his courtship—if it can even be called that—might owe far less to Laura's virtue, which was never really put to the test, than to his own self-censorship.

To dwell on this matter is of course a little perverse, since getting the narrative details clear is not a major part of the business of lyric poetry, and certainly not of Petrarchan lyric poetry. "The first thing to grasp about the sonnet sequence is that it is not a way of telling a story."[8] These are poems focused not on facts but on feelings, not on events but on reactions. One of the reasons Petrarchan sonneteering figures so widely in the Renaissance is that it is a poetry of dramatic, expansive, even tyrannical subjectivity, which gains a certain independence from its context. Yet the event that we can divine in "Pien d'un vago penser" gears significantly with just this disposition. In the failure to speak, in the failure to put desire and hope at the mercy of external reality, we witness in effect a subjectivity electing to remain subjective. To the comparatively obvious negative reasons inhibiting the lover's speech we may add a subtler but possibly more powerful one: the impulse to preserve a private intensity of feeling inviolate in its privacy, which speech would only dissipate, cheapen. In not speaking because he has so much to say, the lover takes on some of the dignity accorded by a proverbial, indeed philosophical tradition that holds silence to be the vehicle of superior emotion and meaning. It is with this tradition that Petrarch's poem merges in subsequent tradition:

> Our Passions are most like to Floods and streames;
> The shallow Murmure; but the Deep are Dumb.
> (Sir Walter Ralegh 18.1–2)[9]

Those moments in which Petrarch can imagine his speechlessness as the means of a higher communion with Laura are perhaps the happiest in the *Canzoniere:* "Connobi allor sì come in paradiso / vede l'un l'altro" ("I learned then how they see each other in Paradise" [123.5]). Yet in important ways the woman's putative cooperation, even her presence, is not essential. Petrarch nurtures his emotional fullness more often than not in total solitude:

> Pien di quella ineffabile dolcezza
> che del bel viso trassen gli occhi miei
> nel dì che volentier chiusi gli avrei
> per non mirar già mai minor bellezza,
>      lassai quel ch'i' più bramo . . .

Full of that ineffable sweetness which my eyes drew from her lovely face on that day when I would gladly have closed them so as never to look on any lesser beauties, I departed from what I most desire. . . . (116.1–5)

There are reasons for saying that the drive to possess the woman Laura is only the ostensible subject of the *Canzoniere.* Petrarch's own contem-

poraries wondered whether Laura was anything more than a literary
fiction, something to write about; and despite Petrarch's protestation
otherwise, we have continued to wonder.[10] Laura is a very shadowy
character in the poems, never more than ambiguously active, present
usually as an image or memory cultivated at a distance:

> quanto in più selvaggio
> loco mi trovo e 'n più deserto lido,
> tanto più bella il mio pensier l'adombra.

in whatever wildest place and most deserted shore I find myself, so much
the more beautiful does my thought shadow her forth. (129.46–48)

The central pun of the sequence—arguably the central pun of Pe-
trarch's life—equates Laura the woman with *lauro,* the laurel crown of
poetic achievement; and it is not at all clear that what Petrarch worships
in worshiping her is not the activity of his own creative imagination.
Renaissance theorists would point specifically to absence as the principal
condition that stimulates and nurtures the imagination:

> Sensation is caused by present objects, provided that they are sen-
> sible. . . . Imagination, on the contrary, performs its function when the
> sensible object is rejected and even removed. Nay rather, it conceives not
> only what now is no more, but as well what it suspects or believes is yet to
> be, and even what it presumes cannot be created by Mother Nature.[11]

Petrarch's failure to speak to the real woman with Laura's name—and
we may as well concede that in all likelihood there was such a person—
is in effect a way of sustaining her absence at close range. The very full-
ness of his own emotion makes it as if, for all practical purposes, she
were not there; and in that cleared space the inward lyricism of Renais-
sance individualism begins to flourish.

Some two centuries later, the golden age of English Renaissance po-
etry begins with a poem about erotic writer's block:

> Loving in truth, and faine in verse my love to show,
> That the deare She might take some pleasure of my paine:
> Pleasure might cause her reade, reading might make her know,
> Knowledge might pitie winne, and pitie grace obtaine,
>      I sought fit words to paint the blackest face of woe,
> Studying inventions fine, her wits to entertaine:
> Oft turning others' leaves, to see if thence would flow
> Some fresh and fruitfull showers upon my sunne-burn'd braine.
>      But words came halting forth, wanting Invention's stay,
> Invention, Nature's child, fled step-dame Studie's blowes,
> And others' feete still seem'd but strangers in my way.

> Thus great with child to speake, and helplesse in my throwes,
>   Biting my trewand pen, beating my selfe for spite,
>   "Foole," said my Muse to me, "looke in thy heart and write."
>     (*Astrophil and Stella* 1)[12]

As an artistic manifesto, Sidney's famous poem seems to announce England's new poetic beginning as a dramatic break with the past. What in Petrarch was ostensibly between him and his lady is here transposed into a literary *agōn,* an explicit instance of the anxiety of influence—indeed, it would appear, specifically the influence of Petrarch. Elsewhere Sidney inveighs directly against those "that poore *Petrarch's* long deceased woes, / With new-borne sighes and denisend wit do sing" (15.7–8), and the polemical context of the opening poem as well is Petrarchan sonneteering in its sixteenth-century vogue, which is actively interfering with the production of true love poetry. We are here into those anti-Petrarchan declarations that mark so much late sixteenth-century and early seventeenth-century love poetry in England, and resonate so strongly in modern ears: "I graunt I never saw a goddesse goe, / My Mistres when shee walkes treads on the ground" (Shakespeare, *Sonnets* 130.11–12).[13] But in fact Sidney predates most English Petrarchism, and anti-Petrarchan protestations are not merely late features of the tradition; they are an established part of Sidney's own Continental heritage:

> J'ay oublié l'art de Petrarquizer.
> Je veulx d'Amour franchement deviser
> Sans vous flatter, & sans me deguizer.

I have forgotten the art of Petrarchizing. I want to speak of love forthrightly, without flattering you or falsifying myself.[14]

*Astrophil and Stella* makes especially clear how closely such disavowals can coexist with Petrarchan conventionality of the most egregious kind:

> Queene *Vertue's* court, which some call *Stella's* face,
>   Prepar'd by Nature's chiefest furniture,
>   Hath his front built of Alablaster pure;
> Gold is the covering of that stately place.
>     (9.1–4)

Criticism, once troubled by this apparent inconsistency, has come to understand that even the opening poem of the sequence is not the profession of unpredicated sincerity it may sound like, since we know from elsewhere that what Astrophil sees when he looks into his heart is Stella's image. The appropriate gloss is provided two poems later:

> For me in sooth, no Muse but one I know:
> Phrases and Problemes from my reach do grow,
> And strange things cost too deare for my poore sprites.
> How then? even thus: in *Stella's* face I reed,
> What Love and Beautie be, then all my deed
> But Copying is, what in her Nature writes.
> (3.9–14)

Which is no more than Petrarch or any number of perfectly tame imitators might say, changing only the lady's name. Sidney's anti-Petrarchan Petrism is not easy to get a fix on.

The case suggests in obvious ways Harold Bloom's powerful model of poetic warfare, in which individual talents struggle against their predecessors, only to involute in unexpected ways back within the structure of their predecessors' achievement. We might put the process in more benign terms, as, in this case, the process whereby Petrarchism stays true to its own values, and even deepens them, as it becomes a tradition. The opening poem of *Astrophil and Stella* turns away from the overt propagation of Petrarchism in order to repeat and enrich one of Petrarchism's essential actions. The world's available canons for poetic eloquence are brought to bear in order to serve the lover's overweening desire to persuade his lady, but the result of trying so hard to be effective is paralysis. The deadlock is resolved by a turning inward, in which personal and poetic authenticity are seen to reside in the rejection of external resource. For the naive modern response to Sidney's last line does have its validity: the convention to which it points, of the woman possessed as a mental image, is itself involved in a poetics of subjective inwardness. To stigmatize Petrarchan imitation, as Astrophil does, with "a want of inward tuch" (15.10) is in fact to keep faith with the dynamic of Petrarch's own poetic enterprise. If anything, Sidney, transposing the encounter of the tongue-tied lover and his beloved into a struggle more fully and obviously within the lover's own mind, makes clearer the gain in his apparent failure. The strenuous ambition to have his way with externals can yield, if he will only look into his own heart, to a blissfully passive copying of what is already his. Poetry, the poetry that counts, makes nothing happen.

This may be to extract a lesson not entirely in key with the rest of the sequence. Once he gets going, Astrophil does not scruple to use his poems to try to seduce Stella; I have already cited his aggressiveness and even crudity as a counterexample to Petrarch's reticence. Astrophil's pushiness nevertheless delivers him by the last poems into a fully Petrarchan solitude— "O absent presence *Stella* is not here" (106.1)—and the acquiescence that there might serve him best does reside in the open-

ing poem as a subtle point of literary tact. The point is dilated upon by
Spenser, realigning Petrarch's topic with Sidney's guidance:

> So when my toung would speak her praises dew,
>     it stopped is with thoughts astonishment:
> and when my pen would write her titles true,
>     it ravisht is with fancies wonderment:
> Yet in my hart I then both speake and write
>     the wonder that my wit cannot endite.
>             (*Amoretti* 3.9–12)[15]

Wit's loss is the heart's gain. And that opposition takes on particular
force in the age's most unpredictable sonnet sequence—though one of
the most revelatory precisely in its unpredictability. Even more than for
Astrophil, Shakespeare's problem is not an intimidating loved one so
much as another poet:

> My toung-tide Muse in manners holds her still,
> While comments of your praise richly compil'd,
> Reserve thy Character with goulden quill,
> And precious phrase by all the Muses fil'd.
> I thinke good thoughts, whilst other write good wordes,
> And like unletter'd clarke still crie Amen,
> To every Himne that able spirit affords,
> In polisht forme of well refined pen.
> Hearing you praisd, I say 'tis so, 'tis true,
> And to the most of praise adde some-thing more,
> But that is in my thought, whose love to you
> (Though words come hind-most) holds his ranke before,
>     Then others, for the breath of words respect,
>     Me for my dombe thoughts, speaking in effect.
>             (*Sonnets* 85)[16]

William Shakespeare's protestation of poetic incapacity is in itself a
mere convention of panegyric, but the context of his struggle with the
rival poet for the young man's affections gives that convention unusual
force. Behind the presenting claim that he cannot write the poetry that
the other poet writes stands the sterner assertion that in this situation he
will not and should not. The drama is to some extent a conflict of poetic
styles, open grandiosity—"the proud full saile of his great verse"
(86.1)—against colloquial simplicity, though in this particular poem
that conflict is shaded by the conceit that Shakespeare in fact assents to
everything the rival poet writes (I mean what he says). The effective op-
position is between language and meaning, words and thoughts, with a
suggestion that they may be radically disjunct. Authentic feeling be-

longs to the tongue-tied, while the one who knows what to say probably is not sincere. We need not assent to that as a general proposition for Shakespeare's cosmos, but it has urgency in a situation where certain kinds of personal aggrandizement are at stake—when the speaking of what is truly felt and thought activates other agendas. Shakespeare is more angrily articulate later:

> My love is strengthned though more weake in seeming,
> I love not lesse, thogh lesse the show appeare,
> That love is marchandiz'd, whose ritch esteeming,
> The owners tongue doth publish every where.
> (102.1–4)

The theme is not limited to the rival-poet episode. That competitive crisis merely focuses a determination voiced near the beginning of the sequence:

> O let me true in love but truly write,
> And then beleeve me, my love is as faire,
> As any mothers childe, though not so bright
> As those gould candells fixt in heavens ayer:
> Let them say more that like of heare-say well,
> I will not prayse that purpose not to sell.
> (21.9–14)

We sense behind the sting of that last word the specific pressure of a social situation where love and patronage treacherously mix. The muse's manners are held in place by a fine moral discrimination concerning the publicity of emotion as a means to an end. These are poems such as Cordelia might have written.

This moral urgency is new to the topic with Shakespeare—the result, we might say, of that topic's having found a context more fully appropriate to its odd rhetorical decorum. That decorum twists the usual rhetorical instruction to aim one's utterance at its addressee, to arrange one's words in some calculating way around the desires and expectations of their intended audience. The poem of unspeakable love, in contrast, is something more drastic than mere aposiopesis: an attempt, rather, to speak as if the seats in the theater were empty, since only then can love clear itself of corrupt intent. Still, the citation of Cordelia brings a reminder that the story here, if played out, is apt to be tragic. The failure to say the effective thing can be disastrous if it is, as seems perfectly likely, misconstrued. The "outcome" in Shakespeare's sonnets is too unclear to call with any confidence, but nothing we learn of the young man suggests that he could understand or recognize the austerity of motive that "My toung-tied Muse" and its companions delineate; and in the morally real world it is in fact important whether or not one's secret speech is divined or overheard by the audience that still, all paradoxes past, counts.

There are love poets who give confident expression to Petrarch's hope that silent speech can be deciphered and reciprocated. For Spenser, the hope figures in the work of courtship as a sounding of the woman's own emotional depth and wisdom:

> Yet I my hart with silence secretly
>> will teach to speak, and my just cause to plead:
>> and eke mine eies with meeke humility,
>> love learned letters to her eyes to read.
> Which her deep wit, that true harts thought can spel,
>> will soone conceive, and learne to construe well.
>> (*Amoretti* 43.9–14)

James Shirley extrapolates a genial scenario of Ovidian play:

> Then silence be my language, which if she
> But understand, and speak again to me,
> We shall secure our Fate, and prove at least
> The miracles of love are not quite ceast.
> Bar frowns from our discourse, and ev'ry where
> A smile may be his own Interpreter.
> Thus we may read in spite of standers by,
> Whole volumes, in the twinckling of an eye.
> ("A Lover that durst not speak to his M.")[17]

The most remarkable development of the topic, however, comes when George Herbert orients it towards another kind of auditor altogether, by way of dramatizing what communication would be like with the most important absent presence to which the Western psyche has sought to speak:

> When first my lines of heav'nly joyes made mention,
> Such was their lustre, they did so excell,
> That I sought out quaint words, and trim invention;
> My thoughts began to burnish, sprout, and swell,
> Curling with metaphors a plain intention,
> Decking the sense, as if it were to sell.
>
> Thousands of notions in my brain did runne,
> Off'ring their service, if I were not sped:
> I often blotted what I had begunne;
> This was not quick enough, and that was dead.
> Nothing could seem too rich to clothe the sunne,
> Much lesse those joyes which trample on his head.

> As flames do work and winde, when they ascend,
> So did I weave my self into the sense.
> But while I bustled, I might heare a friend
> Whisper, *How wide is all this long pretence!*
> *There is in love a sweetnesse readie penn'd:*
> *Copie out onely that, and save expense.*
> ("Jordan" II)[18]

Petrarchism here turns openly to the devotional tradition which it always threatens to parody, as unspeakable love assumes the role that theologians and mystics had long claimed for it: conversation with God.

The poem was originally entitled "Invention"; it is the most famous and important of Herbert's poems about poetry. It is also one of the most specific applications of Herbert's youthful desire to rededicate the expressive resources of profane love poetry to the celebration of divine love:

> Doth Poetry
> Wear *Venus* Livery? only serve her turn?
> Why are not *Sonnets* made of thee? and layes
> Upon thine Altar burnt? Cannot thy love
> Heighten a spirit to sound out thy praise
> As well as any she?[19]

The close relation of "Jordan" II to *Astrophil and Stella* 1 and 3 has long been recognized;[20] but there are Shakespearean echoes as well ("Decking the sense, as if it were to sell"), and the whole history of the topic of unspeakable love bears on Herbert's fable of scuttled eloquence. That topic, of course, is probably not among the ones the young Herbert had in mind, since its mature application is a critique of his own early confidence that writing love poetry to God called simply for intensifying the traditional activity of rhetorical inventiveness, as if what God needed was simply more of what profane beloveds received: "Nothing could seem too rich to clothe the sunne." The older Herbert does not insist that such an effort is impossible. He reports no writer's block in its pursuit—quite the contrary, it would seem. This itself may be one consequence of Herbert's having God as his love object: an addressee less scary than Petrarch's and Astrophil's, and less suspect and undependable than Shakespeare's. Nevertheless, the point of the poem is that this effort of confident expressiveness lapses, and for good reasons. It is too "expensive," and there is a modest but wholly adequate alternative.

Discussion of the poem has had its tangles.[21] It looks as if it ought to be some kind of manifesto about poetic language, and has been taken as a description of Herbert's artistic conversion to something called the plain style. But that style has proved hard to define, and the manifesto is as difficult to square with the rest of *The Temple* as is Sidney's anti-Petrarchan preface with the rest of *Astrophil and Stella*. Herbert's best work is not short on quaint words, trim invention, metaphors. It is not even entirely clear that what is being renounced at the end of "Jordan" II is not poetry itself. At analogous moments elsewhere we are offered brief liturgical phrases as the example of what Herbert is left with after disabusing his verse of unnecessary embellishment: *"My God, My King"* in "Jordan" I, *"Thou art still my God"* in "The Forerunners." We are clearly on more secure ground attending to the discrimination of motives being effected in "Jordan" II. What is wrong with the poetic decoration described there is that it yokes the author's meaning to his ego: "So did I weave my self into the sense." The point of the peripeteia—coming just after the prosodically significant fourteenth line[22]—is that the poet's own ambitious will is replaced by something anonymously other: by the recommendation of a friend (whom we are not actually told is Christ) and then by whoever authored the sweetness that is already penned. In writing about the writing of poetry, Herbert is actually writing about the effacement of the self as a lesson in humility.

The lesson is in many ways a particularly Protestant one. New antipathy to human pride and new subtlety in its detection are among the characteristic features of Reformation theology. Part of the rationale for the doctrine of justification by faith is that it deprives the individual of any sense that his will can ever preempt God's. Good works are a willful bid for a kind of salvational entitlement, an attempt to force God's hand. The calculus of such suspiciousness takes the Protestant conscience well beyond the familiar array of conventional sins into the most intimate operations of feeling and thought. Luther distrusted reason itself as the weapon of a human propensity for dickering with God—or, to use Herbert's term, "articling" ("Artillerie," l. 31). On such points scrupulous passivity is a desideratum, an important moral value. Without it, the most admirable actions and sentiments are subtly but dangerously corrupt. One extrapolation of this is a stern iconoclasm in matters of art and literature in some of the more extreme Protestant sects; and though Herbert is altogether gentler, "Jordan" II is, in its way, of their company, depicting the abandonment of self-conscious poetic prowess because it is an attempt to persuade God of Herbert's love. That love may well be genuine and is certainly what Herbert ought to feel; but in the light of Protestant moral thought, saying that he feels it can be a treacherous act.

We may speak here of a characteristic principle of many of Herbert's poems, what Nuttall calls "moral regression":

In Herbert, the praying subject endeavours to deserve God's love by being good and then withdraws as he realizes that his effort to deserve is itself absurd, and then withdraws *again* as he realizes that his ostentatious waiving of desert might itself be construed as a covert assertion of merit. The scheme is in principle indefinitely extendable.[23]

Nuttall is among several recent critics to give renewed attention to Herbert's Protestantism as the animating force behind the self-critical movement of his poetry. Fish sensitized us to that movement in his influential essay of fifteen years ago, and the durable consensus since then has been that Herbert is preeminently the poet of reflexive self-interference, systematically disrupting his patterning and repose, undermining his confidence even as it builds. His poems are "self-consuming artifacts" (Fish) or "collapsing poems" (Harman), and Herbert himself is a precursor of postmodern skepticism about the coherence and autonomy of the individual self. Scrutiny of the operation of the Protestant conscience keeps such claims from seeming like the mere imposition of contemporary predilections. Harman, in the most extensive and sophisticated deconstructive reading of Herbert to date, gives a lucid account of the literary *aporia* at the end of "Jordan" II—"The possibility of a new kind of writing is indicated in the final lines, but is has no representation in them"—while affirming its resolution in such poems as "Aaron" and "The Bunch of Grapes," where the poet's own story is fully assimilated to Protestant typology:

> If collapsing poems make representation possible only by making it subject to recall, and chronicles of dissolution make it possible by dismantling coherent images of the self, typological poems make representation possible by making the speaker's enduring account the story of others rather than the story of the self.[24]

Protestant devotion is in effect a paradigm for the postmodern effacement of selfhood into discourse.

The argument, however, is not quite decisive. It strains against some cogent interpretations of typology and its significance,[25] and—as does Nuttall's analysis—against the attested role of Reformation spirituality as a source of intense personal empowerment. Authoritative expressions of that empowerment can be extravagant: "every Christian is by faith so exalted above all things that, by virtue of a spiritual power, he is lord of all things without exception, so that nothing can do him any harm. As a matter of fact, all things are made subject to him and are compelled to serve him in obtaining salvation." Protestant abjection is inseparable from a sense of omnipotence: "A Christian is a perfectly free lord of all, subject to none. A Christian is a perfectly dutiful servant of all, subject to all."[26] That blunt paradox is a logical contradiction, but the testimony of Protestantism is precisely that it is not an experiential contradiction. Luther insisted that his message of individual depravity was wedded to a message of comfort: a receiving of undeserved grace precisely in our undeserving. Guilt and self-doubt that rationally "ought" to be endless in the infinite regress of the Protestant conscience have a way of suddenly turning over, converting themselves into unaccountable peace and confidence. Making explicable that event is the major challenge that Reformation literature presents to the explanatory resources of modern criticism.[27]

It is Strier's distinction, among recent students of Herbert's religion, to show the benefits of keeping justification by faith intact at the center of the analysis. Doing so halts the deconstructive actions of conscience short of Harman's elision of the personal into the typical, through a different application of Luther's distrust of reason. Herbert's persistent critique of his presumptuousness finds a secure reassurance in the very anguish of that critique when the analytical mind yields to what Strier calls the heart's privileges, which are of a different order and not subject to the same corrosion. Inward feelings that are simply there when we turn to look, that we do not remember having willed, are our contact with God's will; and that in particular is the destination of "Jordan" II:

> The movement of the poem is from brain-work ("Thousands of notions in my braine did runne") to the heart-work which is heaven-work. When the "friend" sets the bustling and eager poet to "copie out" what is "readie penn'd" in love, he is telling him, in effect, to "look in [his] heart and write," for this is where, as Herbert has made clear in many other poems, God primarily does His "penning."[28]

The gesture of attacking the self on one level quietly reaffirms the self on another; and that is ultimately not a problem but the point.

Strier's seems to me the interpretation most in key with the poem's context, and for more than just sectarian reasons. His citation of Sidney—by way of parallel, not contrast—suggests the alignment I have been pursuing here, and a longer view than that of Protestant devotional poetry. The paradox resolved in justification by faith is a tightened version of the enduring and indeed defining paradox of the Christian perspective on the individual self: enjoined to absolute humility and dependence, but also offered the prospect of a personal immortality absent from many major religions. The flashpoint of this double teaching in Protestantism is part of the course of Western individualism, and particularly of its Renaissance passage from Petrarch to the English seventeenth century; and the poems of unspeakable love illustrate, with progressive clarity, a dialectic of contradiction whereby Burckhardt's *geistige Individualität* actually makes its way in the world.[29]

Naive attempts to apply Burckhardt's thesis that Renaissance culture is the culture of a new kind of individualism tend to search for triumphant assertions of domineering selfhood as the way stations of Renaissance psychological progress. But such an account has trouble beginning, as any account of Renaissance culture at its fullest needs to begin, with Petrarch, the great lyric poet of failure and desperation. The relevant ambition to cite would be Petrarch's innovative drive for poetic fame—the laurel—in which he indeed succeeded; but some of his most powerful writing, in the latter part of the *Canzoniere* and his prose *Secretum,* dramatizes the immense guilty anxiety that even this refined enterprise roused in him. The relevant accusation, lodged by the spirit of Saint Augustine in the *Secretum,* is indeed pride, *superbia:* "The story of Narcissus has no warning for you."[30] The Protestant attack on that sin is specially fierce and influential, but it is neither unprecedented nor in its own time a Protestant monopoly; it may be easily paralleled, for instance, in Jesuit devotional teaching, or in the writings of the Catholic skeptic Montaigne.[31] Renaissance individualism comes with a countervailing fear of its own deep illegitimacy. That fear is arguably the proper and necessary pressure of a moral responsibility to what is intractably beyond the individual and his desires, and these poems about blocked speech are acts of deference to that responsibility. In a culture increasingly conscious of cunning and articulate speech as a source of power, the paralysis of that speech in the face of overwhelming longing imposes a discipline on the acquisitive self, a discipline which it is the business of Renaissance culture repeatedly to impose.

Yet the imposing of that discipline also repeatedly augments another sense of what the self is and how much it counts for—a sense all the more compelling for seeming simply there, unpursued, a given. Luther attacks individual presumption and self-esteem only to relocate the arena of significant moral action deep within the individual's unguarded emotional experience. Montaigne demolishes the claims of human reason to know and master reality only to expand drastically our understanding of the range and importance of the subjective, and to increase our respect for the mysterious eccentricities of habit and personality that make us what we are though they were not our idea. And the failed persuaders of the poems of unspeakable love discover in the lapse of their attempt an intensified consciousness of and increasing comfort with the suddenly available reality of their inner landscape. Repeatedly prompting that consciousness and comfort, unsuccess figures significantly in the scenario of exfoliating individualism. We grow in the defeat of our strivings.

## Notes

1. *The Letters of George Santayana,* ed. Daniel Cory (New York: Scribner's, 1955), p. 281 (to Iris Origo, 1933).

2. I quote Petrarch's Italian from *Rime e Trionfi di Francesco Petrarca,* ed. Fredinando Neri, 2d ed. (Turin: UTET, 1960); translations from the *Canzoniere* are by Robert M. Durling, *Petrarch's Lyric Poems* (Cambridge, Mass.: Harvard University Press, 1976). This particular sonnet is one of those translated by Wyatt ("Suche vayn thought as wonted to myslede me"); on the significance of his alterations of sense and inflection, see Anne Ferry, *The "Inward" Language: Sonnets of Wyatt, Sidney, Shakespeare, Donne* (Chicago: University of Chicago Press, 1983), pp. 94–97. In addition to the other Petrarchan poems cited below, see *Canzoniere* 20, 49, 95, and 170; the conclusion of the last—"chi po dir com'egli arde è 'n picciol foco" (he who can say how he burns is in but a little fire)—may have particularly attracted Sidney's attention (*Astrophil and Stella* 54.14; see n. 9 below). Among continental Petrarchists—largely scanted in the account to follow—the topic acquires special importance in Pontus de Tyard, where it has been the object of some acute recent discussion: François Lecercle, "Métamorphose de la parole: Sur deux sonnets des *Erreurs Amoureuses,*" in *Poétiques de la métamorphose,* ed. Guy Demerson (Saint-Etienne: Université Saint-Etienne, 1981), pp. 95–104; and especially Jean-Claude Carron, *Discours de l'errance amoureuse* (Paris: Vrin, 1986), pp. 87–111.

3. "On True Love," trans. Alison Goddard Elliott, *Allegorica* 7.2 (1982): 13. The best guess dates the treatise fourteenth century, more or less contemporary with Petrarch.

4. *The Poetry of Arnaut Daniel,* ed. and trans. James J. Wilhelm (New York: Garland, 1981).

5. *Biblioteca di letteratura popolare italiana,* vol. 1, ed. Severino Ferrari (Florence, 1882), p. 86; translated by Donald R. Guss, in his *John Donne, Petrarchist* (Detroit: Wayne State University Press, 1966), p. 54. Callimaco sings this song in Machiavelli's *Mandragola* (4.9), shortly before his successful adulterous assignation with Lucrezia. I cite the poem, obviously, for effect; anonymous and popular, it admittedly falls outside the strict circuit of Petrarchism, though less colorful fantasies of revenge are common enough in sonnet form.

6. Many of the arguments that follow concerning Petrarch and Petrarchism are set out more fully in my "Love and Fame: The Petrarchan Career," in *Pragmatism's Freud,* ed. Joseph H. Smith and William Kerrigan (Baltimore: Johns Hopkins University Press, 1986), pp. 126–58.

7. Some catastrophic direct encounters are apparently related in a few poems—notably *Canzoniere* 23—but in a form that is cryptic and figurative even for Petrarch. On their significance in this connection, see Braden, "Love and Fame," pp. 148–51.

8. C. S. Lewis, *English Literature in the Sixteenth Century, Excluding Drama* (Oxford: Clarendon, 1954), p. 327.

9. *The Poems of Sir Walter Ralegh,* ed. Agnes M. C. Latham (Cambridge, Mass.: Harvard University Press, 1951). Ralegh's direct debt may well be to Sidney: "Shallow brookes murmure most, deep silent slide away" (*Old Arcadia* 7.11), "Dumbe Swannes, not chatring Pies, do Lovers prove" (*Astrophil and Stella* 54.13); *The Poems of Sir Philip Sidney,* ed. William A. Ringler, Jr. (Oxford: Clarendon, 1962). The most influential source for the sentiment, though, is Senecan tragedy: "curae leues loquuntur, ingentes stupent" (*Phaedra* 607). On the philosophical tradition, see Raymond B. Waddington, "The Iconography of Silence and Chapman's Hercules," *Journal of the Warburg and Courtauld Institutes* 33 (1970): 248–63.

10. See Petrarch's reply to Giacomo Colonna, *Rerum familiarum libri I–VIII,* trans. Aldo S. Bernardo (Albany: SUNY Press, 1975), p. 102 (2.9). On attempts to identify Laura historically, see Emmanuel Davin, "Les différentes Laure de Pétrarque," *Bulletin de l'Association Budé* (1956) 4:83–104. Davin's commonsensical conclusion parallels Colonna's skepticism: "Contentons-nous de son prénom: il est immortel par la poésie" (p. 104).

11. Gianfrancesco Pico della Mirandola, *On the Imagination,* ed. and trans. Harry Caplan (New Haven: Yale University Press, 1930), p. 29. It is the beloved's absence that is specifically cited as the turning point toward enlightenment in Castiglione: "to escape the torment of this absence and to enjoy beauty without suffering, the Courtier, aided by reason, must turn his desire entirely away from the body and to beauty alone, contemplate it in its simple and pure self, in so far as he is able, and in his imagination give it a shape distinct from all matter" (*The Book of the Courtier,* trans. Charles S. Singleton [Garden City: Doubleday, 1959], p. 351).

12. Quotations of Sidney are from Ringler's edition (n. 9, above). The best discussions of Sidney's Petrarchism remain Richard B. Young, "English Petrarke," in Young, W. Todd Furniss, and William G. Madsen, *Three Studies in the Renaissance* (New Haven: Yale University Press, 1958), pp. 1–88; and David Kalstone, *Sidney's Poetry* (Cambridge: Harvard University Press, 1967), pp. 105–32.

13. Quotations of Shakespeare are (with minor adjustments) from *The Complete Works: Original-Spelling Edition,* gen. eds. Stanley Wells and Gary Taylor (Oxford: Clarendon, 1986).

14. Joachim du Bellay, "Contre les petrarquistes," *Oeuvres poétiques,* ed. Henri Chamard (Paris: Hachette, 1908–31), 5:69; there is an earlier version, "A une dame," 4:205. Further instances are cited by Robert J. Clements, "Anti-Petrarchism of the Pléiade," *Modern Philology* 39 (1941): 15–21. Du Bellay's own sources are in turn Italian; see Joseph Vianey, *Le Pétrarchisme en France au xvi^e siècle* (1909; rpt., Geneva: Slatkine, 1969), pp. 165–78. A scabrous Italian anticipation of "My Mistres eyes are nothing like the Sunne" may be found in Aretino as the work of one "messer fa-sonetti": "non vo' dir che voi siate divina, / non pisciando acqua lanfa per orina" (I will not say that you are divine or

piss orange-flower water instead of urine) (*Sei giornate,* ed. Guido Davico Bonino [Turin: Einaudi, 1975], p. 286).

15. I quote Spenser, with minor changes, from *The Poetical Works of Edmund Spenser,* ed. J. C. Smith and E. De Selincourt (London: Oxford University Press, 1912). Janet G. Scott—*Les sonnets élisabéthains* (Paris: Champion, 1929), pp. 319–20—adduces likely sources for *Amoretti* 3 and 43 in Tasso (*Rime* 35, 164–66), Spenser's kindred spirit in many ways, though I think the handling of the wit-heart opposition and the deliberate inclusion of writing in the blockage are specifically indebted to Sidney. Spenser's courtship is of course ultimately—and almost uniquely—successful, but only, it would seem, when he gives up the chase (*Amoretti* 67).

16. Shakespeare's indebtedness to Sidney is assessed with fresh detail and conviction by Ferry, *The Inward Language,* pp. 170–214, 251–55 (pp. 194–97 on Shakespeare 85). She sees Shakespeare as deepening Sidney's interest in an inner experience specifically at odds with, defined in contrast to, any outward expression; her general argument, running from Wyatt to Donne, is relevant to mine at numerous points.

17. James Shirley, *Poems 1646, Together with Poems from the Rawlinson Manuscript* (Menston, England: Scolar Press, 1970), p. 16.

18. I quote Herbert from *The English Poems of George Herbert,* ed. C. A. Patrides (London: Dent, 1974).

19. Ibid., p. 205. On "Jordan" II as a critique of this poem and its companion—including some reworking of their imagery—see Rosemond Tuve, *A Reading of George Herbert* (Chicago: University of Chicago Press, 1952), pp. 190–91.

20. Failure to take *Astrophil and Stella* 3 into account can skew the comparison here. Stanley Fish's claim of a "radical difference" between Sidney and Herbert—"one is advised to call on his own resources; the other is reminded that his resources are not his own"—seems to me to understate the passivity in which Astrophil is being instructed; see Fish, *Self-Consuming Artifacts* (Berkeley: University of California Press, 1972), pp. 198–99.

21. My major points of reference here, in addition to Fish, *Self-Consuming Artifacts,* pp. 196–99, and Tuve, *A Reading of George Herbert,* pp. 188–92, are Barbara Leah Harman, *Costly Monuments: Representations of the Self in George Herbert's Poetry* (Cambridge, Mass.: Harvard University Press, 1982), pp. 43–49; A. D. Nuttall, *Overheard by God: Fiction and Prayer in Herbert, Milton, Dante and St. John* (London: Methuen, 1980), pp. 14–16; Richard Strier, *Love Known: Theology and Experience in George Herbert's Poetry* (Chicago: University of Chicago Press, 1983), pp. 196–98; and Joseph H. Summers, *George Herbert: His Religion and Art* (Cambridge, Mass.: Harvard University Press, 1954), pp. 109–11.

22. Fish, *Self-Consuming Artifacts,* p. 198.

23. Nuttall, *Overheard by God,* p. 42.

24. Harman, *Costly Monuments,* pp. 48, 196.

25. In ibid., Harman explicitly engages Barbara Kiefer Lewalski on the

subject, p. 189. Where Lewalski argues that typology serves to "personalize theology," Harman claims that, at least for Herbert, "it theologizes the personal, and makes unavailable the very notion of a 'radically personal' account." Protestant justification makes the contrast itself difficult to sustain; I suspect the truth lies closer to a superimposition of the two formulas.

26. Luther, "The Freedom of a Christian," trans. W. A. Lambert and Harold J. Grimm, in Luther, *Selections from His Writings,* ed. John Dillenberger (Garden City: Doubleday, 1961), pp. 63, 53.

27. Nuttall, perhaps the most emphatic of Herbert's critics about the aggressiveness of his Protestant conscience, finds a peace at the end of the struggle, but through an implicit abandonment of Protestant doctrine: "Herbert's poetry overthrows Calvinism by subjecting it to the test of ingenuous loyalty" (*Overheard by God,* p. 81). It may be significant that Nuttall's focus is Calvin rather than Luther. The most compelling attempt to parse the extreme Protestant experience in modern terms seems to me to be William Kerrigan's psychoanalytic portrait of Milton: "His father first, then all the derivatives of his father in earthly authority—teachers, bishops, kings, parliaments, theologians—could be deposed and abused by a rebellious son, while Milton at the same time remained the obedient son of his divine father. . . . Milton's great lesson is that obedience is freedom" (*The Sacred Complex: On the Psychogenesis of Paradise Lost* [Cambridge, Mass.: Harvard University Press, 1983], pp. 114–15). Kerrigan disclaims typicality for Milton's case, but it seems to me instructive for a wide range of Reformation—and Renaissance—figures.

28. Strier, *Love Known,* p. 197.

29. The understanding of Burckhardt here at work is set out more fully by William Kerrigan and myself in *The Idea of the Renaissance* (Baltimore: Johns Hopkins University Press, 1989); see especially pp. 31–35.

30. *Petrarch's Secret,* trans. William H. Draper (London: Chatto and Windus, 1911), p. 55.

31. Ilona Bell has indeed come to conclusions very similar to Strier's by studying Herbert's documented relations to the Catholic devotional writer Juan Valdés: "Herbert's Valdésian Vision," *English Literary Renaissance* 17 (1987): 303–28. Valdés's writings were condemned by his own church after his death, but justification by faith has in the long run proved the schismatic issue with which Catholicism has had perhaps the least trouble.

# "That Ancient Heat": Sexuality and Spirituality in *The Temple*

*Michael C. Schoenfeldt*

In a passage from the *Paragone* comparing the affective capacities of poetry and painting, Leonardo da Vinci includes a remarkable anecdote exploring the aesthetic conjunction of erotic and religious desire:

> It once happened that I made a picture representing a divine subject, and it was bought by a man who fell in love with her [*dall' amante di quella*]. He wished to remove the emblems of divinity in order to be able to kiss the picture without scruples [*baciare sanza sospetto*]. But finally conscience overcame his sighs of desire [*li sospiri e la libidine*] and he was obliged to remove the painting from his house.[1]

The viewer's confusion—relished by Leonardo as evidence of painting's emotive power—emblematizes the difficulty of mustering an adequate response to an object imbued at once with religious and erotic significance. Caught at the nexus of two parallel yet potentially opposed forces, Leonardo's patron desires to strip the artifact of all religious connotations in order to give free play to the concupiscence it arouses. Ultimately, however, he withdraws from the unsettling aesthetic experience altogether by having the painting removed from his field of vision.

The divine poetry of George Herbert does not provoke the kinds of libidinal desire that Leonardo's patron feels. But like the viewer of Leonardo's painting, the reader of Herbert's poetry confronts an aesthetic object poised on the cusp of erotic and spiritual longing. Rather than eliminating emblems of divinity in order to indulge a sensuality uncontaminated by religious scruples, however, critics of Herbert have generally suppressed elements of eroticism in order to worship without distraction. As Russell Fraser has recently remarked, "Cultural conditioning has sponsored a wheyfaced Herbert," denuded of the sexual

intimations suffusing his poems.[2] Despite Herbert's announcement in
"The Forerunners" that the substance of his sacred devotions is a lan-
guage that "before / Of stews and brothels onely knew the doores," most
readers have chosen to conceal these erotic origins.[3] Moreover, even
though Herbert has "wash[ed]" this language, "Brought [it] to Church
well drest and clad," he has not totally broken it of its habitual cupidity;
indeed, as he reluctantly concedes, these "sweet phrases, [and] lovely
metaphors" still desire to "leave the Church, and love a stie." In his pas-
sionate attachment to a vocabulary of affection he concedes is sullied,
Herbert registers "the inconsistency between the Christian emphasis
upon love as the chief reality and the strong presence in Christian histo-
ry of a negative attitude to sex."[4] As Herbert confusingly reminds him-
self in "The Size," "Thy Saviour sentenc'd joy, / And in the flesh
condemn'd it as unfit." Throughout *The Temple* and culminating in the
encounter between impotent mortality and amorous divinity in the vol-
ume's final lyric, Herbert discovers in the phallocentric discourse of
Renaissance sexuality a vocabulary which fuses spiritual aspiration and
swelling pride, devotional passion and priapic aggression.[5] Mobilizing a
subtle but incandescent eroticism which chafes against the sacred urges
it both contradicts and embodies, Herbert situates his reader on the vi-
sual and emotional axis occupied by Leonardo's bewildered patron. By
failing to acknowledge this eroticism and the uneasiness it arouses, we
make Herbert's poetry the subject of our own repressions.

Significantly, the relationship between erotic and religious passion is
the subject of Herbert's first two extant poems—sonnets written as a
"New-years gift" to his mother when he was sixteen. In these poems, sex-
uality is not imagined as the repressed source of religious feeling but
rather as the outgrowth of suppressed religious urges. Deploying the son-
net form to excoriate its traditional amorous connections, these lyrics
painstakingly oppose "those many Love-poems, that are daily writ and
consecrated to *Venus*" to the "few [that] are writ, and look towards *God*
and *Heaven*" (*Works*, p. 363). Yet the poems expressing this pious opposi-
tion engage in bawdy word-play which blurs its borders. In asking,
"Doth Poetry / Wear *Venus* Livery? Only serve her turn?" for example,
the adolescent Herbert plays upon the Renaissance sense of "service": to
"serve Venus's turn" intimates sexual intercourse.[6] Similarly, his ques-
tion, "Cannot thy love / Heighten a spirit to sound out thy praise / As well
as any she?" compares God's ability to arouse suitors to the point of an
erection with the capacity of a mortal lover to excite carnal desire ("spirit"
being a common Renaissance euphemism for "penis").[7] In these poems,
Herbert wants to impress his devout and clever mother with his verbal
ingenuity and spiritual piety. But the curiously ribald puns he makes
erode the distinction he draws between the "ancient heat" of religious

martyrs and the lascivious ardor of secular lovers. If Herbert has washed this language, the taint of carnal desire lingers.

In the two sonnets entitled "Love" in *The Temple,* Herbert similarly complains that secular poets allow "mortall love" to usurp the prerogative of devotion due solely to "Immortall Love." Hinting at a pun on "wit" and "penis," the first sonnet remarks how "Wit fancies beautie, beautie raiseth wit"; both poetic craft and phallic desire are castigated for their elevated attention to physical beauty.[8] Aptly capturing Herbert's wordplay, Richard Strier remarks, "Herbert views his erected wit with alarm."[9] Like Sidney, Herbert emphasizes the impropriety of devoting to "mortal love" language fit for an "immortal" object.[10] For Herbert, though, even the erected wit, if not directed exclusively towards God, is the product of infected will. Yet the second sonnet looks forward to the prospect of rectifying this faculty in its prayer that the "greater flame" of God will "kindle in our hearts such true desires, / As may consume our lusts."[11] As a result of obeying such *"true"* desires," Herbert promises that "All knees shall bow to thee; all wits shall rise." By bending poetic ingenuity and erotic energy to God, one can achieve the virtuously heightened spirit and genuinely purifying ardor Herbert forecast in the sonnets to his mother.

"Dulnesse" likewise compares the activities of devotional and secular poets. In this poem, however, the comparison allows Herbert to lash his own lyric torpor rather than the misdirected attentions of secular lovers:

> Why do I languish thus, drooping and dull,
>   As if I were all earth?
>
> . . . . . . .
>
> The wanton lover in a curious strain
>   Can praise his fairest fair;
> And with quaint metaphors her curled hair
>   Curl o're again.
>
> Thou art my lovelinesse, my life, my light,
>   Beautie alone to me:
> Thy bloudy death and undeserv'd, makes thee
>   Pure red and white.
>
> . . . . . . .
>
> Where are my lines then? my approaches? views?
>   Where are my window-songs?
> Lovers are still pretending, & ev'n wrongs
>   Sharpen their Muse:
>
> But I am lost in flesh. . . .

Herbert characterizes his devotional lassitude as a lack of physical virility ("drooping and dull") in contrast to the erotic vigor and "Sharpen[ed]" Muse of the "wanton lover." Moreover, the language used to describe the activity of this lover has bawdy connotations which betray his lascivious intentions. "Strain," for example, can designate not only the secular lover's song of praise but also the close embrace he intends to win through this song.[12] Similarly, "quaint" can suggest the female pudendum, a meaning here underscored by its juxtaposition with "curled hair."[13] Yet Herbert's explanation for his comparative inability to offer appropriate praise to God elides the distinction he intends to assert between such carnal concerns and his own. The phrase "But I am lost in flesh" weirdly designates the activities of the wanton lover to whom he ostensibly contraposes his own devotional torpor. The poem appropriately concludes in the interrogative mode, asking "to *love* thee, who can be, / What angel fit?" The initially glib contrast between religious devotion and erotic affection dissolves into a question of mortal (and even angelic) capacity for properly cherishing God.

Other poems in *The Temple* explore the ways in which Herbert's devotional motives are found as well as lost in flesh. In "The Pearl," Herbert proclaims that he

> know[s] the wayes of Pleasure, the sweet strains,
> The lullings and the relishes of it;
> The propositions of hot bloud and brains;
> What mirth and musick mean; what love and wit
> Have done these twentie hundred yeares, and more:
> My stuffe is flesh, not brasse; my senses live.

As Richard Strier suggests, "'Sweet strains' blends both [musical and sexual] realms brilliantly."[14] Such carnal knowledge provides both a pattern for, and the antithesis of, the statement of impassioned devotion to God that concludes each of the first three stanzas: "Yet I love thee." Like "The Pearl," "Church-musick" aligns physical and musical pleasure. In "Church-musick," furthermore, the rapture of divine song is astonishingly compared with a visit to a brothel:

> Sweetest of sweets, I thank you: when displeasure
> Did through my bodie wound my minde,
> You took me thence, and in your house of pleasure
> A daintie lodging me assign'd.
>
> Now I in you without a bodie move,
> Rising and falling with your wings:
> We both sweetly live and love. . . .

The intangible experience of music is expressed in terms of a liminality that is corporeal as well as architectural—the entry into another, and into the edifice of the church, a true "house of pleasure." "Comfort, I'le die," declares the speaker, anticipating a death which is both spiritual and sexual. The moment of physical consummation, however, is also a disembodied experience: "Now I in you without a bodie move." As in Donne's "The Extasie," abandonment of the flesh occasions abandonment to the flesh.

In "Sinnes round," by contrast, flesh is the site of sinfulness rather than the element of spiritual ecstasy. Jonathan Goldberg has recently suggested that the subtitle of *The Temple*—"Sacred Poems and Private Ejaculations"—aligns the writing of devotional poetry and the "spurting forth of seed and fluid."[15] In "Sinnes round," a poem Goldberg does not discuss, Herbert indeed depicts the cycle of penitence and offence in remarkably onanistic terms:

> Sorrie I am, my God, sorrie I am,
> That my offences course it in a ring.
> My thoughts are working like a busie flame,
> Untill their cockatrice they hatch and bring:
> And when they once have perfected their draughts,
> My words take fire from my inflamed thoughts.
>
> My words take fire from my inflamed thoughts,
> Which spit it forth like the Sicilian Hill.
> They vent the wares, and passe them with their faults,
> And by their breathing ventilate the ill.
> But words suffice not, where are lewd intentions:
> My hands do joyn to finish the inventions.
>
> My hands do joyn to finish the inventions:
> And so my sinnes ascend three stories high,
> As Babel grew, before there were dissentions.
> Yet ill deeds loyter not: for they supplie
> New thoughts of sinning: wherefore, to my shame,
> Sorrie I am, my God, sorrie I am.

Part rooster, part snake, hatched by a serpent from an egg laid by a cock, and able to kill with a glance, the cockatrice consolidates images of masculine sexuality, aberrant generation, and spiritual peril.[16] When this mythical creature—whose name is also a slang term for a prostitute—is juxtaposed with the ejaculatory imagery of "the Sicilian Hill" (the volcanic Mount Etna), the phallic erection of Babel, the flames of concupiscence, the heightened respiration of sexual excitement ("by their breathing ventilate the ill"), and the remark that his "hands do joyn to finish" the "lewd intention" begun in his brain, the suggestion of masturbation is hard to avoid.[17] The poem is an act of self-abuse (in both senses). Even as the speaker confesses his "sin of self-love," the poem's ophidian form completes the closed circuit of shame and desire he describes, turning back upon itself in autoerotic repetition of the sins of the previous line or stanza.[18] "In Western literature—beginning with Christian monasticism—masturbation remains associated with the chimera of the imagination and its dangers," suggests Foucault.[19] Playing on the assonance of "sin" and "ascend" and perhaps deploying an unstated visual pun on "pen" and "penis," Herbert links the "self-willed" product of his creative imagination to the erotic fantasies and barren tumescence of masturbation.[20]

A similar image of erection is explored in "The Flower." Rather than spilling his seed upon the ground, however, the speaker of this poem hopes to become a plant in God's garden. He observes that

> Many a spring I shoot up fair,
> Offring at heav'n, growing and groaning thither:
> Nor doth my flower
> Want a spring-showre,
> My sinnes and I joining together.
>
> But while I grow in a straight line,
> Still upwards bent, as if heav'n were mine own,
> Thy anger comes, and I decline.
> What frost to that? what pole is not the zone,
> Where all things burn,
> When thou dost turn,
> And the least frown of thine is shown?
> (lines 24–35)

Because the poem opens with a lament against barrenness ("Who would have thought my shrivel'd heart / Could have recover'd greennesse?"), one would expect the dilation announced in "Many a spring I shoot up fair" to be celebrated. Such virility, however, is revealed as sinful, akin to the aggressive sexuality castigated in "Sinnes round," and wilting under the climatic "pole" of God's boreal glare. In the final stanza, moreover, priapism is equated with "pride," a word designating, as Strier notes, both a period of heightened sexual desire and an exaggerated sense of self-esteem:

> These are thy wonders, Lord of love,
> To make us see we are but flowers that glide:
> Which when we once can finde and prove,
> Thou hast a garden for us, where to bide.
> Who would be more,
> Swelling through store,
> Forfeit their Paradise by their pride.

"We cannot miss the tentative sexuality of his 'budding' and 'shooting up' and later 'swelling,'" remarks Helen Vendler.[21] This sexuality, and the aspiration for upward mobility it represents, must be sacrificed before he can be placed in God's garden, "where no flower can wither."

"Frailtie" begins where "The Flower" ends, with the speaker complacently enunciating the sort of admirable *contemptus mundi* sentiments we expect in religious poetry:

> Lord, in my silence how do I despise
> What upon trust
> Is styled *honour, riches,* or *fair eyes;*
> But is *fair dust!*
> I surname them *guilded clay,*
> *Deare earth, fine grasse* or *hay;*
> In all, I think my foot doth ever tread
> Upon their head.

Yet even as he rehearses this pious contrast between earthly and heavenly joys, his statement of contempt for the world dissolves into a striking image of his passion for it:

> But when I view abroad both Regiments;
> The worlds, and thine:
> Thine clad with simplenesse, and sad events;
> The other fine,
> Full of glorie and gay weeds,
> Brave language, braver deeds:
> That which was dust before, doth quickly rise,
> And prick mine eyes.

The juxtaposition of *prick* and *rise* betrays Herbert's arousal by the resplendent world whose attractions he would piously dismiss. St. Augustine suggests that postlapsarian corruption is signaled by the inability of reason and will to control the penis; Herbert's mortal "frailty" is likewise indicated by an erection beyond his volition.[22] The poem concludes with the speaker imploring God to forestall this phenomenon by making the pleasure of his own regiment more apparent:

> O brook not this, lest if what even now
> My foot did tread,
> Affront those joyes, wherewith thou didst endow
> And long since wed
> My poore soul, ev'n sick of love:
> It may a Babel prove
> Commodious to conquer heav'n and thee
> Planted in me.

Like the spouse in the Song of Songs, the speaker is truly "sick of love," and longs to be cured by being "wed" to God, that is, by establishing an amorous bond between God and his soul that will preclude his deep desire for the world. As in "Sinnes round," the rearing of Babel represents both a phallic love of earthly pleasure and a priapic threat to heaven. In "Frailtie," however, lust insidiously infiltrates the very pieties that aspire to deny its power.

The frequent identification of the erect penis with sin, rebellion, and aggression in Herbert's poetry can be understood at least in part by recourse to Renaissance discourse about the ritual of circumcision. Donne explains that God made the apparently curious choice of the penis, "so base and uncleane a thing," to seal his covenant with Abraham because "*that* part of the body is the most rebellious part."[23] Suggesting momentarily that man relates to his penis as God relates to his unruly creatures, Donne proposes that "to reproach Mans rebellion to *God, God* hath left one part of Mans body, to rebell against him." As an organ beyond the control of man, the penis represents the continual tendency of God's creatures to rise against him. Because, reasons Donne, "this rebellious part, is the roote of all sinne, . . . therefore did that part need this stigmaticall marke of Circumcision."[24] As the penis becomes a synecdoche for mortal depravity, circumcision comes to represent the severing of our capacity for sin. "In this Circumcision, we must cut the *root,* the *mother-sinne,* that nourishes all our sinnes, and the *branches* too, . . . . It is not the Circumcision of an *Excessive* use of that sinne, that will serve our turne, but such a circumcision, as amounts to an *Excession,* a cutting off the *root,* and *branch,* the *Sinne,* and the *fruits,* the *profits* of that sinne."[25]

In "Paradise" Herbert prays for just such a severance from an aggressive male sexuality imagined likewise in botanical terms. Although the speaker begins by praising a God who prunes in order to produce fruit—"I blesse thee, Lord, because I GROW / Among thy trees, which in a ROW / To thee both fruit and order ow"—the body of the poem emphasizes excision rather than expansion:

> Inclose me still for fear I START.
> Be to me rather sharp and TART,
> Then let me want thy hand & ART.
>
> When thou dost greater judgements SPARE,
> And with thy knife but prune and PARE,
> Ev'n fruitfull trees more fruitfull ARE.
>
> Such sharpnes shows the sweetest FREND:
> Such cuttings rather heal then REND;
> And such beginnings touch their END.

The act of "pare-ing" is at the linguistic and theological core of Herbert's "Paradise." Unlike Milton's Eden with its lushly erotic vegetation, Herbert's paradisal garden is an orchard of neatly ordered, well-pruned trees. For fear that he will literally stand out among such plants, the speaker of "Paradise" asks to be circumscribed by his Lord's arm even as he is circumcised by this Lord's knife. The pun on "sharp" (used twice) punctuates the physical presence of this weapon. Furthermore, the rhyme words themselves produce meaning through amputation of letters, demonstrating the fruition that this salutary emasculation should foster.[26] In this Paradise, less really is more. Shorn of his potent and potentially aggressive sexuality, the speaker, like the "flowers that glide" at the end of "The Flower," approaches what Stanley Stewart terms a "blessed state of passivity."[27]

A related wish to find a mode of religious devotion walled off from refractory erotic passion emerges in "H. Baptisme (II)."[28] The speaker of this poem prays for the opportunity to recapture the imagined pre-sexual purity of childhood.

> O let me still
> Write thee great God, and me a childe:
> Let me be soft and supple to thy will,
> Small to my self. . .
> .   .   .   .   .   .   .   .   .   .
> The growth of flesh is but a blister;
> Childhood is health.

Herbert links the burgeoning flesh of maturation with blistering, the sexual edema portrayed in "Sinnes round" and "The Flower," and contrasts that with his own salubrious desire to remain small, soft, and supple. In *Paradise Lost* Michael associates disobedience with "man's effeminate slackness" (11:634); but for Herbert lack of tumescence designates submission to divine ordinance.[29] Childhood is health because it integrates social subordination and sexlessness, and so does not threaten God with "shooting up," "offring at heaven."

Although Herbert imagines his own sinfulness in terms of an aggressive and largely masculine sexuality, he nevertheless attempts to comprehend the mystery of Christ's descent into vulnerable flesh as an adoption of tacitly feminine traits. "Throughout the Old Testament," remarks Elaine Scarry, "God's power and authority are in part extreme and continually amplified elaborations of the fact that people have bodies and He has no body."[30] In "The Bag," Herbert's uncharacteristically grotesque portrait of the wounded Christ forces his readers to comprehend the complete strangeness of the New Testament's reversal of this relationship. In a nursery-rhyme style that belies the latent eroticism and blatant violence of its treatment of Christ, Herbert tells how his "Lord Jesus, . . . The God of power," traveled to earth, "undressing all the way," confident that "He had new clothes a making here below." The *kenosis* of Christ is rendered as a kind of striptease. The disrobed God is wounded by a soldier's spear, transforming his body into the bag of the title, a receptacle for carrying messages "Unto my Fathers hands and sight." Moreover, he invites his torturers to follow the spear in penetrating his body so they may "put [their messages] very neare my heart," and enticingly reminds them that "the doore /Shall still be open." Robert Graves perhaps overstates the case, but he is close to the truth when he suggests that "The Divine Figure in 'The Bag' is fused with the figure of the temptress and at the end of the poem subordinate to her, when it has distinct feminine characteristics."[31] The poems' details—the action of "undressing," the placement in a "inne," the emphasis upon pregnability, the seductive promise that "the doore / Shall still be open"—all connote a sexual scenario which never fully surfaces, but which suffuses the process by which the almighty God of power becomes a compassionate and vulnerable deity. The wound functions as a kind of vaginal orifice, feminizing a traditionally masculine Christ. In "Marie Magdalene," Herbert suggests that Christ "did vouchsafe and deigne / To bear her filth." "The Bag" reveals the process by which Christ voluntarily becomes the container of mortal filth, literally bearing it to heaven. "The God-man," argues Kenneth Burke, "must become immeasurably the worst criminal of all, in taking upon himself the full guilt of humankind."[32] Christ's willingness to assume a vulnerable body and be entered by all opens him up to the contamination of a fallen, and surprisingly feminine, sexuality.

Several Latin poems by Herbert also envision piercing the divine body, and intimate the possibility of a feminized Christ. *Passio Discerpta* 4, *"In Latus perfossum,"* depicts the "remorseless steel . . . open[ing] up a path" in Christ, a path the speaker hopes his heart will follow.[33] *Lucas* 30, *"In Thomam Didymum,"* opens with a striking image of a mortal penetrating the divine body—"The servant puts his fingers in you"— and views Jesus' allowance of such penetration as a gesture of love:

> Do you Redeemer, permit this sign?
> For sure you are all love, and the pith of it.
> You make a shelter and sweet rest
> For a grudging faith and a narrow mind.[34]

*Lucas* 34, addressed "To John leaning on the Lord's breast," imagines an overtly female Christ, nourishing with milk and blood his mortal disciples. Like a jealous sibling, Herbert's speaker declares to John:

> Ah now, glutton, let me suck too!
> You won't really hoard the whole
> Breast for yourself! Do you thieve
> Away from everyone that common well?
> He also shed his blood for me,
> And thus, having rightful
> Access to the breast, I claim the milk
> Mingled with the blood.[35]

E. Pearlman rightly calls attention to this extraordinary "vision of a female or bisexual Jesus whose breast is not only comforting but in fact a source of milk."[36] As strange as this figure may seem, however, it suits perfectly the widespread medieval image of "mother Jesus" recently explored by Caroline Walker Bynum. Bynum uncovers a remarkable number of representations of Christ as a nourishing mother, and argues that "What writers in the high Middle Ages wished to say about Christ the savior who feeds the individual soul with his own blood was precisely and concisely said in the image of the nursing mother whose milk *is* her blood, offered to the child."[37] Herbert's Christ exudes blood and milk at one, blending maternal and sacrificial capacities. As the subtly seductive femininity of "The Bag" consoles in its open absorption of sinful humanity, the outright maternity of "To John" reassures in its outpouring of feminine nurture. Whether inviting another into itself or nourishing another with its substance, the female body provides a conduit of heavenly grace.

Despite such surprising complicity between notions of divinity and images of femininity, *The Temple* is littered with conventional *contemptus mulieris* sentiments which make the final vision of an androgynous divinity in "Love (III)" all the more striking.[38] Among the worldly figures who gather to "geere at" the speaker of "The Quip" is a tempting female "Beautie," who "crept into a rose, / Which when I pluckt not, Sir, said she, / Tell me, I pray, Whose hands are those?" The speaker of "Home" wishes to dismiss such enticing femininity altogether, asking: "What is this woman-kinde, which I can wink / Into a blacknesse and distaste?" "Constancie" links "sick folks, women, those whom passions sway," while "Dotage" groups "Foolish night-fires, womens and childrens wishes." Culturally understood as figures of feebleness and temptation, women supply Herbert with a repertoire of images for the allurements of the world and the frailty of the flesh.

Such disturbingly conventional expressions of Renaissance misogyny, however, issue for Herbert in rather unconventional images of disgust at mortal sexuality. In "The Forerunners," Herbert depicts all desire not directed to God as devotion to a "stie" and "dung." "Filth" is the prod-

uct of the sensuality represented by "Marie Magdalene" before her turn
to God as well as the mortal matter lurking just under the surface of
even "the best face" in Herbert's second sonnet to his mother. The
speaker of "Miserie" asks, "What strange pollutions doth he [man] wed,
/ And make his own?" "Beware of lust," warns the avuncular speaker of
"The Church-porch," "it doth pollute and foul."

Indeed, "The Church-porch" expends much energy in the attempt to
contain concupiscence. Herbert offers the youthful audience of this
gnomic poem a commonplace choice of Pauline avenues for avoiding the
pollutions of lust: "Abstain wholly or wed."[39] An even deeper anxiety
about sexuality arises in his discussion of drunkenness. Excessive con-
sumption of alcohol ("Drink not the third glasse" opines the sententious
speaker three times in twenty-four lines) is to be avoided because it al-
lows the desires one normally represses to surface. In one of the
strangest passages in all of Herbert, he imagines the liberating effects of
alcohol on behavior:

> He that is drunken, may his mother kill
> Bigge with his sister: he hath lost the reins,
> Is outlawd by himself.
> (lines 31–33)

As Strier suggests, this is "a completely arbitrary instance of drunken
behavior that the young George Herbert would have found especially
appalling and perhaps, in some Freudian depth, appealing."[40] In a
phrase that chillingly blends incest and matricide, Herbert views the self
as seething with turbulent desires kept under tenuous control by the
internalized laws of society. Without such "reins," innate concupiscence
seeks to satisfy its most violent and salacious drives. The natural gravity
pulling one towards dissipation must continually be resisted:

> Who keeps no guard upon himself, is slack,
> And rots to nothing at the next great thaw.
> Man is a shop of rules, a well truss'd pack,
> Whose every parcell under-writes a law.
>     Lose not thy self, nor give thy humours way:
>     God gave them to thee under lock and key.
> (lines 139–44)

This sense of a self necessarily maintained in a state of perpetual house
arrest assumes profound misgivings about the body and its urges.

Yet the domain of femininity about which Herbert expresses such
misgivings also supplies him with the materials for representing the two
institutions he served—the university and the church. In a letter to

Robert Creighton, his successor as university orator at Cambridge, Herbert advises Creighton to imagine the institution on whose behalf he writes as "a matron holy, reverend, of antique and august countenance."[41] For Herbert, the university truly was an *alma mater*. In "Church-rents and schismes," correspondingly, Herbert employs the traditional topos of *mater ecclesia*.[42] Curiously, though, the poem depicts the church not only as a "Mother" who blushes at the doctrinal disputes raging about her but also as a "Brave rose" which has been invaded by "a worm." The juxtaposition of the worm and the rose functions—as in William Blake's "The Sick Rose"—to underwrite an implicit if unmistakable image of sexual violation which rests uncomfortably next to the identification of church and mother. Doctrinal dispute, Herbert seems to suggest, is a kind of incestuous rape.[43]

In "The British Church," by contrast, Herbert segregates sexual and maternal imagery in order to discover in his mother church a nonsexual, matriarchal edifice which transcends the erotic attractions of both Catholicism and Puritanism.[44] Rome, for Herbert, is a painted prostitute, seducing her followers with false promises and dazzling cosmetics:

> She on the hills, which wantonly
> Allureth all in hope to be
> > By her preferr'd,
> Hath kiss'd so long her painted shrines,
> That ev'n her face by kissing shines,
> > For her reward.

Geneva, by contrast, affects a plainness which is nearly as salacious as Roman makeup—nudity:

> She in the valley is so shie
> Of dressing, that her hair doth lie
> > About her eares:
> While she avoids her neighbours pride,
> She wholly goes on th' other wide,
> > And nothing wears.

Where Rome is erotically "painted," Geneva wears nothing at all. Both breach the decorum of female conduct in the period. Like Donne in "Satyre 3" and the Holy Sonnet "Show me deare Christ," Herbert converts religious choice into a question of sexual preference. But for Herbert, unlike Donne, the choice is clear; the British Church, his "deare Mother," epitomizes the genuine allure Rome and Geneva imitate so unsuccessfully even as it repudiates their erotic enticements. Possessed of "perfect lineaments and hue," the British Church is one in whom "Beautie . . . takes up her place, / And dates her letters from thy face, / When she doth write." Unlike the meretricious availability of Rome and Geneva, furthermore, Herbert's mother church is blessed with geographical and (by implication) sexual inaccessibility; God has chosen "To double-moat thee with his grace, / And none but thee." The *via media* of Anglicanism does not so much mediate between the respective sensual claims of Rome and Geneva as rest comfortably outside them. As femininity subsumes both the Whore of Babylon and the Spouse of the Lamb in the book of Revelation, so for Herbert does it embody at once the whorish church of Rome and Geneva and the maternal ideal of the English church.

In "Love (III)," the final lyric of *The Temple,* Herbert consolidates and reappraises the various strands of eroticism that we have been examining. If, as Elizabeth Stambler and others have argued, "*The Temple* as a whole resembles a volume of courtly love poetry," then "Love (III)" functions as a kind of epithalamion, consummating, like Spenser's *Epithalamion* appended to the *Amoretti,* a frustrating and difficult courtship.[45] Behind Herbert's portrait of his encounter with God in "Love (III)" are the biblical parable of the wedding feast and the sensuous imagery of the Song of Songs.[46] Throughout the poem, Herbert awakens rather than represses the eroticism implicit in these biblical motifs to represent the full richness and complexity of the confrontation with divine love. Because God is in part represented as a social superior addressed as "Lord" as well as an innkeeper asking "What d'ye lack?" a majority of the interpreters of this remarkable poem have been able to sustain discussion of it without reference to the sexual.[47] The poem is probably the finest example of Herbert's ability to fold into a single text a variety of discourses and situations. Yet to read the poem without attending to its sexual climate is to dodge the disquiet it intends to enforce, and to miss some of its finest effects.

Even those readers who have begun to excavate the layers of eroticism in the poem have done so with some trepidation. Chana Bloch, for example, astutely notes "the suggestion . . . of a sexual encounter between an inhibited or impotent man and a gently loving, patient woman."[48] Yet "it is unlikely," she adds, "that [Herbert] would have intended an explicitly sexual scene," and suggests that he may have been "unconsciously guided by the memory or imagination of a human sexual encounter." Janis Lull also acknowledges the poem's eroticism, but argues that "it is only in the first lines of the poem that God is thus envisioned as a woman reassuring an inhibited and guilty male lover."[49] The poem, suggests Lull, "considers and rejects sexuality as an image of humanity's love relationship with God"; the speaker "must discard the sexual metaphor altogether" (pp. 14, 13). Where Lull claims that Herbert intentionally rejects the sexual as a medium of devotion, Bloch asserts that Herbert unintentionally adopts it.

Despite the sensitivity of their readings, both critics, in order to assuage the genuine discomfort that the eroticism of the poem generates, must deny that Herbert intended to express the meeting with divine love as an erotic situation. Yet the poem continually veers towards the sexual in a way that must in some sense be intentional. Together with the speaker's first and final term of address—"my deare"—the first four words of the poem—"Love bade me welcome"—stir the erotic meanings dormant in Herbert's devotional language, conjuring an image of sociable reception which shades into sexual invitation.[50] The initial epithet with which Love is described—"quick-ey'd"—not only designates the animated and solicitous favor present in Love's gaze but also echoes the extravagant attention given to the eyes of the beloved in secular love poetry. The physical gesture by which Love responds to the speaker's statement of his inability to look on Love—"Love took my hand"—signifies both the decreasing physical distance between Love and the speaker and the act of marriage, which is often expressed in the phrase "to take the hand of."[51] This line shrewdly resuscitates the matrimonial imagery enveloping the theological occasion.

Yet there is in "Love (III)" an even deeper eroticism than the phenomena we have been observing, phenomena which could simply be termed sacred parody.[52] Rather, Herbert's portrait of his encounter with divine love is charged with questions of sexual potency which underscore his concern for his own social potency in relation to God. In the context of a sexual tryst, to "grow slack / From my first entrance in" indicates a loss of erection just after penetration.[53] Moreover, to "grow slack" is inherently oxymoronic, a physical version of the proud humility that the speaker's assertions of unworthiness involve. Similarly, Love's "sweetly questioning" if the speaker "lack'd any thing" plays upon the common Renaissance euphemism of "thing" for "penis."[54] If the speaker has grown sexually slack, he does indeed lack a proper thing, an erect penis. The apprehension the speaker feels about his own spiritual worth is translated into an anxiety about his sexual performance. Because of his slackness, he is a guest unworthy to be where he is—in the private chambers of love.

The speaker protests that he is too abashed to "look on" Love, that even if Love did make his eyes, the speaker has "marr'd them." His expression of embarrassment in ocular terms is multivalent, for in the Renaissance, as William Kerrigan suggests, "the activity of seeing was itself invested with sexual significance. . . . The word 'propagation' referred to the multiplication of the visual image in the spatial continuum between the object and the eye—seeing was making love to the world. . . . And certainly the Italianate love poetry of the sixteenth century had established gazing, glancing, glimpsing, peering, peeking, and peeping as a kind of sexual activity, a foreplaying near in effect to a consummation."[55] Moreover, Renaissance physiology made the eye a central sexual organ. According to Robert Burton, erotic melancholy had ocular origins: "by often gazing one on the other, [lovers] direct sight to sight, join eye to eye, and so drink and suck in Love between them . . . the beginning of this disease is the Eye."[56] The refusal to look on Love—and the implicit contrast with Love's "quick" eyes—are concurrently a product, and another version, of the speaker's inability to perform as he would like.

Because of this inability, the speaker requests that his "shame" be allowed to "Go where it doth deserve." "Shame" here designates both what the *OED* terms "the privy member" (on the model of *pudendum,* the Latin word for "shame" and "genitalia") and the deep disgrace he feels at this organ's current incapacity.[57] Love responds by assuming full responsibility for the speaker's present state: "And know you not, sayes Love, who bore the blame." The sacrifice of Christ that engrosses human sinfulness and dismisses the theological question of worthiness is here portrayed in the kind of words of one who understands a lover's incapacity. The speaker's subsequent offer of service—"My deare, then I will serve"—plays, as does Herbert's sonnet to his mother, upon bawdy and devout senses of "service." In offering to serve, then, the speaker expresses his desire to preserve some vestige of social and sexual sufficiency. Love answers with a command that both dismisses and fulfills this desire—"You must sit down, sayes Love, and taste my meat." Oral dependency supplants genital potency as an expression of love and union.[58] The final two sets of rhymes in the poem—"deserve/serve" and "meat/eat"—are produced, as in "Paradise," by pruning, and represent the whittling away of the speaker's pretensions of social and sexual power.

In the last two lines, terminology which is perfectly appropriate for describing the Eucharist—"taste," "meat," "sit," "eat"—assumes striking venereal significance from the sexual scenario suffusing the previous lines. "Eating" of course possessed strong sexual connotations in the Renaissance (although not in the modern American sense of specifically oral sex).[59] Partridge, for example, cites the bawdy jest of Apemantus in *Timon of Athens*—"O they [ladies] eat lords; so they come by great bellies" (1.1.206)—and Emilia's pointed characterization of men's sexual appetites in *Othello* (3.4.112–15): "They are all but stomach, and we all but food; / They eat us hungerly, and when they are full / They belch us."[60] Moreover, as the following passage from Jacques Bossuet, a seven-teenth-century French theologian, suggests, an erotic interpretation of eucharistic feasting was available even to the devout:

> The Eucharist explains to us all the words of love, of correspondence, of union, which are between Jesus Christ and his Church, between the Bridegroom and the Bride, between him and us.
>
> In the ecstasy of human love, who is unaware that we eat and devour each other, that we long to become part of each other in every way, and, as the poet said, to carry off even with our teeth the thing we love in order to possess it, feed upon it, become one with it, live on it? That which is frenzy, that which is impotence in corporeal love[,] is truth, is wisdom in the love of Jesus: "Take, eat, this is my body": devour, swallow up not a part, not a piece but the whole.[61]

The Eucharist, Bossuet argues, perfects the incomplete incorporation of another that all seek in erotic experience. Love is a hunger for consumption of another, a hunger inevitably frustrated in mortal love but fully satisfied through the Eucharist, in which Christ, like a lover, offers the meat of his body to his beloved. As Theodoret, the fifth-century bishop of Cyrrhus, remarks:

> at the moment of the sacrament when we receive the members of the Spouse, we kiss and embrace him . . . and we imagine a kind of nuptial embrace . . . we unite ourselves to him by embracing and kissing him.[62]

The Eucharist is both the pattern and the fulfillment of sexual desire.

"Love (III)" exploits just such a conflation of the imagery of eating and of sexual intercourse. In offering himself to all at each celebration of the Eucharist, Christ is like a desirable and desiring lover, promis-cuously permitting suitors to possess him again and again. Because the Christian God willingly dons human flesh, all bodily phenomena can be viewed as potential manifestations of grace. In an uncharacteristically sybaritic passage, Richard Hooker describes the incarnation as a "copu-lation [of flesh] with Deity," and imagines receiving the Eucharist as the moment when "in the wounds of our Redeemer we there dip our tongues, we are dyed red both within and without, our hunger is satis-fied and our thirst for ever quenched."[63] Lancelot Andrewes, too, waxes sensual on the subject; he remarks that in the incarnation, "He, and we, become not only *one flesh* (as *man* and *wife* do, by *conjugal union*); but even one *bloud* too."[64] Like Andrewes and Hooker, Herbert finds sexual union and sensual pleasure to be compelling models for the intimacy between humanity and God signaled by the incarnation, and celebrated in the Eucharist. "The Glimpse" describes a tantalizing God whose "short abode and stay / Feeds not, but addes to the desire of meat." In

"Ungratefulnesse," Herbert declares that God assumed human flesh in order to "allure us with delights," and describes "The *Trinitie,* and *Incarnation*" as "jewels to betroth / The work of thy creation / Unto thy self in everlasting pleasure." "The Invitation," as Strier trenchantly remarks, "presents the Eucharist as the ideal fulfillment of the passions involved in sinning."[65] It welcomes all to "feast" on a "God, in whom all dainties are," and tells those "whose love / Is your dove" that "Here is love, which having breath / Ev'n in death, / After death can never die." By representing eucharistic tasting as sexual indulgence, "Love (III)" highlights the voluptuous qualities of the feast of love stressed in "The Glimpse," "Ungratefulnesse" and "The Invitation"; it also flaunts the divine willingness to take on a body that is explored in "The Bag" and "Marie Magdalene." In both senses, it accents the carnality immanent in the incarnation.

In two of his Holy Sonnets Donne engages in a superficially similar sexualization of his relationship with God. But in Donne, the stunning blend of erotic and religious impulses is easily comprehended precisely because the eroticism is so explicit. In "Show me dear Christ thy spouse," the vast differences between earthly and heavenly promiscuity are underscored by the apparent contradiction of the final couplet, in which Christ's spouse, the church, is "most trew, and pleasing to thee, then / When she'is embrac'd and open to most men." Similarly, in "Batter my heart, three-person'd God," the paradox of a rape which makes one chaste is readily understood as a form of divine rapture stated in erotic terms:

> Take mee to you, imprison mee, for I
> Except you'enthrall mee, never shall be free,
> Nor ever chast, except you ravish mee.

With Donne we are meant to see, as William Kerrigan has eloquently demonstrated, the "awful discrimination" of heavenly and earthly love.[66]

But in "Love (III)" the reader experiences far greater discomfort because the eroticism is so much more deeply engrained in the divine. Rather than apprehending the awful discrimination of heavenly and earthly love, Herbert's reader is forced to grasp their equally awe-inspiring similarity. Like the speaker, the reader is at a loss for a fit response to this figure of divine Love. This uneasiness embodies a diminished version of the apprehension the speaker of "Love (III)" feels at this unexpected intimacy between him and his God. Indeed, the temptation to "draw back" from this aspect of "Love (III)" is great. For the erotic and the religious, although never separated in the poem, work against each other even as they are expressed in precisely the same language. In order to make simple sense of the poem, one must either suppress the erotic or cultivate it at the expense of the sacred. If this figure is an enticing lover, it is proper for the speaker to draw back, to grow slack, to refuse the seduction. But if this figure is God, then to draw back, to grow slack, to refuse to enter, is morally bad, evidence of unregenerate pride. The poem is, and is about, an impasse.

Such complications have led E. Pearlman to argue that the poem is best understood as an example of "the radical confusion in Herbert's mind between things maternal and things divine."[67] In feeding another, especially with the substance of his own body, divine Love does perform a traditionally maternal task. But when the speaker of "Love (III)" addresses his God as both "My deare" and "Lord," Herbert is not simply confusing his mother and his God. Rather, he is celebrating the remarkable intimacy with which God continues to astonish his creatures. In "Redemption," for example, the speaker seeks his Lord "in great resorts; / In cities, theatres, gardens parks, and courts" only to find him amidst "a ragged noise and mirth / Of theeves and murderers." Throughout *The Temple,* Herbert has been looking for Love in all the wrong places. In "Love (III)" he discovers it in an unanticipated form— the guise of a seductive lover—thereby transforming a comedy of errors into a comedy of eros. In this way, "Love (III)" exposes the process by which "sin," in Julia Kristeva's phrase, is "turned upside down into love."[68] Paradoxically, the very humanness and familiarity of this incarnated God makes him so peculiar.[69] The life and death of Christ truly is, as "The Bag" suggests, "a strange storie." As in "Marie Magdalene," Herbert's God astonishes by his ability to assimilate the sin he cancels, and to welcome the sinner his law would condemn.

In a sermon on Psalms 2.12 ("Kisse the Son, lest he be angry") Donne praises a God who similarly "stoops even to the words of our foule and unchaste love, that thereby he might raise us to the heavenly love of himselfe." Yet such condescension, Donne argues, places intense interpretive pressure on the mortal reader: "Take heed lest those phrases of love and kisses which should raise thee to him, do not bury thee in the memory and contemplation of sinfull love, and of licentious kisses." Donne promises the wary reader that "There is corne under the chaffe. . . . There is a heavenly love, under these ordinary phrases."[70] For Donne, the reader's task is to distinguish spiritual and carnal senses. Yet in "Love (III)" the corn keeps adhering to the chaff; the carnal continues to infiltrate the spiritual. Such distinctions, however, are rendered irrelevant by Herbert's open-armed deity. Divine acceptance of the speaker, albeit "guilty of dust and sin," entails an embrace of sexuality, that which makes him feel guilty. And the embrace of sexuality, finally, is also a cordial reception of the sexually impotent, he who cannot perform as he would like for divine love.[71] Where Donne's God adopts erotic terminology to test the interpretive and moral capacities of his followers, Herbert's God assumes sexuality to attest his total absorption of sinful humanity.

Such absorption also manifests itself in the curious blending of gender-specific traits implicit in Herbert's representations of divinity. Although Pearlman argues that Herbert's God "is threatening when envisioned as father, consoling when envisioned as mother," rarely are the masculine and feminine characteristics of Herbert's deity this distinct.[72] "Longing," for example, exhibits considerable lability among the images it uses to envision God. Herbert depicts the "Lord of my soul, love of my minde" (line 20) as a nourishing mother— "Mothers are kinde, because thou art, / And dost dispose / To them a part: / Their infants, them; and they suck thee / More free" (lines 13–18)—and a great lord who feasts all comers— "Thy board is full, yet humble guests / Finde nests" (lines 54–55)—as well as a king who left his "throne" in order to "relieve" humanity. Herbert represents himself not only as a "humble guest" and God's "childe" but also as a "beggar" (line 77) and "thy dust . . . Thy pile of dust" (lines 37, 41). In the final stanza, furthermore, God is envisaged both as the speaker's beloved and as Cupid, the wounding God of Love, at whose feet the speaker prostrates himself:

> My love, my sweetnesse, heare!
> By these thy feet, at which my heart
>   Lies all the yeare,
>   Pluck out thy dart,
> And heal my troubled breast which cryes,
>   Which dyes.[73]

For Herbert God is simultaneously an image of patriarchal power and a figure of maternal nourishment, the object of an inferior's supplication and the audience of a suitor's erotic pleas, an injuring Cupid and the injured savior. God is at once threatening and consoling, piercing and impaled, hospitable and coercive, powerful and submissive.

In *The Courtier,* Castiglione indicates just how necessary such a blending of gender-specific imagery can be to the proper representation of divinity:

And for so much as one kinde [gender] alone betokeneth an imperfection, the Divines of olde time referre both the one and the other to God: Wherefore Orpheus saide that Jupiter was both male and female: and it is read in scripture that God fashioned male and female to his likenesse. And the Poets many times speaking of the Gods, meddle the kindes together.[74]

The presence of masculine and feminine traits in Herbert's deity is a manifestation of godlike perfection, not the product of poetic deficiency or psychological confusion. Among the *Outlandish Proverbs* collected by Herbert is the common Renaissance expression that "words are women, deedes are men."[75] Perhaps Herbert's apprehension about performing before God is expressed so often in images of male potency because of this cultural equation of masculinity and accomplishment. In the encounter with the Word-made-Flesh in "Love (III)," though, Herbert's overwhelmingly beneficent deity robs him of both feminine words and masculine deeds, telling him neither to serve nor to speak, but to "sit and eat." The theological anxiety generated by the need to serve an omnipotent God, then, finds an erotic corollary in the scenario of an amorous and androgynous divinity welcoming an impotent mortal. Love literally becomes "the Master Mistris" of the speaker's passion, the object of his sexual and social desires, an image of erotic invitation and political domination.

Stephen Greenblatt has recently argued that Shakespearean comedy, despite its array of women disguised as men, fails to represent male characters dressed up as women "in part because a passage from male to female was coded ideologically as a descent from superior to inferior and hence as an unnatural act or a social disgrace."[76] But this is precisely the trajectory taken by Herbert's condescending deity, stooping to a culturally gendered inferiority while condescending to serve an inferior. By fusing masculine and feminine attributes, then, divine Love breaks down normally discrete social and sexual categories, just as Love closes to nothing the physical distance separating mortal from God.[77] In "To Mr. Tilman after he had taken orders," Donne terms the priest a "blest Hermaphrodite" because he couples heaven and earth (line 54); for Herbert, however, the hermaphrodite is not the priest but God, whose conjugation of heaven and earth is replicated in the marriage of masculine and feminine traits.[78]

The apparition of an enticing, hermaphroditic deity brings us back to the work of Leonardo da Vinci, the figure with whom we began. In Leonardo's striking painting of a sexually ambiguous John the Baptist, divine invitation similarly occurs in the guise of sexual solicitation. The gesture of the right hand provocatively summons the viewer even as it points to a heaven above. Identified as a religious figure only by a thin cross nearly rendered invisible against the saint's luminous flesh, Leonardo's androgynous *St. John* unsettles the viewer he welcomes. "I felt far from comfortable in the presence of this apparition looming tenebrously out of the murky darkness," remembers Bernard Berenson of his first encounter with the painting. "I could not conceive why this fleshy female should pretend to be the virile, sun-dried Baptist, half starved in the wilderness."[79] Surprised by sensuality in a devotional context, the viewer of Leonardo's *St. John,* like the reader of Herbert's "Love (III)," must reconcile normally adverse impulses. The enigmatic smile, lurid but saintly, joins masculine and feminine, heaven and earth, flesh and spirit, temptation and transcendence. Like Herbert's smiling deity in "Love (III)," Leonardo's *St. John* embodies the sexual mystery at the core of religious experience.[80]

"The terms of the social order," remarks Kenneth Burke, "incongruously shape our idea of God, inviting [mortals] to conceive of communication with God after the analogy of their worldly embarrassments."[81] In "Love (III)" and throughout *The Temple* Herbert explores the intersection of social order, worldly embarrassment, and religious experience, playing on and developing a complex set of homologies among divine, social, and sexual courtship.[82] The English Renaissance was particularly well poised to appreciate these homologies. While Queen Elizabeth appropriated a rhetoric of masculine sovereignty, King James assimilated images of matriarchal nurture.[83] Under both monarchs, furthermore, amorous language provided a medium of political courtship; political favor, in turn, was often expressed in erotic terms. The Renaissance conflation of social, sexual, and divine courtship provided writers such as Herbert with a vibrant devotional vocabulary. A composite of masculine and feminine authority and the object of political and sexual desire, Herbert's androgynous divinity functions as the absolute audience of the Renaissance lyric.

Recent scholarship has begun to exhume the importance of gender-specific and erotic imagery for past concepts of God. Leo Steinberg, for example, has called attention to a remarkable number of Renaissance depictions of Christ that emphasize the savior's genital potency as a measure of his adoption of human weakness.[84] Caroline Walker Bynum, conversely, has discovered an astonishing range and flexibility of gender imagery in medieval devotional discourse.[85] Moreover, Herbert's historical moment—the early seventeenth century—has recently been identified by Michel Foucault and Lawrence Stone as inaugurating the withdrawal of sexuality into architectural privacy and linguistic euphemism.[86] In their engagement with and recoil from a discourse of sexuality, Herbert's lyrics rest precariously on the fault lines of this cultural movement. To draw back from their anxious eroticism is finally to retreat from history, that miscellany of texts and practices infiltrating

Leonardo da Vinci, *St. John the Baptist* (1513–16). In Paris, Louvre.

and enabling Herbert's devotional performances. The love that Herbert anatomizes and practices throughout *The Temple* is not just *caritas* but also *cupiditas;* not just *agape* but also *eros.*[87] Rather than functioning as an impertinent distraction from devotion, sexuality is the warp of that carefully woven fabric through which Herbert attempts to comprehend and express the divine. "To reproach mystics with loving God by means of the faculty of sexual love," remarks Simone Weil, "is as though one were to reproach a painter with making pictures by means of colors composed of material substances. We haven't anything else with which to love."[88] We should not then be as surprised as we nevertheless are to discover the plethora of erotic references pervading Herbert's religious poetry. We should, rather, admire the spiritual stamina of a poet who continually resists the temptation to draw back from the unsettling aspects of his encounter with the divine, and prize the capacity of his poetry to aspire to spirituality by embracing rather than repressing a remarkable range of corporeal experience.

## Notes

1. Leonardo da Vinci, *Treatise on Painting,* trans. A Philip McMahon, 2 vols. (Princeton: Princeton University Press, 1956), 1:22. The Italian text is quoted from *The Literary Works of Leonardo da Vinci,* ed. Jean Paul Richter, 2 vols. (London: Phaidon, 1970), 1:64.

2. Russell Fraser, "George Herbert's Poetry," *Sewanee Review* 95 (1987): 581. Fraser supplies a fascinating reading of the "occulted sexual energy" (p. 575) of Herbert's "Vertue." In "Reading (Herbert's 'Vertue') Otherwise," *Mississippi Review* 33 (1983): 61, Jonathan Goldberg also sees "Vertue" as "a sexual scene, sweet, perfumed, filled with roses and spring." Robert Rogers, *Metaphor: A Psychoanalytic View* (Berkeley: University of California Press, 1978), pp. 55–57, likewise attends to the poem's erotic overtones.

Yvor Winters' pronouncements on the irrelevance of sexual knowledge to religious experience in *Forms of Discovery* (Chicago: Swallow Press, 1967), p. 92, articulately voice the cultural assumptions Fraser speaks of: "the poet who insists on dealing with [religious] experience and who becomes involved emotionally in the sexual analogy runs the risk of corrupting his devotional poetry with sexual imagery. It is not that sexual experience is 'immoral'; but it is irrelevant to the religious experience, and in so far as it is introduced into the religious experience, can result in nothing but confusion." Winters has the excesses of Richard Crashaw in mind, but argues that such excesses are the inevitable product of mixing religion and sex rather than symptoms of Crashaw's particular poetic. In "Changing the Object: Herbert and Excess," *George Herbert Journal* 2, no. 1 (1978); 24–37, Richard Strier distinguishes between Crashaw's "Counter-Reformation cultivation of ecstasy" and Herbert's Protestant sensibility.

3. All citations of Herbert's English works are from *The Works of George Herbert,* ed. F. E. Hutchinson (Oxford: Clarendon Press, 1941). In *The Poetry of*

*George Herbert* (Cambridge: Harvard University Press, 1975), Helen Vendler suggests that "Herbert may say in 'The Forerunners' that his words, before his employ, knew only stews and brothels, but it would seem that he knew just enough to have a perfect horror of such places and of their inhabitants" (p. 162).

4. Charles Davis, *Body as Spirit: The Nature of Religious Feeling* (New York: Seabury, 1976), pp. 130–31. Two recent works explore the genesis of this inconsistency in early Christian attitudes: Elaine Pagels, *Adam, Eve, and the Serpent* (New York: Random House, 1988), and Peter Brown, *The Body and Society: Men, Women and Sexual Renunciation in Early Christianity* (New York: Columbia University Press, 1988). Evidence that this inconsistency continues unabated was supplied in the summer of 1988, in the controversy generated by the representation of Christ as a being with sexual urges in Martin Scorsese's film of Nikos Kazantzakis' novel, *The Last Temptation of Christ*.

5. On this discourse, see Stephen Greenblatt, *Shakespearean Negotiations: The Circulation of Social Energy in Renaissance England* (Berkeley: University of California Press, 1988), pp. 66–93, and Thomas Laqueur, "Orgasm, Generation, and the Politics of Reproductive Biology," *Representations* 14 (1986): 1–41. Both Greenblatt and Laqueur explore how Renaissance phallocentric assumptions encouraged a view of women as inverted or incomplete men.

6. On the sexual meaning of "to serve," see Stephen Booth, ed., *Shakespeare's Sonnets* (New Haven: Yale University Press, 1977), p. 487, note on Sonnet 141, line 10. Under "turn," sb. 30b., the *OED* identifies the meaning of the phrase "to serve one's turn" as "to suffice for or satisfy a need." To serve Venus's turn is thus to satisfy her needs. In the Introduction to his edition of *Philaster, or, Love Lies a-Bleeding* (1609) by Francis Beaumont and John Fletcher (London: Methuen, 1969), pp. lxiv–lxv, Andrew Gurr explores the relationships between heroic and erotic ideas of service in the play.

7. See Booth, *Sonnets,* pp. 441–42, note on Sonnet 129, line 1; and Herbert Alexander Ellis, *Shakespeare's Lusty Punning in "Love's Labour's Lost"* (Mouton: The Hague, 1973), pp. 95–97. Ellis cites the following words of Mercutio in *Romeo and Juliet* (1.2.23–6): " 'Twould anger him / To raise a *spirit* in his mistress' circle / Of some strange nature, letting it there stand / Till she had laid it and conjur'd it down." Except for the sonnets, which I cite from Booth, all citations of Shakespeare are from *The Riverside Shakespeare,* ed. G. Blakemore Evans et al. (Boston: Houghton Mifflin, 1974).

8. Booth, *Sonnets,* p. 177, and Ellis, *Shakespeare's Lusty Punning,* pp. 103–10.

9. Richard Strier, *Love Known: Theology and Experience in George Herbert's Poetry* (Chicago: University of Chicago Press, 1983), p. 39, n. 30.

10. In *Transformations of the Word: Spenser, Herbert, Vaughan* (Athens: University of Georgia Press, 1988), pp. 224–37, John N. Wall explores in detail the influence of Sidney's *Astrophil and Stella* on Herbert's *Temple,* and argues that "Love for Herbert does not exclude the erotic dimension" (p. 225).

11. In his Holy Sonnet "I am a little world made cunningly," Donne provides a similar contrast between carnal and purifying flames, comparing "the fire / Of lust and envie" to the "fiery zeale" of God, "which doth in eating

heale" (*The Divine Poems of John Donne,* ed. Helen Gardner [Oxford: Clarendon Press, 1978], p. 13).

12. On "strain" as a verb meaning "to embrace closely," see Eric Partridge,
*Shakespeare's Bawdy* (New York: Dutton, 1960), p. 196.

13. This meaning, employed frequently and with great relish by Chaucer's
Wife of Bath, is still available in Shakespeare's Sonnet 20, in which the young
man is "not acquainted" (line 3) because nature has "pricked [him] out for
women's pleasure" (line 13). In addition, the "quaint Honour" that the speaker
of Marvell's "To His Coy Mistress" (line 29) prophesies will "turn to dust" is
both his mistress's pudendum and a mocking reference to the societal value
conferred by her control over it (*The Poems and Letters of Andrew Marvell,* ed.
H. M. Margoliouth, 2 vols. [Oxford: Clarendon Press, 1971], 1:28).

14. Strier, *Love Known,* p. 89. Janis Lull finds a similar pun on "strain" in
the conclusion of "Employment (I)": "Lord place me in thy consort; give one
strain / To my poore reed." Lull remarks: "the reed, 'poore' or not, is another
symbol of male egotism—at once phallus, musical instrument, and pen"
("George Herbert's Revisions in 'The Church' and the Carnality of 'Love'
[III]," *George Herbert Journal* 9, no. 1 [1985]: 5).

15. Jonathan Goldberg, *Voice Terminal Echo: Postmodernism and English
Renaissance Texts* (New York: Methuen, 1986), p. 110. Goldberg does not deal
with the fact that Herbert almost certainly had nothing to do with this subtitle;
it is in neither of the manuscripts. He does, however, speculate on a range of
autoerotic interpretive possibilities in poems such as "Artillerie," "Home," and
"The Bag."

16. On the sexual confusion and unnatural generation represented by the
cockatrice, see Thomas Rogers Forbes, *The Midwife and the Witch* (New
Haven: Yale University Press, 1966), pp. 1–17. The relevance of alchemical
concepts of the cockatrice is explored in Laurence Breiner, "Herbert's Cockatrice," *Modern Philology* 77 (1979): 10–17. Hutchinson cites Isaiah 59.5, where
the wicked "hatch cockatrice egges . . . he that eateth of their egges dieth"
(*Works,* p. 520).

17. On "cockatrice" as "prostitute," see James T. Henke, *Courtesans and
Cuckolds: A Glossary of Renaissance Dramatic Bawdy (Exclusive of Shakespeare)*
(New York: Garland, 1979), p. 43; and Ben Jonson, "On Lieutenant Shift"
(lines 21–24), *Epigrammes* 12, in *Ben Jonson,* ed. C. H. Herford and Percy and
Evelyn Simpson, 11 vols. (Oxford: Oxford University Press, 1925–52), 8:31.
John Garrett, "Sin and Shame in George Herbert's Poetry," *Rivesta Canaria de
Estudios Ingleses* 8 (1984): 141–43, offers a clumsy but interesting attempt to
read the poem in strictly Freudian terms.

18. The phrase is from Shakespeare's Sonnet 62, line 1. Dissuasion from
masturbation as a theme in the sonnets is examined by Booth, *Sonnets,* pp. 140,
142–43, and Joseph Pequigney, *"Such Is My Love": A Study of Shakespeare's Sonnets* (Chicago: University of Chicago Press, 1985), pp. 15–18.

19. Michel Foucault, *The Care of the Self,* vol. 3 of *The History of Sexuality,*
trans. Robert Hurley (New York: Random House, 1986), p. 140.

20. The phrase is from Sonnet 6, line 13. On the pen/penis pun, see Par

tridge, *Shakespeare's Bawdy*, p. 163; Booth, *Sonnets*, p. 270, note on Sonnet 78, lines 3, 7, 11; and Hilda M. Hulme, *Explorations in Shakespeare's Language* (New York: Barnes and Noble, 1963), pp. 135–36. All three point to Gratiano's jealous threat in *Merchant of Venice* (5.1.237) to "mar the . . . pen" of the "young clerk" whom Nerissa teasingly promises to sleep with.

21. Strier, *Love Known*, p. 252; Vendler, *The Poetry of George Herbert*, p. 51; in addition, see Fraser, "George Herbert's Poetry," p. 576. Strier, *Love Known*, p. 252, n. 63, also calls attention to Herbert's "use of 'store' in an at least implicitly sexual context" in "The Pearl," line 26: "the projects of unbridled store." In Thomas Nashe's *The Choice of Valentines* (commonly known as *Nashe His Dildo*), "store" suggests seminal fluid; the sexually exhausted speaker complains of his voracious mistress that "all my store seemes to hir, penurie" (*The Works of Thomas Nashe*, ed. R. B. McKerrow, 5 vols. [London, 1904–10], 3:415, line 300).

22. Augustine, *The City of God* (14.16–18), trans. John Healey (1610), 2 vols. (London: Dent, 1945), 2:47–49; see Gerard O'Daly, *Augustine's Philosophy of Mind* (London: Duckworth, 1987), p. 53. Lull, "Herbert's Revisions," p. 3, suggests that "the substitution in *W* [the Williams manusript] of 'And prick mine eyes' for 'Troubling mine eyes' was inspired by the phallic connotations of 'Babel'—the quick growing tower of self-delusion in the poem's final lines."

23. *The Sermons of John Donne,* ed. Evelyn Simpson and George R. Potter 10 vols. (Berkeley: University of California Press, 1954–62), 6:190–91.

24. Ibid., 6:192.

25. Ibid., 6:200.

26. Vendler seems cautiously attracted by a "Psychoanalytic interpretation" which "might see this poem as a masochistic acquiescence in castration; to accept castration is to be reconciled with the father by no longer possessing a rival masculine member" (*The Poetry of George Herbert*, p. 295, n. 12). But one need only glimpse the aggression that Herbert, Donne, and others associate with sexual potency to comprehend the theological and emotional power of this castration. Legend suggests that Origen, on reading Matthew 19.12—"and there be Eunuches, which have made themselves Eunuches for the kingdome of heavens sake"—castrated himself. Also relevant is Paul's admonition in Galatians 5.12—"I would they were even cut off which trouble you." In *"Justus quidem tu es, Domine,"* line 13, Gerard Manley Hopkins describes himself as "Time's eunuch" (*A Hopkins Reader,* ed. John Pick [London: Oxford University Press, 1953], p. 30).

27. Stanley Stewart, *The Enclosed Garden: The Tradition and the Image in Seventeenth-Century Poetry* (Madison: University of Wisconsin Press, 1966), p. 53.

28. In *Childhood and Cultural Despair: A Theme and Variations in Seventeenth-Century Literature* (Pittsburgh: University of Pittsburgh Press, 1978), pp. 94–120, Leah S. Marcus incisively examines the manner in which "becoming the child of God" was the major goal of Herbert's devotional life, but she does not explore the ways in which childhood was bound up for Herbert in notions of asexual purity.

29. John Milton, *Paradise Lost,* ed. Scott Elledge (New York: Norton, 1975), p. 257.

30. Elaine Scarry, *The Body in Pain: The Making and Unmaking of the World* (Oxford: Oxford University Press, 1985), p. 210.

31. Robert Graves, *Poetic Unreason and Other Studies* (London: Cecil Palmer, 1925), p. 62. Graves views "The Bag" as a poem of "the Jekyll and Hyde variety . . . where the manifest content and the latent content represent opposite sides of a conflict" (p. 57).

32. Kenneth Burke, *A Rhetoric of Motives* (Berkeley: University of California Press, 1969), p. 328. Burke is paraphrasing Luther.

33. I quote from the translation of Mark McCloskey and Paul R. Murphy, *The Latin Poetry of George Herbert: A Bilingual Edition* (Athens: Ohio University Press, 1965), p. 65. The *Soliloquies* attributed to Bonaventura likewise stress divine penetrability; Christ's wound, observes the author, is "opened to suffer thee to enter therein" (*Soliloquies* [London, 1655], p. 88, sig. E7v, quoted in Richard Todd, *The Opacity of Signs: Acts of Interpretation in George Herbert's 'The Temple,'* [Columbia: University of Missouri Press, 1986], p. 25, n. 10).

34. McCloskey and Murphy, *Latin Poetry,* p. 107.

35. Ibid., p. 119. A similar image occurs in the conclusion of "Perseverance," a poem Herbert did not include in *The Temple:* "Onely my soule hangs on thy promises / With face and hands clinging unto thy brest, / clinging and crying, crying without cease . . ." (*Works,* p. 205). It is, I think, significant that such explicit imagery exists only in a Latin poem and in a poem Herbert rejected from *The Temple;* as Fred J. Nichols suggests, the Latin poetry of the Renaissance is often far more "intimate and personal" than works in the vernacular (*An Anthology of Neo-Latin Poetry,* ed. Nichols [New Haven: Yale University Press, 1979], pp. 1–3).

36. E. Pearlman, "George Herbert's God," *English Literary Renaissance* 13 (1983): 108. Isaiah 49.23 offers some license for such imagery, where God promises his people: "And kings shall be thy nursing fathers, and their queenes thy nursing mothers."

37. Caroline Walker Bynum, *Jesus as Mother: Studies in the Spirituality of the High Middle Ages* (Berkeley: University of California Press, 1982), p. 133; see also Bynum, *Holy Feast and Holy Fast: The Religious Significance of Food to Medieval Women* (Berkeley: University of California Press, 1987), pp. 270–71; and Marsha L. Dutton, "Christ Our Mother: Aelred's Iconography for Contemplative Union," *Goad and Nail: Studies in Medieval Cistercian History,* ed. E. Rozanne Elder (Kalamazoo, Mich.: Cistercian Publications, 1985), pp. 21–45.

38. On the tradition of such sentiments, see R. Howard Bloch, "Medieval Misogyny," *Representations* 20 (1987): 1–24.

39. An earlier version of this poem concedes that such advice may "seeme Monkish," but goes on to recommend:

> Let not each fansy make thee to detest
> A Virgin-bed, wch hath a speciall Crowne
> If it concurr wth vertue.
>
> (*W,* lines 19–21)

40. Richard Strier, "Sanctifying the Aristocracy: 'Devout Humanism' in François de Sales, John Donne, and George Herbert," *Journal of Religion* 69 (1989): 46, n. 41.

41. I cite the translation of A. B. Grosart in *The Complete Works in Verse and Prose of George Herbert*, ed. Grosart, 3 vols. (London: Fuller Worthies' Library, 1874), 3:475–76; *Works*, pp. 470–71.

42. On the background of this topos, see Joseph C. Plumpe, *Mater Ecclesia: An Enquiry into the Concept of Church as Mother in Early Christianity* (Washington, D.C.: Catholic University of America Press, 1943).

43. In his discussion of the phallic connotations of the phrase "staffe of flesh" in "Divinitie," Richard Strier suggests that "Herbert seems to have conceived of the intellect in terms of aggressive sexuality" (*Love Known*, p. 48, n. 45).

44. The literary and biblical contexts of this poem are explored in rich detail by Claude J. Summers, "The Bride of the Apocalypse and the Quest for True Religion: Donne, Herbert, and Spenser," in *"Bright Shootes of Everlastingnesse": The Seventeenth-Century Religious Lyric*, ed. Claude J. Summers and Ted-Larry Pebworth (Columbia: University of Missouri Press, 1987), pp. 72–95. In *Equivocal Predication: George Herbert's Way to God* (Toronto: University of Toronto Press, 1981), pp. 94–110, Heather A. R. Asals speculates on the connections among Mother Church, Magdalene Herbert, and Mary Magdalene, in Herbert's mind.

45. Elizabeth Stambler, "The Unity of Herbert's *Temple*," in *Essential Articles for the Study of George Herbert's Poetry*, ed. John R. Roberts (Hamden: Archon, 1979), p. 329. See also Louis L. Martz, *The Poetry of Meditation: A Study in English Religious Literature of the Seventeenth Century* (New Haven: Yale University Press, 1962), pp. 259–73.

46. Stewart, *The Enclosed Garden*, offers a learned account of the reception of the Song of Songs in the seventeenth century. See also George L. Scheper, "Reformation Attitudes toward Allegory and the Song of Songs," *PMLA* 89 (1974): 551–62. Chana Bloch, *Spelling the Word: George Herbert and the Bible* (Berkeley: University of California Press, 1985), exhaustively explores the variety of biblical sources that infiltrate "Love (III)."

47. See, for example, Arnold Stein, *George Herbert's Lyrics* (Baltimore: Johns Hopkins University Press, 1968), pp. 190–95; Stanley Fish, *The Living Temple: George Herbert and Catechizing* (Berkeley: University of California Press, 1979), pp. 131–34; Strier, *Love Known*, pp. 73–83; Vendler, *The Poetry of George Herbert*, pp. 58–60, 274–76; Marcus, *Childhood and Cultural Despair*, pp. 116–17; Anne Williams, "Gracious Accommodations: Herbert's 'Love (III),'" *Modern Philology* 82 (1984): 13–22; and my "Standing on Ceremony: The Comedy of Manners in Herbert's 'Love (III),'" in *"Bright Shootes of Everlastingnesse*," ed. Summers and Pebworth, pp. 116–33.

48. Bloch, *Spelling the Word*, p. 339. Reuben Brower similarly describes the encounter as one of "almost feminine intimacy" (*The Fields of Light: An Experiment in Critical Reading* [London: Oxford University Press, 1951], pp 28–31). See also Robert Bagg, "The Electromagnet and the Shred of Platinum," *Arion* 8 (1969): 428–29:

The charm of the poem is the almost geisha-like care and
thoughtfulness of Love; shyness and unworthiness before Christ is felt as
unworthiness in an encounter full of sexual ambience. . . . Redemption
is the point of the drama, but the medium wherein it takes place is Her-
bert's sexual anxiety . . . he feels his acceptance by Christ through a
dream in which masculine self-doubt is soothed away by extraordinary
tenderness.

49. Lull, "Herbert's Revisions," p. 11.

50. The opening line of "Womans Honour," a poem by the notorious John
Wilmot, earl of Rochester—"Love bade me hope, and I obeyed"—parodies
the erotic connotations of this image. This allusion to Herbert not only re-
minds the reader of Rochester's poem "that Rochester's speaker desires a sexual
version of the submission in which Herbert's meditation ends" (Jeremy
Treglown, "Satirical Inversion of Some English Sources in Rochester's Poetry,"
*Review of English Studies* 24 [1973]: 43); it also awakens the dormant eroticism
of "Love (III)"'s situation and opening line.

51. Spenser's *Epithalamion,* lines 238–39, uses a version of the phrase in just
this way when the speaker asks his hesitant bride: "Why blush ye love to give to
me your hand, / The pledge of all our band?" (*Spenser: Poetical Works,* ed. J. C.
Smith and E. de Selincourt [London: Oxford University Press, 1912], p. 582).

52. In "Sacred 'Parody' of Love Poetry, and Herbert," *Essays by Rosemond
Tuve,* ed. Thomas P. Roche, Jr. (Princeton: Princeton University Press, 1970),
pp. 207–51, Rosemond Tuve explores the kind of sacred parody available to and
practiced by Herbert.

53. The sexual implication of "slack" is noted, but not explored, by John R.
Mulder, "George Herbert's *Temple:* Design and Methodology," *Seventeenth-
Century News* 31, no. 2 (1973): 43; Greg Crossan, "Herbert's 'Love (III),'"
*Explicator* 37, no. 1 (1978): 40–41; Todd, *The Opacity of Signs,* pp. 189–90;
William A. Sessions, "Abandonment and the Religious Lyric," in *"Bright
Shootes of Everlastingnesse,"* ed. Summers and Pebworth, pp. 13–14; and Gar-
rett, "Sin and Shame," pp. 144–46.

54. Shakespeare's Sonnet 20, for example, bemoans the fact that nature, by
"prick[ing]" the young man "out for women's pleasure," has "add[ed] one *thing*
to my purpose nothing" (lines 12–13; my emphasis). Booth, *Shakespeare's Son-
nets,* p. 472, cites the following verse from "Fain wold I have a pretie thing to
give unto my Ladie," a song published in *A Handful of Pleasant Delights* [1584],
ed. Hyder E. Rollins, (Cambridge: Harvard University Press, 1924), p. 58,
which suggests a potential erotic model for the dialogue of "Love (III)": "The
Mercers pull me going by, / the Silkie wiues say, *what lack ye? / The thing you
haue not,* then say I" (my emphasis). See also the range of quotations collected
by Partridge, *Shakespeare's Bawdy,* p. 203, and Henke, *Courtesans and Cuckolds,*
p. 270.

55. William Kerrigan, "The Fearful Accommodations of John Donne,"
*English Literary Renaissance* 4 (1974): 357. Perhaps also relevant is Booth's claim
that "diminished eyesight was particularly associated with the diminishment of
'spirits'" (*Shakespeare's Sonnets,* p. 442).

56. Robert Burton, *The Anatomy of Melancholy,* pt. 3, sec. 2, mem. 2, subs. 2; quoted in Donald Beecher, "The Lover's Body: The Somatogenesis of Love in Renaissance Medical Treatises," *Renaissance and Reformation* 24 (1988): 9.

57. *OED,* 1:7. See, for example, Isaiah 47.3 (AV)—"Thy nakednes shalbe uncovered, yea thy shame shalbe seene"—and Revelations 16.15—"Blessed is he that . . . keepeth his garments, least hee walke naked, and they see his shame."

58. "The extrasensory *taste* of God," remarks William Kerrigan, "had approximately the emotional centrality for Herbert that the similarly extrasensory vision of God had for Milton" ("Ritual Man: On the Outside of Herbert's Poetry," *Psychiatry* 48 [1985]: 70).

59. Henke, *Courtesans and Cuckolds,* p. 78, suggests that the use of "eat" to indicate "cunnilingus or fellatio" is an American coinage.

60. Partridge, *Shakespeare's Bawdy,* pp. 105, 195.

61. *Méditations sur l'Evangile: Sermons de Notre-Seigneur, XXIV journée,* in *Oeuvres Complètes de Bossuet,* 6 vols. (Paris, 1862), 6:369. I owe this reference, and the latter paragraph of the translation, to Nicholas J. Perella, *The Kiss Sacred and Profane: An Interpretive History of Kiss Symbolism and Related Religio-Erotic Themes* (Berkeley: University of California Press, 1969), p. 3. In *Holy Feast and Holy Fast,* Caroline Walker Bynum suggestively explores the devotional importance of eating in the Middle Ages.

62. Quoted in Perella, *The Kiss,* p. 46.

63. Richard Hooker, *Of the Laws of Ecclesiastical Polity* (5.65.5, and 5.67.12), ed. Christopher Morris, 2 vols. (London: Dent, 1965), 2:215, and 2:231.

64. Lancelot Andrewes, "Sermon 1 of the Nativitie: Christmas 1605," in *Sermons,* ed. G. M. Story (London: Oxford University Press, 1967), p. 11.

65. Strier, "Changing the Object," p. 28. Strier, though, argues that the poem's translation of sensuality into spirituality is atypical of Herbert, where I find it symptomatic.

66. Kerrigan, "Fearful Accommodations," pp. 337–63.

67. Pearlman, "George Herbert's God," p. 111.

68. Julia Kristeva, *Powers of Horror: An Essay on Abjection,* trans. Leon S. Roudiez (New York: Columbia University Press, 1982), pp. 122–23. I have learned much from this provocative book, and from Kristeva's *Tales of Love,* trans. Leon S. Roudiez (New York: Columbia University Press, 1987).

69. Strier, *Love Known,* pp. 57–58, explores how Herbert's God violates decorum to demonstrate the strangeness of the means of divine grace.

70. Donne, *Sermons,* 3:318–19 (quoted in part in Kerrigan, "Fearful Accommodations," p. 350). On the Protestant anxiety about the eroticism of the Song of Songs, see Scheper, "Reformation Attitudes toward Allegory and the Song of Songs, pp. 557–59.

71. As Pierre Darmon has demonstrated, the impotent were social outcasts in early modern Europe (*Trial by Impotence: Virility and Marriage in Pre-Revolutionary France,* trans. Paul Keegan [London: Chatto and Windus, 1985]). The embrace of the impotent, then, is a prototypically Christian acceptance of the socially marginal.

72. Pearlman, "George Herbert's God," p. 103, n. 14. Vendler similarly suggests that "Herbert's tendency is certainly to see God, in any benevolent aspect, as more female than male" (*The Poetry of George Herbert,* p. 292, n. 14).

73. Strier, "Changing the Object," pp. 25–27, makes the important distinction between the masochistic ecstasy of Crashaw's St. Theresa poems and Herbert's asexual treatment of the dart of Love in these lines, arguing that Herbert, unlike St. Theresa, desires "not a prolongation of his pain but a surcease from it."

74. Baldassare Castiglione, *The Book of the Courtier,* trans. Thomas Hoby (1561), ed. W. H. D. Rouse and Drayton Henderson (London: Dent, 1928), p. 199. The scriptural precedent in Genesis is discussed in detail by James Grantham Turner, *One Flesh: Paradisal Marriage and Sexual Relations in the Age of Milton* (Oxford: Clarendon Press, 1987), chap. 1, and by Mary Nyquist, "The Genesis of Gendered Subjectivity in the Divorce Tracts and in *Paradise Lost,*" in *Re-membering Milton,* ed. Mary Nyquist and Margaret Ferguson (London: Methuen, 1988), pp. 99–127.

75. *Works,* no. 843, p. 349. In *Literary Fat Ladies: Rhetoric, Gender, Property* (London: Methuen, 1987), pp. 23–24, Patricia Parker analyzes this traditional opposition between womanly words and manly deeds in *Hamlet.*

76. Greenblatt, *Shakespearean Negotiations,* p. 92.

77. In "Androgyny, Mimesis, and the Marriage of the Boy Heroine on the English Renaissance Stage," *PMLA* 102 (1987): 29, Phyllis Rackin suggests: "The androgyne could be an image of transcendence—of surpassing the bounds that limit the human condition in a fallen world, of breaking through the constraints that material existence imposes on spiritual aspiration or the personal restrictions that define our roles in society. But the androgyne could also be an object of ridicule or an image of monstrous deformity, of social and physical abnormality." Herbert's implicitly androgynous divinity fuses, I would argue, what Rackin terms "the spiritualized conception of the *super*natural androgyne" with the "image of the *un*natural hermaphrodite" (p. 29).

78. In a sermon on Proverbs 8.17 ("I love them that love me, and they that seek me early shall find me"), Donne explores the androgyny of Christ's love in ways similar to Herbert in "Love (III)":

> To shew the constancy and durableness of this love, the lover is a he, that is Christ; to show the vehemency and earnestness of it, the lover is a shee, that is wisdom . . . all that is good then, either in the love of man or woman is in this love; for he is expressed in both sexes, man and woman; and all that can be ill in the love of either sex, is purged away. (*Sermons,* 1:239).

With Herbert's androgynous God, however, the "ill" is not purged but absorbed. In "Adam, Christ, and Mr. Tilman: God's Blest Hermaphrodites," *American Benedictine Review* 40 (1989): 250–60, Frances M. Malpezzi surveys traditional analogues to Donne's striking image.

79. Bernard Berenson, "An Attempt at Revaluation" (1916) in *Leonardo da Vinci: Aspects of the Renaissance Genius,* ed. Morris Philipson [New York:

George Braziller, 1966], pp. 115, 120). Perhaps because of its unsettling blend of carnality and spirituality, masculine and feminine, this painting is one of the least admired of Leonardo's works. Even Kenneth Clark, who offers probably the fullest appreciation of the painting, concludes that "it remains an unsatisfactory work" (*Leonardo da Vinci: An Account of His Development as an Artist* [Cambridge: Cambridge University Press, 1952], pp. 171–75). The painting, however, was certainly dear to the artist, being one of the few works to make the voyage with him from Italy to France. It was also, according to Clark, his "most influential," and most often copied, work (p. 174).

80. Fascinatingly, a painting of Bacchus (also in the Louvre) ascribed to Leonardo's studio began as a representation of John the Baptist. The seventeenth-century addition of a crown of vine leaves and a leopard's skin, and the conversion of the cross into a thyrsis, complete the metamorphosis from sacred to profane object desired by Leonardo's patron in the anecdote from the *Paragone* with which we began.

81. Burke, *A Rhetoric of Motives*, p. 234. In a review-essay of Rosemond Tuve's *A Reading of George Herbert*, Burke glances at the possibility of androgyny in Herbert's God via Herbert's relationship to his mother ("On Covery, Re- and Dis-," *Accent* 13 [1953]: 225–26).

82. "The vocabularies of social and sexual courtship," Kenneth Burke argues, "are so readily interchangeable, not because one is a mere 'substitute' for the other, but because sexual courtship is intrinsically fused with the motives of social hierarchy" (*A Rhetoric of Motives*, p. 217).

83. On Elizabeth's use of masculine terminology, see Leah S. Marcus, "Shakespeare's Comic Heroines, Elizabeth I, and the Political Uses of Androgyny," in *Women in the Middle Ages and the Renaissance: Literary and Historical Perspectives*, ed. Mary Beth Rose (Syracuse: Syracuse University Press, 1986), pp. 135–53. On the Jacobean imagination of the king as a nourishing father, combining male and female modes of authority, see especially Jonathan Goldberg "Fatherly Authority: The Politics of Stuart Family Images," in *Rewriting the Renaissance: The Discourses of Sexual Difference in Early Modern Europe*, ed. Margaret W. Ferguson, Maureen Quilligan, and Nancy J. Vickers (Chicago: University of Chicago Press, 1986), pp. 3–32; and Stephen Orgel, "Prospero's Wife," *Representations* 8 (1984): 1–13. In *Pagan Mysteries in the Renaissance* (New York: Norton, 1958; rev. 1968), pp. 211–17, Edgar Wind explores the intellectual and artistic traditions of androgyny, and calls attention to a striking portrait of Francis I as a "bearded warrior" with "the anatomy of a *virago.*"

84. Leo Steinberg, *The Sexuality of Christ in Renaissance Art and in Modern Oblivion* (New York: Pantheon, 1983). See also Bynum's fine commentary on Steinberg, "The Body of Christ in the Later Middle Ages: A Reply to Leo Steinberg," *Renaissance Quarterly* 39 (1986): 399–439. Among the many rich anecdotes available in Natalie Zemon Davis, *Fiction in the Archives: Pardon Tales and Their Tellers in Sixteenth-Century France* (Stanford: Stanford University Press, 1987), is a bizarre tale in which an act of homicide originates in a bawdy joke about the sexual virility of God. A supplicant who had been "play-

ing and representing the figure of Our Lord in his tomb" is approached by another, the ultimate victim, who sneers: "I see the god on earth. Did you keep your virile and shameful member stiff in playing God?" (pp. 30–32).

85. Bynum, *Jesus as Mother* (1982), and *Holy Feast and Holy Fast* (1987). See also the recovery of female images of the biblical God by feminist theologians in Phyllis Trible, *God and the Rhetoric of Sexuality* (Philadelphia: Fortress Press, 1978), and Virginia Ramey Mollenkott, *The Divine Feminine: The Biblical Imagery of God as Female* (New York: Crossroad, 1984).

86. Michel Foucault, *The History of Sexuality,* vol. 1, *An Introduction,* trans. Robert Hurley (New York: Random House, 1978), especially, pp. 3–13, 53–74, 115–31. See also Lawrence Stone, *The Family, Sex and Marriage in England, 1500–1800* (New York: Harper and Row, 1977), especially pp. 519–27.

87. Tuve's otherwise impressive essay, "George Herbert and *Caritas,*" offers the consummate statement of a desexualized love in Herbert: "when the love exchanged is between God and man, . . . the identical words and similar phrases of profane poetry cease to bear a comparable significance" (*Essays,* p. 181). In *Protestant Poetics and the Seventeenth-Century Religious Lyric* (Princeton: Princeton University Press, 1979), p. 293, Barbara Lewalski similarly remarks that Herbert "makes little direct use" of the Bridegroom-Bride metaphor for his relationship with God, "and when he does, avoids its erotic connotation."

The term *agape* and *eros* are of course from Anders Nygren's monumental *Agape and Eros,* trans. Philip S. Watson (New York: Harper, 1969).

88. *The Notebooks of Simone Weil,* trans. Arthur Wills, 2 vols. (London, 1956), 2:472; quoted in Bynum, "A Reply to Leo Steinberg," p. 410, n. 26. In "Simone Weil et George Herbert," *Etudes* 340 (1974): 250, Jean Mambrino cites Weil's judgment on "Love (III)" as "le plus beau poème du monde."

# The Constant Subject:
# Instability and Female Authority in
# Wroth's *Urania* Poems

*Maureen Quilligan*

Lady Mary Wroth was Sir Philip Sidney's niece; this familial fact had great bearing on her work. While he was the first to write a sonnet cycle in English, she was the last to do so in the Renaissance, publishing the first such sequence by a woman in 1621. "Pamphilia to Amphilanthus," a series of 103 poems, was appended to Wroth's prosimetric pastoral romance, *The Countess of Mountgomerie's Urania,* by which title the book designedly recalled Sidney's *Countess of Pembroke's Arcadia.* Additionally then, if he was the first to write a Greek romance, she wrote another, and in so doing was the first woman to publish a work of prose fiction in English. Wroth's membership in the Sidney family goes a long way towards explaining how she could overcome the massive social injunctions against female authority that functioned throughout the Renaissance to silence female would-be writers.[1] The eldest child of Sidney's younger brother Robert and thus the daughter of an earl, raised at celebrated Penshurst, patron of poets, an early and prominent member of the Jacobean court, for fourteen years a favorite of Queen Anne's, Lady Mary Wroth was born to a social legitimacy even her uncle did not possess.[2] Perhaps more importantly, she was also niece to Mary Sidney Herbert, the countess of Pembroke, who had earned fame as a writer herself as well as for her patronage of literature. The highly visible social acceptance of Mary Sidney's writing, even though offered as adjuncts to her dead brother's canon, seems to have established the possibility of public female authorship for Wroth as an early and intimately familial fact. Poets such as John Davies, Joshua Sylvester, and Ben Jonson praised her and her poetry and saw her achievements specifically in terms of her membership in the Sidney family.[3]

Wroth elected to write not in her aunt's religious genres, but in her uncle's exotic and erotic mode, thereby making her as vulnerable as she proved later to be to a powerful Jacobean courtier's attack. Thus, although Wroth had a female model, she did not follow it, and consequently took real political risks in writing as she did.[4] Lord Denny castigated her for the unwomanly project of writing at all: for him, such an act virtually negated her sex:

> Hermaphrodite in show, in deed a monster
> As by thy words and works all men may conster
> .   .   .   .   .   .   .   .   .   .
> Work o' the Workes leave idle books alone
> For wise and worthyer women have writte none.
> (Roberts, pp. 32–33)

At the start of the scandal, in a letter to the duke of Buckingham, Wroth offered to recall the book, but there is no evidence that any effort was actually made to stop publication. Later, apparently, she answered Denny's poem, point for point: "Your spitefull words against a harmless booke / Shows that an ass much like the sire doth looke"—a poem she sent to him and also to friends who, she hoped, would intercede for her in the controversy.[5]

While the power Sidney's (initially scandalous) work has for Wroth as her major precursor may for some be thought to be a liability in that it limits the kind of claim she can make for artistic originality, the close relationship which her work bears to her uncle's writing has a distinctly positive function for a criticism that seeks to assess the significance of gender on her authorial practice. Because Mary Wroth uses her uncle's texts in a process that sometimes becomes one of virtually self-conscious revision, we may gauge the sexual difference of their authorities in the specific details of her many revisionary moves. The shared family gives them an experience as similar as we are likely to get for two writers of the period; what differs in their experience of that shared society, then, is quintessentially, if not solely, their gender; through Sidney and Wroth we may perceive the radically different ways in which their sex determined what their experience could be.

Wroth's revision of her uncle's forms may also show us something more locally significant than the large-scale historical question of sexual difference in poetic authority. Because Wroth's *Urania,* like her uncle's *Arcadia,* scatters poems throughout the prose, a comparison of the two may provide hints about how the social practice of versifying changed

from the Elizabethan to the Jacobean courts. Wroth's different place-
ment of the poems, her assignment of verses in a different manner, as
well as the different manner and matter of the verses themselves, thus
tell us something about the social function of unprinted poetry as it cir-
culated throughout a (changing) social elite. In this sense, Philip
Sidney's *Arcadia* poems are more pivotally important than the sonnet
sequence by her father, Robert Sidney. Like the verse scattered through-
out the *Arcadia,* the *Urania* poems are controlled by their prose
contexts.[6] Sir Philip Sidney has recently become of central interest to
contemporary criticism of Renaissance culture, with its renewed con-
cern for the social and political praxis of Renaissance poetry, primarily
because his social role as Elizabethan courtier put him in a position to
make at least a potential intervention into actual power relations. It has
therefore become possible to make new claims for a rereading of
Sidney's poetry particularly as the lyrics themselves address their own
social function.[7] This is, of course, true of the enormously influential
sonnet cycle *Astrophil and Stella,* but it is also true of the often over-
looked verse of the *Arcadia.* The importance of these lyrics, then, may be
not so much their actual content and formal experimentation as the cues
they offer us for understanding the social function of poetry by their
presence within their own fictionalized social context—that is, the fic-
tive world in which they were written to be read.[8] Similarly, Wroth's
work reflects on a court culture she knew firsthand, and offers clues to
the political importance (or lack of it) enjoyed by versifying within it.

Because Wroth's rewrite of her uncle's romance recasts a text which
he had already revised, it will also be useful to keep in mind Sidney's
changing plans for his book; as family member, Wroth would have had
direct access to the two separate versions and all that their conflicting
states might imply about Sidney's own changing sense of his authority.[9]
The more comic and scandalous first manuscript version, *The Old Ar-
cadia,* being the private family possession, would doubtless have had a
special appeal for Wroth. Not only is it a text she could easily have
known (thus making her the only writer in the history of English liter-
ature for whom it *is* an important version), the holograph manuscript
itself is one her book-loving cousin William Herbert, as his mother's
heir, might have expected to inherit and value. As a first cousin who
bore him two illegitimate children, Wroth may have known this privi-
leged copy well. However, she begins her published romance with a
direct allusion to the far better known published revision, *The New Ar-
cadia.*

In the opening scene of *The Countess of Mountgomerie's Urania*—a
work which runs to 558 pages in its printed section and is continued in

another unpublished part about two-thirds as long—Wroth places at
center stage a character who is absent from Sidney's opening scene. The
revised *New Arcadia* begins by presenting two shepherds, Strephon and
Claius, who lament the absence of their beloved Urania, a shepherd lass
whose love has ennobled them and raised them from the status of lowly
shepherds to true poets. The absent Urania thus may have signaled for
Sidney the revision of his text upward in status, from lowly pastoral and
private family toy, to fully heroic, potentially public romance.[10] In
Wroth's text this same character inaugurates a further revision of the
romance form; this time Urania is not absent but present. It is the shep-
herdess herself who appears, alone in the pastoral landscape, and
laments:

> Alas Urania said she . . . of any miserie that can befall woman, is not
> this the most and greatest which thou art falne into? Can there be any
> neare the unhappiness of being ignorant, and that in the highest kind,
> not being certaine of mine own estate or birth? (I.i.i)

The shift in pronouns from the "thou" of an apostrophized self-address
to the more logical first-person "I" immediately betrays the radically
unstable speaking position of this character, so specifically gendered
female, in having suffered the greatest misfortune that can befall
"woman."[11] Where Strephon and Claius celebrate their high-aspiring
knowledge while lamenting their Urania's absence, Wroth's Urania
loses the base of her identity by learning that she is highborn:

> Why was I not stil continued in the beleefe I was, as I appeare, a Shep-
> herdes, and Daughter to a Shepherd? My ambition then went no higher
> then this estate, now flies it to a knowledge; then was I contented, now
> perplexed. O ignorance, can thy dulness yet procure so sharpe a pain?
> and that such a thought as makes me now aspire unto knowledge? How
> did I ioy in this poore life being quiet? blest in the love of those I took for
> parents, but now by them I know the contrary, and by that knowledge,
> not to know my selfe. (I.i.i)

Where Sidney's shepherds gain from an absent Urania a self-awareness
that is the truest sign of humanist discourse—because it carries a sense
of self-worth beyond class—Wroth's shepherdess Urania discovers a
knowledge that knows it does not know itself. Thus, while Wroth
places the female character center-stage, she has her speak a complete
lack of self-presence. Her new knowledge is that, in not knowing her
family (and therefore her class), she does not know herself.

Undomesticated in her grief, unfamiliar, unknown, "her very soul
turned into morning" (p. 2), Urania speaks extempore a fourteen-line
English sonnet in which she laments her similarity to Echo:

> Unseene, unknowne, I here alone complaine
> To Rocks, to Hills, to Meadowes, and to Springs,
> Which can no helpe returne to ease my paine,
> But back my sorrowes the sad Eccho brings.[12]

Although the poem is about Echo, it is not an echo-poem, such as, for instance, Philisides' hexameters in Sidney's Second Eclogues, to which Urania's poem bears resemblance.[13] There is no enacted response to Urania's lamentations, and therefore no antiphonal opposition between Echo and the speaker whereby Echo recasts the last words of the male poet to create her own meaning. The missing female part of the text is itself significant. There is no description of what Echo does but rather an insinuation of the uncanny resemblance between the speaker and the selfless nymph, whose voices, however doubly resounding, tend to collapse into a single "monefull voice," as in a self-consciously bonded female experience.

> Thus still encreasing are my woes to me,
> Doubly resounded by that monefull voice,
> Which seems to second me in miserie,
> And answere gives like friend of mine owne choice.

It is not so much that Echo reflects the speaker's misery, as that the speaker and Echo are shown to be so similar in their grieving that together they become a unit to which alternate features of the landscape are "others."

> Thus only she doth my companion prove,
> The others [Rocks, Hills, etc.] silently doe offer ease:
> But those that grieve, a grieving note doe love;
> Pleasures to dying eies bring but disease.

Finally, in the couplet both share a death-in-life lack of existence:

> And such am I, who daily ending live,
> Wayling a state which can no comfort give.

This is recognizably Petrarchan discourse, the language of a lover lamenting the absence of the beloved; but here Urania speaks not to bewail a lost lover, but a lost sense of self as a (female) member of a family. One could say that Wroth subtly stages here her own imitation of her uncle's text (Philisides is Philip Sidney's persona for himself), and thus dramatizes her differently gendered mimicry of a tradition by allying herself with one of the few possible speaking parts for a female voice within that tradition—the character of Echo. Importantly, however, Wroth's use of Petrarchan discourse in which a female speaker laments her own lack of self-presence paradoxically works to insert that female into the generically well-defined position of the Petrarchan speaker. Even though she is but a late echo of an already defunct genre, Wroth thus appears to appropriate quite self-consciously its discursive possibility for expressing a self, commenting as she does so (in the figure of Echo) on the very lateness of her start. Without a family for context, and therefore without a definite class position (although the reader understands the generically determined upward drift), the speaker is momentarily free to define her subject position by all its lacks. Imprecisely located as to class and family, the speaker speaks from a subject position identified only as female (that which can "befall woman").

This regendered appropriation of Petrarchan discourse is Wroth's typical maneuver throughout the text of the *Urania*. The creation of a speaking self for Urania does not, however, work to allow her a fully autonomous sense of subjectivity. Urania generates no plot for herself, and can only await a male's rescue (by her brother's surrogate) from her initial predicament of self-ignorance.[14] Yet the appropriation does allow a potential interiority for the female character, which, however empty, provides both a generically recognizable subject about which to speak as a female, as well as a fully developed poetic language for speaking.[15] In that sense, the use of Echo is a remarkably apt emblem for Wroth's achievement: Echo twists an already fixed meaning into a *different* sense. She may only repeat; yet by repeating afterwards and only incompletely, she differs and thereby gains her own differently gendered meaning. Echo stages the problem of the Jacobean female author so neatly one wonders if the decision to make Echo figure so prominently in the first lyric was not specifically and self-consciously determined by Wroth's own sense of her relation to her uncle's text.[16]

To glance briefly at the first two poems in the *Arcadia* is to grasp more immediately Urania's rhetorical predicament as a putative heroine of a female-authored Jacobean romance. Elizabethan Sidney opens his family toy—the unpublished *Old Arcadia*—with a prophecy about disordered family relations, the Delphic oracle's warning to Basilius that his family will appear to self-destruct. The patriarch's comic inability to cope with this threatened disorder sets up the plot—which persistently deals with the problems of patriarchal rule in the female-dominated Tudor dynasty.[17] Following directly upon this "poem" is the hero's decision to cross-dress and present himself as an Amazon warrior princess. The first real sonnet in the text, then, is Pyrocles'/Philoclea's consideration of his own transformation addressed to his beloved (but absent) lady.[18] "Transformed in show, but more transformed in mind" (p. 26), Pyrocles/Philoclea confesses himself to have been false to himself, overthrown by love:

> Thus reason to his servants gives his right
> Thus is my power transformed to your will.
> What marvel, then, I take a woman's hue,
> Since what I see, think, know, is all but you?

Having risked a simultaneous class and gender derogation, surrendering greater right to a social inferior's will, the speaker is apparently transformed into the thing he loves, a woman. He has suffered none of these things of course; rather the transvestism of Pyrocles' disguise allows Sidney a great deal of comic fun, freeing him to play with the notion of patriarchy, which gives power not only to males over females but to older males over younger males (and thus old Basilius ridiculously falls in love with young Pyrocles/Philoclea). All the complications of male mastery of the female other in Petrarchan discourse, itself masquerading as submission, are made risibly manifest in Pyrocles' cross-dressing.

Any problematic downshift in social status Pyrocles might have taken on in his cross-dressing is handled by the immediate appearance of a parodic blazon of feminine beauty in dispraise of Mopsa. The language of gender difference is reregistered as class difference in a burlesque "sonnet" written in the plodding (but very popular) Poulter's measure:

> What length of verse can serve brave Mopsa's good to show,
> Whose virtues strange, and beauties such, as no man them may know.
> .  .  .  .  .  .  .  .  .  .  .  .  .  .  .
> Her forehead jacinth like, her cheeks of opal hue
> Her twinkling eyes bedecked with pearl, her lips of sapphire blue.
> (Pp. 27–28)

The control over the female body exerted by the parodic blazon is here more remarkably aggressive than usual, perhaps because of the strange rhetorical positions of the cross-dressed and class-disguised heroes.[19]

In the opening two poems in both texts, gender and class identity are juxtaposed and repositioned. Prince Pyrocles cross-dresses and borrows the erotic power of the female, but is protected against loss of status by the immediate parodic denigration of the lower-class female, as well as by his previous identification as prince (in contrast to Urania). The fluidity of the relationship between the male self and female other in Petrarchism is established as an elite discourse for aristocratic or royal figures. (Mopsa, the lower-class female figure, serves the same function again, making safe from real class transgression Musidorus' disguise as a shepherd; in the pastoralism of Musidorus' masquerade the class question of Pyrocles' gender transformation is echoed and made explicit.)[20]

Urania's problematic shift in class position, by finding voice instantly in the Petrarchan language of a spurned lover, reregisters cross-class movement as gender shift; her loss of female class identity is like the male lover's discovery of a new interiority through his engulfing love and his lady's refusal. I do not think it is necessary to posit a great deal of critical self-consciousness on the part of Wroth's chiastic relation to Sidney's text, she substituting for his approach to class instability through the terms of gender, her consideration of gender redefinition in terms of class identity. It is not necessary to assume that Wroth understood what Sidney was doing in order for her to reverse his ideological formula with such neatness. The two languages of politics and gender come closely coded together in any society and seem to have been especially intertwined in the absolutist period of the Elizabethan and Jacobean courts.[21] Each can easily be substituted, and confused, for the other. Suffice it to say that Wroth revises the Perdita-like position of her actually royal shepherdess to make it specifically consider gender; Wroth loses no time having any characters contend that they suspected Urania's real class from her "natural" behavior. Instead Urania confronts, in as socially neutralized a context as can be generically managed, her female individuality. The language that is culturally accessible for expressing this problem of new *female* interiority is Petrarchan discourse.

In providing the narrative context for the second poem in the *Urania*, Wroth makes this shared speaking position absolutely explicit. In a direct imitation of Pyrocles' discovery of Gynecia's candle-lit sonnet on a sheet of paper left in a cave in the *Old Arcadia*, on page two of Wroth's romance Urania comes upon a similar sheet of inscribed candle-lit paper in a cave. On the paper is a conventional Petrarchan poem by Perissus, who, lovelorn, has withdrawn into the cave to lament his sorrow "all alone in silence":

> Hatefull all thought of comfort is to me,
> Despised day, let me still night possesse;
> Let me all torments feel in their excesse,
> And but this light allow my state to see.
> Which still doth wast, and wasting as this light,
> Are my sad dayes unto eternall night.
>
> (Roberts, pp. 148)

Urania immediately announces the similarity of her own predicament: "Alas Urania (sigh'd she)! How well doe these words, this place, and all agree with thy fortune? sure poore soule thou wert heere appointed to spend thy daies, and these roomes ordain'd to keep thy tortures" (I.i.3).

Yet however much she protests, Urania's position is not finally coherent with the Petrarchan speaker's. She is not yet in love, and therefore lacks the "other" term to which she may oppose, and so identify, herself. Pyrocles addresses himself to the female other whose powerful otherness (even if absent) assures his masculinity, whatever his disguise. Benighted Perissus addresses despised day and the loss of his married mistress. Urania addresses no one but herself, occasioning the unstable pronoun slippages which mark all her soliloquies. The plot calls attention to the distinct difference between Urania and Perissus, when Urania advises him to go out and seek his beloved, to have faith that the woman still lives and can be saved. Urania does not accompany him in his quest (as, say, Britomart accompanied Scudamour in a similar plot maneuver); instead, she remains where she is and waits passively to be discovered.[22] Nor is she disappointed for long, as—soon enough—a knight named Parselius comes upon her in her self-ignorant state. It turns out that he is on a quest, seeking the lost sister of his best friend, Amphilanthus. Parselius correctly guesses that Urania is this lost sister and so he decides to take her back to Amphilanthus' family to get a more certain identification. On the long journey back, Urania falls in love with Parselius; they are soon separated by the magic enchantments of romantic plot deferrals, in this case a violent storm that blows them from the Bay of Naples to Cyprus, Venus' isle. And in any event, once in love, Urania sings no more songs.

It is given to another character, the heroine of the romance, to occupy the privileged position of the Petrarchan poet. Pamphilia is a queen, sister to Parselius, soon friend to Urania, and the most self-conscious, poetry-producing "author" among all the characters. Together the two women provide double heroines to match Musidorus and Pyrocles. Like Sidney's men, they are cousins, and at least initially each falls in love with the other's brother (Urania, however, loses her love for Parselius, Pamphilia's brother, when she is washed by her brother Amphilanthus in a magic water that purges her of her passion; she ultimately falls in love with someone else, much to Pamphilia's surprise).

A poet with a reputation of her own, Pamphilia writes her first poem in the text on the occasion of becoming jealous of what she fears is Amphilanthus' love for another woman. A potential rivalry thus sets the stage for the most self-conscious poetic performance in the text. Although, as the narrator points out, Pamphilia is "excellent in writing," few of the papers in her "little Cabinet" please her, so she "writ these verses." There follows a Petrarchan poem perfectly conventional in all respects, save for gender; thus, the male lover's eyes "killingly disclose / Plagues, famines, murder in the fullest store / But threaten more" (I.i.51; Roberts, *Poems of Lady Wroth*, p. 148). Soon after writing this sonnet, Pamphilia is as ashamed of her "idleness" in love and in writing about love as ever Astrophil was: "Fie passion (said she) how foolish canst thou make us? and when with much paine and business thou hast gain'd us, how dost thou then dispose us unto folly, making our choicest wits testimony to our faces of our weaknesses, and, as at this time doest, bring my own hands to witnesse against me, unblushingly showing my idlenesses to mee." Her response to the predicament is harsher than Astrophil's, fulfilling the harsher social commands against publishing female desire: "Then took shee the new-writ lines, and as soone almost as shee had given them life, she likewise gave them buriall" (I.i.52).

Pamphilia's predicament as a female sonneteer is made more specifically immediate in the next sonnet she writes; because it is a close imitation of Pamela's sonnet "Do not disdaine, O straight upraised pine" (*OA*, p. 174; Ringler, p. 77), we may the more concretely gauge Wroth's revisionary act of writing about the predicament of her gender. It is important first to note the overarching difference between the two contexts for the poems: in Sidney's text, Pamela has happily allowed herself to be taken off with Musidorus, trusting to his self-restraint and loyalty. Her poem is part of a love duet, for he writes a companion poem on other trees. Her poem insists upon her virtue—a problematic thing at the moment, for having allowed herself to be carried off, her virtue is profoundly at risk. Immediately after the recitation of the poems in the *Old Arcadia*, Musidorus plans to rape Pamela; he does not follow through on his intentions only because he is interrupted by the sudden appearance of a peasant mob (the scene was thoroughly revised by the countess of Pembroke before being published in her version of the *Arcadia*). By contrast, in the *Urania*, Pamphilia has withdrawn to her secret garden to continue engraving on a tree a poem she has started earlier. Sidney's poem emphasizes the difference, the implicit agon, between the speaker and the apostrophized tree, who vie with each other in virtue, however much they share a superficial similarity. Wroth's poem insists upon the pain Pamphilia shares with the tree; again Wroth collapses rather than creates differences: the speaker and the tree share a similar torment.

Sidney's Italian sonnet opens with a conceit that stresses the straightness of both tree and Pamela's virtue. However, because her thoughts are more deeply wounded than it, she cannot think that "My inward hurt should spare thy outward rine":

> Do not disdaine, O straight upraised pine,
> That wounding thee, my thoughts in thee I grave;
> Since that my thoughts, as straight as straightness thine,
> No smaller wound—alas! far deeper have.

The sestet presents the twist that, however opposed tree and speaker are, "yet still, fair tree, lift up thy stately line"—a line which includes not only the tree's long-lived height but now the stately verses that the tree continues to testify about Pamela's virtue. The poem closes with a couplet that tightly draws the paradox of the female in Pamela's position; in typical Sidney fashion, it overturns the logic of the first twelve lines and leaves the conceit of the tree utterly behind.

> My heart my word, my word hath giv'n my heart.
> The giver giv'n from gift shall never part.

The crux of the whole plot of the *Old Arcadia,* of course, is that the proper giver of Pamela—that is, her father, Basilius—has specifically refused to give her, having withdrawn in terror of the prophecy which forecast misfortune with Pamela's courtship. She is heir to the throne and as such would have been far more limited in her choice of suitable suitor than any other female in the realm. Being most inappropriately both giver and gift, Pamela may wish to bestow herself where she desires, but in doing so, she risks all—as the attempted rape and rebellion subsequently reveal. Sidney's tree-poems artfully outline the problem Pamela faces: even though the "root" of her desire is virtuous and constant, her virtue offers no solution to the problem posed by her attempt to be giver of herself as a gift. The illogic of the couplet's "paradox" makes the Elizabethan sex/gender system explicit.

While Pamela comes up against something of a systemic limit in the last two lines of the poem, through her Sidney ventriloquizes a very active speaking subject. In contrast, although Wroth's Pamphilia commands her tree to do any number of things, her poem enforces a similarity rather than a dramatic agon between arborial addressee and speaker. Wroth's speaker is nearly as immobile as a tree.

> Beare part with me most straight and pleasant Tree,
> And imitate the Torments of my smart
> Which cruell Love doth send into my heart,
> Keepe in thy skin this testament of me:
>             (I.i.75; Roberts, p. 149)

Wroth's poet asks the tree to join in sympathy with, and to imitate, the speaker in her pain. Sidney's Pamela—herself a cruel mistress who denies Musidorus—confesses that she has given herself her own wounds ("Thus cruel to myself"); Wroth's Pamphilia more traditionally complains that she has been a passive subject of love's mastery. In the second half of the octave, it is indeed difficult to say at first which is being engraved—the tree or the speaker:

> Which Love ingraven hath with miserie,
> Cutting with grief the unresisting part,
> Which would with pleasure soone have leanrd loves art,
> But wounds still cureless, must my rulers bee.

Only as we read on do we understand how that which love has engraved is the "testament" of the grieving speaker and not the tree.

Wroth's sestet pursues a similarity Sidney's poem neglects altogether, that is, the sap of the tree being like a lover's tears. Wroth makes use of this baroque possibility in the prose introduction to the poem; thus Pamphilia "finished a Sonnet, which at other times shee had begunne to ingrave in the barke of one of those fayre and straight Ashes, causing that sapp to accompany her teares for love" (I.i.75). In the poem itself, the sap becomes the tree's tears; its weeping is similar to the speaker's heart-blood that "drops."

> Thy sap doth weepingly bewray thy paine,
> My heart-blood drops with stormes it doth sustaine,
> Love senceless, neither good nor mercy knows
> Pitiles I do wound thee, while that I
> Unpitied, and unthought on, wounded crie:
> Then out-live me, and testifie my woes.
>                          (Roberts, pp. 149–50)

The blood-drops recur throughout the poetry in the *Urania,* becoming something of a signature, as well as, perhaps, a debt-acknowledging reference to Spenser's baroque image for sadomasochistic sonneteering itself.[23] The ultimate difference between the tree and the speaker, however, is that the tree will live on, the speaker being a mere human mortal. The implication is that the speaker expects to "die" of love's torments sooner rather than later. The notion of the long-lived tree—testimony to Pamela's long-delayed gratification of desire—here records in Wroth's poem not only the speaker's love-death, but it also implicitly affirms the immortality of the verse. Pamela does not expect to be remembered as a poet. Pamphilia at least considers the possibility.

The scene of Pamphilia's writing a poem on the tree soon turns to a confrontation not between two lovers, as in the context of the *Arcadia,* but between Pamphilia and Antissia, a rival for Amphilanthus' love. Taxed by Antissia's logical argument that the testimony of "your owne hand in yonder faire Ashe is witness against you," Pamphilia still denies that she is in love with Amphilanthus or anyone else, arguing that "many Poets write as well by imitation, as by sense of passion; therefore this is no proofe against me" (I.i.67 [sic]). Overturning her uncle's possibly disingenuous argument in favor of *energia* in the *Apology for Poetry,* Wroth makes Pamphilia claim the possibility of a vocational rather than a personal motivation to write. She mendaciously claims that she writes not because she is in love but because she wants to write. "It is well said (answered Antissia) in your own defence." Antissia is not, of course, persuaded of the truth of Pamphilia's claims, but they finally come to a jealous truce, uncomfortable friends who walk out of the garden, "holding each other by the arm, with as much love," the narrator ironically remarks, "as love in them could joyn" (I.i.79). Pamphilia's attempt to hide the painfully real source of her writing from Antissia by proclaiming an ambition to be a poet ironically reverses Astrophil's persistent claims to the contrary: unlike the rival (hack) poets who fake love, he does not write for fame at all, but only to persuade Stella to love him. The reversal suggests that there might be different literary risks for the different genders in Petrarchan poetry at this time: a woman disguises her tabooed desire as conventional artistry, while a man masquerades his verbal mastery as petitioning passion.

Later, having passed a restless and tormented night, Antissia herself comes into the garden alone and sits under the same ash tree on which Pamphilia had written her sonnet. There "she was invited, either by her own passion, or the imitation of that excellent Lady, to put some of her thoughts in some kind of measure, so as shee perplexed with love, jealousie, and losse as shee beleeved, made this Sonnet" (I.i.94). Antissia is no mere rival poet, but a tragic character in her own right. The sestet emphasizes a restlessness which later turns to madness:

> Obedience, feare, and love doe all conspire
> A worth-less conquest gain'd to ruine me,
> Who did but feele the height of blest desire
> When danger, doubt, and losse, I straight did see.
> Restlesse I live, consulting what to do,
> And more I study, more I still undoe.
> (I.i.94; Roberts, p. 151)

Antissia's rivalry with Pamphilia, and the introduction of Pamphilia's first instance of poetic production in the context of that rivalry, establishes the profession of poetry as an agonistic activity, even among females. The proliferation of sonnet cycles in the last decade of the sixteenth century exemplified the competitive nature of the Petrarchan enterprise.[24] What Wroth has done is reflect that rivalry in her jealous women poets. Do they feel jealousy and therefore write or do they feel jealous in order to write? The narrator quite specifically refuses to choose, thereby asserting that the passion of the female heroines may be no more mimetically real, or any less purely discursive a strategy, than it was for a male Petrarchan poet.[25]

The insertion of a female response into the tradition of Petrarchan lyric—Wroth's self-scrutinizing originality in the genre—is shared out among myriad other female poets. A specific instance is a fishergirl's spontaneous lyric while she fishes streamside, overheard by the hero Amphilanthus and his friend. In context, then, the poem is a representative female response to the male-authored tradition of the blazon poem:

> Lying bare
> To despaire,
> When you thus anotamise [sic]
> All my body, my heart prise:
> Being true
> Just to you.
> Close the Truncke, embalme the Chest,
> Where your power still shall rest,
> Joy entombe,
> Loves just doome.
> (U22; Roberts, p. 162)

A critique and a correction, the response both points out the sadism even as it masochistically embraces the pain, turning suffering into a monumental claim for female stability and constancy beyond death.[26]

In her analysis of "feminine identity" in the *Urania,* Carolyn Ruth Swift concludes that "Wroth viewed society as destructive of a woman's sense of self."[27] This is particularly so, according to Swift, because Wroth does not allow her heroine Pamphilia to experience an autonomous existence, one separate from her obsessive love for Amphilanthus, Urania's most noble brother: "Wroth shows that a woman's self-worth may rest on the admiration of a man whom she may in many ways dislike, she also shows that this good opinion can therefore arise only when a woman rejects her own feelings, desires, and abilities. The resulting confusion renders true self-awareness impossible" (p. 343).[28] Such a formulation of the problem, however, assumes that there is an essential "true self-awareness" the power to have which society either gives or takes away. If, instead of burdening Wroth's fiction with expectations that it will deliver a full, modern sense of (female) self, we look for an attempt to construct that autonomous "self" out of the discursive possibilities already available in the culture, we may find ourselves less disappointed with Wroth's articulation of woman's position.

It is entirely possible that by exaggerating—in a feminine voice—the very masochistic-sounding laments of her borrowed Petrarchan poetics, Wroth is in the process of forging a language for the very "self" that might potentially exist separate from the institutions (such as marriage) that inexorably organized women's social lives. As Swift herself notes, Wroth's heroines seldom find love within marriage, often valuing "libertie more than marriages bondage" (p. 342). Although, as Paul Salzman points out, "Wroth breaks romance convention by depicting marriage rather than courtship," strikingly enough, Wroth is not in the least concerned with the conduct of a woman fulfilling the social role of *wife*.[29] While vast numbers of her female characters are married, we only discover this fact as an ancillary social detail which explains—insofar as the situation needs explaining (and it often does not)—why a given woman may not contemplate a full sexual union with a given man.[30] Wroth presents a full portrait of marriage as she traces the individually varying, but socially constant, end result of the traffic in women; but she is not interested in the individual wife, that is, in her experiences *as* wife.[31] Rather she is persistently interested in the predicament whereby a woman is "married" to one man but "wedded in affection" to another (I.iii.413). In the deferral of the consummation with the second, or in the gap between the two objects of female attention, one proper (the husband), and other improper (the beloved), Wroth locates the space for attending to the female herself. In the published *Urania,* that discursive space can be said to have stretched to 558 pages.

If, as we have come to learn, a sense of "self" is itself socially constructed and cannot therefore exist prior to its social construction (or destruction), then what we may in fact see in Wroth's text is her attempt to articulate a woman's social experience that is specifically not that of the wife, the one role upon which all discussion of female experience focused in the seventeenth century. Pamphilia loves Amphilanthus without hope of marrying him. Furthermore, there is no good reason given for her not marrying him; being a crowned royal, she does not need to marry. It would appear that the only reason for their not marrying is their remarkable reticence in declaring their love to each other (he does love her deeply, even though, as fickle man, he is constantly involved with numbers of other women). The reason for their thoroughly unmotivated deferral of desire, however, is not far to seek: were Pamphilia to have married Amphilanthus, she would have become a wife, and an entirely different set of terms would have impinged on their relations.[32] Her erotic attachment apparently aims at a result different from wifedom, or rather, at the Petrarchan lack of any result, the purely unconsummated, unchanging continuation, an "end" endemic to continually dilating romance which can generically imagine closure only as apocalypse.[33] Pamphilia's affection for Amphilanthus is so relentless it becomes an issue in the text. Urania tries to talk Pamphilia out of her constancy. Again, by juxtaposing a comparable scene from Sidney's earlier texts we may be better able to see what Wroth might have been after.

In what must be a replay of Musidorus' attempt to dissuade Pyrocles' from loving in the *Arcadia,* Urania tries to talk Pamphilia out of her excessive fidelity to the quintessentially faithless Amphilanthus, whose very name means "lover of two" (p. 250).

> Where is that judgment, and discreet govern'd spirit, for which this and all other places that have been happy with the knowledge of your name hath made you famous? will you now fall under the low groanes of the meanest esteemed passion? Where is that resolution, which full of brave knowledge, despised the greatest Princes when they wore loves livery; must this sinke, while his tossing follies swimme? shall your excellent vertues bee drowned in the Sea of weaknesse? call your powers together, you that have been admired for a Masculine spirit, will you descend below the poorest Feminine in love? (p. 398)

Because Pamphilia is a crowned queen, Urania can even use one argument Musidorus cannot use with mere Prince Pyrocles: "if your people knew this, how can they hope of your government, that can no better governe one poor passion? how can you command others, that cannot master your selfe; or make laws, that cannot counsel, or soveraignize over a poore thought?" (p. 398). Pamphilia's defense is different from that of Pyrocles, who against Musidorus' attack, defends women as a species, and ends, finally, by fainting (proving his weakness). Instead, Pamphilia insists that her constancy, *especially* in the face of his inconstancy, constitutes her claim to a stable self:

> To leave him for being false would shew my love was not for his sake, but mine owne, that because he loved me, I therefore loved him, but when hee leaves I can do so to. O no deere Cousen I loved him for himselfe, and would have loved him had hee not loued mee, and will love though he dispise me. . . . Pamphilia must be of a new composition before she can let such thoughts fall into her constant breast, which is a Sanctuary of zealous affection, and so well hath love instructed me, as I can never leave my master nor his precepts, but still maintaine a vertuous constancy. (p. 400)

As paradoxical as it may indeed sound, Pamphilia's point is that in loving him when he does not love her in return, she shows her constant self, by contrast. If she loved him only as a return for his loving her, the desire would have its origin in the male, female desire remaining a mere reflective repetition of male desire. In order to locate an active desire in her female self, she needs *it*—her own will—to be autonomous. While she appears to depend on him, taking her identity from him, she in fact insists upon her identity as opposed to his. Her constancy is an act of willful self-definition. She "will love though he despise me."

Urania, for her part, continues to lament such crazed constancy:

> 'Tis pitie said Urania, that ever that fruitlesse thing Constancy was taught you as a vertue, since for vertues sake you will loue it, as having true possession of your soule, but understand, this vertue hath limits to hold it in, being a vertue, but thus that it is a vice in them that breake it, but those with whom it is broken, are by the breach free to leave or choose againe where more staidnes may be found. (p. 400)

If Wroth can here have Urania sound so sensible, we do not have to mis-take Pamphilia's acceptance of the tenet of absolute constancy for the author's own mystification. It remains doubly important to notice what Wroth has achieved: Pamphilia enacts a traditional, Griselda-like vir-tue, yet for the woman who is specifically not fulfilling the duties of a wife. We are forced to ask, what purpose could Pamphilia's obstinate constancy be serving? One answer is surely that her constancy becomes the stable position from which she can complain (poetically) of her lover's *in*constancy; Pamphilia pleads that Urania forgive her and "when you have me with you, you must let me complain unto my selfe" (p. 400). Pamphilia's "self" here is constructed as her own audience for her complaint. Urania's presence is a facilitating part of Pamphilia's ad-dress to herself, while Urania's complained-against brother Amphilan-thus is, by his sister's presence, at least implicitly on the horizon (one expects he will some day get the message: it will be sent). Virtuous female complaint is a powerful mode, authorized in its virtue by the very delay in publishing it to a male audience.

Upon the dichotomy between constancy and inconstancy Wroth erects her own categories of gender difference. Females are, by gender redefinition, constitutionally constant. By contrast, as the opposing oth-ers, males are helplessly inconstant. As Veralinda explains to Musalina (a lady with whom Amphilanthus has a passing attachment):

> take heed brave Lady, trust not too much; for believe it, the kindest, lovingest, passionatest, worthiest, loveliest, valiantest, sweetest, and best man, will, and must change, not that he, it may bee, doth it purposely, but tis their naturall infirmitie, and cannot be helped. (I.iii.375)

Veralinda is aware that this counsel—perhaps even its mystification of calling "natural" any culturally sanctioned behavior—is the neat re-verse of former gender differences:

> It was laid to our charge in times passed to bee false, and changing, but
> they who excell us in all perfections, would not for their honours sake, let
> us surpasse them in any one thing, though that, and now are much more
> perfect, and excellent in that then wee, there is nothing left us, that they
> excell us not in, although in our greatest fault. (I.iii.375)

By the simple expedient of self-consciously and ironically reversing the
usual dichotomy, Wroth wittily reorganizes gender difference. The very
self-conscious wittiness of Veralinda's sententia should not, however,
blind us to the fine fit it makes with the rest of the text. Her remarks are
not merely a joke. In newly becoming the inconstant other, masculine
fickleness stabilizes by its "natural" instability the constant sameness of
the female. Poem after poem of complaint about male inconstancy af-
firms the productive position this stance allows: a constant female self
lamenting male change. All Pamphilia's poems speak to this one theme:
"Cruell Remembrance alas now be still, / Put me not on the Racke to
torture me" (Roberts, p. 170); "Unquiet griefe search farder, in my
hart, / If place be found which thou has nott possest" (Roberts pp. 170–
71);

> Losse my molester at last patient be,
> And satisfied with thy curst selfe, or more
> Thy mournefull force thus oft on perjurd love,
> To wast a life which lives by mischeifes fee.
> (Roberts p. 171)

Paul Salzman calls Wroth's approach "a feminist reading of the
romance form."[34] According to him, her critique of the "less salubrious
underside of the heroic and courtly code" does not merely overturn ro-
mance conventions; she also uses the genre "to explore the situation of
women in the courtly society which she knew so well" (p. 143). Wroth's
ironical reversal of gender relations is de-idealizing, of course, and is of
a piece with the flare-up of the *querelle des femmes* surrounding Joseph
Swetnam's publication of a misogynistic tract in 1615, a half-decade or
so before Wroth published the *Urania*.[35] Wroth's critique of masculine
disloyalty and her concomitant praise of female fidelity—her very priv-
ileging of Pamphilia's "too feminine" patience—puts her distinctly in
the pro-woman camp, although the romance is anything but polemical.
One of Wroth's investments in the book, as the scandal of its publication
made clear, was the retailing in narrative event the lives she observed. In
pursuing her verisimilar plotting, Wroth necessarily ends with repre-
senting the traffic in women as an inexorable shaper of their lives, the
only virtuous escape from which appears to have been into the cul-de-
sac of private poesis. It is indeed interesting that the one event we know

to be a roman à clef, the one to which Edward Denny so vehemently objected, involved paternal violence toward an only daughter who had made her husband jealous, justly or unjustly the narrator cannot say. The narrative emphasizes the violence of the two men: the husband ends up protecting his possibly errant wife from the savage attack of her father, even though it was he who had earlier broken open her cabinets, hunting for incriminating letters. The condemnation falls heaviest on the father (Denny's kinsman) for his rabid and unnatural violence, but the narrator (the husband's friend) acknowledges from the outset that young passion is very unsteady. The couple reconcile, however, and have two children, after which the wife dies, and the husband remarries, only to become estranged again, from his new wife. While the tone of the narrative is more rueful than cynical, Pamphilia smilingly concludes that such a story of unsteady desire will easily be matched by another eager suitor. The story thus confirms the danger to women of a masculine unsteadiness. The extratextual event of Denny's response only restaged in another arena the antifemale violence within the text.

Salzman finds her versimilarity to be one of Wroth's most original contributions to the development of prose fiction; it offered a "a new engagement with the minutiae of contemporary life, which makes it possible for the later political romances to encompass events of the Civil War in detail" (p. 141). Yet it is not merely in her versimilitude that Wroth's prose tactics offer effects for use in later royal romances; her Petrarchan poetics, based as they are on the poetic practice of a queen, have their own distinctly absolutist politics. These politics have some potential bearing on the problem of the subject.

It is not so much that erotic desire—which powers all of the plots in the *Urania*—did design much of the goings on in the Stuart court, but that erotic desire is another language for the nuanced flux of hierarchically organized power relations. Very early in the sixteenth century, Petrarchism had of course become an overtly political language, developing into a substitute political discourse, especially during the reign of Elizabeth. Courtly compliment to an unmarried queen easily took the form of Petrarchan address, and worldly ambition efficiently wore the livery of love during the cult of Elizabeth.[36]

A series of seven sonnets in the *Urania,* grouped under the heading of "Lindamira's Complaint," and standing in, as it were, for the eclogues that would ordinarily close the third book, form a very interesting testimony to the still interlinked discourses of Petrarchan eroticism and absolutist power, especially as the two involved the power of satellite royal females. The seven sonnets are introduced by a very pronounced set of hints that Lindamira's story is true; thus Pamphilia tells it "faigning it to be written in a French Story" (I.iii.423). One of the more famous Renaissance collections of French stories was, of course, the *Heptameron* by Marguerite de Valois, herself a real queen of Navarre, and sister of Francis I. Most significantly, the *Heptameron* very specifically insisted upon the truth of its tales. Its major difference from Boccaccio's *Decameron,* its named precursor, was that its stories were true: "une chose differente de Boccace, c'est de n'escrire nouvelle qui ne fust véritable histoire."[37] Wroth's choice to rehearse her own life's story in terms of a French story—especially because a signal event in Lindamira's life is the loss of her queen's favor—may owe something to French royal example. Wroth and Marguerite Valois share a "revolutionary" interest in verisimilar plotting.[38] After fourteen years' loyal service, Lindamira loses her queen's favor for no apparent reason, "all her favor was withdrawn as suddenly and directly, as if never had: Lindamira remaining," the narrator poignantly explains, "like one in a gay Masque, the night pass'd, they are in the old clothes again, and no appearance of what was; she yet was grieved to the heart because she truly lov'd her mistris" (I.iii.424). What is thus intriguing about the "story," especially as it is furthered by the poetry, is the peculiar doubleness of its relationship to Wroth's position as subject—speaking subject in her own text and political subject of her queen. Queen Pamphilia confesses that she found Lindamira's complaint outlined an "estate so neere [to] agree with mine, I put [it] into Sonnets" (I.iii.425). Lindamira's loss of her queen's favor is equal to Pamphilia's erotic loss. The double addressee, then, makes the poems work very ambiguously, to express a lament for both a male lover and for the lost favor of a female political superior. The economy of such a double purpose is made possible, of course, by the fiction of the "mistris" in both. Tyrannized over by a fickle queen or master/mistress, the speaker suffers the same pride of self in his or her humiliation, the female taking on the same subjection and subjectivity as the male.

> Some doe, perhaps, both wrong my love, and care,
> Taxing me with mistrust and Jelousie,
> From both which sinne in love like freedome, free
> I live, these slanders but new raised are.
> What though from griefe, my soule I doe not spare,
> When I percieve neglect's slight on me?
> While unto some the loving smiles I see
> I am not Jealous, they so well do fare.
> But doubt my selfe lest I lesse worthy am,
> Or that it was but flashes, no true flame,
> Dazzl'd my eyes, and so my humour fed.

If this be jealouise, then do I yeeld,
And doe confess I thus go arm'd to field,
For by such Jealousie my love is led.
                    (U43; Roberts, p. 178)

In a possible pun on her married name, jealous of her own self worth, Wroth shows herself a Sidney. She does not hesitate to blame the fickleness of Lindamira's queen as much as she blames Pamphilia's Amphilanthus. Their situations agree not only in the shared pain but in the insistent self-definition created in a relationship betrayed by the powerful other. Both of these self-instituting losses are furthermore underwritten by Pamphilia's self-sovereignty. Pamphilia as crowned royalty is not "trafficed" in; she is her own sovereign subject, a queen. From this position as monarch, she as female may the more easily inhabit the speaking position of the male "subject." In tracing the absolutist sympathies of Margaret Cavendish and Mary Astell, two polemically political seventeenth-century protofeminist woman authors, Catherine Gallagher has pointed out that "women were excluded from all state offices except that of monarch."[39] More important than this historical actuality, an identification with monarchical absolutism aids in the development of a female subjectivity: "The monarch becomes a figure for the self-enclosed, autonomous nature of any person" (p. 26), and the "ideology of the absolute monarch" in the seventeenth century allows a transition to "an ideology of the absolute self" (p. 25). Both Cavendish and Astell were polemically active Tories; while Wroth was merely a courtier, her focus in Lindamira's complaint on monarch-subject relations may be, in part, a poetic version of the other women's explicit arguments. In this sense, then, the history of Petrarchism in England did not disallow its use in a monarchical discourse.

It has been argued that a profoundly disturbing implication of Petrarchism is that, in the supposed coherence allowed the male speaking subject by his love of the absent female he continues to disperse, we are tricked into thinking that a union between a male and female presence has been experienced. The female addressee, in being the subject of the poem, is subjected to the cultural silence required by the discourse of Petrarchism. The Caelicas, Ideas, and Lauras do not need to exist in order for the poems to be.

While the practice of female poets in mid-sixteenth-century Italy and France would seem to give the lie to the proposal that Petrarchism aggressively enjoins the silence of the female, Wroth's own use of the mode does work to silence the male beloved, specifically Amphilanthus.[40] Although she assigns a vast number of her ambidextrous sonnets to male speakers throughout the text of the *Urania*, she never gives one to Amphilanthus. Her explicit motive is modesty about her poetic abilities; as the narrator explains, she is incapable of giving him a poem worthy of his talents:

> he put the rest of his thoughts into excellent verse, making such excelling ones, as none could any more imitate or match them, then equall his valour: so exquisite was he in all true virtues, and skill in Poetry, a quallitie among the best much prized and esteemed, Princes brought up in that, next to the use of Arms. . . . Many more, and far more excellent discourses, had he with himself, and such as I am altogether unable to set down, therefore leave them to be guessed at by those who are able to comprehend his worth. (I.i.112)

Such a suppression of what is here obviously offered as *the* privileged male voice of lyric authority provides a fascinating commentary on Mary Wroth's sense of the authority of her own lyric achievement. But first it is necessary to recognize that there is a possible biographical explanation for Wroth's refusal to grant us a poem by Amphilanthus. In the unpublished continuation of the romance, which exists only in Wroth's autograph manuscript (and which thus, as far as positive evidence goes, *had* no real publication). Amphilanthus does produce a poem, the second one in the manuscript, "Had I loved butt att that rate." It is a poem identified as William Herbert's in a number of manuscript collections. In part on the basis of this poem, Roberts positively identifies Amphilanthus as William Herbert.[41] It may thus be that Wroth intended her readers to recognize an identification for Amphilanthus but was reluctant to make it explicit through citation in the published part of the text. Had she supplied him with a poem of her own creation, the identification would have, in effect, been denied; however, it was apparently too risky to hint as directly as she does in the unpublished part by providing him one of Herbert's known verses.

Whatever might have been the motive biographically—and any such reasoning about it must remain merely speculative—the net effect is a silencing of Amphilanthus in the published volume of the romance. What is left of his authority after this silencing is a remarkable residue: to call it pure authority is to insist upon the centrality of his poetry to his vocation as central hero, a studied skill "next" only to his martial abilities. A crowned king himself, Amphilanthus' royalty, like Pamphilia's, grants to his invisible versifying a far higher vocational status than it had even in Sidney's *Arcadia*—where poems drop more inadvertently from the principals, like crowns and crownets from Mark Antony's pockets.

The nonappearance of Amphilanthus' poems has the practical effect of a subtle genre-shift as well; the narrator often paraphrases the (conventionally Petrarchan) conceits of Amphilanthus' complaints. We get the prose paraphrase in the text, but not the poem itself. (Just as the poems of Lindamira's complaint are Pamphilia's versifications of Lindamira's presumed prose laments.) Such a practice of substituting prose for poetry may derive from Sidney's argument that there is no difference between them—verse being only an "ornament" to properly poetic foreconceits, which are themselves necessarily paraphraseable in prose. Such paraphrase is also, however, a claim for the further legitimacy of prose fiction—and that a romance by a female might provisionally claim for itself the same kind of aristocratic power as that belonging to very privileged male-humanist-authored poetry.

In providing only prose paraphrases of Amphilanthus' verse, Wroth presents the Petrarchan poet in his pure author-function, that is, as part of what Foucault has called the establishment and continuation of the endless possibility of discourse. What we get is not Amphilanthus' poem but his discursive practice. In thus refusing to imitate a poem, Wroth instead represents the discourse and makes more immediate her attempt to insert her own female authority into it. Of course, because Petrarchan discourse is so resolutely gendered from its inception—a defining characteristic of it being, indeed, its play with gender—to re-gender it is to effect "a return to the origin," as Foucault puts it, the possibility for such a return being one of the proofs that a discourse is, in fact, a discourse. Such an act does not, in Foucault's terms, make of Mary Wroth an author (only Petrarch is "author" of Petrarchism). But Foucault's terms do allow us to see that Wroth has asked an essential question of Petrarchism: "what placements are determined for possible subjects?"[42] She has undertaken to discover, in effect, what sort of narrative maneuvers are necessary in order to make a place for the female subject within such a proto-modern discourse. To make greater claims for Wroth's authority than this is, perhaps, not useful at this time, especially when it still seems hardly more difficult for a female to be an author in the early seventeenth century than in the terms outlined by Foucault's essay: the very test case for the nonauthor in the essay being Ann Radcliffe, whose creation of the genre of gothic novel does not fit the requirements Foucault establishes for the author of a discursive practice. As the first female writer of a romance in the English language—a text which shares at least the overarching genre of romance with Radcliffe's—Wroth may not be an author of anything more than her own text. But she was one of the first to attempt to determine the various placements initially necessary for female authority in English; that in her case the place turned out to be within Petrarchist prose fiction, pioneered by her uncle, says not only a great deal about the social determination of any writing practice, but also about the fundamentally gendered nature of that poetry and its potential for creating the subject of modern prose fiction.

## Notes

1. Suzanne W. Hull, *Chaste, Silent, and Obedient: English Books for Women, 1475–1640* (San Marino: Huntington Library, 1982) summarizes in her title the main message of all the books printed for a female reading audience in the period. For a quick indication of just how repressive the injunctions could be felt to be, see the prefaces by various female authors collected in Betty Travitsky, ed., *The Paradise of Women: Writings by Englishwomen of the Renaissance* (Westport, Conn.: Greenwood Press, 1981).

2. It was a social legitimacy she did not retain, bearing two out-of-wedlock children to her first cousin, William Herbert, losing her sovereign's favor for some unspecified offense, and causing a scandal by publishing a roman à clef. For the details of her life, see Josephine A. Roberts, ed. *The Poems of Lady Wroth* (Baton Rouge: Louisiana State University Press, 1983), Introduction. All quotations of Wroth's poetry is from this edition, hereafter cited in the text.

3. The title page of the *Urania* made the family connection triply clear: "The Countess of Mountgomerie's URANIA. Written by the right honorable the Lady MARY WROTH, Daughter to the right Noble Robert, Earle of Leicester. And Neece to the ever famous and renowned Sir Philip Sidney knighte. And to the most excellent Lady Mary Countess of Pembroke, late deceased" (John Marriott and John Grismand: London, 1621); hereafter cited in the text by book and page number from Part I of *Urania*. For the poets' tributes, see Roberts, pp. 18–22.

4. The courtier who attacked Wroth for publishing *Urania* did so because an episode in the *Urania* retailed one of his family's scandals. More globally, however, and with a rather humorously transparent hypocrisy that says as much about the sexual politics of their shared court culture as it does about his character, Lord Denny condemned her for not following her illustrious aunt's example, instead writing on scurrilous topics: he writes to her praying that "you may redeeme the tym with writing as large a volume of heavenly layes and holy love as you have of lascivious tales and amorous toyes that at the last you may followe the rare, and pious example of your vertuous and learned Aunt, who translated so many godly books and especially the holly psalms of David, that no doubt now shee sings in the quier of Heaven those devine meditations which shee so sweetly tuned heer belowe, and which being left to us heer on earth will begett hir dayly more and more glory in heaven as others by them shalbe enlightened, who as so many trophies shall appear to her further exaltation in gods favour, with which prayer for you I end and rest / Your most wellwishing frend/ Edward Denny/ who for the great honor I bear somme of your noble allies and my deerly honored frends doe forbeare to write what I might" (Appendix, Roberts, p. 239).

5. See Roberts, pp. 33–36.

6. Roberts notes that many verbal echoes of Robert Sidney's poems.

7. See in particular Louis A. Montrose, "Celebration and Insinuation: Sir Philip Sidney and the Motives of Elizabethan Courtship." *Renaissance Drama,* n. s. 8 (1977):3–35; Arthur Marotti, "'Love is not Love': Elizabethan Sonnet Sequences and the Social Order," *ELH* 49 (1982): 396–429; Leonard Tennenhouse, *Power on Display: the Politics of Shakespeare's Genres* (New York and London: Methuen, 1986), pp. 17–42; Richard McCoy, *Sir Philip Sidney: Rebellion in Arcadia* (New Brunswick, N.J.: Rutgers University Press, 1979).

8. The Menippean form Sidney borrows from Sannazaro does not answer for all the social situations of the lyrics as texts. The fiction of Sannazaro's *Arcadia* is that the songs are sung in singing contests among, for the most part, unlettered herdsmen. Sidney immediately dispells this fiction in the remarkably *scripted* nature of verse production in Sidney's *Arcadia.* Cleophila's first song in the *Old Arcadia,* for example, is "made" before she sings it in the text. See Sir Philip Sidney, *The Old Arcadia,* ed. Katherine Duncan-Jones (Oxford: Oxford University Press, 1985), p. 26; hereafter cited in text as *OA.*

9. For a discussion of the complicated printing history of the *Old* and *New Arcadia,* see William A. Ringler, *The Poems of Sir Philip Sidney* (Oxford: Clarendon Press, 1962), p. 364; ten manuscripts of the *Old Arcadia* survive, suggesting that it had a nonprint publication of its own.

10. For a fuller argument about the change in status, see Maureen Quilligan, "Lady Mary Wroth: Female Authority and Family Romance," in *Unfolded Tales,* ed. George Logan and Gordon Teskey (Ithaca: Cornell University Press, 1989).

11. For a discussion of the problematically unstable speaking position of females at this point in history, see the fascinating and suggestive argument by Catherine Belsey in *The Subject of Tragedy: Identity and Difference in Renaissance Drama* (London and New York: Methuen, 1985), esp. pp. 149ff.

12. Roberts, p. 146.

13. Oh! I do know what guest I have met; it is echo. / 'Tis echo. Well met, echo, approach; then tell me thy will too. / I will too.
Sir Philip Sidney, *OA,* pp. 140–41; see "Pamphilia to Amphilanthus," no. 97, for an entire poem in Echo's voice (Roberts, p. 139).

14. Significantly, while there is an episode of male cross-dressing, no female character in the *Urania* cross-dresses as a male. The freedom Britomart—or Rosalind—gains by masculine disguise is not one Wroth allows her heroines. For a discussion of the anthropological importance of brothers in the portrait of patriarchy Wroth provides, see Quilligan (1989).

15. For a brief summary argument about the "recognizably modern mode of subjectivity" to be found in Petrarchism, see Louis A. Montrose, "The Elizabethan Subject and the Spenserian Text," in *Literary Theory/Renaissance Texts,* ed. Patricia Parker and David Quint (Baltimore: Johns Hopkins University Press, 1986), p. 325: "The Petrarchan persona is a distinctly masculine subject explicitly fashioned in relation to a feminine other . . . . he masters his mistress by inscribing her within his text, where she is repeatedly put together and taken apart—and, sometimes, killed."

16. The time lag—that is, the deferral—in Echo's sounding seems also to

stage "difference" in Derrida's sense. Echo enacts the fact that sexual difference in any period is based on the social construction of an opposition between male and female, with the female always providing the secondary, unstable, "opposite" term, which thereby allows a sense of the fixed significance to the positive *male* term. Wroth stages an explicitly gendered difference from her uncle Philip in "Pamphilia to Amphilanthus," no. 37 (Roberts, p. 111), addressed to "you blessed stars"; the speaker prefers to the lights reminiscent of Astrophil's Stella the sight of a specifically male beloved, "his grace," "his sight." For further application of a poststructuralist sense of sexual difference to Renaissance English culture, see Catherine Belsey, "Disrupting Sexual Difference: Meaning and Gender in the Comedies," in John Drakakis, ed. *Alternative Shakespeares* (New York and London: Methuen, 1985), pp. 167–90. For the rhetoric of secondariness in gender difference, see Patricia Parker, *Literary Fat Ladies: Rhetoric, Gender, Property* (New York: Methuen, 1987), esp. chap. 9, "Coming Second: Woman's Place."

17. For a discussion of the relationship between the plot of the *Arcadia* and Elizabethan problems with patriarchal rule, see Tennenhouse, p. 25.

18. Because Sidney added only a few poems to the expanded *New Arcadia,* it will be more convenient to refer to the poems and their contexts in terms of the far shorter *Old Arcadia.*

19. For a germinal discussion of the compensatory function of the blazon in Petrarchan poetics, see Nancy J. Vickers, "Diana Described: Scattered Woman and Scattered Rime," in *Writing and Sexual Difference,* ed. Elizabeth Abel (Chicago: University of Chicago Press, 1985); for the male poet's mastery over the female "subject"/addressee, see Ann Rosalind Jones and Peter Stallybrass, "Courtship and Courtiership: the Politics of *Astrophil and Stella," Studies in English Literature* 24 (1984): 53–68. For a discussion of the different tactics involved in positing all females as belonging to a coherent gender-group of "others," or in constructing them as striated into different social classes, the legitimacy of which they thereby naturalize, see Peter Stallybrass, "Patriarchal Territories: The Body Enclosed," in *Rewriting the Renaissance: The Discourses of Sexual Difference in Early Modern Europe,* ed. Margaret Ferguson, Maureen Quilligan, Nancy Vickers (Chicago: University of Chicago Press, 1986), esp. p. 133.

20. To make the political problem clearer (and his ultimate loyalties more obvious), Pyrocles makes his post-shipwreck appearance in the revised *New Arcadia* at the head of a peasant uprising. He relinquishes his leadership only after he has helped the group to resubmit to proper authority; see *New Arcadia,* pp. 94–99.

21. See in particular the essays by Jonathan Goldberg, Peter Stallybrass, and Sheila ffolliott in *Rewriting the Renaissance.*

22. Arguing that the cave episode becomes "a point of reference throughout the *Urania,"* Naomi J. Miller sees it as one which stages a very different problem of gender from its precursor in the *Arcadia:* "whereas in [Sidney] an imagined difference between women turns out to be nonexistent, in [Wroth] the imagined sameness of all women . . . breaks down in the face of Urania's individual identity as a woman" ("'Not much to be marked': Narrative of the Woman's Part in Lady Mary Wroth's *Urania,"* SEL [1989]:128).

23. See, in particular, Roberts pp. 147–50; *Urania* I.i.3, 51, 75. The first poem in the *Amoretti* refers to "hearts' close-bleeding book"; and the climactic moment of Amoret's torture in Book III of *The Faerie Queene* stages the scene of writing as a sadistic lettering with Amoret's literalized heart's blood. Wroth rewrites Spenser's crucial and baroque scene of torture at *Urania*, I.iiii.494. It is not Wroth's use of the imagery of tears which marks her poem as female-authored. John Donne, for instance, uses the imagery of tears in "Twickenham Garden," but he uses it ultimately to question the sincerity of woman's crying; his difference from Wroth lies, then, not only in his witty critique of female tears but also in the audience addressed by the poem—a group of men ("Nor can you more judge woman's thoughts by tears"). Conversely, Wroth's poem does not indicate, beyond the tree, whom the speaker addresses: indeed a great part of Pamphilia's problem is that "publishing" her poetry, even to circulate it to friends, is a borderline transgression.

24. In France the rivalry was institutionalized by royal command in a competition of blazon poems: Maurice Scève won with his poem on the eyebrow. See Nancy Vickers, *The Anatomy of Beauty: Poetry at the Court of Francis I* (Cambridge: Harvard University Press, forthcoming).

25. Antissia cannot simply be dismissed as a bad poet; her only fault is being loved by Amphilanthus while not being as good as Pamphilia, whose greater merits she all too well understands. In the Newberry manuscript part of the text however, Antissia goes quite mad, a sign of her madness being her desire, along with a male tutor, to better Ovid. Her nephew judges her: "indeed she was butt weake in true sence, but colorick ever, and rash, and now such a height of poetry wch att the best is butt a frency, and yett in Louers itt is a most commendable, and fine qualitie beeing a way most excellent to express their pretious thoughts." She has gone beyond all into "flatt madnes" (Newberry Library, *Urania*, pt. II,f.7).

26. The baroque image of the disembodied heart—with the pun on "prise" as in cherish and pry open—Wroth may again owe to the scene of Amoret's torture, which is itself a part of Spenser's critique of Petrarchism. An instructive contrast with Donne may be found in his use of the body-without-a-heart in "The Legacy," where the male speaker finds he has no heart. In contrast to Wroth's fishergirl, addressing the male lover who anatomizes her body into parts, Donne's speaker is in a most emphatically active position in this poem, disposing of his own body: "I bid me send my heart, when I was gone, / But alas could there find none, / When I had ripp'd me, and search'd where hearts did lie" (12–14). Wroth's difference from her male contemporary would seem to lie not so much in a use of different kind of imagery, but in a different deployment of rhetorical positions.

27. Carolyn Ruth Swift, "Feminine Identity in Lady Mary Wroth's Romance *Urania*," *ELR* 14 (1984): 331.

28. Swift argues, "Pamphilia's unnecessary choice to wait for an inconstant Amphilanthus is weakness in a woman whose discretion" is otherwise admirable (p. 342).

29. Paul Salzman, *English Prose Fiction, 1558–1700: A Critical History* (Oxford: Clarendon Press, 1985), p. 141.

30. After a lady met by the way has told her entire life history, an interlocutor asks, as a footnote, "if she had a husband." "I had Madam, said shee, which was none of my least afflictions or molestations, then kissing her, the rest likewise took leave and so went on their journey, the Lady returning to her house" (I.iii.376). The episode ends with these words.

31. The generically appropriate subject of her narrative romance, then, differs radically from the closet drama, *The Tragedy of Mariam,* published by Elizabeth Carey in 1613. Wife to Herod, Mariam suffers the tragedy of a wife who must, but cannot, obey her husband in silence. For a fascinating discussion of the play's analysis of the problematic contradictions in seventeenth-century wifedom, see Margaret Ferguson, "Running on with an Almost Public Voice: The Case of "E.C." (forthcoming).

32. Pamphilia and Amphilanthus are also first cousins; in part on the basis of this fact, Roberts reasons that their romantic attachment can be understood as Worth's representation of her affair with her first cousin, William Herbert. Because this identification seems accurate, one must wonder if the narrative silence about the suitability of Pamphilia's marrying Amphilanthus may reflect anxiety about an incest taboo. Although Henry VIII had legalized first-cousin marriage in the Church of England, to some Protestant reformers it still remained incestuous. Wroth never mentions the problem of first-cousin incest (although a single episode of the romance appears to deal with the more generically usual father-daughter incest), but the manifold kinship ties insist upon the importance to Wroth of *family*—which is significantly central to all the multiple brother-sister plots in the *Urania.* For a discussion of evolving incest laws in Europe, see Jack Goody, *The Development of the Family and Marriage in Europe* (Cambridge University Press, 1983)., esp. pp. 157–82. For an argument about incest in Jacobean tragedy as a means of representing anxieties about the fluctuating boundaries of the social elite, see Frank Whigham, "Sexual and Social Mobility in *The Duchess of Malfi,*" *PMLA* 100 (1985): 167–186. For some suggestions about the transgression of the incest taboo as a way of opening up a discursive space for female authority, see Quilligan (1989).

33. For a discussion of this aspect of the genre throughout a number of different periods, see Patricia Parker, *Inescapable Romance* (Princeton: Princeton University Press, 1979).

34. Salzman, p. 141.

35. At least three different women responded to the challenge with tracts of their own: Ester Sowernam (a pseudonym, as was perhaps also Joan Sharpe), Constantia Munda, and Rachel Speght. For excerpts, see Moira Ferguson, ed., *First Feminists: British Women Writers, 1578–1799* (Bloomington, Ind.: Indiana University Press, 1985).

36. For studies of the cult of Elizabeth, see Frances A. Yates, *Astraea* (London: Routledge and Kegan Paul, 1975); Roy Strong, *The Cult of Elizabeth* (London: Thames and Hudson, 1977); and Louis A. Montrose, "Eliza Queene of Shepheardes, and the Pastoral of Power," *ELR* 10 (1980): 153–82. In contrast, James I had little taste for the genre, and sonnet sequences immediately went out of fashion, save for the late publication of Wroth's cycle.

37. *L'Heptameron des Nouvelles de tres illustre et tres excellent princess Marguerite de Valois, Royne de Navarre* (Jean Caveiller, 1559), p. 6. A copy of the 1559 edition of the *Heptameron* in Beinecke Library, Yale University, is signed "Roger Twysdon, 1624," demonstrating that the book was being read by an Englishman in the 1620s.

38. Roberts also points out that "The account of Lindamira's life exactly parallels that of Lady Mary Wroth in such details as family background, education, marriage, and participation in court activities" (Roberts, p. 175). An earlier fifteenth-century female humanist, Christine de Pizan, had also rewritten Boccaccio from the point of view of actual verisimilarity. Such an early emphasis on what could be called "realism" from women may be explained as a female author's need to tell stories in ways that are not to be found in any male-authored texts. The very lack of a scripted tradition is a signal characteristic of women's culture; each female author must logically rehearse the same move, basing her authority in her own experience. Wroth—most interestingly—reverses the maneuver, alerting her reader to her stories' referentiality by appeal to a scripted tradition.

39. Catherine Gallagher, "Embracing the Absolute: The Politics of the Female Subject in Seventeenth Century England," *Genders* 1 (1988): 27.

40. Louise Labé, Pernette Guillet, Veronica Franco wrote poems in the Petrarchan mode, making it fit their purposes, as Wroth was to do later. For interesting discussions of Labé and Franco see the articles by Ann Jones and François Rigolot in Ferguson et al., *Rewriting the Renaissance.*

41. Roberts prints the poem, p. 217; for the argument as to identification, see pp. 43–44.

42. Michel Foucault, "What Is an Author?" in *Language, Counter-Memory, Practice,* trans. Donald F. Bouchard and Sherry Simon (Ithaca: Cornell University Press, 1977), p. 139.

# Contributors

*Gordon Braden,* professor of English at the University of Virginia, is the author of *Renaissance Tragedy and the Senecan Tradition: Anger's Privilege, The Classics and English Renaissance Poetry: Three Case Studies,* and, with William Kerrigan, *The Idea of the Renaissance.* His essay is part of a longer work in progress on the Petrarchan tradition.

*Stanley Fish* is Arts and Sciences Distinguished Professor of English and Law and chairman of the English Department at Duke University. His books include *Is There a Text in This Class? The Authority of Interpretive Communities, The Living Temple: George Herbert and Catechizing, Self-Consuming Artifacts: The Experience of Seventeenth-Century Literature, Surprised by Sin: The Reader in Paradise Lost,* and *John Skelton's Poetry.*

*Jonathan Goldberg* is Sir William Osler Professor of English at the Johns Hopkins University, and author of *Voice Terminal Echo: Postmodernism and English Renaissance Texts, James I and the Politics of Literature: Jonson, Shakespeare, Donne, and Their Contemporaries,* and *Endlesse Worke: Spenser and the Structures of Discourse.* His most recent book-length project is on handwriting in the Renaissance.

*John Guillory,* associate professor of English at The Johns Hopkins University, is the author of *Poetic Authority: Spenser, Milton, and Literary History* and is writing a study of the formation of the literary canon.

*Rosemary Kegl,* an assistant professor at the University of Rochester, is writing a book on the poetics of concealment in the English Renaissance. Her essay on George Puttenham is published in *ELR.*

*Arthur Marotti* is professor of English at Wayne State University. He is the author of *John Donne, Coterie Poet* and of essays on Jonson, Sidney, psychoanalytic criticism, and literary patronage in the sixteenth and seventeenth centuries. His essay is part of a larger project on the reception of Shakespeare in the seventeenth century.

*David Norbrook* is tutor in English at Magdalen College, Oxford. His publications include *Poetry and Politics in the English Renaissance* and articles in *TLS* and *The London Review of Books*.

*Stephen Orgel* is professor of English at Stanford University. He is the author of *The Illusion of Power* and *The Jonsonian Masque*, the coauthor of *The Theater of the Stuart Court* and the coeditor of *Patronage in the Renaissance*. He is at work on an edition of Milton and a book on transvestite theater in the Renaissance.

*Annabel Patterson* is professor of English at Duke University. She is the author of *Pastoral and Ideology, Censorship and Interpretation: The Conditions of Writing and Reading in Early Modern England, Marvell and the Civic Crown, Hermogenes and the Renaissance: Seven Ideas of Style,* and articles on many facets of Renaissance and Restoration culture.

*Maureen Quilligan* is professor of English at the University of Pennsylvania. She is the author of *Milton's Spenser: The Politics of Reading* and *The Language of Allegory: Defining the Genre,* and coeditor of *Rewriting the Renaissance: The Discourse of Sexual Difference In Early Modern Europe.* She is currently engaged in a study of female sovereignty in sixteenth-century Europe.

*Michael C. Schoenfeldt,* assistant professor of English at the University of Michigan, is the author of a number of articles on Herbert and Jonson. He has recently completed a book entitled *"The Distance of the Meek": George Herbert and His God.*

Jane Tylus is an assistant professor of Comparative Literature at the University of Wisconsin. She has published essays on Ariosto, Spenser and Virgil, and Tasso. She has just finished a book on Renaissance conceptions of pastoral which is provisionally entitled *Domesticating the Subject: Pastoral and Theater in Late Renaissance Europe.*

*Elizabeth D. Harvey* has written articles on Sidney, Spenser, and Donne and has edited a volume of essays on women and rationality. She is currently completing a book entitled *Ventriloquized Voices* that examines male appropriations of the feminine voice in Renaissance literature. She is an assistant professor in the English Department at the University of Western Ontario.

*Katharine Eisaman Maus,* associate professor of English at the University of Virginia, is the author of *Ben Jonson and the Roman Frame of Mind* and numerous essays on sixteenth- and seventeenth-century English poetry and drama.

# Index of Names